WRITING VIOLENCE

Writing Violence

THE POLITICS OF FORM IN
EARLY MODERN JAPANESE LITERATURE

David C. Atherton

Columbia University Press
New York

Columbia University Press
Publishers Since 1893
New York   Chichester, West Sussex
cup.columbia.edu
Copyright © 2023 Columbia University Press
All rights reserved

Library of Congress Cataloging-in-Publication Data
Names: Atherton, David (David C.), author.
Title: Writing violence : the politics of form in early modern Japanese literature / David C. Atherton.
Description: New York : Columbia University Press, [2023] | Includes bibliographical references and index.
Identifiers: LCCN 2023012062 (print) | LCCN 2023012063 (ebook) | ISBN 9780231211543 (hardback) | ISBN 9780231211550 (trade paperback) | ISBN 9780231558969 (ebook)
Subjects: LCSH: Japanese fiction—Edo period, 1600–1868—History and criticism. | Violence in literature. | Literature and society—Japan.
Classification: LCC PL747.37.S62 A84 2023 (print) | LCC PL747.37.S62 (ebook) | DDC 895.63—dc23/eng/20230601
LC record available at https://lccn.loc.gov/2023012062
LC ebook record available at https://lccn.loc.gov/2023012063

Cover design: Chang Jae Lee
Cover image: "Komagine Hachibyōe," from Tsukioka Yoshitoshi's woodblock print series *One Hundred Selected Portraits of Those Who Dash Ahead* (*Kaidai hyakusensō*, 1868–1869). National Diet Library Digital Collections

For my father, Stephen Otis Atherton (1938–2015), who would have been so proud

Contents

Acknowledgments ix
Note to Readers xiii

INTRODUCTION
The Problem, Promise, and Politics of Early Modern Literary Form 1

I Creative Destruction
Remaking the World in Seventeenth-Century Disaster Literature 32

II The Vengeance Variations
Revenge as Form in the Fiction of Ihara Saikaku 65

III The (Un)crucified Lovers
Adultery, Punishment, and the "Truth" of Transgression 98

IV Ueda Akinari and the Form of Fiction
In Which a Brother Is Celebrated for Beheading His Sister 133

V Frontier Violence
Late Yomihon *Form and the Bodies and Bounds of the Realm* 177

EPILOGUE
Forms in Context, Forms Beyond Context 209

Notes 221
Bibliography 259
Index 275

Acknowledgments

The image of the lone scholar may persist, but anyone who sets out to write a book soon learns that it is very much a group effort. This book could not exist were it not for the support and assistance of many people and institutions—many more than I can name here.

The distant roots of this project lie in the work I did as a graduate student at Columbia University. There, I was tremendously fortunate to have as my advisor Haruo Shirane, who took me on despite my lack of training in Japanese studies. His generosity with his guidance and support continues to this day. Tomi Suzuki was one of my keenest teachers and has been a staunch advocate in innumerable ways. The learning that I did in the classrooms of Michael Como, Wiebke Denecke, Matthew McKelway, and Max Moerman continues to hold me in good stead. Very special thanks go to David Lurie, who remains one of my most important mentors even as he has become a close friend. He read drafts of nearly all of the chapters in this book and provided encouragement when I needed it most.

This book also bears the imprint, in myriad ways, of my outstanding community of fellow graduate students and *senpai*—now friends and colleagues—including Michael Emmerich, Jenny Guest, Nan Ma Hartmann, Robert Hewitt, Pau Pitarch Fernández, Yumi Kim, Pat Noonan, Satoko Shimazaki, Nate Shockey, Ariel Stilerman, Shiho Takai, Rob Tuck, Charles Woolley, Christina Yi, and Hitomi Yoshio. My sincere thanks to Daniel Poch, who read drafts of multiple chapters and offered critical feedback and encouragement at multiple stages, and to Tom Gaubatz, an Edo literature brother-in-arms, who read and talked through multiple parts of this book and helped me keep my *mondai ishiki* sharp.

I began work on the book as an assistant professor at the University of Colorado Boulder, where I benefited from an exceptional group of colleagues, including Sabahat Adil, Katherine Alexander, Aun Hasan Ali, Haytham Bahoora, Janice Brown, Adam Hosein, Miriam Kingsberg Kadia, Faye Kleeman, Terry Kleeman, Paul Kroll, Rahul Parson, Antje Richter, Matthias Richter, Laurel Rodd, Suyoung Son, Andrew Stuckey, and Marcia Yonemoto. Special thanks to Keller Kimbrough for being a generous mentor as I began my professional career.

My good fortune has continued at Harvard, where I have found a community of scholars who are both intellectually extraordinary and highly supportive. Sarah Dimick, Tom Kelly, Annabel Kim, Nicole Sütterlin, Naomi Weiss, Alex Zahlten, and Saul Zaritt all gave extremely helpful feedback on portions of the manuscript—as did Annette Lienau, in addition to being an inspiring writing and accountability partner. Thanks to Ryuichi Abe, Matthew Fraleigh, David Howell, Shigehisa Kuriyama, Jie Li, Kio Lippit, Deidre Lynch, Hannah Marcus, Melissa McCormick, Matt Ocheltree, Si Nae Park, James Robson, Karen Thornber, Leah Whittington, and Tomiko Yoda for support and inspiration in many forms. Particular thanks to Victor Seow for riverside walks, collegial solidarity, and warm friendship, and to Karthik Pandian for regular check-ins about what really matters. Special thanks also to Kimmy Sanders, including for inviting me into a writing community on a visit to Japan just when this manuscript needed it most, and to KC Diaz for thoughtful conversations about process and balance. I am deeply grateful for the institutional support I have received at Harvard and for the people who make that support possible: in particular, Gus Espada, Alison Howe, Susan Kashiwa, John Park, and Naia Poyer (in the Department of East Asian Languages and Civilizations); Kuniko McVey (at the Harvard-Yenching Library); and Hannah Perry, Yitsy Ooi, Yukari Swanson, Jenni Ting, Gavin Whitelaw, and the extraordinary Stacie Matsumoto (at the Reischauer Institute for Japanese Studies).

Beyond Harvard's gates, Laura Moretti has been a source of support and inspiration in innumerable ways. Jayanthi Selinger has shared constant solidarity and good cheer. Will Hedberg generously read portions of the manuscript when I was still figuring out what it was about and gave very helpful and encouraging feedback. Rebecca Schuman helped make a massive project feel manageable. And Irene Pavitt read the full manuscript with exquisite care and offered edits that improved it immeasurably.

In Japan, I have benefitted from deeply generous mentorship and support. Komine Kazuaki has continued to encourage me even though my research focus long ago shifted from the medieval to the Edo period. Nakajima Takashi has been a brilliant and inspiring guide into the labyrinths of early modern popular fiction, and particularly that of Ihara Saikaku (a labyrinth unto himself). It was in his seminar at Waseda University that I first saw the excitement of putting different early modern writers and genres into dialogue with one another. And Toeda Hirokazu generously invited me to Waseda for three stays as a visiting researcher—trips that proved crucial to the completion of the manuscript. Together with Tanaka Yukari, he helped me to feel at home even as these visits took me far from my family.

Thanks also to audiences at the University of Colorado, Harvard University, Yale University, Bowdoin College, the University of Southern California, and the annual meetings of the Association for Japanese Literary Studies and the Association for Asian Studies for helpful feedback on presentations of various portions of the manuscript. My sincere thanks to the graduate students in my classes at Boulder and Harvard for inspiration, insight, and intellectual fellowship. It has been a true pleasure to learn with you.

Portions of chapters 2 and 5 draw upon dissertation research that was supported by the Japan Foundation, Waseda University, and the Japan Society for the Promotion of Science. Support from the Center for the Humanities and Arts at CU Boulder and the Reischauer Institute of Japanese Studies at Harvard enabled me to take teaching leaves that were crucial to the completion of the manuscript. I am grateful as well to the Faculty of Arts and Sciences at Harvard for a generous publishing subvention.

I am grateful to Christine Dunbar at Columbia University Press for her enthusiasm for this project when it was still taking shape and for her guidance on its path to becoming a book. The book is significantly stronger for the critical and supportive feedback provided by the two anonymous reviewers. Thanks to Christian Winting for his editorial support, Chang Jae Lee for the book's design, Zack Friedman for helping finalize the title, Leslie Kriesel for seeing the book through production, Mary Bagg for her meticulous and insightful copyediting, and Do Mi Stauber for producing the index.

The friendship of John Kowalski, Erwin Rosinberg, Latsavongsakda Sethaphong, Uttam Tambar, and Gaurav Upadhyay saw me through some of the hardest times of writing. Nancy and Abdul Hannan have been extraordinary neighbors. I am deeply grateful to the entire Tsuneda family—Masahiro, Yoriko, Ryutaro, Fumi, and Akihiro—for their unstinting generosity and support. Highest thanks go to my family, including Kath, Justin, Sam, and Tobin, Lizzy and Rodger, Nonie, Mary and Alan, the extended Salt Lake Athertons (with a special shoutout to Mikey), Alfie, and especially my parents, Katie and Stephen. This book is dedicated to my father's memory; he would have been so proud to see it in print. Thanks with all my heart to Michiko, who knew just the words to support me in the darkest days, and to Yuma, who grew so much faster than the manuscript did, and who knows how to make fun of me in the way that will make me laugh the hardest.

Note to Readers

Japanese personal names appear in the order of family name followed by given name. For premodern writers, after the first reference I follow the customary practice of referring to them by their given name or artistic name. Ihara Saikaku, for example, is abbreviated as Saikaku.

To foster accessibility and readability for a wide audience, I have used English translations of Japanese titles in the main text. Japanese titles appear in parentheses upon first mention and are used in endnotes and the bibliography.

Romanization of Japanese words follows the modified Hepburn system. All translations, unless otherwise noted, are my own.

WRITING VIOLENCE

Introduction

The Problem, Promise, and Politics of Early Modern Literary Form

How are we to make sense of the relationship between the formal features of literary works and the social world beyond their pages? This problem (relevant to our own moment of blurred lines between fiction and reality) confronts anyone who picks up a work of fiction produced during Japan's Edo period (1603–1867). The Edo (or early modern) period was a golden age for commercial fiction. After four centuries of nearly continuous warfare, the establishment of the Tokugawa shogunate in 1603 and its promulgation of new regimes of social organization and control ushered in over two and a half centuries of peace: a peace in which cities grew into major metropolises, the ranks of the literate increased exponentially, and the commercialization of woodblock-print technology facilitated the appearance of a robust market for popular literature. A host of new and ever-transforming narrative genres cast a sophisticated gaze across the social landscape, probed the realms of history and the fantastic, and breathed new life into the corpus of literary tradition.

One *senses* that these works, in all their diversity of genre and content, have meaningful things to say about the world beyond their covers. But their formal features—all those elements that enact, align with, or pull against recognizable patterns, which I understand broadly as encompassing language, voice, characterization, plotting, intertextual reference, organization, and generic structure—can prove prohibitive. Unlike the European realist novel's "contradictory generic achievements" of "depth psychology and social expansiveness" over the course of the same centuries, early modern Japanese fiction, while deeply invested in social typology, displays almost no concern for psychological interiority.[1] And rather than prizing the illusion of transparent mimesis, the favored formal dynamics of Edo-period fiction—the formulaicness, narrative modularity and tropic recycling, linguistic and intertextual play, and heavy allusion to literary tradition—can appear to hold the "real" world at arm's length. Some scholars, as we will see, caution us to treat these texts as sophisticated indulgences in aesthetic play, and to read them in those terms alone. For the critic looking to find something more, however, the terms of engagement can feel daunting—or simply obscure.

I felt the depth of the problem some years ago when I read *The Miraculous Destiny of Moon and Ice* (*Geppyō kien*, 1803), the first work of serious fiction in the genre called *yomihon* (reading books) by the celebrated writer Kyokutei Bakin (1767–1848).[2] The book's convoluted story of blood revenge, samurai families, and the fantastic so prizes character typology over individual psychology that a table in its first pages groups its twenty-seven main characters by type or social position: "Warriors," "Ladies," "Filial Children," "Unemployed Samurai," "Doctors," "Priests," "Thieves," and so on.[3] And its settings are constructed from heavily intertextual parts. A climactic scene arrives, for example, on the wintry banks of the Yoshino River, at the site where it courses between Mount Imo and Mount Se (Imoseyama). The Yoshino River and Imoseyama were "poem pillows" (*utamakura*): long-standing places of accumulated poetic lore, as much a set of canonized poetic references as physical geographic locations. And the action of the climax is pitched not in the key of mimetic realism, but in a blend of emotional excess and tortuously specific violence. A samurai woman named Akome learns that her husband, to whom she has been happily married for twenty years, was an accomplice in the murder of her first husband, who was killed on their wedding night. She reacts by drawing her son's sword, giving her husband a two-inch cut on his shoulder, and then plunging the sword into her belly. Dying, she explains:

> I shared only a moment of closeness with my first husband, but twenty years of affection with my second husband. In terms of love, who should be more precious to me? Yet in terms of the proper ways of the world, my second husband is the enemy of my first. How could I not express my resentment with at least one cut? . . . Even if I die,

it will not absolve me of my sin toward my first husband, and if I live, I will be a terrible example for my child. By inflicting a wound upon my second husband, I have expressed my apology to my first husband, and by killing myself, I will repay my second husband for his twenty years of kindness.[4]

I was still puzzling over this convoluted logic, which read to me like the violent solution to a socioemotional math problem, when I discovered that Bakin had lifted the dynamics of the entire scene from a completely different text: the puppet play *Lovers Pond in Settsu Province* (*Tsu no kuni meoto ike*, 1721), written by Chikamatsu Monzaemon (1653–1724) eight decades earlier.[5] Bakin simply altered the names, the setting, and other key elements—in Chikamatsu's play, the wife severs her husband's ear rather than stabbing him in the shoulder—and kneaded the scene into his otherwise different narrative. The scene is arresting and clearly complex. But its interlocking formal pieces left me lost as to how to make sense of it.

Stock characters, intertextual showmanship, labyrinthine plotting, modularity and recycling, unrealism, excess, quasiplagiarism: these elements, in various combinations and to greater or lesser degrees, confront the reader who opens any work of Edo-period commercial fiction. Do these texts have critical things to say about their world? That is, do they have a politics? And if so, where—and how—are we to locate it amid the threads of modular and conventionalized forms of which the texts are woven? How should we comprehend the relationship between the figural and the social, the aesthetic and the political, text and context? And how might work on early modern fiction engage the tussle between formalism and historicism that continues to resonate through the field of literary study more broadly?

On these questions, the field remains divided. One long-standing strain urges us to locate the politics of Edo popular literature in the subversion of state authority and ideology. The proponents of this approach typically characterize the Tokugawa shogunate as rigid, authoritarian, and controlling. They treat literary politics as the clever circumvention of restrictions; or as the satiric, parodic, or otherwise "camouflaged" critique of authority; or (in a more recent formulation) as the "dialogic" presentation of fluid social dynamics that subvert the shogunate's putative insistence on harmonious stasis.[6] A contrasting model, voiced most stridently by the influential scholar Nakano Mitsutoshi, characterizes early modern literature as fundamentally uncritical and apolitical. Nakano argues that those who lived during the Edo period, regardless of social position, held a common faith in the hierarchical structures of the age. Everyone accepted the superiority of samurai culture and elite values and respected the legitimacy of samurai to administer the realm. In literature and the arts, everyone honored the superiority of high (*ga*) over common (*zoku*) culture and afforded the classics an unquestioned authority. The role of prose works, within this context of shared and unquestioned values, was to entertain and to edify. Literary creativity involved not the creation of new meanings (much less of critique), but the seeking of new forms of expression—a variegated "art for art's sake" (*geijutsu no tame no geijutsu*)—against a background wherein values and meanings went largely uncontested.[7] The impact of this stance continues to be felt across the field in a broad move away from interpretation and toward positivist literary and book history.[8]

I find the assumption about literary politics inherent in these approaches—that politics is a matter of subversion of or alignment with authority—limiting. Here I treat literary politics as something much more capacious and generative. I understand literary works as proposing models of the world.[9] The formal features of literary works—which, again, I define capaciously in terms of elements that reproduce or pull against recognizable patterns, at scales ranging from phrasing to character, trope, intertextual reference, and plot structure—create arrangements of order and relation that open and foreclose possibilities of perception. They suggest what the world contains and excludes; how it is connected, organized, and made to cohere (or not); what kinds of voices it amplifies or diminishes; and what dynamics of relation and antagonism animate it. Understanding literary politics in this way enables us to move beyond tired models of opposition and complicity—and instead to recognize popular literature as an agent, active in shaping what Jacques Rancière calls the "distribution of the sensible": the "delimitation of spaces and times, of the visible and the invisible, of speech and noise."[10] What can be seen? Who can be heard? What can be thought? What are the perceptual boundaries of the world, and how is it—or how might it be—organized? What dynamics, unnoticed in the flow of the everyday, might be brought into relief and made apprehensible? And what might be pushed from perception, rendered invisible, or silenced?

The political purview of literature, conceived in these terms, is limitless. Subversion has a place here, as does acquiescence to authority. But neither accounts for the whole story. Literary politics reach into realms of experience that have little to do with official political authority at all, but much to do with the politics of everyday life: the sexual politics of the household; the ethical and economic exchanges of an emergent capitalistic society; the geographies and borderlines of community, vast and intimate; the relationship of the present to the past and the future; the place of the sacred and the unseen within the spaces of the mundane; the licit or illicit nature of violence on scales grand and small. Understanding literature through the way it proposes forms of order and models of the world opens a host of doors for our comprehension of the relationship between texts and the world beyond them. And it enables us to avoid the historian's occasional mistake of interpreting literature as a mere reflection of historical trends or social *mentalités*. Instead, we can grasp literature as a process, active in the formation of the world and its horizon of possibilities.[11]

Seen in this way, the formal elements of early modern literature that might appear static, conservative, modular, repetitive, or unrealistic reveal themselves in a new light. Central to my argument is the idea that in proposing versions of the world, Edo popular literature employs logic and materials shared with the social and political world beyond the page. These include a deep investment in tradition; a fascination with typology, taxonomy, categories, catalogues, and containers; and a belief that the proper performance of normative forms can affect, or even *effect*, reality: a faith, indeed, that reality inheres in recognizable, normative forms, and that the world becomes more real the closer one cleaves to them. When Akome, in Bakin's text, gives a precise (two-inch!) cut to her husband's shoulder with a specific sword and then stabs herself in the belly as a solution to a messy tangle of social and emotional relationships, her character partakes (with melodramatic exaggeration) of a broader social logic that took external formalization as an arbiter of order, personhood—even reality itself. *Writing Violence* argues that the conventionalized, modular, and formulaic formal ingredients of early modern Japanese fiction did not hold the world at a remove; they shared in the formalized logic that animated social life, and thus were poised to intervene in its perception.

Form was paramount in early modern Japan. Formalized behaviors served the preservation of order in a society that derived its structure from military models and relied heavily on visual signs to make that structure—and everyone's place in it—visible.[12] But as patterns against which experience could be measured and appraised, forms also helped to define the very edges of perception, expression, and imagination, thus shaping the real itself. In this book, I show how early modern fiction proposes its visions of the world in ways that align with this logic: not in the celebration of experimental novelty or through an apparently transparent realism, but by combining, colliding, overlapping, bending, stretching, and remixing established forms.

We are accustomed to thinking of "form" as a matter of aesthetics. Here, however, I employ the term in its broadest sense of pattern, order, shape, style, type, mold, precedent, or convention—the basic principle that makes something identifiable. I do not consider "form" as something opposed to "content;" form, rather, is the *shape* that its material takes. That is, unlike a container "filled" with content, form is "simply a way of being of the material, the glass's way of being a wineglass as opposed to an eyeglass or a window."[13] This "way of being of the material" applies as well to a glass as to a sonnet or a *waka* verse or a plot structure, and as well to a sword as to a handshake or a dance. Everything *has* a form. But our perception of any given form relies upon the forms that precede it, in the way it repeats or deviates from them. It is in this sense that Sianne Ngai defines form as "socially pre-shaped perception—a structured way of seeing."[14] But as Raymond Williams notes, "form" actually encompasses two senses: "a visible or outward shape, and an inherent shaping impulse," or the established norm and the creative principle.[15] Grasping the theoretical import of form, he argues, requires apprehending the dialectical relationship between these two senses, for "form is inevitably a relationship. Form depends, that is to say, on its perception as well as its creation. Like every other communicative element, from the most local to the most general, it is always in this sense a social process."[16]

Put another way, form is located at the razor-thin line where stasis and innovation meet. Forms appear static because they are repeatable and can, in that sense, be abstracted: we can recognize a wineglass as a wineglass, or a verse with thirty-one syllables in a 5-7-5-7-7 pattern as a *waka*. But their repetitions introduce variations that render forms in fact ever in motion, always in flow.[17] And each new instance has the potential to reinforce or to alter the sense of what characterizes a particular form—or to transform it into a new form altogether. Each new *waka* alters the possibility of what a *waka* can be. And so, the study of form always involves a delicate tacking between abstraction and specificity, as well as between different frames of reference (for example, between the arrangement of words in a specific *waka* versus the arrangement of multiple *waka* in an anthology). It is in this sense that I identify as "forms" in Bakin's *yomihon* elements that might more traditionally be classified as "content": character types, *utamakura*, plot structures, the practice of *seppuku*. Each of these takes a shape in the *yomihon* that is recognizable because it builds upon earlier instances from other texts and (in the case of *seppuku*) social practice. But we can also track the way the shapes of these established forms are altered and arranged in this particular instance.

We can find a point of resonance with this dialectical understanding of form in the Japanese term *kata*, which covers a semantic range broadly akin to that of "form."[18] *Kata*, like "form," can be used in a strictly aesthetic sense, but it applies as easily to social practices and patterns of behavior. In traditional Japanese arts and practices, indeed, *kata* often straddle the aesthetic and the social, denoting the preordained normative practices, styles, or movements that a student must learn to reproduce through a rigorous process of training, but that encompass elements as diverse as the stances practiced by martial artists, the ceremonial gestures of tea specialists, the patterns of flower arrangement in ikebana, the body movements of dancers, even the ritualized body movements of monks. *Kata* do not merely enforce rote reproduction (though that is one possible outcome), but also enable *kata-yaburi* (form-breaking), the creative innovations that would be imperceptible without the background—the "socially pre-shaped perception"—of established *kata*.

Although the purview of "form" in my discussion extends beyond the codified *kata* of the various arts, I take inspiration from the dynamic that they represent: one of modularity, repetition, and permutation. And, just as *kata* can encompass both the aesthetic and the social, I take inspiration as well from Caroline Levine's expansion of "form" beyond the aesthetic realm to include "all shapes and configurations, all ordering principles, all patterns of repetition and difference," including those of social and political structures.[19] Approaching form in broad terms helps us to apprehend the points of continuity among aesthetic, social, and political forms. Grouping elements as diverse as the thirty-one-syllable *waka* verse, a character type ("Filial Child"), an *utamakura* poetic topos like Imoseyama, the two swords worn at a samurai's side, the shape of an Edo city ward, and the nested political units of the *bakuhan* political system under the term "form" may seem to be overly generalizing. But, as Levine argues, a broad definition of "form" enables us to recognize that all forms proffer a variety of order, each attended by its own set of possibilities and constraints. And it helps us to appreciate the ways in which these varied forms and their models of order overlap, collide with, cooperate with, blend with, collapse into, or push against one another.[20] The politics of literature emerge from within these formal relations.

Stretching our understanding of form to straddle both text and context, I argue that popular fiction's creative dynamic of permutation within conventionalized forms made it a potent site for intervention into the perception of social forms. Indeed, those aspects of early modern aesthetic form that have seemingly kept the world at a remove are the very ones with the greatest potential to intervene in the perception of the real, as they introduce unaccustomed variations into familiarized patterns. Evaluating the politics of early modern Japanese fiction thus involves seeking not the mimetic realism of the European novel, but the places where established forms rearrange into novel constellations, opening new perceptual possibilities. Seen in this way, we can begin to appreciate popular fiction's role in the "distribution of the sensible." The formal mutations of commercial fiction possessed the power to rework the relationship among present, past, and future; to defamiliarize social conventions; to make latent social, economic, and affective forces apprehensible; to mold the contours of different forms of community; and to authorize the voices that could be heard within those communities—voices that might otherwise be inaudible beyond the page. And fiction's formal sophistication made it a powerful site for navigating one of the most pervasive dilemmas faced by a society that placed such store in codified forms: how to differentiate the merely seeming (*kyo*) from the real (*jitsu*).[21]

To make apparent the stakes and rewards of my approach, I center this book on the theme of violence. Violence has a fraught relationship to form. It may seem as though the two are rivals: that whereas form is a matter of order and patterning, violence undoes patterns and wreaks disorder. But, as Peter Haidu cautions us, "Violence must not be hypostasized. It is a relational concept, not a thing."[22] And so it is more appropriate to say that form *fosters the perception* of violence: it teaches us what does and what does not count as violent, and it mediates the line separating licit from transgressive violence. Cultures can formalize—indeed, institutionalize—certain forms of harm in a way that normalizes them, while treating others as dangerous irruptions into an ostensible background of nonviolence. They can treat violence as a natural feature of human experience, or as something to be "mastered and eliminated."[23] Likewise, the formal organization of works of art and literature can foster many and various perceptions of harm: celebrating it, sequestering it, normalizing it, treating it as tragic, making it an occasion for hilarity. The Russian formalist Viktor Shklovsky, in "Art as Device" (1917/1919), his seminal essay on the capacity of literary form to defamiliarize our "automatized" perceptions of life, turns to the treatment of violence as a primary example. He demonstrates how Tolstoy, in the essay "Shame!" (1895), elaborately depicts a flogging and highlights its interchangeability with less familiar but equally cruel punishments so as to stimulate the reader's conscience about a routine practice in tsarist Russia.[24] Without altering anything in the form of flogging itself, Tolstoy's literary treatment shifts the possibility of its perception, relocating it from the category of the mundane to that of a violation.

Violence is a particularly potent entry point for considering form in early modern Japan. It was an overdetermined category in a warrior-ruled polity that made the preservation of peace central to its ideology. Military logic and the specter of warfare were written into the DNA of that polity, shaping social structures, culture, and space in ways great and small. One means of taming violence's threat to order was through rigorous formalization, as in the cases of ritual suicide and blood revenge, each of which took on features distant from their atavistic origins.[25] But violence that broke free from formalized patterns—riots, brawls, assaults, cold-blooded murders—raised the fear of dreaded disorder. Approaching violence at the level of form thus helps us to appraise the continuity between aesthetic and social formalization. In a society in which the body served as a charged site of social signification, for example, the depiction of violated bodies bore potent implications for the imagination of communal cohesion. Likewise, the literary treatment of such practices as blood revenge, honor killing, and capital punishment involved engagement with both literary and social conventions. And because violence, as a "relational concept," is always recognized as violent only by social agreement, its status was a product of continual renewal and renegotiation. That process, it follows, necessarily involved the renewal and renegotiation of a host of other social values. Attention to the formal treatment of violence—and to the violence of literary deformation—helps us to recognize the critical role that popular literature played in the imagination of such vital issues as the place of the sacred, the boundaries of the family, the moral relations of gender difference, and the integrity of the body politic.

If we return to Bakin's *Miraculous Destiny of Moon and Ice* with this framework in mind, a new picture emerges. We can recognize, for example, that the text's approach to character parallels the early modern understanding of personhood, which relied heavily on categorization and normative, externalized markers of categorical identity. Typology was part of how society presented itself to itself and apprehended itself. That does not mean that early modern society was static; identity could be highly fluid and society quite mobile. But it relied, always, on highly formalized categories and markers.[26] From an early modern perspective, the text's explicit basing of characters on type—even if those types were as generic as "Filial Children" and "Thieves"—brought them closer to reality rather than distanced them from it.

We can see, too, how Bakin's use of Imoseyama as the setting for the climactic scene is no mere intertextual window dressing. The passage opens with the horror of Akome's son and his lover at the discovery that they may be siblings who were separated at birth. As Akome and her husband explain why this is not so, the scene snowballs into an avalanche of family revelations, including a secret adoption, culminating in Akome's discovery that her husband was an accomplice to her first husband's murder. The sundering of the "female" and "male" peaks (Mount Imo and Mount Se) by the Yoshino River had inspired centuries of poetry on the estrangement that can infect even the closest relationships between men and women, and *imose* can mean either "sister-brother" or "wife-husband."[27] This legacy and the double meaning of the compound word lend thematic heft to a scene that probes the sometimes-capricious bonds that hold together lovers and families. The characters may be sketched as types, but the landscape and its constellation of introspective poetic associations import into the scene a sense of psychology and emotional interiority.

Although Bakin pinched the general parameters of this climax from Chikamatsu's puppet play *Lovers Pond in Settsu Province*, his reworking of it, far from comprising gross plagiarism, epitomizes early modern literary creativity, which, as I will discuss, championed innovation within established forms over wholesale novelty. It was Bakin's innovation, for example, to transpose the action to Imoseyama.[28] And it is in such alteration of formal details within Chikamatsu's general framework that the scene's politics come into sharper focus. Whereas the wife in Chikamatsu's play, for example, stabs herself in the throat—a mode of suicide traditionally associated with samurai women—Akome plunges the blade into her belly (*hara*): a symbolically overdetermined part of the body that was associated both with the male samurai practice of ritual suicide by disembowelment (*seppuku*) and with a woman's sexuality and reproduction.

Taken together, the formal elements that at first appear so alienating—the scene's typified characters, invocation of poetic tradition, plagiaristic borrowing, and oddly precise violence—now reveal themselves as working in concert to present a startling vision of family politics: the tussle of personal affections and relational obligations in a community that is bound variously through blood, marriage, and adoption. The scene underscores the relationality of familial identity: like the twin peaks of Imoseyama, one could be a "husband" only in relation to a "wife." But like the mountains' sundered peaks, an element of estrangement and difference necessarily cuts across such relations, threatening to yawn into emotional, moral, even existential rifts. And when Akome plunges the sword into her womb, the act astonishingly evokes the stark gender divisions of the early modern household and the overdetermined role of a wife within it. A wife's reproductive labor was crucial to the household's perpetuation. But this also made her sexuality an object of anxiety, surveillance, and moralizing discourse. These conditions of unease and scrutiny sat alongside whatever emotional intimacy and affection (*shitashimi, on'ai*), both cited in Akome's speech, she might share with her husband. The scene powerfully evokes the tangling of these many elements and the potential for danger when they jostle and pull against one another. Even as Akome appears to resolve them through a set of highly formalized maneuvers—a two-inch cut, on a nonthreatening part of her husband's body, with a particular blade, followed by the stab to her belly—the gender-bending those maneuvers entail underscores the very messiness that they purport to resolve. A household that has relied on a woman's *hara* for its reproductive lifeblood will have the violent and sexual corruptions instigated by its patriarch redressed, and thus be safeguarded for the next generation, by the woman's cutting open her womb (in the manner of a man's *seppuku*) and embracing death. Bakin's writing is often filed away under the moralistic-sounding category of "rewarding virtue and castigating vice" (*kanzen chōaku*). But when we step away from facile labels and attend to details—to the specifics of how the text is put together—we begin to apprehend the text's complexity, its provocativeness, its politics. Not the politics of complicity or subversion, but the politics of perception: here, probing the dynamics of latent violence that haunt the household's gendered structure and ideology.

This is writing that rewards close attention. Form matters in early modern fiction. For it is in the formal details that the text brushes most closely against the grain of the living world and its thresholds of perception. *Writing Violence* takes up the challenge of how to read for early modern form.

Form in Context, Form as Context

Taking up that challenge requires first apprehending the paramount role and complex functioning of form in early modern Japanese society. Certainly, every culture relies on visual markers and behavioral norms. But in Edo Japan, external signs of identity; normative practices of gesture, dress, and speech; and ritualized behaviors of social and political intercourse were crucial to societal functioning to an extraordinary degree. We can trace the emergence of this dynamic to the society's military origins. The Tokugawa order emerged from over a century of intense warfare among warlords who commanded gargantuan armies. As Oda Nobunaga (1534–1582), Toyotomi Hideyoshi (1537–1598), and, finally, Tokugawa Ieyasu (1542–1616) successively sought (and achieved) hegemony over their rivals, they instituted policies born from the logic of warfare that were intended to preserve order and maintain their power. A chief concern of many of these programs was to still the intense social fluidity and turmoil of the age. The disarming of the populace, the sequestering of samurai in castle towns, the cataloguing of each member of the populace in registers of religious affiliation: all worked to create legible divisions among different communities and strata of the population. Together, they laid the groundwork for a new ordering of society *and* a new way of perceiving it.[29] Out of these and other policies that reached into the middle decades of the seventeenth century emerged a system based on status (*mibun*), in which everyone occupied an identifiable place among a vast constellation of differentiated occupational groups, which in turn derived their identities and legal statuses from the services they were expected to provide to the state.[30]

This was a "taxonomic revolution."[31] It took place in both top-down and bottom-up fashion, through intentional institutional policies, and through the organic adaptations of social groups to a new societal and political reality.[32] And it did not freeze society; the boundaries of the status system's social containers were permeable. But the idea of a social identity outside the taxonomic order became unthinkable. An early modern subject would not have experienced status as an alien appendage forced onto his or her identity from without. Status was the grammar in which society spoke itself. And this grammar was made outwardly apprehensible—as a language is written in script—through visual and behavioral forms: styles of hair, types of dress, features of speech, modes of comportment. Herman Ooms notes the visual formalism of social status:

> This social order relied heavily on the eye for support. It was a matter not only of division, of cutting up society into separate status groups, but also of vision, of establishing clear signs that unmistakably displayed this order. The proper order should always be unambiguously connoted by unequivocal signs of everyone's place in it. Every part was meant to evoke the whole, precisely because it was not just some contingent social unit or occupation but a constituent "part." A peasant was not simply someone who earned a living by working in the fields; he occupied a position and a function in a hierarchical order.[33]

Everyone—even beggars and itinerants—had a place, and each place was marked by legible signs of belonging: to a household, a status group, a retainer band, a domain. These social containers were the building blocks of society.

The taxonomic revolution extended as well to other spheres of life and knowledge, catalyzed by the commercialization of print by the mid-seventeenth century. Mary Elizabeth Berry writes eloquently of the emergence of a "library of public information" contained in printed books, which treated subjects ranging from agronomy to urban geography, cooking, poetic composition, money making, social typology, and much more: "The vehicle of this holistic coverage was classification—the breaking down of big subjects into manageable components. The list . . . ruled."[34] The print market played a pronounced role in promulgating social forms and typologies. Already by 1690, the *Illustrated Overview of Humanity* (*Jinrin kinmō zui*) offered a commercial catalogue of nearly five hundred different statuses and occupations—from aristocrats, warriors, and monks to lumberjacks, barge pullers, and hat makers—complete with brief descriptions and illustrations. The pictures are simple iconographic representations that summarize the appearance and labor of different social types: *waka* poets in splendid robes arranged around a set of writing implements; a carver of Buddhist statuary sitting beside the chisels of his trade and holding up his product to a monk; a publisher proffering a book to a customer amid stacked and scattered volumes.[35] To each person, a social category; to each category, a contour of iconographic form.

And form extended to behaviors, each of which, likewise, could be broken into constituent formal pieces. Laura Moretti notes the popularity of etiquette guides sold on the book market. They instructed readers in comportment by indexing codified behaviors: "Take up your chopsticks. While holding your chopsticks take the bowl in your right hand, then pass it to your left and eat the pieces of food in the soup. Under no circumstances should you begin by drinking the soup."[36] These manuals not only provided readers with practical knowledge (though Moretti notes that the information, which describes the comportment of those of highborn samurai status, sometimes was irrelevant to the immediate life of the general reader),[37] but also afforded a vision of where everyone fit within the larger social framework, and of how formalized behaviors marked those positions.

For even as this classifying consciousness broke things down into their constituent parts, it posited ways of understanding how they all fit together. Taxonomy could scale upward and downward, providing different levels of perception into how part and whole constituted each other. Two swords at the side marked a samurai, but infinite variations were possible within the physical form of the swords, the ways they were carried, and the ways they matched (or not) the dress, accoutrements, and comportment of the man carrying them. The intersections of these forms afforded finer nuances of identity marking—and identity reading—of where a person fit into the larger, interlocking, and multilayered whole of social positions.

This enmeshment of parts, wholes, and form had implications for the experience of social reality. The experience of identity—indeed, of personhood—was deeply connected to form. As Hino Tatsuo argues, formalized behaviors, which he calls "modes of being" (*sonzai no yōshiki*), were a site where image and reality converged, fostering a "typological" sense of personhood, such that "living in accordance with agreed-upon behaviors—a warrior in a warrior-like manner [*bushirashiku*], a townsman in a townsman-like manner [*chōninrashiku*]—was considered the supreme virtue."[38] Normative social forms were a standard of (self-)measure; selfhood was understood in terms of alignment with or divergence from the formalized norm. The production of such typological subjects can be employed as a variety of control, Hino notes; but he argues that early modern subjects actively embraced such a posture because it afforded a sense of order and self-objectification for selves that were (like all selves) subject to boundless diffusion amid the flow of reality: "For people of the early modern period, image [*imēji*] and life [*seikatsu*] fused, and life itself became the medium by which the self was objectified. Therein lies the early modern aesthetics of personhood [*kinseiteki jinkaku no bigaku*]: the self made into an object even as the self was, simultaneously, a living being."[39]

Fiction was potent in a world in which behaviors were so deeply informed by idealized—and hence, to a degree, fictional—forms. Fiction, indeed, straddled life and art. Hino references the early kabuki play *The Rōnin's Saké Cup* (*Rōnin sakazuki*, seventeenth century), in which two old samurai acquaintances, one of whom has lost formal employment, encounter each other on the road. They wish to drink to better fortunes, but, lacking saké and cups, they must resort to mimicking the exchange of cups using a fan. When they part ways, they do so with drunken steps, although they have been "drinking" no more than empty air. Hino identifies in the play an emblem for "early modern life, in which the border with fiction [*kyokō*] was ambiguous. The image of the saké cup displaced onto the fan has the capacity to make the two men drunk, and thus fulfills a function for their lives, while the fictional saké they drink objectifies their happiness at encountering each other."[40] Actors foregrounding the blurry boundary between reality and fiction onstage may seem in keeping with the world of theater, but the point is that not only fiction but also early modern life itself possessed a strong theatrical element. Daily life involved the constant performance of formalized fictions—and these fictions, in turn, shaped reality.

And not just the pedestrian reality of daily life. Luke Roberts, in *Performing the Great Peace*, highlights the centrality of performance to early modern politics writ large. Because the political structures of early modern Japan consisted of a series of largely "sealed-off" hierarchical containers—from the semi-independent domains, which structured the administrative landscape, to the households, which organized social life at the micro level—political life was divided between the realities located in the containers' insides (*uchi*) and those performed at the outward or surface (*omote*) level in accordance with the expectations of hierarchical superiors. Roberts writes of his dawning awareness of the political import of this inside-outside dynamic as he scrutinized clan diaries: "I came to learn that . . . the 'play' was the thing of government. The ability to command *performance* of duty—in the thespian sense when actual performance of duty might be lacking—was a crucial tool of Tokugawa power that effectively worked toward preserving the peace in the realm. Real political struggle between parties occurred in the connections between *performance* and performance."[41]

The crucial element in Tokugawa politics was proper adherence at the *omote* level to the formalized signs of subservience and order. This "*performance* of signs" was not static: "the boundary between acceptable and intolerable deviation was subtle and sometimes shifting, and the stuff of politics was discovering just where this boundary lay for whom and at what moment."[42] These formalized *omote* performances, even if they might strike us as empty charades (particularly so, given that all the players were not infrequently aware of the discrepancy between the *omote* performance and the *uchi* reality) carried very real consequences, often for matters of high political import: the issue of succession; the settling of disputes; indeed, the maintenance of the Tokugawa Great Peace itself. But the performances also blurred the distinction between fact and fiction, making reality provisional, such that "a daimyo [lord] could be both dead and alive at the same time, as long as the conditions were divided by the political spacing of 'inside the clan' and 'outside the clan.'"[43] Like a plain fan that could make a *rōnin* drunk on the theatrical stage, the daimyo's body might be dead, but as long as the forms of aliveness were performed about him on the political stage, the daimyo was, for all intents and purposes, alive.

The Aesthetics and Politics of Early Modern Literary Form

In *Writing Violence* I argue that these complex dynamics of early modern social and political form can help us to understand the dynamics of early modern literary form. I do not mean to suggest that literature was "reflective" of society in a derivative way. Instead, I understand literature as another facet of the shared plane of social life: a textual co-participant in the ongoing creation of social imagination and, through imagination, reality. A shared formal logic circulated between the pages of texts and the world beyond them. And literary logic, like social logic, was organized around typologies, authoritative models, set pieces, and modules that could be arranged and rearranged into greater wholes, and against which innovation and difference could be measured, akin to Hino's samurai measuring himself against an idea of samurai-ness. In literature, these typological ingredients encompassed genre forms, classical precedents, character types, literary geographies (such as *utamakura*), conventions grand and small, linguistic forms, styles and registers, and historical figures and events. They extended as well to material features, such as book sizes and formats, paper qualities, calligraphic styles, illustration types, and the differences between printed books and manuscripts. These were the units of which texts were structured and against which they, their quality, and their innovations could be recognized and appraised. In all, precedent and authority were paramount. Literary innovation resided in the skill with which one introduced permutations into established formal codes.

In short, a fundamental mode underlay the highly diverse literary output of the early modern period. Idealized forms—aesthetic and social—were held in the commons of the popular imagination, and literary creation involved the novel reassembly, blending, fracturing, and distortion of these forms, some of which then crystalized into new norms and became the substrate for new innovations. This mode was dynamic, as evidenced by the flourishing profusion of texts and genres and their change over time. But its most basic logic of repetition inflected by difference remained remarkably consistent, even across genres, geographies, and generations: a reflection, perhaps, of the general institutional stability and cultural cohesion of the age.[44] Within this relentless recapitulation and reworking of established forms—in the slippage between repetition and alteration, however subtle—new avenues of perception could be opened and others foreclosed. The politics of form in early modern literature lies in this slippage; apprehending it therefore requires understanding the elements of this mode and the dynamics of early modern literary creativity.

Only a few scholars have attempted to theorize Edo literature in terms of such a pervasive mode, and they have generally stopped short of considering its political import. One of these few is Nakamura Yukihiko, a towering figure in postwar Edo literary studies. In an essay titled "*Kata* and Literary Style" (Kata no bunshō, 1967), he makes the argument that the literary arts of the period, for all their variety, possess a shared stylistic logic that was entwined with the social dynamics of the age and therefore produced a literature that was noticeably different from the literatures of the periods that proceeded and followed it. He identifies this logic in typological form, or *kata*. "In a word," he explains, "early modern literature mirrors early modern society in that it is, in a variety of ways, a typological literature [*ruikei no bungaku*]."[45] Though he gestures here to a homological correspondence between literary and social forms, he leaves this aspect untheorized; aside from this reference, the essay focuses exclusively on literary dynamics.

To a remarkable and pervasive extent, Nakamura argues, early modern literary production relied on formalized models and their modification. This dynamic was not unprecedented. Classical poetics had long depended on conscious engagement with a well-defined traditional corpus. By the medieval period, *waka* had become highly modular and intertextual, as epitomized by the practice of *honkadori* (construction of a new verse by reworking elements of an earlier "base poem"), and largely restricted in subject matter to variations on a set of well-defined topics and in expression to a circumscribed vocabulary. But in the Edo period, modular composition, intertextual recycling and recombination, and consciousness of a well-established body of traditional texts to draw on touched all corners of popular literature—poetic, prosaic, and theatrical—and became fundamental to their modus operandi.

Nakamura argues that *all* early modern literature relied on the imitation and manipulation of established *kata*—even as he registers his hesitation at reducing to a single word the nuance, complexity, and multidimensionality of the dynamic he seeks to describe. He finds a dependence on *kata* operative in literature high and low, vernacular and Sinitic, reaching from the microscale of a word, verse link, or sentence up to the macroscale of a theatrical play or work of sprawling narrative fiction. Genres, schools, even distinctive stylistic tones (such as the "*Monkey's Raincoat* style" of Matsuo Bashō's poetic school) were all apprehended as typological models that could be broken down into smaller taxonomic units. The appreciation of a literary work, Nakamura argues, involved two layers: not only the appreciation of the text's expression and meaning, but the identification and appreciation of the *kata* that it employed, and its relative skill in doing so. A linked-verse sequence by a member of Bashō's school, for example, would involve attention not only to how well the formal demands of the thirty-six-verse *kasen* linked-verse form had been executed, but also to the stylistic tenor of the sequence: how it adhered to, deviated from, or innovated within the established "*Monkey's Raincoat* style," which had itself taken shape and achieved significance through a process of innovating within and remixing earlier established styles:[46] "Writers revealed their individuality from within those various *kata* and while preserving those *kata*."[47] Nakamura offers the example of style guides that taught writers of Sinitic verse how to recognize different ways of combining words to convey a sense of being "Tang poetry–like, Ming poetry–like, Song poetry–like" (*Tōshirashiku, Minshi-rashiku, Sōshi-rashiku*): a dynamic of relying on and measuring oneself against normative models that resonates with Hino's characterization of social identities as being performed around models of the "warrior-like" or "townsman-like."[48] Literary virtuosity was located in those writers who were fluent in the *kata* of multiple literary forms and registers—Sinitic and vernacular, high and low—and could mix and match them into a "hybrid harmony" (*konzen ittai*).[49]

Suwa Haruo summarizes this creative dynamic in a similarly ambitious essay titled "What Is Edo Literature?" (Edo bungaku to wa nanika?): "The spirit of the times was such that to take a plot, an idea, or an expression thought up by another and twist it to a more effective use redounded to the honor of the writer. It was universally understood that in creating a work, basing it on a precise source was more important than individual originality."[50] Suwa does not theorize the political potential of this dynamic, except to note that it relies upon the secular authority of literary tradition, which he vaguely likens to the authority of Tokugawa governance.[51] But he provides striking examples of the creative mode in practice, such as Ueda Akinari's (1734–1809) *Tales of Moonlight and Rain* (*Ugetsu monogatari*, 1776). Celebrated as one of the greatest fiction collections of the Edo period, Akinari's nine stories are spectacularly reliant on established models, incorporating nearly sixty Chinese sources and one hundred Japanese ones in a complex dynamic of allusion, adaptation, remixing, and translation that Suwa likens to the assembly of a literary "mosaic."[52] Yet, like a mosaic, the collection coheres into something much greater than the sum of its derivative parts. And early modern writers did not limit their dependence on existing forms to only those of the past. Suwa cites as well Chikamatsu Monzaemon's *jōruri* play *The Love Suicides at Amijima* (*Shinjū ten no Amijima*, 1721). Celebrated today as one of the playwright's greatest works, the play borrows many elements of its plot, setting, and characterization directly from *The Love Suicides at Umeda* (*Umeda shinjū*, 1706), written by Chikamatsu's rival Ki no Kaion (1663–1742); its first two scenes border on outright plagiarism of Kaion's play. Far from being condemned for such imitation and creative filching, however, Chikamatsu was hailed within three years of his death as the "patron god of writers" (*sakusha no ujigami*).[53]

The age abounds with aesthetic devices that involved mashing up or layering traditional forms into new arrangements. The fundamental device of early modern literary creativity was the *shukō*: the innovation or twist introduced by a writer into an existing form or constellation of forms. The term is best known from its use in kabuki, where it is typically paired with *sekai* (world). The "world" was the established historical or cultural setting for the play, built out of familiar patterns that would be immediately recognizable to audiences; the *shukō* was the "fresh twist ... that made the old pattern new again."[54] But the importance of the *shukō* as a creative swerve pervaded all the arts, as noted by Nakamura: "We can spot [*shukō*] as a key literary term in all forms and all stages of the Edo period."[55] And it did not depend on a fully realized *sekai*; all that was needed was *some* kind of recognizable, existing pattern that could make the swerve perceptible.[56] Bashō's celebrated verse, "Old pond: a frog jumps in—the sound of water" (*Furuike ya kawazu tobikomu mizu no oto*), is one such example. The verse was immediately arresting because it transformed a codified poetic tradition that associated the frog with fresh flowing water, love, croaking, song, poetry, and bright *yamabuki* flowers into a poem about stagnant water, solitude, and sound and silence. It introduced a profound swerve into the formalized poetic essence (*hon'i*) of frogs, accreted over the course of centuries; yet the innovation of this swerve would have been imperceptible without this tradition, within which it unlocked new possibilities.[57]

Variations on this creative dynamic of alteration within recognized forms appear throughout the early modern arts. One of the most prevalent aesthetic devices is *mitate*: the layering of two scenes or motifs so that their contours align to create an effect of double vision, often in a way that melds classical or elite (*ga*) culture with contemporary or vernacular (*zoku*) culture. The technique pervades the popular visual arts (a famous example is woodblock prints jointly produced by Utagawa Hiroshige [1797–1858] and Utagawa Kunisada [1786–1864] that depict courtesans and their customers arranged to evoke scenes from *The Tale of Genji*). Such visual layering and aligning devices have received the most critical attention, but *mitate* abounds in literature as well. Other aesthetic devices rely on a similar formal logic while upping the complexity. Whereas *mitate* produces a double exposure, techniques such as *fukiyose* (medley) and *naimaze* (jumble) involve throwing together characters, scenarios, styles, and storylines from a variety of different literary and historical worlds to form a cohesive, multivalent whole. All these mash-ups depend on formal congruences, great or small, to enable their connections and enmeshments.[58] Such devices may seem to be a matter of "mere" play, and they can certainly be playful—even hilarious, for much early modern humor hinges on the delight of unexpected associations. But playful or not, connection is their key. *Mitate*, *fukiyose*, and *naimaze* are all ways of seeing links, of drawing disparate parts of the world together, and thus of forming visions *of* the world. And they do so by identifying correspondences of form.

As these dynamics suggest, the forms operative in the early modern literary mode are relatively stable, but they are not immutable or essentialized; they are neither the essential Forms (*eidē*) of Plato's cave nor the endlessly transmissible shapes (*morphai*) of Aristotle. Form, rather, is both pattern *and* process. Unlike a mold that imprints itself on material or a container that is filled with "content," form here is better understood as a relational standard: a measure that is itself constantly transformed in relation to that which is measured against it. Because early modern literature prized—and, indeed, could not operate without—standards of literary tradition and authority, early modern literary form can appear conservative, static, or beholden to precedent. But here I find Devin Griffiths's ecological articulation of form salutary: "Rather than a discrete combination of shape and substance, form is a constellation of things and repeated actions. . . . The simple distinction between *form* and *content* does not adequately capture the dynamic and expanded nature of these relations. . . . [Form] works through wider networks of relation and of the material, energetic, and social interactions that give it life."[59] Bashō's frog takes its leap within a relatively stable body of poetic tradition about frogs; but its leap sends new ripples through that tradition, altering its shape and scope of possibilities. And so, it is important to focus on the modular and formulaic pieces that a work of early modern literature comprises, as well as to focus on the innovations introduced into them, the relations established among them, and the patterns they draw on as reference. For it is within and among those relations—in their in-betweenness—that associations could be stretched, models of order and arrangement proposed, authority and precedent transformed, and new perceptions made possible. It is in the interrelation of forms that we can touch the politics of early modern Japanese literature.

Here I would like to highlight three points that I see as crucial for understanding the politics of early modern form. First, I must reiterate that by "politics" I do not mean subversion, and I do not limit its purview to low or commercial literary forms. Second, we must set aside models that juxtapose reality and representation and instead understand forms as circulating between literature and life, which shared a deep investment in formalism. And third, the centrality of normative form to early modern social and political life made form itself a problem, one entangled with the relationship between truth and fiction. Let me unpack each of these points in turn.

The capacity of formal arrangements to shape modes of perception could serve (or ignore) authority as well as subvert it, and it operated in high literature as well as low. Take, for example, *In the Shelter of the Pine* (*Matsukage nikki*), a literary memoir that depicts, for the years 1690 to 1710, the household of the powerful Yanagisawa Yoshiyasu (1658–1714), adjutant (*yōnin*) to the shogun Tokugawa Tsunayoshi (1646–1709, r. 1680–1709).[60] The memoir's author, Ōgimachi Machiko (1678?–1724), was Yoshiyasu's second concubine. She was born into an aristocratic family in Kyoto and was brought into the adjutant's household in part for her cultural pedigree; she composed the account at Yoshiyasu's request. As G. G. Rowley notes in the introduction to her recent translation, Machiko suffuses *In the Shelter of the Pine* with sophisticated allusions to classical literature, modeling the memoir on *The Tale of Genji* in particular. Her style relentlessly adheres to that of Heian aristocratic vernacular prose (*wabun*), avoiding the Sinitic compounds that were part of the everyday vocabulary of power and administration in the shogun's capital. She refers to people by only their aristocratic court titles, not their shogunal titles. She never once uses the word "castle" or mentions Edo by name—although the memoir is set in Edo, and Yoshiyasu, the book's central figure, worked in Edo Castle—as such terms would have been foreign to the classical aristocratic world.[61] We might be tempted to read here a subversive formal politics at the level of vocabulary, elision, and allusion: an aristocratic woman's assertion, in the face of shogunal and samurai power, of the cultural superiority of Kyoto and its imperial court.

Yet to do so would be a misreading. For missing from *In the Shelter of the Pine* is the human and emotional messiness of court politics that *The Tale of Genji* makes palpable: spirit possession, sexual transgression, rear-court machinations, women and children sacrificed on the altar of politics. It is more appropriate to regard *In the Shelter of the Pine* as a grand *mitate*, in which Yoshiyasu and his household are transposed into the "world" (*sekai*) of *The Tale of Genji*. This *sekai* is a selective one: it contains the pomp, grandeur, and elegance of *Genji*'s world and the emotional depth of its characters—particularly in moments of celebration and mourning—but it completely excises its dark side. In this way, *In the Shelter of the Pine* is a deeply political text, but one that is the *opposite* of subversive. It imbues figures of present-day political power with the aura of classical cultural grandeur, presenting the shogun's circle as a seamless equivalent of the imperial court by casting its dramatis personae in the role of perfect aristocrats, effecting a vision of power at its zenith.

Second, we must understand forms as straddling literature and life. The celebrated *jōruri* play *The Treasury of Loyal Retainers* (*Kanadehon chūshingura*, 1748) famously recasts the Akō Vendetta (1701–1703) in the "world" of the medieval war epic *The Chronicle of Great Peace* (*Taiheiki*, fourteenth century); this work melds contemporary affairs with literary tradition in a way not dissimilar to Machiko's stylistic dressing of Yoshiyasu's household in *Genji*'s trappings (albeit one motivated as well by the taboo against representing politically sensitive subject matter onstage).[62] But the historian Miyazawa Seiichi has argued that *The Chronicle of Great Peace* may have shaped the Akō Vendetta itself. Through an examination of the avengers' correspondence and a biography of their league written by one of its members, Miyazawa makes the case that the *rōnin* measured their situation and (violent) actions in part against the model of the medieval literary epic, representing their decisions in ways that adopted its moral framework and literary style.[63] Henry D. Smith, discussing Miyazawa's work together with research in a similar vein by the historian Taniguchi Shinko, concludes that the vendetta was, in part, a "literary event."[64] And this bloody literary event, of course, went on to inspire a host of literary works of its own.

This startling dialogue between literature and life indicates the formal logic shared between the two realms. Just as some of the avengers resorted to literary models to make sense of their experiences and assess their actions, artists relied on the formal affordances of the same models to give the violent incident literary shape and meaning. In the following chapters I examine literary works that depict real-life events (the Great Meireki Fire; the crucifixion of the adulterous lovers Osan and Mohei; the beheading of Watanabe Yae by her brother, Genta) or practices (blood revenge). But rather than view the event or practice as primary and the literary work as secondary, it is more productive to comprehend the two as interrelated, each drawing on the other, both realms alike relying on formal models and precedents for feeling, shape, and meaning. Blood revenge was both a literary trope and a legally regulated social practice, but in chapter 2 we see that the idea of revenge existed somewhere between the two, as an atavistic practice that possessed an implicit narrative shape. Similarly, in chapter 3 we see that a crucifixion was a highly formalized—and even textual—event, while the literary treatments of the crucified lovers Osan and Mohei did not so much "represent" their transgression and punishment as rework and rearrange a spectrum of formal elements taken from both literature and life. And I suggest in chapter 1 how a fire or an earthquake was already, at a certain level, a "literary event" at the moment of its occurrence, its significance shaped by centuries of literary depictions of disaster.

Third, the heavy investment in formalism in both literature and life made form, in some instances, a problem for each realm, one that was entangled with the differentiation between truth and fiction. For if adherence to formal models and norms could effect a kind of reality, how was one to differentiate an empty formalism—a mere surface performance that might mask an alternative reality—from a formalism that enhanced, rather than obscured, reality? Ooms summarizes the problem: "Manner often overwhelmed matter; content lost substance and disappeared, as it were, leaving room only for form. . . . Form, norm, and formality are close neighbors, and together they may sometimes seem to take up too much space. One can argue that this was the case in Tokugawa Japan."[65] Fictional genres were exceptionally positioned to engage this problem, and they did so in ways that sometimes introduced into their pages a metareflective approach to their own fictionality and conventionality. This reflective quality could involve a satirical tack, as in Santō Kyōden's illustrated booklet (*kibyōshi*) *Revenge After the Fact* (*Katakiuchi ato no matsuri*, 1788). The book's samurai protagonist, Yōtarō, succeeds in taking blood revenge for his father's murder mere moments after it occurs. His lord congratulates him on fulfilling his filial duty, but Yōtarō feels uneasy:

> When Yōtarō thought it over, [he realized that] in books about revenge since days of yore, in order to strike down the killer of one's lord or parent, an avenger must sleep in the mountains and fields, wreck his body, sell his daughter and wife into prostitution, stifle

his regrets, conceal himself, give no thought to poverty, and meet with miseries and sorrows: this is what makes it an act of loyalty or filial piety.... The logic was the same whether he did it all before or after. And so, he made up his mind to undergo all those sufferings now.[66]

Having fulfilled the *act* of blood revenge but not its normative *form* (a form pointedly mediated by books about vengeance), Yōtarō feels that he has not actually completed his revenge. He embarks on a quest to undertake, after the fact, the hardships that will make his retribution true to form.

Yōtarō's quest—in search of an enemy he has already slain—is ridiculous. But the relationship between truth and fiction, which was closely tied to that between form and perception, could make for high drama. One of the most poignant scenes in *The Treasury of Loyal Retainers* involves Yuranosuke, leader of the league of Akō avengers, eating octopus on the eve of the anniversary of his lord's death—a time of abstention and vegetarian fare—to convince an antagonist that he no longer harbors any feelings for his lord or thoughts of revenge. The power of the scene hinges on the entanglement of truth and fiction with form and perception. The antagonist goads Yuranosuke into eating the octopus on the assumption that violating such a loaded norm would be too wrenching to carry out unless he had genuinely abandoned the lord-retainer relationship: the performance of the outward form, he expects, will serve as a channel to the obscured recesses of Yuranosuke's heart. Even the suspicious antagonist is "stunned into silence" as Yuranosuke blithely gulps down the octopus. But later, when Yuranosuke is able to throw pretense aside and punish the man for provoking him to undertake this violation, he voices the pain involved in such a deviation of outer form from inner feeling:

And tonight especially, on the eve of my lord's death anniversary! Even as I uttered all sorts of filthy words, I, Yuranosuke, was doing all I could to stay true to my abstention. And you dared to press the flesh of a fish upon me! Powerless to say no, unable to say yes: how I suffered in my breast! And what do you think my heart felt as the flesh passed my throat, on the night of the anniversary of a lord whose family favored my family for three generations? My entire body was racked with torment, and my bones felt as though they were shattering.[67]

The scene pits the "truth" effected by outward form against the truth held within the human heart. It suggests that only a hero of exceptional will could violate the form without his sense of identity ("I, Yuranosuke") coming apart at the seams. The relationship between the apparent and the real in a world of paramount form runs throughout the rest of the chapters in *Writing Violence*, surfacing most explicitly in the highly reflexive chapter 4, where it is the writer Ueda Akinari himself who must seek the literary form that will enable him to conjure forth the truth from the fictions he spins.

Texts That Bite Back

Writing Violence thus argues that we can recognize a definitive mode animating literary and cultural production throughout the Edo period: one that invested heavily in codified, typological forms and the traces of literary tradition but, through their dynamic and processual interrelation, permutation, and transformation, constantly opened new perceptual possibilities, proposing visions—great or small, innovative or conservative—of the world, its composition, its values, and its potentials. In this relationship between form and perception, I argue, we can access and appraise the politics of early modern literary works. To make clear the stakes involved in this mode, I center the book on forms of violence, as violence was ideologically complicated in a society ruled by warriors, and its licit forms were highly formalized. But the mode I engage in the chapters to follow was operative as well in other early modern genres and texts, and it applies far beyond works that consider the theme of violence. And so, with *Writing Violence* I suggest an approach to reading early modern works that is not limited to its immediate subject matter.

This approach insists, however, that particularities matter; the devil is in the formal details. I have therefore organized *Writing Violence* in a way that emphasizes both breadth of scale and specificity of focus. My scope reaches from the early days of seventeenth-century commercial print culture through the early nineteenth century. But each chapter focuses tightly on a particular moment, topos, or cluster of connected texts that rewards close examination of aesthetic forms and their imbrication with social and political forms. I address major authors—Asai Ryōi, Ihara Saikaku, Chikamatsu Monzaemon, Takebe Ayatari, Ueda Akinari, and Santō Kyōden—but with a focus on works that have confounded scholars because they do not fit neatly into the field's dominant narratives, or that evince interpretive possibilities that the field has overlooked. Put another way, I have chosen to focus on works that first got under my skin because their formal features confounded me, and that rewarded my sustained efforts to meet their formal dynamics on their own terms.

But what does it mean to meet a text's formal dynamics on its own terms? And where does that leave historical context? As should now be clear, I am not interested in hiving off the formal features of texts from the broader historical (social, cultural, political) contexts of their production in a kind of blinkered, intrinsic criticism. But neither do I regard those contexts as determinative. As Griffiths argues, "All those features we generally assign to forms, including their self-similarity, mobility, and capacity to produce specific modes of encounter, are actually features of collective interaction, events repeatedly produced and reproduced by the interaction of things in the world, from material substrates to natural agents to people."[68] My insistence on placing texts and contexts on a shared plane affirms this "eventful" understanding of cultural production in the dynamic terms of interaction, not of reflection or determination but of collective and shared process. This perspective makes it possible to tack swiftly between the microlevel specificities of texts and the macrolevel of social and historical contexts, recognizing both as coparticipants in the ongoing construction of meaning and the continuing inflection of a shared cultural grammar.

My method in seeking to grasp the dynamics of process, however, works decidedly from the inside of the texts outward, first paying attention to the formal aspects that arrest and confound me, and then comprehending the larger literary, material, and historical ecologies in which they are coparticipants. That is, I let the texts teach me what questions to ask of them and their world. Part of the point of this book is to argue against the subordination of idiosyncratic texts, each of which tests new formal and perceptual possibilities, to the smoothed-out contours of literary history. I am not as interested in mapping a royal road as in meandering down byways seldom taken, in enjoying the prospects and possibilities afforded by texts that, from the grand narratives of literary history, may appear to be dead ends. And I do not hesitate to ask: Are they dead ends? Or have we become so accustomed to certain modes of reading and argumentation that we overlook the complexities of their visions? Throughout, I have been guided by Ellen Rooney's reminder of the necessity of continuing to read texts carefully "long after one has acquired theoretical assumptions and ideological commitments. When the text bites back, it rewrites those assumptions and commitments, it theorizes and reads theory, history, ideology as it is being read and theorized. Form is its sharpened tooth."[69]

What follows are five chapters about texts that bit back, unsettling my assumptions about how early modern narratives are supposed to work and what they are supposed to do, and, in so doing, called my attention to the sharpened teeth of their forms. Each chapter results from a deep dive into a text or cluster of texts in a particular moment or genre. In each one I explore a different violent trope (disaster, revenge, crucifixion, honor killing, and murder and cannibalism). Within each chapter I seek to avoid formal myopia by demonstrating the broader political stakes of such attention to detail and by elucidating a different facet of early modern formal dynamics. Taken together, however, the chapters do *not* constitute a historical narrative—part of the book's point is the importance of difference and specificity, not totalization—and they may be read separately. Indeed, the chapters serve more like a compass than a systematized method, pointing us into the processual workings of texts without proposing a definitive picture or exhaustive history. But by placing my focus on the formal mode that animates the texts and links them to the world beyond their pages, the chapters *do*, collectively, point to a larger picture of how early modern fiction works. And so that compass may prove helpful to readers seeking their ways into the formal thickets of other early modern texts, each of which will bite back in its own way.

To demonstrate the political and perceptual stakes of literary form, I focus chapter 1 on *Stirrups of Musashi* (*Musashi abumi*, ca. 1661), a work by the pioneering popular writer Asai Ryōi (d. 1691) that depicts the Great Meireki Fire, a cataclysm that decimated the shogun's capital of Edo in 1657. Throughout the medieval period, disasters such as fires, floods, and earthquakes had been closely linked to violence in the popular and political imagination, interpreted either as portents of approaching warfare or as otherworldly vengeance by the victims of politically motivated deaths. But Ryōi's work divests the fire of these violent associations. He employed established medieval formal elements to depict the fire, but he collided them with the formal affordances of a new print-based informational economy in such a way that the scale of the damage and the subsequent recovery reveal the integrity of the ruling order and urban community. The chapter's focus on the formal representation—and transformation—of disaster thereby sounds the nature of the medieval to early modern transition and highlights the means whereby formal innovation could alter the perception of time, space, and politics.

In chapter 2, I turn to one of the few licit acts of violence during the early modern period: blood revenge, which was permitted for samurai to avenge the murder of a senior family member. Readers eagerly consumed stories, some fictional and others based in fact, of avengers undergoing grueling hardships to track down killers. While scholars have focused on the lurid subject matter to explain the early modern fascination with revenge, I approach revenge as an idealized form that straddled narrative and practice. I argue that the fascination with this "revenge form" reflected a broader social faith in the power of form itself: a belief that the proper performance of formalized behaviors—even violent ones—could hold social disorder at bay. I focus on the formally unusual revenge works of Ihara Saikaku (1642–1693) published in *Inheritance of the Martial Way* (*Budō denraiki*, 1687), which were critiqued in their own day for deviating from the representation of revenge proper. I argue that we should understand Saikaku's stories as interrogating, by means of the subject of revenge, this popular and political investment in form as a social bulwark. Saikaku's stories demonstrate how easily social forms could be manipulated to mask collateral violences or become warped by the unpredictable exchanges of commerce. The chapter thus demonstrates how the deformation of narrative conventions could intervene in the perception of social conventions.

In chapter 3, I consider the story of the lovers Osan and Mohei, who were crucified in 1683 for the crime of adultery and whose story became a fixture of street performances, fiction, and theater. I take the crucifixion itself as my point of departure, approaching it as a performance, staged by the authorities, that rendered the adulterers' bodies as forms: mute signifiers of a message about transgression and social control. I then turn to oral ballads (*utazaimon*), a story by Ihara Saikaku collected in *Five Amorous Women* (*Kōshoku gonin onna*, 1686), and *The Calendar-Maker and the Old Calendar* (*Daikyōji mukashigoyomi*, 1715), a puppet play by Chikamatsu Monzaemon (1653–1724)—all of which treated Osan and Mohei's story. Analyzing the various ways in which these works rearranged the story's formal elements—and reworked the meanings imparted to the protagonists' bodies—I demonstrate that they not only returned a sense of subjectivity, agency, and voice to the lovers, but inverted the message that their crucified bodies were intended to convey, making them the emblems (and victims) of an increasingly corrupted social order. The chapter reveals the body as a point of contact between social signification and literary signification, and as a site where textual representations could alter the meanings that bodies were believed to exemplify in the world.

In 1767, a young man named Genta beheaded his sister Yae in the courtyard of a man with whom she had been romantically involved. The murder was unusual in many respects, but the authorities ignored its peculiar elements to fit it into the familiar form of a patriarchal honor killing, and they absolved Genta. In chapter 4, I examine Ueda Akinari's (1734–1809) attempts to navigate the relationship among fiction, reality, violence, and expressivity through his writing—and rewriting—of the story of the murder: first in the essay "The Tale of a *Masurao*" (Masurao monogatari, 1807), and then in a story published in *Tales of the Spring Rain* (*Harusame monogatari*, 1808). Akinari had long wrestled with such questions: not only as a writer, but in his capacity as a scholar of *kokugaku* (study of the country), one of the most dynamic intellectual currents of the eighteenth century. Akinari identified in Genta's violent act not an honor killing, but the traces of primordial Japanese culture, characterized in *kokugaku* discourse by sincerity of heart and directness of expression. I demonstrate how Akinari's fascination with the unusual form of the murder became an opening for him to interrogate literary form's relationship to Japan's past and present, and the problem of "truth" more broadly, and ultimately to pioneer a new formal approach to fiction intended to restore archaic expressivity to his latter-day age.

The emergence of a nascent sense of nationhood underlies chapter 5, which addresses the fictional representation of Japan's early modern frontier and the question of how literary works theorized "Japan" as a coherent geographic and cultural entity: a protonational form. My object is Santō Kyōden's (1761–1816) *Revenge and Strange Tales: The Asaka Marsh* (*Fukushū kidan Asaka no numa*, 1803), a text that introduced many of the formal features that would come to define Edo *yomihon*, a genre of historical romance that wove together local lore, historical references, classical intertexts, and aspects of Chinese vernacular fiction in the construction of convoluted plots. Much of *The Asaka Marsh* takes place in Japan's northern outland, a geography celebrated in classical poetry but ambivalently related to the traditional centers of Japanese culture and political power, and it involves a protagonist who discovers, at the polity's ragged edge, a terrifying form of violence with critical implications for the health of the body politic. The forms of bodies and boundaries, centers and peripheries shape my analysis, which demonstrates the ways that the modular structure and intertextuality of the *yomihon* inform the questions it raises about normative bodies, social interconnectedness, and the shape of Japan itself.

I hope that readers leave *Writing Violence* with a new sense of possibility regarding how we read Edo-period literature and thus feel inspired to approach early modern literary works with new eyes, to chart fresh interpretive pathways into an expansive textual field, and to reevaluate the critical capacity of traditional aesthetic forms.

CHAPTER 1

Creative Destruction

Remaking the World in Seventeenth-Century Disaster Literature

> Then, in the first year of the Genkō era, flames emerged from the North Valley of the Eastern Pagoda of the Mountain Gate, and the Cloister of the Four Kings, the Cloister of Prolonged Life, the Great Lecture Hall, the Lotus Hall, and the Hall of Amida Recitation were all reduced to ashes in an instant. "These are portents of disaster in the land," everyone thought, and their souls ran cold.... With terrified hearts, they thought, "These fires at temples and earthquakes in various places are no ordinary happenings. Unthinkable things are coming."
>
> —THE CHRONICLE OF GREAT PEACE (TAIHEIKI)

Three days after the massive earthquake and tsunami that struck Japan on March 11, 2011—killing nearly 20,000 people, devastating the northeast, and setting off a nuclear crisis—Ishihara Shintarō, then governor of Tokyo, told reporters that the disaster was "divine punishment" (*tenbatsu*) for a culture of "selfish greed" (*gayoku*) that had taken hold of contemporary Japanese society.[1] Outrage ensued, and Ishihara quickly apologized. But his suggestion, that behind the violent destructiveness of the cataclysm lay a different kind of violence—an intentional, signifying violence—partook of an archaic mode of making sense of the caprices of the natural world. His words would not have been out of place in the medieval period, when (as in the *Chronicle of Great Peace* [*Taiheiki*], late fourteenth century) such calamities were widely interpreted as signifiers of the unhealthy status of human political and moral affairs. Ishihara's words seem callous and misguided in an age in which we understand the impersonality of geologic forces, but disasters nonetheless invite interpretation because, as Anthony Oliver-Smith puts it, they "disclose fundamental features of society and culture, laying bare crucial relationships and core values in the intensity of impact and the stress of recovery and reconstruction."[2] Disasters shake things up; they shake things out. Their shock forces humans to take stock of aspects of life that pass unseen in the steady flow of the everyday. The ways they are interpreted—not just in a politician's offhand remarks, but through the mediation of literary and artistic representation—have the capacity to alter perceptions. In the way their destructiveness is read and represented, disasters can go beyond destruction. They can remake the world.

The interpretation of disasters was particularly fraught in the early Edo period, precisely because of the long-standing association between cataclysms and human violence. Medieval modes of interpretation posited an intimate link between the political sphere and the natural world, which was "ethically reactive to human behavior."[3] If struggles or corruption among the powerful were bound to end in bloodshed, the devastation wrought by a disaster was understood to be an early symptom. Quakes and fires, storms and floods strike throughout the medieval military epics (*gunkimono*), pointing always to political turmoil to come. So conventional did the scene of ominous catastrophe become that it sometimes was included in these works even if, historically, none had actually occurred.[4] Yet the violence of disaster could also be more than a symptom: it could represent an intentional punishment, inflicted on the living by rancorous, otherworldly agents. The belief that those who had suffered politically connected deaths could return to punish those in power reached back to the ancient period and sometimes motivated the initiation of considerable protective measures. When the capital was besieged by floods, fires, and a deadly lightning strike following the death in exile of the minister Sugawara no Michizane (845–903), for example, reparative measures culminated in his deification as the god Tenjin and his enshrinement at Kitano, on Kyoto's northern outskirts. The warfare of the medieval period only added to the ranks of such "angry spirits" (*onryō*), who haunted the living through the forces of geology and weather.[5] When an earthquake strikes the capital near the conclusion of the Kakuichi version of the *Tale of the Heike* (*Heike monogatari*, fourteenth century) following the defeat of the Heike clan, temples collapse, the palace is damaged, landslides and tsunamis cause widespread devastation, the earth cracks open, and people are crushed in multitudes:

> The emperor, possessed of the ten virtues, had departed the Capital and sunk to the depths of the sea. Great ministers and nobles had been dragged through the avenues and their heads hung from the gates. From old times until now, people have feared the wrath of angry spirits. Among those of understanding, there was none who

did not now wonder with grief and lamentation what might happen next in the world.[6]

The survivors interpret the earthquake as the work of the vengeful Heike dead and, at the same time, as a portent of fresh violence to come. Just when it seems that order has returned after years of civil war, the quake threatens the continuation of war by other means.

The Tokugawa had come to power through the violence of warfare—as well as through the betrayal of the great hegemon Toyotomi Hideyoshi's (1537–1598) heir, Hideyori (1593–1615), whom the Tokugawa founder, Ieyasu, had once sworn to protect. Having brought an end to centuries of disorder and disunity, moreover, the new regime was deeply sensitive to any sign that the unrest of the past might return. When a gargantuan fire struck Edo in 1657 (the third year of the Meireki era), leveling more than half of the shogun's young capital and killing perhaps as many as 100,000 people just over fifty years after the establishment of the shogunate, the event was therefore rife with unwelcome symbolic danger atop the physical and human costs. Centuries of precedent existed to invite the interpretation that behind the Great Meireki Fire, as the conflagration is known today, might lie the impending danger of human violence to come, or the otherworldly vengeance of the Toyotomi or other victims of the Tokugawa rise to power.

The literary landscape that would mediate the representation of the fire, however, differed from anything that had appeared before. Print technology, which had existed in the archipelago for centuries, had received new life at the beginning of the seventeenth century, first through imperial and shogunal investment, and then through private enterprise. By the 1650s—the decade of the fire—a burgeoning commercial-printing industry had come into being, and, in the interest of accessibility, many of the books it produced were written with heavy reliance on the phonetic kana syllabary.[7] These vernacular "kana booklets" (*kanazōshi*) could be read even by those unfamiliar with all but the most basic kanji.[8] The disaster, brimming with signifying potential, therefore coincided not only with a new social and political order, but with a new landscape for representation and dissemination.

The narrative of the Great Meireki Fire produced for the commercial-print market was written by one of that market's most innovative figures, Asai Ryōi (d. 1691), a prolific author of fictional and nonfictional works on a wide range of subjects in the mid-seventeenth century. *Stirrups of Musashi* (*Musashi abumi*) was likely published in 1661, four years after the fire, and it would continue to influence the popular perception of the blaze through reprints in 1676 and 1772.[9] Its illustrations, now recognized as early examples of the dynamic potential of woodblock-printed images, remain emblematic of the fire to this day.[10]

Stirrups of Musashi lacks neither spectacle nor pathos: monuments burn, innocents suffer ghastly deaths, tears are shed, loved ones are mourned. And yet, something is different. The work is narrated by a tragicomic figure who serially misreads everything before him, evoking laughter amid the tears. His story, meanwhile, is periodically swamped by a deluge of statistics and informational lists that can stretch on for page after page. The book repeatedly invokes medieval modes of meaning-making, only to undermine them. And the conflagration, though represented as a tragedy in the short term, is revealed as a long-term comedy: a signifier, finally, of benevolent rule, power, and prosperity in a present that stretches steadily into an indefinite future. If this disaster is being made to disclose a world, it certainly differs from the world evoked in the treatment of disasters in literary works of the preceding centuries.

Consideration of the relationship between disaster and violence thus points to larger questions of the relationship between medieval and early modern modes of literary meaning-making. The periodization scheme of Japanese literary historiography draws a sharp line at the start of the seventeenth century: it is as though, together with the Western Army, "medieval literature" fell on the battlefield at Sekigahara in 1600, never to rise again, and "early modern literature"—armed with new genres, print technology, and a wider readership—marched away victorious. The meteoric rise of commercial printing typically counts among the key factors understood to separate the early modern from the medieval world. Print enabled the dissemination of widely shared bodies of information, facilitating the emergence of publics that reached beyond barriers of geography and status, and fostered among readers a stance of objective curiosity about the world they inhabited.[11] In keeping with the suggestion that print's first cultural intervention is an informational one, the modern reception of *Stirrups of Musashi* has largely analyzed the work in terms of reportage: an instance of print culture's new information economy.[12]

But what happens if we look at this work not as an instance but as an agent, a piece of literary craft that seeks to transform the "symbolic intentionality" of disaster and, in so doing, to call into being new ways of reading the world?[13] For *Stirrups of Musashi* posits novel relationships between local specificities and macroscopic wholes; between natural forces and political power; between the present, the past, and the future; and between the individuals and the spaces that together make up the community of Edo. And though it does so in part by drawing on the affordances of a brave new media landscape, it relies no less on recourse to archaic modes of representation and interpretation, dressing up old literary tropes in new meanings. In so doing, it transforms the symbolic intentionality of the fire so that it becomes not a variety of violence but the seal of a world at peace.

The key to grasping this process is to meet the work at the formal level, attending to the particularities and the peculiarities with which it organizes the chaos of the conflagration into a representable whole. Why does the text periodically veer away from narrative and descend into informational lists—lists that can stretch on for page after page? How should we understand its weaving together of statistics together with medieval tropes? Why does the seemingly serious figure who commences the text's narration later transform into an object of ridicule? Positioning the text at the nexus of seventeenth-century print culture, information and ideology, and aesthetic form will help us to see 1600 less as a barrier than as a point of flow, exemplifying how the dynamics, modes, and conventions that came to define early modern literature initially emerged, like new growth, from within the rich soil of earlier literature. But it also helps us to analyze the very real differences between medieval and early modern literature that tend to be treated as a priori differences, and thus remain undertheorized. And it ultimately enables us to think anew about the politics of early printed fiction—not merely in relation to technological, social, or political contexts external to literary works themselves, but at the level of literary form. For the formal details are what will prove crucial to grasping the version of the world that *Stirrups of Musashi* proposes.

Medievality and Disaster

In a provocative article that attempts to theorize the relationship between medieval (*chūsei*) and early modern (*kinsei*) Japanese literature—one of the few rigorous attempts to do so—Matsuda Osamu suggests that we consider the difference in terms of conceptions of time and space. He argues that medieval space should be seen as multidimensional, with different varieties of space (from diverse regional spaces to such otherworldly spaces as hells and demonic realms) layered on top of and around one another, each with its own ethical system and sometimes its own literature. In medieval temporality, past, present, and future are subsumed within one another and gain value through their interrelationship, but with the past being of the highest value and a sense of degeneration moving from the past into the present and future. In the early modern period, in contrast, both time and space become flattened out. All space exists on one shared plane and partakes of the same ethical system, while temporally, the present is paramount, with the future an extension of it and the past exerting a weaker force.[14]

Matsuda's heuristic proves fruitful when we think about medieval conceptualizations of disaster. In his understanding, the medieval world is always greater than it appears: the unseen and the dead may exist alongside and affect the affairs of the living; past, present, and future point backward and forward across one another, touching and interacting.[15] Disaster brings these interrelationships into dramatic focus: properly read a fire, and comprehend political ruin; properly observe an earthquake, and glimpse forces of numinous affect, bound to this world through a history of violence that will continue to unravel into the future. At their most profound level, cataclysms may even point to truths that pervade all times and all spaces. The most famous medieval depiction of disaster is the succession of catastrophes—fire, whirlwind, famine, pestilence, earthquake—that strike Kyoto in Kamo no Chōmei's (1155?–1216) essay "An Account of My Hermitage" (Hōjōki, 1212). Flames spread through the capital like the unfolding of a fan; roof tiles fly into the sky like dry leaves; a child suckles at the breast of its mother's emaciated corpse in a city's street. For Chōmei, these are potent manifestations of the Buddhist truth of uncertainty and changeability that lies beneath all phenomena all the time, and they point up the folly of the humans who live complacently without seeking the refuge of spiritual awakening. Significantly, the disasters of fire, whirlwind, famine, and earthquake map onto fire, air, water, and earth: the four elements that make up all matter in the Buddhist cosmology.[16]

In this sense, medieval treatments of catastrophe adopt what Eric Hayot, in a comprehensive study of literary world-making, describes as a mode of high aesthetic "amplitude." Hayot defines amplitude as the relationship between narrative foreground and background, characterized by the "relative spread of narrative attention across the diegesis, and particularly the distribution of that attention relative to the narrative importance of any given object in diegetic space."[17] In the high-amplitude mode of a medieval work like "An Account of My Hermitage," selected details of a disaster are brought into sharp relief, but their significance derives from a grander interpretive background that is sketched only in the barest of strokes. In this mode, not all details count, just those that express most potently their connection to the implied, numinous ground from which all real meaning derives. In an early modern disaster work like *Stirrups of Musashi*, by contrast, the depiction of disaster changes, as we will see; its amplitude becomes lower, crowded with information and details that compete for attention and that orient the text toward the shared, flattened out, this-worldly space-time described by Matsuda. Yet the text does continue, at critical moments, to invoke the high-amplitude mode of medieval works. As Hayot notes, differences in amplitude can mark "shifts in the theory of reality and of the social space that are reflected, conceived, or imagined into possibility by . . . work[s] of art."[18] The toggling between older and newer forms of amplitude in *Stirrups of Musashi*, that is, points to a newly emergent way of theorizing the nature of reality beyond the page.

Print Transformations and Asai Ryōi

If the disaster narratives of the seventeenth century adopt a low-amplitude mode that differs from the medieval period's high-amplitude depictions of disaster, one cause is surely the transforming relationship to information wrought by the rise of commercial printing. By midcentury, the scope of the material printed for the emergent publishing market was dizzying, encompassing native and continental books, new and old, written in classical Chinese; reprints of Japanese literary classics that had for centuries circulated only in manuscript; new fictional and nonfictional works written in Japanese on all variety of topics, using the phonetic kana syllabary with minimal use of kanji (the aforementioned "kana booklets"); and sundry images, maps, and ephemera.[19] Scholarship on the cultural effects of this new sea of texts has focused on the ways they transformed readers' relationship to information, and hence transformed the ways readers made sense of their world. Mary Elizabeth Berry characterizes this new volume of print as a "library of public information," and she discovers within it new and pervasive "habits of mind" oriented toward rational knowability and taxonomic order. "The texts," she argues, "affirm the knowability through observation of worldly phenomena. They presume the coherence of those phenomena through holistic and taxonomic modes of analysis. And they declare the entitlement of anonymous and ordinary readers to know what is known."[20] This shift toward "rational knowability" had implications for the treatment of disaster as well.

The rise of the commercial-print market was not solely an informational revolution, but also a revolution of literary form. The profit motive drove experimentation as publishers and writers sought to produce works that people would buy. At the same time, printing made widely available older texts that had circulated only in manuscript, and their various formal ingredients, including structures, characters, tropes, plots, verbiage, and conventions, provided fodder for writers' experimentation. The advent of commercial fiction, in particular, did not involve the creation of entirely new types of writing out of nothing. It entailed instead the joining, rejoining, and re-rejoining of units of culture—whether information, character types, or literary tropes—into new assemblages, each unit selected for what it might afford to the book as a whole. The combination of forms might include layering contemporary satirical references onto the structure of a classical text, as in *Fake Tales* (*Nise monogatari*, ca. 1630s): a parodical rewriting, down to the level of the sentence, of the Heian classic *Tales of Ise* (*Ise monogatari*, ca. ninth-tenth centuries). It might, as in *Guide to Famous Places Along the Eastern Highway* (*Tōkaidō meishoki*, ca. 1660), mean devising a protagonist—adapted from the wandering, comic protagonist of an earlier work—to conduct the reader through a travel guide that aggregates not just information but poems, stories, and observations.[21] Or it might involve adapting vernacular Chinese tales to Japanese settings, woven through with references to classical Japanese poetry, as in *Companion Dolls* (*Otogi bōko*, 1666). Bringing together existing pieces in new ways, books made new meanings, and these meanings emerged through the tensions between overlapping, mashed-up forms.

The author of the disaster work I discuss here, Asai Ryōi, exemplifies this spirit of formal inventiveness. Ryōi was the son of an abbot of the Ōtani sect of True Pure Land Buddhism, but his father's defrocking led to peripatetic years in which he seems to have relied on writing to get by. Indeed, as many as seventy titles in six hundred fascicles are attributed to him, ranging from True Pure Land Buddhist tracts, to adaptations of Confucian essays from Korea, to geographic works and travel writings, moralistic tales, didactic essays, and commentaries.[22] Eventually, Ryōi was welcomed back into the faith and became the abbot of a monastery in

Kyoto; by the time of his death in 1691, he had acquired a reputation as a Buddhist proselytizer and man of wide knowledge. He was clearly well versed in a broad spectrum of texts in both Japanese and Chinese, and we might best think of him as a translator in the broadest sense: someone capable of metamorphosing difficult-of-access material (Chinese tales, Buddhist doctrine, the language of old classics, unfamiliar geographies) into forms that audiences could apprehend. In so doing, he helped shape the landscape of commercial fiction. In the words of Matsuda Osamu, "Truly, for the volume and quality of his works and for his multi-dimensionality [takakusei], to talk about Asai Ryōi is to talk about kana booklets themselves."[23]

Stirrups of Musashi exemplifies the confluence of information, translation, and profit-driven experimentation. Sakamaki Kōta posits that the book's publisher, Kawano Michikiyo, commissioned it in response to curiosity in the Kamigata region—Ryōi's home and the heartland of seventeenth-century publishing—about the Great Meireki Fire in the shogun's capital. He speculates that Kawano dispatched Ryōi to Edo to gather information and examine the rebuilt city for himself and to translate the facts and experience of the conflagration into a holistic, readable form that would meet a market demand.[24] Shortly after the work's publication, Kawano published another book by Ryōi—*A Guide to the Famous Places of Edo* (*Edo meishoki*, 1662)—and a detailed map of the newly reconstructed city, and he also may have published Ryōi's *Guide to Famous Places Along the Eastern Highway* two years earlier. This set of publications responded to Kamigata-based readers' desire for information about the great metropolis in the east, its destruction, and its rebirth from the ashes.[25] We will see, however, that in *Stirrups of Musashi* Ryōi does more than just palatably assemble the facts. He strategically brings together diverse forms that fundamentally transform what a disaster could signify and how it could do so.

The Burning of the Shogun's Capital

Readers in Kyoto and Osaka had good reason to wonder about the shogun's capital, for the city, which was little more than ruins and wasteland when Tokugawa Ieyasu took possession of it in 1590, had grown into a spectacular metropolis. Ieyasu's engineers constructed Edo on an innovative spiral design along canals that circled away from the mid-fifteenth-century castle—a plan that could accommodate unchecked urban expansion into the Musashi Plain—and the very shape of the city embodied the politics of the new age.[26] Ieyasu requested that the wives and children of daimyo remain resident in his capital as hostages to guarantee fealty, and his successors dictated that the daimyo divide their time in alternating years between their home domains and Edo, where they would perform service to the shogun and remain under his watchful eye. This system of alternate attendance (*sankin kōtai*) had crystallized for all daimyo by 1642, and it swelled the population of the city. Lords, who came to number over two hundred, were expected to maintain at least two, often three—and for higher-ranking daimyo, as many as five or six—residences in Edo, and these mansions sprawled along the city's highlands, occupied by their families and large staffs of samurai. Merchants poured into Edo to serve this population of captive consumers; the houses of townsmen were crammed into blocks in the city's lowlands. By 1644, Edo had grown to more than double the size of Kyoto.[27] Above its sprawling geography of blocks and mansions, gates and canals, the keep of the shogun's castle complex towered 275 feet above the city, its turrets tiled with lead and its walls painted with lacquer to shield it from the dangers of wind and flame.

These were potent dangers. Each year, from late winter into spring, fierce dry winds blew from the north and northwest into Edo's labyrinth of narrow streets and wood-and-paper structures; a stray spark could wreak havoc on a blustery day. A drought had exacerbated the danger, parching the city's structures, when, on a late winter day in early 1657, a fire broke out in the Hongō neighborhood and spread rapidly through the city. Rising, falling, and shifting course with changes in the typhoon-strength winds, the flames burned for three days. More than half the city was reduced to ash, including most of Edo Castle. As many as 100,000 people—one-quarter of Edo's population—are thought to have perished.[28] The Great Meireki Fire was unprecedented in scale and symbolically fraught. How would Ryōi translate it for a curious Kamigata readership?

Stirrups of Musashi

Between Fact and Fiction

Ryōi presented the Great Meireki Fire through a set of formal collisions, mashing up existing tropes with the affordances of the new, print-based information economy. As a result, *Stirrups of Musashi* not only conveys the facts and experience of the fire but, ultimately, also transforms its symbolic intentionality. We can see Ryōi's strategy at work in the book's opening passage:

> Not so much one who had abandoned the world as one abandoned by it, left now with nothing else to do, he shaved his hair, dyed his robes black, and, taking the name of Rakusaibō or some such, followed the direction his heart would take him and let his feet carry him up to the Capital, where he prayed here and there before making his way to the famous shrine at Kitano. He prostrated himself to the deity, the same Tenjin as that enshrined at Yushima in his hometown. After, as he looked about the precincts, he came across an old acquaintance: a peddler, who had for many years made trips out to the east. This man was astounded. "How is it," he asked, "that I meet you now in the guise of a monk?" Answered Rakusaibō: "I experienced an unanticipated disgrace, and, unable to remain as I was, changed my appearance to that you now see." "And what was this ignominy you speak of so vaguely?" asked the peddler. "To speak of it is all the more painful," replied Rakusaibō. "Surely by now, you have heard about the terrible fire of the third year of Meireki, the firebird year?" Replied the peddler, "It is well known. At the time of the disaster, there were many young clerks from the Capital who had gone down [to Edo] together and who perished in the fire. Many are the parents and children who still mourn and grieve for them. The accounts I have heard of [the fire] are overwhelming [*obitadashi*]. Monk, for the sake of your own confession [*zangi sange*], tell me about what it was all like." "I feel as though suffering and sadness are afflicting me alone," answered Rakusaibō. "Like the poem about the stirrups of Musashi: not to be asked about such a thing is painful; yet to be asked is burdensome [*urusashi*]. I had thought not to speak a word about it to others. But, when I think that it may serve as a confession, [I realize] I should let you hear roughly what happened."[29]

This opening may seem little more than the establishment of a frame narrative: the account of the great conflagration, we learn, will be told in the voice of a character who ostensibly lived through it—Rakusaibō, the mournful monk, driven to tonsure by a great "disgrace" (*haji*). But this opening in fact embodies a series of collisions: between different media, different modes of narration, different literary desires and affects, differences of distance and proximity, and different ways of investing experience with meaning.

Stirrups of Musashi may have emerged from the seventeenth century's new economies of print and information, but here it adopts the conceit of an older form of information circulation: oral performance (*katarimono*). Oral narratives had served as an important medium for the dissemination of information for centuries and continued to thrive in various forms into the age of print. The setting at the Kitano Shrine is significant, for as both Sakamaki and Mizue Renko have noted, the shrine was an important site for the performance of various storytelling arts.[30] And, as the shrine first erected in 947 to pacify the angry spirit of the courtier Sugawara no Michizane, its use as the location of the men's encounter also hints at the connection between disasters and vengeful spirits, implicitly raising the question of the possibly violent, political signification of the Great Meireki Fire.

The peddler who solicits Rakusaibō's tale can be regarded as a stand-in for the reader, a Kamigata townsman who is curious, for reasons both personal and professional, about the fire in Edo. What he desires is information. But he coaxes it from Rakusaibō by framing the latter's narration as a "confession" (*sange*). The "confession tale" (*sangemono*) was a medieval trope. It took shape as a subcategory of late medieval fiction (*otogizōshi*) featuring monks and nuns who narrate their past sins and the events that turned them to the Buddhist path; a number of these medieval works were printed in the seventeenth century.[31] Rakusaibō's recent tonsure, his allusions to his recent shame, and his assertion that he feels as if "suffering and sadness are afflicting me alone," place him squarely within the medieval trope of individual suffering and Buddhist redemption. Ryōi thus signals that the account of the fire will be told in an intensely personal register, one laden with emotion and religious significance.

Yet the peddler's concerns are profits, the circulation of goods, and the practical information that can affect business outcomes. For him, Kyoto and Edo are bound by the routes along which merchandise and information flow, here marked by the clerks sent to the Edo branches of Kyoto businesses. For Rakusaibō, by contrast, spatial connection takes the older form of sacred networks. He has come to pay his respects to Tenjin because the deity is the "same Tenjin" enshrined in his hometown: a god who creates patterns of connection by existing in multiple places at the same time. Whereas the peddler desires informational details, Rakusaibō adopts a high-amplitude mode in which part is made to speak for whole: "I feel as though suffering and sadness are afflicting me alone." The frame narrative thus encapsulates a number of tensions: between oral performance and printed text, personal and objective experience, intimate and grand scales, and religious confession and worldly information. The vision of the Great Meireki Fire that follows is woven from their intersection.

This dynamic demands a startling bifurcation of the narrative voice itself. When Rakusaibō commences his purported "confession," the overwrought voice of the oral raconteur abruptly recedes, and the objective voice replacing it describes the fire on a scale that supersedes any single individual's experience. This omniscient narrator dominates *Stirrups of Musashi*, but Rakusaibō's lugubrious voice reappears twice: first at the halfway point—the end of the fire's first day and the book's first volume—and again as a final coda to the second volume. This tension between voices is vital to the way *Stirrups of Musashi* characterizes the signifying potential of disaster, and so we must make sense of what each voice accomplishes. I will first discuss the misadventures of Rakusaibō, and then return to compare him with the omniscient narrator who subsumes his voice.

Seeing with Medieval Eyes: The Confession of Rakusaibō

At the outset of *Stirrups of Musashi*, Rakusaibō may seem to be an impressive figure: a survivor of catastrophe who finds within it the seeds of religious awakening. In fact, Rakusaibō is a buffoon, the protagonist of a comedy of errors. Each of these errors, crucially, involves the *mis*reading of the fire. His story is therefore deeply connected to matters of perception, and to the question of how meaning should be wrung from the experience of disaster.

Rakusaibō's first misreading involves his own mother. After his encounter with the peddler, Rakusaibō returns to the narrative when his family regroups at the end of the first day of the fire. They discover that his mother is missing, and they come across a charred corpse that resembles her. They bring the corpse home and begin to perform funerary rites for it, when the real matriarch (not dead at all) walks in. Rakusaibō is aghast:

What is this? Have you already become a ghost [*mōrei*]? Is this a visitation? Why, then, have we been reciting the Hail Amida? Here we thought you must already have let go of your delusions and been reborn in the highest paradise! But it turns out you've kept your attachments to this world of woe, and now you show up as a ghost? This is terrible! Quickly, begone! We'll pray properly for your repose, so don't linger a moment longer at the forking of the Six Ways![32]

The facts should be clear: the family has misidentified the body. But Rakusaibō insists on clinging to the narrative that he has constructed, forcing his mother into the role of ghost rather than recalibrating his own assumptions. Only when she continues to protest does he look closely and realize that the corpse "was just the body of some nobody." The family unceremoniously disposes of the corpse and celebrates the mother's return.

Rakusaibō then reappears at the end of the second volume, this time to misread *himself* as dead. After celebrating his mother's return with drink, he is too intoxicated to flee when fire breaks out again the following morning. His family members thrust him into a wheeled chest and drag him through the burning city, but they are forced to abandon him when the streets become too congested. Soon thieves come prowling through the abandoned carts and chests, prying them open and looting the contents. Rakusaibō, awakening to find himself enclosed in a chest, thinks, "I have died and am being taken in a coffin to the charnel grounds. The coffin is being torn apart by hell minions, intent on tormenting me!"[33] He leaps from the chest, sending the thieves flying. Surveying the landscape, he confirms his suspicion:

> When I stood and looked about, everything around me was dark, but far to the east flames were burning furiously, and I could hear the shouts and cries of people. In my heart I thought, "That must be the Avīci Hell, and the sounds are those of sinners burning in the terrible flames and being tormented by hell minions. Oh, how horrible! How can I find my way to paradise?" Thinking this way, I continued along, when a large number of horses that had got loose came galloping my way. "This must be the Hell of Beasts," I thought.[34]

He continues to misread the landscape of burning Edo as a journey through the Buddhist cosmology of the Six Realms (*rokudō*) of existence, traveling from the human realm through (he believes) hell, including King Enma's court (actually, the Hall of the Ten Kings in Shibaguchi), the Realm of Beasts (the loose horses), the violent Asura Realm (a pursuer cutting down a looter), the Realm of Hungry Ghosts (officials distributing gruel to refugees), and the heavenly realms (a house where worshippers are singing and praying to Amida Buddha). Only when dawn comes does reality sink in. He later learns that his entire family has perished in the fire while he was drunkenly wandering through "hell." This, he concludes to his peddler acquaintance, is the great disgrace that has driven him to tonsure.

The tragicomedy of Rakusaibō's way of seeing is that it is calibrated to the wrong scale: a high-amplitude medieval one. Like the prognosticators in the medieval military epics, he invests selected details with profound signifying power, extrapolating to cosmic vastness—but he does so by looking past other details that could amend his view. When his mother walks through the door, he conjures up a cosmological vision of heavens and hells, delusion and attachment, prayers and salvation, yet misses the most obvious conclusion. His mistaking of Edo for the Six Realms relies on his coming across flames, animals, statues, and singers, but he overlooks the abundant data that might contradict his narrative. As Peter Kornicki has noted, even Rakusaibō's journey through "hell" is a parody of the "hell tour" (*jigoku meguri*), a theme popular in medieval literature and connected to oral storytelling and picture explication (*etoki*). In the hell tour, a living protagonist descends to the underworld and returns alive to report what he has witnessed there; one of the most famous versions involves the origin of the Kitano Shrine—the ostensible site of *Stirrups of Musashi*'s narration.[35] Rakusaibō's tonsure in reaction to the catastrophe, too, is a medieval gesture, resembling the actions of the protagonist of a confession tale or of Kamo no Chōmei himself, casting off the world in pursuit of a greater salvation.

Yet within *Stirrups of Musashi*, each of Rakusaibō's medievally inflected maneuvers is relativized or negated. His faulty perceptions meet with outright dismissal from other characters within the text. When he stumbles on the gathering of Amida worshipers, for example, mistaking it for paradise, he pounds on the door of the house and cries out for salvation to the bodhisattva Kannon: "From within came a great clamor of laughter. 'It must be someone whose wits have been addled by the shock of the fire!' they said."[36] And at the end of it all, as Rakusaibō explains to the peddler how the events led him to monkhood, he identifies a larger significance behind everything he has experienced: "To have lost my entire family in the fire is a bitter experience. But as a means to Buddhist awakening [*bodai no en*], is it not akin to the virtuous friend [who aids one on the spiritual path] [*zen chishiki*]?" The peddler is almost callous in his practical response: "Truly, this kind of great disaster, unprecedented and unforeseen, must have been a shock to your heart. Such foolishness is not unheard of. You should not think of it as such a matter of shame. But tell me, has there ever in the past been an instance of so many people perishing together?" Whereas Rakusaibō situates himself as the protagonist of a tale of Buddhist awakening, seeking spiritual significance in his suffering, the peddler identifies a case of shock and an ill-advised life choice. He abruptly switches the focus from the singularity of Rakusaibō's travails to a larger scale, zooming out to the scope of the disaster in aggregate and inquiring about its place among other historical referents.

In this way, Rakusaibō acts in *Stirrups of Musashi* as an embodiment of older modes of interpretation, reading disaster in a purely negative mode and linking its signification to a cosmology that supersedes the human realm. But by performing the role of serial *mis*reader and serving as the object of negation and relativization, he becomes the means by which such interpretations and values may be dismissed from the fire; as the butt of the joke, he lends credence, in negative, to the alternative mode of reading put forth throughout the remainder of the text. To fully grasp this dynamic, however, we must turn to the other parts of *Stirrups of Musashi* and grapple with the narrative voice that infiltrates Rakusaibō's purported "confession" and supersedes his personal story.

Creating and Destroying a Metropolis in Words

When Rakusaibō commences his "confession" to his peddler friend at the Kitano Shrine, the voice of the mournful monk disappears at once and is replaced by something quite different:

> Now then, in the Fiery Rooster year, the third year of Meireki, on the eighteenth day of the First Month, at precisely the Hour of the Dragon [7:00–9:00 a.m.], the wind began to blow from the northwest, swelling to become a great gale. Dust and dirt gusted into the heavens and trailed across the sky. Was it clouds? Swirling smoke? The

trailing haze of spring? Even as they wondered, the high and the low throughout Edo were unable to open their doors; though day had broken, it was still dark as night. No one stirred in the streets.[37]

The viewpoint has shifted from that of a single witness to that of city dwellers high and low. In the next lines, even this collective perspective is superseded: "When it reached the Hour of the Sheep [1:00–3:00 p.m.], a fire suddenly broke out at the western entrance to the fourth ward of Hongō, at a Nichiren temple called Honmyōji. Black smoke darkened the sky as the temple went up in flames all at once. Just then, an ill wind blew in all directions, and in an instant the flames burned toward Yushima and leaped the wide canal from Hatagoyachō to Surugadai . . ."[38] The viewpoint now exceeds direct human observation, as though the narrative perspective has receded into the smoky sky above the city and begun to trace the path of the flames through the urban geography with spatial and temporal precision. Strikingly, the coordinates it employs in this process of textual mapping are the residences of the various daimyo, whose mansions occupied so much of the space of Edo, each one of which is marked simply with the name of its resident lord. The previous sentence continues after the flames had leapt across the canal to Surugadai: ". . . where they ran about through [the mansions of] Nagai Protector of Shinano, Toda Uneme, Naitō Protector of Hida, Matsudaira Protector of Shimōsa, Lord Tsugaru, and others beginning with Satake Yoshinobu, and on through Daimyo Alley in Takajōmachi, where several hundred structures were instantly reduced to dust and ashes."[39] As the flames rip through the city, narrative recedes, and the text becomes a list of names: each name a mansion, each mansion an urban coordinate, and each coordinate charting the path of the flames. The effect is at once numbing and sublime, as when fire bursts out again on the second day:

> Within a short time, the buildings of the great mansion of the Middle Counselor of Mito, built so splendidly side by side, caught fire and burned violently, wrapped in flames and smoke. On the far side of the canal, below the grove of Hontakajō-machi, the Tenjuin Palace in Iidamachi, the two mansions of the Tenkyūkō of the Left and Right, the keep of the main citadel of Edo Castle all burned, and beginning with the Second Citadel and the Third Citadel, Matsudaira Protector of Kaga, Matsudaira Protector of Izu, Doi Protector

of Tōtomi, Mizu Protector of Dewa, Recorder Honda, Sakai Protector of Settsu, Tōdō Director of the Daigaku, Right Minister Ogasawara, Andō Protector of Tsushima, Tsuchiya [Minbu shōbu], Inoue Protector of Kawachi, Sakai Lord of Uta, Matsudaira Protector of Izumi . . .

The list continues for nearly *three pages*, dense with names and titles, before concluding with the predicate: "all burst into flames as one" (*ichidō ni moeagari*).[40]

What a contrast this vision of the city makes with Rakusaibō's misguided hell tour. Whereas Rakusaibō's misreading hinges on his extrapolation from selected details to grander cosmologies, here a precise map of Edo and its ravishment emerges from a constellation of pixels. The text has switched to a low-amplitude mode, crammed with multitudinous details that vie for attention on an equal footing. The narrator offers no interpretation, no signaling of significance—virtually no story. And yet, from this vision of a city made of names, a portrait emerges of a vast metropolis that collects the powerful and mighty of the realm's width and breadth, assembled in mansion upon mansion around the castle of the one who has summoned them there. The fire is made to operate like a negative: destroying the city, it reveals the city. It makes Edo tangible, not just as a vast physical space, but as an embodiment of shogunal power. No otherworldly cosmologies are necessary: real power is tangible here in the world, in the shape of the city itself.

The ingredients from which this depiction of the city is built are an admixture of old and new, including information made available by print culture. Beginning in the 1640s, the "library of public information" began to fill with cheaply printed rosters of daimyo houses. The entries in these "military mirrors" (*bukan*) included basic facts about the various daimyo, from their nomenclature and titles to the location, geography, and productivity of their domains.[41] As Berry has argued, the rosters made legible "the grain of power" to readers concerned with navigating the political landscape of the samurai capital; in the aggregate, they disclosed not only information but an ideological understanding of the functioning of authority. Similar details began to appear in commercial maps of the city, which regularly labeled daimyo mansions.[42] Such resources, which made Edo's physical geography navigable in terms of political geography, afforded Ryōi a mode of narration that could hover above the burning city, tracing the flames from a perspective disconnected from any single human viewpoint.

Statistical precision augments the effect. When the flames first die down, the narrator offers numbers to assess the damage. Burned: five hundred daimyo mansions, six hundred lodgings for lesser lords, countless commoner dwellings, the castle keep, over thirty watchtowers, sixty bridges, nine thousand storehouses. Killed: more than 102,000 people. Near the end, statistics are again invoked to situate the fire's magnitude in time and space, as the narrator tallies other great catastrophes in China and the archipelago: 22,300 killed by a Chinese earthquake in 1037; 21,829 homes washed away by a flood in fourteenth-century China; 10,000 killed in Kamakura by a quake in 1293. "But the tens of thousands burned to death in the recent conflagration are unheard of in any previous age."[43] The numbers are listed with minimal adornment, but from their aggregation emerges an image of an immense city of mansions, towers, bridges, and storehouses, brimming with inhabitants from all walks of life: a city that endured a catastrophe unequaled in all history, at home or abroad. From the data of destruction rises, phoenix-like, the apparition of a nonpareil metropolis.

But while this vision of Edo relies in part on the informational affordances of print culture, the lists are woven simultaneously of something more archaic: the "exhaustive list" (*monozukushi*), a trope of pre-Edo poetry, song, and—in the famous lists of Sei Shōnagon's *Pillow Book* (*Makura no sōshi*, 1002)—prose.[44] A form of combinatory play, *monozukushi* relied on an organizing conceit to bring together disparate pieces into a (sometimes surprising) whole, as in the following *imayō* song from the twelfth-century collection *Songs to Make the Dust on the Rafters Dance* (*Ryōjin hishō*):

Temples that show the mark of Kannon:
Kiyomizu, Ishiyama, Hasedera's sacred mountain,
Kokawa and, in Ōmi, Mount Hikone,
And visible here close at hand the Rokkakudō.[45]

Here an invisible force—the sacred power of the bodhisattva Kannon—links sites near and far into a rhythmic web of connection. The list conjures both Kannon's power and a sacred geography into legibility, echoing the pilgrimage routes followed by the faithful to points both in and beyond the capital and suggesting, in turn, the ways human movement enacts the connectivity of a sacred landscape.⁴⁶ Literary lists had been a distinctive figure of literary practice since the ancient poetry anthology *Man'yōshū* (*Collection of Ten Thousand Leaves*, after 759), but Suzuki Hideo identifies the medieval period as the real heyday of the *monozukushi*, finding in the trope a reflection of a society in which aristocrat and commoner, urban and rural cultures were coming into contact in new ways and giving birth to novel ways of imagining connection.⁴⁷ Key to the *monozukushi* is the implied point of linkage that binds the items, which Suzuki locates in the act of seeing itself. Each list suggests a perspective that looks into a world of differences and identifies a logic that unites particularities—of items, places, people, and scenes—into a greater web.⁴⁸

When *Stirrups of Musashi* charts the progress of the fire through exhaustive lists of daimyo, it partakes not just of the new "classificatory consciousness" highlighted by Berry, but of the encompassing vision and implied bonds of the *monozukushi*. Just as the power of Kannon in the *imayō* song creates a sacred web across the Kamigata region, so the authority of the Tokugawa house is implicit within the *monozukushi* of daimyo names. For while the fire's destruction makes the unparalleled assemblage of lords and their retinues visible, it is shogunal authority that has summoned them to the city in the first place. And since each daimyo's title points beyond the city to provincial geographies ("Matsudaira Protector of Izu, Doi Protector of Tōtomi, Mizu Protector of Dewa"), the implied web of authority reaches out to embrace the entire realm.

Indeed, once we begin to notice it, an emphasis on the moral authority of the Tokugawa pervades *Stirrups of Musashi*. This fire is not a product of past violences, nor is it a portent of unrest to come. It is a revelation: a calamity that makes shogunal power visible.

Auspicious Flames

The omniscient narration of *Stirrups of Musashi* does not restrict itself to exhaustive lists. Occasionally, it zooms in to depict focused vignettes: flames the size of cartwheels falling on refugees in the graveyard at Reiganji Temple; people freezing to death after throwing themselves into Edo Bay to escape burning to death; carts and chests blocking the city's narrow streets as residents attempt to flee. Yet it is not all death and destruction. When the flames close in on the prison at Kodenmachō, the warden addresses the prisoners, many of whom are already facing death sentences:

> There's no doubt you lot are going to burn to death. It's a wretched thing. But to kill you here and now would also be heartless. Therefore, we will grant you a temporary reprieve. Follow your feet, flee from here, and preserve your lives. Once the flames have died down, you must, to a man, report at Renkeiji Temple in Shitaya. If you do as instructed, I'll see to it that your lives are spared, even if I must give my own life in exchange. But if you break this agreement and don't show up, we'll hunt you down, even among the clouds, and punish not just you but your entire families.[49]

The warden's words weigh the formal duties of his job, the legal status of the prisoners, and the confining purpose of a prison against the morally charged wretchedness (*fubin*) and heartlessness (*muzan*) that those considerations will push him to if he insists on them in the face of the fire. He opens the gates, and the prisoners flee, shedding tears of gratitude. When they later present themselves at Renkeiji as promised, the warden is overjoyed. "You truly possess a sense of righteousness [*gi*]," he praises them. "No matter how severe your crimes, how could we put to death anyone who preserves righteousness?" He appeals to the city elders on their behalf, and the prisoners are pardoned. Those who hear of it exclaim: "The warden had compassion [*nasake*]. The prisoners had righteousness. And the elders had benevolence [*jin*]. It is clear that our country follows the proper Way [*michi*]." The narrator, too, praises the outcome as the manifestation of proper governance and claims that it is "the sign of a reign that adheres to the Way."[50] And so the fire gives life even as it takes life; it redeems old violences and prevents new ones. As though burning away all excess, it lays bare the fundamental virtues that inhere not only in those of authority, but in the lowest of the low—all of which are signs that are made to point back to the shogun: the highest of the high.[51]

Similar signs manifest even in the book's arresting illustrations, many of which depict the grand topography of the city—mansions, row houses, storehouses, gate towers, roofs of thatch and tile—engulfed in flames. In the foreground of the final illustration of the fire, for example, boats laden with burning cargo and rice bales nudge the shore, where firefighters attempt to extinguish the blaze atop a cluster of storehouses. Above the

Figure 1.1 "Momijiyama," in Asai Ryōi, *Stirrups of Musashi* (*Musashi abumi*, vol. 2, fol. 9b)
Source: National Diet Library Digital Collections

flames, however, serene against the outline of a hill, sits a cluster of shrine buildings in a grove, identified by a cartouche as "Momijiyama" (figure 1.1). The Momijiyama Shrine, located on a hillock between the main and western enceintes of Edo Castle, enshrined the Easterly Illuminating Great Avatar (*Tōshō daigongen*), the deified spirit of Tokugawa Ieyasu. On the fire's last day, "the wind blew more and more fiercely from the west, and the raging flames roared right up to the shrine of the Easterly Illuminating Avatar at Momijiyama. But just at the moment of danger, the avatar must have lent his protective power, for suddenly the wind blew from the north, and the Western Enceinte survived unscathed. Auspicious indeed!"[52]

The account is a mere pause amid another catalogue of destruction. But in the illustration, the episode has been elevated, literally, to the top of the page, where the shrine hovers untouched, an intimation of the "protective power" of the ruling house. "Protective power" (ōgo no goriki) is a Buddhistic term, suggesting a buddha's or bodhisattva's ability to protect all living beings. And the visual arrangement of the illustration resembles the sacred iconography of a mandala. Mandalas of the Kasuga Shrine, for example, frequently depict the primary shrine buildings at the top against the outline of sacred Mount Mikasa, with lesser structures below. The use of the same arrangement here—but with the secular landscape aflame—may seem perverse, but the image in fact represents munificence and power. Momijiyama lay at the heart of Edo Castle, at the center of the spiraling, mandala-like structure of Edo itself, schematically represented in the figure as a landscape of prosperity by the towering storehouses and laden cargo boats. And the firefighters, under the guidance of a mounted commander, suggest order and control amid chaos. The image—in its synthesis of secular and sacred, danger and protection, destruction and continuity—presents an irony: in an age free from warfare, it takes a natural calamity to make visible the protective powers of political authority.

These powers come to the fore in the pages devoted to the recovery efforts in the aftermath of the fire, which crescendo from grief, to healing and reconstruction, to resurgence. In the first phase, mourning is a collective process mediated by the benevolent authorities, who establish a new temple, the Ekōin—Temple of Prayers for the Dead—to inter unclaimed corpses. They enlist monastics to recite sutras unceasingly for the lost souls, and "throughout Edo, old and young, men and women came to pay their respects together, sleeve brushing sleeve, raising their voices together to recite the *nenbutsu* and pray for the repose of the dead: an awe-inspiring sight."[53] In the illustration of the towering tomb mound and the performance of rites, grieving and pious citizens from different walks of life crowd the scene, and shared grief becomes an ennobling bond that reaches across lines of class, gender, and experience to unite the citizens of

Figure 1.2 "Ekōin," in Asai Ryōi, *Stirrups of Musashi* (*Musashi abumi*, vol. 2, fol. 18a)
Source: National Diet Library Digital Collections

Edo into an emotional community buttressed by mutual compassion and support (figure 1.2).

From here, the depiction of recovery accelerates. The shogunate distributes rice gruel to the hungry and homeless and silver to merchants to encourage rebuilding and trade, a sign of the rulers' adherence to "the Way of proper governance" (*seidō tadashiki onkoto*) in an age of "an ordered realm and a pacified populace" (*chisei anmin*). The authorities refashion the city with wider roads, firebreaks, and embankments; relocate the inhabitants of overcrowded districts; and disburse funds for daimyo to rebuild their mansions. The crescendo peaks with an auspicious depiction of the flourishing city: "From the lords above to the people below, through the universal mercy of the rulers, the city of Edo returned in no time to the peace and prosperity of before. The great houses and highborn behaved with proper respect, the low commoners were satiated with the profits from their assets, and the auspicious flourishing of the city increased a hundredfold with each passing day."[54] The recovery from the catastrophic fire is illustrated by boxes of goods stacked high before an official (figure 1.3)—the same type of box shown burning in the boats below the Momijiyama Shrine (see figure 1.1). Yet another irony: the losses of the fire have made possible a greater munificence.

So in the wake of catastrophe—and made legible *by* that catastrophe—*Stirrups of Musashi* builds to an auspicious vision of each person in his or her proper place, yet united with others as a community and reaping the rewards of a peaceful age, beneficent rule, and a prospering city. Though it contains no prognostications of woe to come, this happy ending is not diametrically opposed to medieval interpretations of disaster, for it, too, treats disaster as an indicator of the moral soundness of those in power. Whereas the medieval works find in disaster signs of moral corruption at the top, cataclysm in *Stirrups of Musashi* makes legible the sureness of the political and moral authority of the rulers. It also presents a new relationship among present, past, and future. Rather than searching past events for the origin of the Great Meireki Fire or treating the conflagration as a portent of worse to come, the work concludes by making the present the seed of a future that will carry prosperity forward with only greater munificence, increasing "a hundredfold with each passing day." Only bumbling Rakusaibō, throwing himself down before a wooden image of King Enma and asking what he has done to deserve the karmic punishment of hell, looks to the past to make sense of the present. Only Rakusaibō, the fool, interprets the fire as a reason to renounce the world. For the omniscient voice that overtakes Rakusaibō's confession, the fire brings present and future more deeply into the world's embrace.

Figure 1.3 Prosperity following the fire, in Asai Ryōi, *Stirrups of Musashi* (*Musashi abumi*, vol. 2, fol. 24a)
Source: National Diet Library Digital Collections

Songs of Different Ages

And yet Rakusaibō does, in a sense, have the last word.

Stirrups of Musashi concludes back at the Kitano Shrine, following the account of Edo's recovery. Only here, at the last, does it explicitly raise the question of ill omens. Rakusaibō tells the peddler about *shibagaki* (literally, "brushwood fence"): a type of song and dance, likely derived from a northern rice-threshing song, that became popular at drinking gatherings in Edo shortly before the Great Meireki Fire. It was an unsettling fad:

> A low-looking, unrefined, coarse man would come forth; strip to the waist, revealing his black, filthy skin; and with an indescribable look on his face, bulging his eyes and twisting his lips, strike his shoulders and beat his chest, and knead his body like a crazy man. As he wrenched himself to right and left, raising and lowering his face and flailing around, those assembled would lend their voices, clap their hands, and all enjoy themselves together. It was unpleasant and off-putting even to an onlooker.[55]

The *shibagaki* craze was real, and many linked it to the burning of the shogun's capital, not least for the references to smoldering (*kogaru*) and scorching (*kogasu*) in the most popular version of the lyrics:

> I hear the voice of the man I long for,
> But the brushwood fence between us keeps him from my sight.
> Would we could meet, would I could see him, oh how I long!
> The fire that smolders in my lone breast:
> Would that it would scorch the one I love.[56]

An alternative version includes the ominous lyrics, "I've bound together a brushwood fence, but soon I won't be able to live here anymore."[57] And indeed, Rakusaibō muses, many of those who sang and danced the *shibagaki* don't live in Edo anymore, for their houses burned or they were killed in the fire—and so the *shibagaki* craze died out. He contrasts the popularity of this eerie fashion with the singing of auspicious songs of praise (*ōka*) that express a wish for the ruler's reign to flourish. If such songs cultivate favorable effects, he says, small wonder that those who indulged in the gloomy *shibagaki* suffered in the fire. Then he concludes:

"But as I said earlier, because of the sage blessings of the ruler, Edo once again prospered and flourished . . .

The provinces, too, are wealthy, and they follow Edo's lead
In a world well governed, as marked by the pine
Which shelters now the younger pines, growing by its base,
Their branches luxuriant and brightly evergreen
One will never tire of gazing upward in this everlasting reign.

That is the song to which we have returned. That is all for now," he said, and took his leave, passing through the torii gate, southward bound.[58]

And there ends *Stirrups of Musashi*—not with the presaging of dire events to come, but with a paean to the current rulers. In Rakusaibō's logic, the fire punished those who were foolish enough to have indulged in the inauspicious *shibagaki*. Better by far, he suggests, to give thanks to those who preside over an age of peace and prosperity, and who have brought Edo to ever-greater munificence in the wake of the disaster—a munificence that stretches forth into an everlasting (*hisashiki*) future. With this song of praise, Rakusaibō—until now the voice of chagrin and the misreader of signs—departs through the torii gate, as though ritually removing pessimism and misunderstanding with his physical departure.

Who, then, is Rakusaibō? Earlier, I read him as an embodiment of medieval values and interpretive positions, a kind of burlesqued Kamo no Chōmei who construes a pessimistic significance from disaster and turns to Buddhist frameworks in search of salvation. With his formal departure, the text affirms an alternative, optimistic reading in which disaster reveals the capacity of secular political authority—grounded in the concrete, practical details of the here and now—to keep the polity safe and prosperous into an indefinite future. Yet it is also Rakusaibō who sings the song of praise to the ruling house as he departs: a song that enunciates (in Matsuda's terms) a temporal shift *away* from the medieval propensity to read the present in terms of the past, and *toward* a view that looks at the future as the timeless continuation of a well-ordered present. In this sense, Rakusaibō is actually a figure on the threshold, straddling two different times and perspectives, just as his "confession" swings between a recognizably personal voice and an omniscient voice rooted in information. Tragic and comic, knowledgeable and ignorant, outdated and of the moment, Rakusaibō embodies the confluence of old and new texts, tropes, and forms that defined the literary marketplace of the mid-seventeenth century.

He is not alone. Nishida Kōzō identifies Rakusaibō as but one example of a new type of protagonist that appeared in the seventeenth century. An early example is Chikusai, the quack doctor who travels through Kyoto (starting at the Kitano Shrine) and then up the eastern seaboard, observing customs and composing witty doggerel, and who made his debut in the 1620s, with many variants and sequels to follow.[59] Another is Rakuami, the protagonist of Ryōi's own *Guide to Famous Places Along the Eastern Highway*. Nishida summarizes: "Even as they travel through the midst of society, they find no social acceptance. They are burdened, yet there is a nimbleness [*migaru*] to them. Seeming to possess ability and knowledge, they lack them; yet when they appear to lack them, they have them. They are shunned by others and yet treated as necessary."[60] Such figures, marked by in-betweenness and motion and often traversing newly vital circuits and spaces (Edo, the Tōkaidō), seem to me guides for a society undergoing a major shift, from older to newer modes of inhabiting and making sense of the world and navigating a plethora of old and new forms presented via commercial printing. In this sense, Rakusaibō is one of several early modern characters made out of medieval pieces—and perhaps, therefore, is a clue to the nature of literary early modernity itself. For what we call early modernity does not so much make a clear break with the past as enfold it and discover ways to make novel things from the affordances bequeathed by its relics. Just so, *Stirrups of Musashi* creates fresh significance for disaster—and reconfigures temporal and spatial relationships in the process—by investing new meanings and shapes into such older tropes as confessions, exhaustive lists, and hell tours.

Perhaps the greatest example of the early modern investment of old forms with new meanings appears in another work by Ryōi: *Tales of the Floating World* (*Ukiyo monogatari*), likely published within a few years of *Stirrups of Musashi*. Whereas *Stirrups* concludes with a comparison of songs, *Tales of the Floating World* famously opens with a similar comparison, as two voices debate the nature of the world. The first, citing the sense of futility expressed in melancholy songs of the past, considers it a "sorrowful world" (*ukiyo*), in which "nothing matches one's heart's wish, nothing goes as one desires.... Even though I am myself, my own heart and body do not obey me. How vexing!" The other begs to differ:

> No, that's not the meaning of it! Living in the world, we see and hear the good and bad in everything, and it's all interesting. There's nothing but darkness one inch before us, but why should we care one whit about that? Dwelling on it will only give you a bellyache. Just take it moment by moment. Indulge in the moon, the snow, the blossoms, and the autumn leaves. Sing songs and drink wine. Take delight in just floating along. Even if you go broke, you won't suffer. To drift about with an unsinkable outlook, like a gourd upon the waters: this is what we call the floating world![61]

This exchange has long been read as encapsulating the difference between a medieval and an early modern outlook. The second voice, by replacing "sorrowful world" with "floating world," both pronounced *ukiyo*, is typically thought to articulate a world-affirming epicureanism characteristic of the early modern period, in contrast to a world-denying lugubriousness typical of the medieval era. *Ukiyo* as "sorrowful world"—a world from which one could expect pain, disappointment, dissatisfaction—possessed a history in poetry and fiction that reached back centuries.[62] The new usage, "floating world," quickly became a key signifier within early modern popular culture, carrying the nuance of being entertaining, fashionable, up-to-date, or sensuous. Yet, as Taniwaki Masachika has noted, *both* versions of *ukiyo* share the assumption that there's "nothing but darkness one inch before us." They differ only in the matter of how to respond to this darkness: by seeking salvation beyond it or by losing oneself in its ephemeral pleasures.[63] The "floating world" does not overturn the "sorrowful world." It emerges from the older conception, retaining its traces even in the process of its reinvention.

Conclusion

In this chapter I have considered—by means of *Stirrups of Musashi*'s transformation of the violent associations of disaster—the role of commercial literature in the transition between medievality and early modernity. In its depiction of the Great Meireki Fire, *Stirrups of Musashi* undercuts the long-standing association of disaster with impending political violence or otherworldly revenge, transforming the conflagration into an event that, *through* its destruction, makes visible the integrity and benevolence of the political order. Ironically, in an age free from warfare and strife, it is disaster that can disclose these features of the sociopolitical order by placing them under stress. In the process, the text relocates the ground of significance from the sacred or unseen to the secular and informational realm; it reconfigures the temporal relationship among past, present, and future; and it presents a new spatial vision of Edo as an instantiation of political geography, reaching out to the entire realm in a web of authority and commerce. And though the text relies on commercial print's informational economy to achieve these moves, it depends heavily on the affordances of older forms. The religious renunciant, the ominous disaster, the hell tour, the exhaustive list: all make their appearance here, but the meanings they are imbued with differ wholly from anything seen in the medieval period. *Stirrups of Musashi*, like its main character, is a pivot point that looks in two directions at once. It does not stand firmly on one side of the medieval–early modern divide but instead reveals that supposed boundary as a point of flow, a place of ongoing process where the old is gradually transformed into the new.

Also like Rakusaibō, *Stirrups of Musashi* does not stand alone in this regard. Ryōi's book *The Pivot Stone* (*Kanameishi*, 1662), which also treats disaster (an earthquake that struck Kyoto and environs in 1662, killing nearly one thousand people), accomplishes similar effects, though drawing on different strategies and forms. The text explicitly raises the possibility that the quake may have been the doing of Hideyoshi's angry spirit—only to undercut the claim by attributing the disaster to the impersonal "energies of the earth" (*chiki*). It presents the shogunate's inspectors, canvassing the city to assess the damage, as inspiring more awe and reassurance than any otherworldly being, whether Hideyoshi's spirit or the (comically hapless) gods who populate Kyoto's many shrines. And it caps its vignettes—even its tragic ones—with a verse of comic doggerel (*kyōka*), each modeled on a classical *waka* poem: the device invokes a traditional heritage held in common (and increasingly disseminated through print) as a bulwark that keeps the community integral, even as it is rocked by impersonal geophysical forces.[64]

We can certainly view such works as participants in larger cultural and political developments. In the comic undercutting of Rakusaibō's Buddhistic worldview, we may find echoes of the effect of Tokugawa policies that transformed Buddhist schools into sanctioned, centralized sects under the control of a state shaped by Neo-Confucian ideology, altering their intellectual dynamism and authority.[65] In the replacement of numinous beings and spaces in favor of secular powers as loci of authority, we can recognize instantiations of Matsuda's concept of the early modern flattening out of space into a single, this-worldly plain. Suwa Haruo similarly characterizes the advent of early modernity in terms of the replacement of the authority of gods (*kami*) with that of political officials and classical traditions occupying a hierarchically superior (*kami*) position.[66] And Herman Ooms, in a close reading of the polemical best seller *The Tale of Kiyomizu* (*Kiyomizu monogatari*, 1638), has drawn attention to the role of commercial fiction in undergirding aspects of Tokugawa ideology in its formative years.[67]

I wish to emphasize, however, that early commercial literature is not merely reflective of larger sociopolitical trends, or political only in a narrowly polemical way. We may better understand *Stirrups of Musashi* as a "political" text by recognizing its participation in shaping Rancière's "distribution of the sensible": the "modes of perception" governing the inclusions and exclusions that shape any community and its politics.[68] For Rancière, aesthetics in the broad sense is a series of "forms determining what presents itself to sense experience," determining "the place and stakes of politics as a form of experience. Politics revolves around what is seen and what can be said about it, around who has the ability to see and the talent to speak, around the properties of spaces and the possibilities of time."[69] By transforming the import of disaster, conjuring Edo as a set of power relations, revealing communal and political integrity through destruction, and banishing the authority of the unseen, *Stirrups of Musashi* establishes new perceptual coordinates for grasping the way time, space, information, power, and interpretation converge to form a shared and legible world. If this text seems but one entry in the larger (re)distribution of the sensible that marks the transition from a medieval to an early modern episteme, I suggest we view it as a compass, one that points to avenues yet to be explored in assessing the role of seventeenth-century commercial texts in this transformation. And I urge that our assessment look not only outward through recourse to broader "contexts," but also inward, recognizing how much the text's perceptual reconfigurations take place at the level of form, including forms that predate the early modern period by many centuries.

The politics of form remain central to the next chapter. But rather than examining the transformation of older forms, we will see how the form of blood revenge, which had acquired a new sociocultural shape in the early Edo period, could be reworked in commercial fiction to alter the significance of its violence—and to thereby draw attention to the dangers of placing too much faith in form itself.

CHAPTER II

The Vengeance Variations

Revenge as Form in the Fiction of Ihara Saikaku

In 1696, the writer Ihara Saikaku (1642–1693)—Osaka merchant, flamboyant poet, and celebrated innovator of the style and substance of commercial fiction—received what we might call a poor review. In the preface to a collection of revenge stories titled *A Mirror of Japanese Warriors* (*Nihon bushi kagami*), the now-obscure writer Mukunashi Issetsu (1631–1709?) lambastes Saikaku for a book he had published a decade earlier. Issetsu writes: "In recent years, a book with the title *Inheritance of the Martial Way* [*Budō denraiki*] has spread through the world. Upon looking into it, it possesses not a single truth and contains nothing but obscene falsehoods. It is therefore not appropriate to serve as a teaching to people."[1] Writing against this impudent work—and even appropriating its subtitle, "Revenges Throughout the Provinces" (*Shokoku katakiuchi*)—Issetsu emphasizes that he has compiled his own collection of stories with an emphasis on "truth."

Saikaku's modern canonical status rests primarily on his works about eros, the licensed quarters, and the money-making schemes of merchants: a body of work so pioneering in style and subject matter as to be recognized in its own time as a watershed for commercial fiction.[2] But, as Issetsu's condemnation makes clear, he was also a writer of revenge tales. Blood revenge (*katakiuchi*) peppers various of Saikaku's story collections, particularly those he published in 1687 and 1688 that focus on samurai.[3] And it thematically structures the entirety of his monumental *Inheritance of the*

[65]

Martial Way (1687), the object of Issetsu's ire. Each of this work's thirty-two stories contains an act of blood revenge. Some are loosely inspired by real events, but most are purely fictional.[4] We should perhaps not be surprised that the commercially savvy Saikaku devoted so much ink to the depiction of vengeance, for blood revenge was a source of tremendous popular interest during the Edo period. But as Issetsu's critique suggests—particularly in his pitting of Saikaku's "obscene falsehoods" (*midarigawashiki kyomō*) against his own claims to "truth" (*jitsugi*)—the stakes involved in revenge and its representation involved more than salacious readerly tastes.

Blood revenge was freighted with heavy ideological baggage during the early modern period. The human propensity for violence—and its centrality to samurai culture—presented a conundrum for the polity's warrior rulers. The Tokugawa shogunate, which had established peace in the wake of centuries of warfare, relied on the social and political privileging of warriors who were left with no more wars to fight. The administrators of the "age of peace" were, ironically, the inheritors of a long cultural legacy of violence. The state sought ways to attenuate the individualistic, honor-based violence that had shaped samurai culture during the medieval period and, instead, to promote allegiance to hierarchical relationships and communal identities.[5] But one means of transforming violence was to embrace it. Certain violent samurai prerogatives were preserved, but heavily formalized: circumscribed by regulations that held them in check and invested them with values that oriented them toward order rather than havoc.[6] Blood revenge was one such practice.

In the case of the murder of a (typically male) familial senior and the killer's evasion of capture by the authorities, (typically male) familial juniors—sons, nephews, younger brothers—could request permission to track down the murderer and take lethal revenge. A bureaucratic application and registration process regulated the practice, ensuring that the avengers, if successful in locating and killing the target, would not be treated as murderers themselves.[7] Instead, they would more typically be hailed as heroes: moral exemplars who had borne hardship and risk for the sake of filial piety (*kō*).

Real instances of blood revenge were rare, and successful ones even more so.[8] But as one of the few licit acts of private violence permitted in the Edo period, the practice caught the popular imagination, and narratives of revenge—many of them purely fictional—took shape in the pages of books, the stories of raconteurs, and the performances of puppet and kabuki plays. This fascination with revenge signified more than a captivation with violence; the act of virtuous vengeance came to bear complex ideological stakes. We can glimpse the values with which it became invested in the same preface in which Issetsu chastises Saikaku:

> No one will recognize an evergreen if it shows not its color. If one does not take revenge upon the enemy of one's parent, how could the refusal to live under the same heaven as one's enemy be called a warrior virtue? For the weight of righteousness [*gi*] and the support of filial piety [*kō*], nothing is greater than [revenge]. . . . Those born into warrior households should bear this spirit in mind without cease. One should utter not the slightest falsehood, remain modest before others, and exhibit the deepest circumspection in all things. Enjoy yourself while your parents live, it is said, but if you get into pointless fights and lose your life, there will be no escaping the charge of being disloyal and unfilial. And if, while the killer of one's parent or sibling lives, one heedlessly strikes down this man and that, becoming one of the *ashura* [*shura no kenzoku*], how wretched that will be! Patience is the basis of success; a short temper spells doom. One should pursue one's great enemy at once.[9]

Issetsu's words encapsulate the dominant ideological understanding of blood revenge throughout the Edo period. In his characterization, blood revenge represents not wanton violence, but its opposite. As the fruit of self-mastery, revenge makes the virtue of a warrior as legible as the steadfast color of an evergreen, even in an age without wars. Because it requires the sublimation of personal desires to sacrifice on behalf of others, revenge upholds the paramount hierarchical values of loyalty and filial piety. And rooted in patience, modesty, and circumspection, revenge stands in stark contrast to the selfish violence of those who get into pointless fights and kill heedlessly like *ashura*, the demigods infamous for their insatiable lust for combat. The virtuous violence of revenge checks the menace of violence run amok.

Given this characterization, it is not difficult to understand why Issetsu found Saikaku's revenge tales so irksome. Like Issetsu's book, *Inheritance of the Martial Way* dresses itself in the language of warrior idealism and virtues. Yet many of its tales of revenge refuse to fit into the ideal box that

Issetsu advocates. Retribution is accomplished in less-than-exemplary ways. The ethical positions of enemy and avenger sometimes become flipped. Inappropriate people take vengeance. In some tales, the enemy emerges triumphant. And revenge, rather than a bulwark against violence, can seem to be merely one iteration of disorder in a landscape teeming with antagonism and bloodshed. And yet the avengers and their actions are depicted sympathetically—even beautifully—keeping the collection precariously poised between valorization and burlesque. Far from conveying a transparent moral lesson (a value Issetsu asserts for his own collection), in Saikaku's anthology the tension between the rhetorical idealization of revenge and the narrative distortion of revenge proper presents major problems for interpretation.

Scholars have attempted to analyze this ambiguity primarily by understanding the text as a merchant writer's commentary upon the samurai and their culture. Arguments variously approach the text as a product of mere ignorance, as a romantic idealization, as outright mockery, or as slyly camouflaged satire.[10] Consensus, however, has proven elusive. In the conclusion to an article that attempts to wrestle with these varying interpretations, Yano Kimio, a leading Saikaku scholar, appears to throw up his hands: "Did he attempt to depict the tragedy of samurai at the mercy of an irrational warrior society? Or did he set out to make a laughingstock of the way they obsess over their honor to the point of absurdity? Or is it both? Answering these questions will likely require repeated, detailed analysis."[11]

In this chapter, I take a different approach. Rather than treat *Inheritance of the Martial Way* as a commentary on the samurai per se, I read it as a critical engagement with the *formalization* of revenge and the ideological investments that formalization was made to bear. By formalization, I refer not simply to the bureaucratic procedures that came to regulate vengeance, but to the narrative formalization that grew around the practice in literary representation, giving it an ideologically charged, idealized shape in the popular imagination, situated somewhere between historical practice and conventionalized plotline. Recall how Issetsu characterizes revenge in his critique of *Inheritance of the Martial Way*. He insists that his stories will depict the "truth" of revenge. But his characterization makes clear that what he means by "truth" is actually an idealized *form*: a set of normative attitudes, behaviors, and practices that differentiates vengeance from other types of violence. Ideological investment in this *revenge form* (as I call it) presumed the capacity of virtuous violence to constrain heedless violence, as though the form of revenge proper could hold in check the dreaded formlessness threatened by unrestrained violence.

Across a wide range of works (not just those of Issetsu), the revenge form crystallizes this belief into a narrative shape: a plot bookended by the counterpoint of an illicit killing and a virtuous counterkilling, between which stretches a movement of exile and return. And it endows this plot with ideological stakes that exceed the antagonistic relationship between enemy and avenger. For, as I will explain, illicit violence not only inflicted harm on its immediate victim; it threatened the integrity of the hierarchical webs of relationships woven into the social fabric of the early modern period. The revenge form dramatizes the resilience of those relationships by requiring the avenger temporarily to untether himself from their protection and to confront the danger of his own social negation for the sake of a killing that, if accomplished, will vouchsafe the coherence of the communal values that the initial killing imperiled. The revenge form, that is, enacts a drama of collective danger, individual sacrifice, and communal resilience, pitched in the key of violence.

Saikaku's *Inheritance of the Martial Way* calls into question this association between the idealization of form and the preservation of communal integrity, and it does so by playing with the contours of the revenge form itself. By stretching and compressing the counterpoint of killing and counterkilling, relativizing revenge by situating it within larger narrative shapes, and colliding it with other formal structures, I argue that the collection raises the question of what is at stake in the faith placed in formalization, whether on the page or in the world beyond it. Can a set of idealized conventions—whether of plot and character or of virtues and performed behaviors—suffice to keep violence in check? Can formalized norms be trusted to guarantee proper ends? What unsettling truths and consequences might an idealized form obscure? Saikaku's stories aim to entertain, to be sure. But they evince as well a trickster-like capacity to turn the revenge form to ironic ends. And, as Issetsu's invocation of "obscene falsehoods" versus "truth" indicates, there is a politics to such irony. For in a social world that understood adherence to normative forms as a measure of reality, the distortion of form could place reality in question, making visible alternate possibilities that normative "truth" occluded. By bending and inverting narrative form, Saikaku points to the ways in which rigid adherence to form could in fact become a *source* of violence and a challenge to order. His revenge tales demonstrate how the celebration of form for form's sake could render invisible both danger and virtue alike. And ultimately, I argue, his tales suggest that blood revenge's exchange of violence for violence is no match for the unpredictable and vagabond disruptions wrought by the exchanges of a burgeoning capitalist economy—exchanges that made the relationship between truth and fiction murkier than ever.

The Revenge Form and the Containment of Violence

To understand Saikaku's treatment of the revenge form, it is important first to unpack more thoroughly the ideological stakes the form was invested with in practice and imagination. The legalization and bureaucratization of blood revenge, which had largely taken shape by the mid-seventeenth century, emerged at the most basic level from the practical, law-and-order concerns of the Tokugawa state.[12] It removed the violence of private samurai redress from the individual and, with its application procedure, made it reliant on state permission and oversight.[13] It also addressed the problem of law enforcement in a state constituted of semi-independent domains. Domanial authorities could not pursue criminals into other domains, and the various shogunal magistrates—*machibugyō* and *daikan*—oversaw vast populations with shoestring staffs.[14] Formalized blood revenge conveniently displaced the onus of tracking down and punishing murderers onto kin.

But beyond these practical impetuses, blood revenge also came to carry an ideological charge. The conception of blood revenge as an ethical obligation had ancient roots in the Confucian Chinese *Record of Rites* (Ch. *Liji*, J. *Raiki*) and its famous decree: "With the enemy who has slain his father, one should not live under the same heaven."[15] This characterization of revenge as an act of filial piety accorded with the broader conceptual shift—articulated in Tokugawa ideology and in the writings of samurai Confucian scholars such as Yamaga Sokō (1622–1685)—to conceive of the peacetime samurai as moral paragons.[16] Circumscribing this act of atavistic violence within a procedural apparatus and an ethical framework, the Tokugawa sought to convert it into a minimally disruptive act that made visible the martial preparedness and ethical stature of the samurai in an age of peace—a standpoint echoed in Issetsu's preface.[17]

The popular fascination with blood revenge, however, likely sprang not solely from these practical and ideological concerns, but from the practice's deep connection to early modern conceptions of community and selfhood.

These were rooted in reciprocal, hierarchical relationships that John W. Hall memorably characterizes as "a series of boxes or containers which confined the individual but also served to limit the arbitrary exercise of authority upon him."[18] Kurachi Katsunao inventively explains these relational containers by imagining what an early modern name card (*meishi*) would look like, had such documents existed during the Edo period. Whereas a modern name card prominently displays an individual's name and identifies his or her place within a professional context, the name card Kurachi proposes for a generic early modern man named "Tarō" lists the fundamental social units that define his identity: first the name of his lord, signifying the specific authority structure under which he lives (the lord of a domain, or the local representative of the shogunate if on shogunal lands); followed by his own village or town (representing not a geographic address, but his corporate status group); then the name of the head of the household to which he belongs, and his own position within that household (son, servant, retainer); and finally his own name, Tarō. As Kurachi summarizes:

> "Tarō" does not stand alone as a naked individual. He is enmeshed in three relationships: with the rule of his lord [*ryōshu shihai*], with his status group [*mibun dantai*], and with his household [*ie*]. These three relationships are relationships of obligation and protection, service and support. Within these relationships, "Tarō" occupies a fundamentally subordinate position, but by virtue of that position he can receive support for his livelihood [*seikatsu*]. To put it the other way, if he were forsaken by these three individual relations, he would lose any guarantee of his own livelihood—indeed, of his very life [*inochi*].[19]

These relationships affected even the individual's appearance: hairstyle, dress, the display of crests, the number of swords worn at the waist, all provided social clues indicating the larger social relationships in which the individual was enmeshed.[20] These relationships defined as well the spatial being of the individual, rooting him or her in a village, a city ward, or a castle town; if he traveled, he did so as a member of these communities, usually carrying documents that described his position within them.[21] The failure to fulfill one's social obligations threatened the social existence of the individual—the protections afforded by the containers—while individual assertion at the expense of these three reciprocal relationships weakened their cohesion.

An unpunished act of murder was a limit case that raised the specter of individual rancor ascendant over hierarchical reciprocity. The killing threatened all three relationships. It inflicted a wound on the household of the victim. Among samurai, it suggested a subversive willingness to place personal enmity above the interests of one's status community and lord. And it called into question the lord's capacity to administer a peaceful domain and protect his subjects. The killer's escape epitomized the rupture with these relationships as he abandoned them—essentially hacking his way out of the containers and casting them off with impunity—to forge a new identity elsewhere.

Whereas the killer's violence threatened the integrity of social reciprocity, the avenger's counterviolence reaffirmed all three relationships through the drama of sacrifice and hardship. Revenge proper meant seeking vengeance on behalf of *another*—a hierarchical senior within the household—affirming this relationship at the risk of one's life. It was understood, moreover, as a broader social duty expected by the status community. A samurai who failed to seek revenge would be counted a failure as a samurai, whereas success would increase his stature among his peers. And the act of revenge was closely connected to the ruling authority: not only did the domain mediate the avenger's application to the shogunate for permission to embark on a revenge, but the avenger's success redounded to the moral integrity of the lord's governance and was met with celebration and promotion.[22]

But the avenger could achieve this affirmation only by temporarily severing himself from the protections afforded by the three social relationships—by leaving the containers behind. The avenger was typically released from service (if he was not a *rōnin* already) until the completion of the revenge. And while siblings or cousins sometimes sought revenge together, or an avenger might be accompanied by a servant, the avenger necessarily took leave of his accustomed role and responsibilities within his household.[23] In a world in which social identity was vividly presented on the body and in clothing, the avenger sought anonymity through disguise so as to seek out the enemy without attracting attention. And whereas identity in the early modern period was spatially rooted, the avenger took to the road, afforded largely unrestricted access to the entire country, but unprotected. In these respects, he temporarily mirrored the enemy himself: anonymous, mobile, and self-reliant. Only by killing the enemy could he exit this parallel exile and achieve social reintegration.

These dynamics easily lent themselves to amplification in fiction and theater. Revenge already possessed a lengthy literary history in the Japanese islands—most famously, in the medieval *Tale of the Soga* (*Soga monogatari*), which narrates the revenge in 1193 of the Soga brothers, Jūrō and Gorō, against the man responsible for their father's death. Yet the features of medieval revenge literature differ markedly from the dynamics I have outlined, placing little emphasis on communal obligations or filial piety. Products of a feuding polity in which might made right, the early versions of the *Tale of the Soga* are much more concerned with the ability of personal rancor (*urami*)—particularly among those ostracized from the political order—to threaten the power of the politically ascendant, even from beyond the grave. In medieval versions of the tale, the Soga brothers, though successful in killing their enemy, do not escape with their lives. And they achieve communal "reintegration" only by being recognized as wrathful spirits (*goryō*) and ritually pacified after their deaths.[24]

Early modern revenge fiction, by contrast, adopted a different, and very distinct shape: a linear hero's quest, bookended by killing and counterkilling, rupture and reintegration, exile and return. And as Konita Seiji has noted, early modern revenge literature, to a greater degree than that of other periods, emphasizes the liminal middle stage.[25] During this stage, the avenger protagonist is loosed from his accustomed social and geographic containers and must struggle to retain—and ultimately reaffirm—the social identity that awaits him at the conclusion of his travails. The setting becomes the road, taking avenger and reader alike into unfamiliar physical and social geographies, from distant mountains and shores to warrior residences or the licensed quarters. During this stage, in which the avenger, disguised, precarious, and in motion, most resembles the enemy, he must exemplify the virtues that Issetsu praises—restraint, patience, circumspection—so that the death blow he strikes represents the victory of such communally oriented values over the selfishness and hotheadedness embodied by the enemy.

Together, these ingredients and their narrative shape—a shape that remained recognizable even as it was repeated with infinite variation across diverse early modern arts—constitute the early modern *revenge form*. We may call it a set of literary conventions; but Issetsu's invocation of "truth" in characterizing revenge proper suggests that it is better understood as an idealized norm, held in common in the popular imagination, against which reality and fiction alike could be measured and appraised. The revenge form's structure afforded ample room for innovation, exemplified by the Soga story itself, which underwent a dazzling range of transformations, from tragedy to farce, in early modern literature and theater.[26] But even the Soga were transformed, in the early modern period, from resentment-possessed agents, who could threaten the shogun's order, to righteous (if sometimes flamboyant) enforcers of communal values against the violence of corrupt and self-serving individuals. The revenge form's basic shape, and the ideological values that shape encoded, remained consistent.

Issetsu's own stories exemplify the elements I have described. The opening of "Kuka Heizaemon Avenges His Father" (Kuka Heizaemon chichi no kataki o utsu koto) pits the self-centered rancor of a *rōnin* against the reciprocal relationship between a lord and his retainer. A *rōnin* and an employed samurai have forged a friendship during the campaign to suppress the Shimabara Rebellion (1637–1638) in Kyushu, the last major outbreak of warfare until the battles that attended the shogunate's collapse in the nineteenth century. But when the samurai receives special favor from his lord in acknowledgment of his battlefield exploits, the *rōnin*, jealous, begins to slander him. Despite the samurai's efforts to maintain restraint, he ends up fighting the *rōnin* and is killed. The samurai's lord is incensed. He summons the dead man's two young sons and insists that they track down the *rōnin* and take revenge. The boys leave behind the protections of home and take to the road, but the going is hard: "They took their leave and searched through province after province and place after place, but since they had never even known their enemy by sight, there was no one they could ask. The years and months passed as they relied on mere guesswork, but then the older brother came down with a serious illness and died."[27]

This liminal stage is defined by precarity: the young men, alone, have no clues to follow and no protection against danger, which ultimately claims one of their lives. Only when the remaining brother is on the verge of abandoning the quest does he receive a clue to the enemy's whereabouts. The man has changed his identity and joined a lord's retinue in Edo, and the young avenger does the same in order to stalk him. But upon launching his attack, he renounces his disguise, shouting aloud the name of his slain father and identifying himself as his son: a reassertion of identity that foregrounds the relationships on behalf of which he has undertaken this quest. He succeeds in killing the enemy and is immediately welcomed with joy back into the retinue of his lord. Selfishness and selflessness, killing and counterkilling, exile and return: Mukunashi Issetsu's story epitomizes the shape of the revenge form and the ideological stakes bound up within it.

But this is not how Ihara Saikaku tells a revenge story.

Inheritance of the Martial Way

The Vengeance Variations

Inheritance of the Martial Way plays flamboyantly with the revenge form, but that does not necessarily make it an oppositional literature, intent on subverting, critiquing, or demolishing the status hierarchies and power structures of the day. It is more productive to understand Saikaku's stories as operating in an ironic, or even trickster-like mode that shakes up established perceptions and enables new ones. The tales employ the trusted conventions of the revenge form, but in ways that lead to unexpected ends, show up the contingency of seeming certainties, and materialize the unexpected fruits—positive or negative—the form can produce. I derive this conception in part from Lewis Hyde's meditations on the figure of the trickster across myth and art, particularly his characterization of the trickster's relationship to boundaries:

> Trickster is a boundary-crosser.... He ... attends the internal boundaries by which groups articulate their social life. We constantly distinguish—right and wrong, sacred and profane, clean and dirty, male and female, young and old, living and dead—and in every case trickster will cross the line and confuse the distinction.... Trickster is the mythic embodiment of ambiguity and ambivalence, doubleness and duplicity, contradiction and paradox.[28]

But, Hyde emphasizes, the trickster is not concerned solely with the blurring of boundaries, for "there are also cases in which trickster *creates* a boundary, or brings to the surface a distinction previously hidden from sight."[29] If the revenge form is deeply invested in the imagination of boundaries—between peace and violence, order and disorder, restraint and indulgence, the hierarchically higher and lower, and the inside and outside of communities—then Saikaku's fiction tests the soundness of those boundaries. It brings to light consequences of them that might otherwise pass unmarked. And sometimes it proposes new bounded units altogether.

These dynamics operate not only at the level of the individual narrative, but in the shape of the collection as a whole. As Hirosue Tamotsu has argued, in all of Saikaku's works the individual story cannot be fully grasped unless it is read in terms of the "space" (*kūkan*) of the entire collection: a space in which the apparent certainties of any given narrative are diffused and relativized through dialogue with the others.[30] As its subtitle, *Revenges Throughout the Provinces*, suggests, *Inheritance of the Martial Way* situates each of its stories within a particular province or domain, from Satsuma in southern Kyushu to Matsumae in Ezo (Hokkaido), on the northern frontier. The collection's spatial structure thus resembles an ideological vision of the realm of early modern Japan itself: a whole made up of self-contained enclosures. Yet the collection resists both spatial and narrative enclosure. It is not just that the stories frequently send avengers across different geographies on their missions, but that uncanny *formal* resemblances echo among separate stories. Details and scenarios recur: mistaken identities in the dark, surprise encounters at roadside tea stalls, vengeful widows with infant sons—even the motif of a zither plucked in a rundown dwelling. But a different context or nuance accompanies each recursion, such that the collection resembles less a sequence of discrete narratives than a set of contrapuntal variations. Three stories, for example, feature wealthy recluses, each named using the character *mu* (dream): Ganmu (Dream-Seer), Zuimu (Dream-Follower), and Muraku (Dream-Pleasure).[31] Each name can be interpreted as significant within its individual narrative, but the resemblance invites us to read the stories against one another as well, generating additional meanings through their contrast. The result is a centrifugal pull out of any given story, even as its plot exerts a centripetal pull inward: a reminder of contingency even when immersed in a narrative's seeming absolutes. This modular remixing of formal ingredients ultimately points not to connection or coherence across stories, but to a sense of arbitrariness, eerily evoking the sense that meanings and values that appear immutable in one context can take on a radically different significance in another.

The containing whole of the revenge plot itself, meanwhile, does not always align neatly with the shape of the individual narrative. When Issetsu and others write a revenge story, the rhythm of killing and counterkilling typically maps structurally onto the narrative's beginning and end. But

Saikaku's collection swells and shrinks the revenge plot, sometimes diminishing it to a blink-and-you-miss-it afterthought. The second story, "Poison Put Her Life Into a Box" (Dokuyaku wa hakoiri no inochi), for example, unfolds as a maze of variations on violence and reprisal. It begins with a sexual affair between a samurai and his maid; escalates to a mass poisoning perpetrated by a jealous rival; showcases the unusual punishment of the murderess (sealed into a box and impaled with nails); takes a turn when her brother tries to murder the samurai who orchestrated the punishment; builds to the hostage-taking of the samurai's young son; and reaches a climax when the hostage-taker is wounded by a sharpshooter and then cut to pieces by an incensed crowd. Only after all this, on the story's very last page, does "revenge proper" finally make an appearance. Years after the narrative's primary events have passed, a minor character, a samurai named Morinojō—introduced only shortly before as the lover of a young samurai named Ichimaru—receives a letter from his home province informing him of dire events concerning people who appear nowhere else in the story:

> [Morinojō's] older brother, Moriemon, had got into an unexpected quarrel and drawn his sword against three opponents. He cut one down on the spot, leaving two. He was able to battle them for a while, but perhaps his heavenly fortune was weak: in the end, the two of them cut him down. These two opponents, Tomeyama Gidayū and Torisaki Kankurō, left the spot immediately, absconded from town, and vanished. Morinojō, feeling deeply upset by this news, left the province with the intent to kill his brother's enemies, and Ichimaru accompanied him. In a village at the foot of Mount Tsukuba in Hitachi, they found them, and with Ichimaru acting as second, Morinojō killed the two enemies without mishap. They returned to their home in happiness and relief.[32]

Rupture, exile, and reintegration: revenge done right—but so compressed (taking up barely half a page in a twelve-page story) and so tangential to the main narrative as to seem perfunctory.[33] The successful revenge may evoke "happiness and relief," but, far from containing the eruption of violence in the realm, it constitutes a blip within the narrative's more elaborate depiction of larger cycles of murder and countermurder: the exception rather than the rule. And because the other acts among which it is situated are likewise motivated by vengeful impulses, the story hints that the exceptionalism of revenge proper may be a matter of *mere* form, masking a qualitative similarity to the forms of unruly violence it is meant to counteract.

The story of Morinojō and Ichimaru points as well to the challenges of Saikaku's distinctive style, which is marked throughout by compression and ellipses. His revenge narratives are highly plot-driven, thinning out at times to pure action, as in the quoted passage. In these moments, they resemble Issetsu's idiom: straightforward prose with little embellishment. At other moments, however, the pace can slow, the depiction can suddenly become lavish, or the mood can undergo an abrupt shift. Saikaku's reliance on classical poetic devices, such as pivot words (*kakekotoba*) and associated words (*engo*), enable his sentences to convey polyvalent meanings with minimal verbiage; a single phrase can sometimes mean two or even three different things simultaneously, each of which would require translation as a full sentence in English. Sometimes it is even unclear whether the affordances of such wordplay aren't driving the plot, rather than simply embellishing it. Saikaku mastered these techniques as an innovator within the Danrin school of popular linked verse (*haikai*), which celebrated allusiveness and far-fetched links between verses. This poetic background can be felt in his stories' allusions, asides, subnarratives, jokes, tonal reversals, and rapid shifts of voice. The result is a dynamism that destabilizes any straightforward unity of language, story, and meaning. In the story "A Sudden New Year's of 'Knock Knock, Who's There?'" (*Monomō dore to iu niwaka shōgatsu*), for example, the family of a slain samurai rushes in anger to the home of the man who killed him, only to be met at the front gate by the killer's mother:

> Zendayū's family gathered without even saddling their horses and rushed to Jūtarō's house, where they found the front gate open and before it Jūtarō's mother, alone. She wore patterned-leather armor and a headband of crimson and had unsheathed her halberd and seated herself upon a footstool with a look in her eyes that showed she did not begrudge her life. Those who saw her praised her splendidly, saying, "Surely, Tomoe and Yamabuki must have been just like this!" But since she was a woman, they did not bother with her, and when they heard that Jūtarō had fled the province, they each returned home.[34]

The tension builds rapidly as the description plunges from the charge of Zendayū's enraged family to the intimidating appearance of Jūtarō's mother waiting at the gate. Culminating in the allusion to Tomoe and Yamabuki, the two martially skilled consorts of the warrior Kiso Yoshinaka (1154–1184) who are said to have stood by him on the battlefield, a few concise phrases conjure up the impressiveness of this battle-ready woman and an expectation of conflict between her and the furious family. And then, in midsentence, it all deflates: the onlookers praise her and almost in the same breath dismiss her "since she was a woman," and go home. Has the entire, brief scene been the buildup to a punch line? If so, what does this punch line—the discounting of a seemingly imposing woman *because* she is a woman—signify? The rapidity of such shifts, which set up a scenario only to add a detail that necessitates a sudden reinterpretation—much as the addition of a verse in a *haikai* sequence reimagines the meaning of the previous verse—makes it difficult to know how to analyze any piece of a narrative by Saikaku in terms of the whole. Yet at the same time, the fragment floats off to join fragments from other stories in the collection—other instances of women behaving in ways typically gendered male, for example—forming a web of possible meanings that reach across individual stories. The defining characteristic of this collection dedicated to the formalized practice of revenge is fluidity: no form is ever final.

No form is ever final, but recognizing the formal modularity of the stories, and the ways they strain against the structure of the revenge form even as they recapitulate it, can help us to make sense of the collection. For its import is to show us that *no* form is stable or reliable—and particularly not when the destabilizing force of violence is involved. To elucidate these dynamics in closer detail, I offer examinations of three stories from *Inheritance of the Martial Way* that showcase the ironic ways the collection plays with the revenge form, each employing a distinct strategy, but all of them turning the seeming reassurances of the form to unconventional and unsettling ends.

Colliding Hierarchies and Formal Inversions

"A Woman's *Shakuhachi*, Played with Feeling" (Omoiire onna shakuhachi) is—or *should* be—a story of profound transgression. Reduced to bare plot, it concerns a young woman, Kogō, the daughter of a high-ranking samurai in Hiroshima, who commences a secret, illicit affair with a young samurai. She does not desist even when her father betroths her to another man, nor does she repent when she becomes pregnant by her lover. When her husband-to-be catches her paramour sneaking into her bedroom and slays him, she abandons her family and dedicates herself to the killing of her erstwhile fiancé. And she ultimately succeeds, aided by her bastard child, her wetnurse, and a former, male lover of her murdered flame. This is decidedly *not* a story of revenge proper. Instead, the actions of the tale's transgressive heroine defy all the values the revenge form was commonly understood to uphold. Viewed from a critical distance, Kogō is a socially deviant agent of anarchy. And yet that is not the way the story reads. For it adopts the narrative shape of the revenge form in such a way that Kogō appears to be a proper avenger; and it dresses both her romance and her vengeance in high-classical formal ingredients, lending to her actions the aura of legitimacy.

One of the predominant ways the story achieves this effect is by embroidering its questionable revenge plot with aesthetic forms that possess a logic and value hierarchy of their own. At the opening of the story, a craze for the aristocratic game of kickball (*kemari*) has overtaken Hiroshima with the arrival of a kickball master in the domain:

> **Willow** strands dangled in the houses of all the lord's retainers. On windless **evenings**, all would rush [to play], and the sound of kicking could be heard from every mansion.... Here lived a man named Fukushima Ansei; a relative of the lord, he lived in pleasure without position and was particularly fond of kickball. When he assembled his acquaintances for a **Tanabata** match, among them was Torikawa Haemon's **younger brother** Muranosuke, eighteen this year. Though his forehead was shaved at the corners, the fragrance of the **blossom** of the way of beauty [*bidō*] lingered about him.[35]

These may read as straightforward, if rather poetic, lines of exposition: a kickball fad, a gathering on the eve of the Tanabata Festival, a young man on the threshold of adulthood (marked by his partially shaven locks) but still bearing traces of the erotic appeal he had held for older men as a youth (*wakashu*). Each of the words I have rendered in boldface, however, appear under the entry for *mari* (kickball) in the *Ruisenshū* (1676), a dictionary of *haikai* poetic links.³⁶ Works like the *Ruisenshū* assisted *haikai* poets in creating effective links; the entry for "kickball" lists twenty-two possibilities that a poet could draw on to craft a verse that would complete the preceding verse in a compelling way. In this passage Saikaku deploys the lexicon not to craft a verse but to evoke a cascade of associations that intimate the shape and tone of the narrative to follow. "Younger brother" (*otōto*) abbreviates the *Ruisenshū*'s *misomeshi otōto* (falling in love at first sight with the younger brother). "Tanabata," the festival celebrating the yearly rendezvous of the Cowherd and the Weaver Girl (the stars Altair and Vega) and an important topos in classical *waka* poetry, hints at lovers brought together fleetingly across a distance. Other words and associations that the *Ruisenshū* lists under *mari* will soon come into play as well. *Kaki* (hedge or fence), for example, underscores the suggestion of barriers—and possibly their crossing. Ominously, the *Ruisenshū* also lists "Kashiwagi" (*Kashiwagi no emon*), an allusion to the character in *The Tale of Genji* who famously glimpses the Third Princess during a game of kickball and launches a disastrous affair. This brief opening thus evokes other narratives—the Tanabata and Kashiwagi love stories—that imbue the story with an aura of aristocratic romance and suggest a trajectory of rendezvous across formidable boundaries.

Those evocations come to fruition as Muranosuke and Kogō first meet. Dusk deepens, and the last kick of the match flies astray, out of the kickball enclosure, over the bamboo hedge (*kaki*), and into the garden of the adjoining mansion. Muranosuke, sent to retrieve it, spies the daughter of the neighboring house—like a "heavenly being sketched from life" (another Tanabata allusion)—as she steps onto the garden bridge to set afloat her Tanabata wish. He calls to the young woman, asking her to return the ball: "Without heed of the dew as she parted the grasses, she took the ball in hand, and as she passed it to him at a spot where they could exchange words, he held fast her hand and they looked into each other's faces. Thus their love began."³⁷ Defying, like the Tanabata lovers, the obstacles that would keep them apart, the two begin a secret rendezvous that involves surmounting "high hedges" and stealing the keys to locked doors.³⁸ Before long, Kogō is pregnant. A young man's breaching of the physical and social barriers of a high-ranking warrior's household—and of his daughter's womb—would, under any circumstances, constitute a social calamity meriting severe punishment. But the figures Saikaku employs to depict these events—aristocratic love, Tanabata, a sensual young man, a "heavenly" maiden, the Kashiwagi story—instead cloak them with the sympathetic allure of doomed love.

And doomed it is, for Kogō's father, en route back from Edo and unaware of his daughter's affair, stops along the way to arrange her marriage to a samurai named Jinpei. If Muranosuke and Kogō's love is characterized by desire and boundary-crossing, her betrothal to Jinpei is a matter of social practicality and containment. Jinpei is a family insider. He is Kogō's own cousin; even his name resembles that of her father, Jindayū, who intends to adopt him as his heir and retire, making Jinpei the head of the household. In one stroke, Jinpei will step into a position akin to that of Kogō's father, brother, and husband. He is selected in part because his brawniness suggests to Kogō's father "a reliable future" as a samurai. And because Jindayū has secured the lord's formal approval for the marriage and adoption, which will also make Jinpei the lord's retainer, the union is official not only within the household but in the eyes of the lord and the samurai band. Put another way, the betrothal is oriented entirely toward the three hierarchical, communal relationships—to household, status group, and ruling authority—that the revenge form was ideologically understood to uphold. And its formalized status pushes Kogō and Muranosuke's relationship into the legal category of adultery (*mittsū*).

From a conventional perspective, it is therefore wholly appropriate that when Jinpei learns of Kogō's relationship with Muranosuke, he lies in wait for him and cuts him down without a word of warning. The killing of an adulterous lover, like blood revenge, remained a sanctioned form of samurai violence under the Tokugawa shogunate.[39] In ideologically proper terms, the story "should" end here—not as a revenge narrative, but as a tale of adultery and its punishment. The ideological ends would remain the same: the punishment of self-oriented transgression and the reassertion of communal values and proper relationships.

But instead, the narrative shifts seamlessly *into* the revenge form. It treats Muranosuke's death as the first stage of that form's narrative rhythm of killing, exile, and counterkilling. Kogō, infuriated at Muranosuke's death, immediately commits herself to blood revenge against Jinpei, her own fiancé. She and her wet nurse, who serves as her accomplice, refer to him as "enemy" (*kataki*), and they take to the road, facing hardship and plotting Jinpei's demise in a way that resembles the conventional avenger's temporary exile. When her child's birth is at hand, she invokes the language typical of an aggrieved widow in a revenge narrative: "O gods, take pity on me! Grant me a male child who will strike down Jinpei, the enemy of his father, Muranosuke! If it's a girl, I will not leave this place but cut open my belly and die."[40] Slipping fluidly into the conventions of the revenge form, the story draws no overt attention to the ironic perversity of Kogō's prayer: a wish for her bastard child to murder her publicly recognized groom.

This irony is further naturalized by the story's continued invocation of elite forms to characterize Kogō. The high-classical register that marked Muranosuke and Kogō's first encounter—kickball, Tanabata, *Genji*—continues upon the birth of their son, Muramaru. The boy is born at Akashi and studies at Suma, sites associated with Prince Genji's exile prior to his triumphant return in *The Tale of Genji*. Once Muramaru comes of age, mother, son, and wet nurse disguise themselves as itinerant priests and wander the roads playing the *shakuhachi* flute—a revenge trope—but they also visit famous poetic sites (*utamakura*) and pay their respects before the portrait of Murasaki Shikibu at Ishiyama Temple. Their peregrinations, which progress "with the sound of the waves and storms in the pines," resemble the travel passages (*michiyuki*) of the *nō* theater, lending their quest a heft both emotional and aesthetic. Coloring these characters with classical elegance further obscures the unrighteousness (from a conventional perspective) of their endeavor. Jinpei, by contrast, is sketched in abbreviated strokes as an unsympathetic brute. He also possesses great physical strength, a characteristic of the enemy in revenge literature as far back as the medieval period.

These ironic inversions continue through the narrative's climax. At Ishiyama Temple, the trio encounters a man who recognizes them; in years past, he was Muranosuke's lover and he, too, has been seeking revenge against the killer. Tears flow at the formation of this eccentric grouping—male and female lovers, wet nurse, illegitimate child—bound not by asymmetrical ties of hierarchy, but by shared affection for the slain Muranosuke. The older man has a tip to Jinpei's whereabouts; together, they locate him in the mountains of Yamato, and, in a swift denouement, the old lover helps Muramaru strike down the enemy: "Everything went perfectly from beginning to end, and they slipped away from the village without mishap." A story of illegitimate retribution ends on a felicitous note of a revenge well achieved. Beguiled by the story's sly manipulations of its revenge-form shape, a reader can easily reach the end without noticing that revenge's conventional values have been turned entirely inside out.

But perhaps most striking is the subtle meditation the story evinces on the nature of containment itself. The narrative is full of containers both physical and social, from the kickball enclosure at the beginning, to the samurai mansion with its hedged garden and locked doors, to the patriarchal household structure the mansion represents. From the first stray kick of the ball, the narrative explores the consequences of trajectories that cross enclosures meant to contain them. The ball's course inaugurates the transgressive relationship of the young lovers, but it also foreshadows Kogō's own eventual trajectory beyond the confines of the household, onto the open road, and, ultimately, into a community of choice grounded in shared feeling. Adversity marks this community, but so does freedom of movement and sentiment. And so, too, does felicitation, for the story grants these "avengers" a happy ending. Kogō's father, by contrast—the man who wants to keep everything "in house" by marrying his daughter to her cousin against her will—ends the story enclosed himself: sentenced by his lord to house arrest (*enryo*) for the turmoil in his household. In all these instances, "A Woman's *Shakuhachi*, Played with Feeling" raises the question of whether containment truly provides the security it promises: a question that it implicitly extrapolates to the revenge form itself by filling up its familiar narrative shape with transgressive content. Therein might we locate the narrative's perceptual politics. Reader, beware: the familiarity of form can beguile, and trusted containers may foster the very violence they purport to guard against.

A Relationship Without a Name

Inheritance of the Martial Way's focus on samurai culture affords the collection rich material for probing this possibility that social forms, rather than mediating interpersonal relations and attenuating violence, may become channels of disruption. Even leaving aside limit cases like blood revenge, normalized social forms played an outsized role in the hierarchical, militarized culture of the Edo period's warrior-bureaucrats. Certainly, one could imagine a merchant writer like Saikaku lampooning samurai in their rigid commitment to ritualized behaviors. Doing so would be easy. But instead, the collection treats such commitments as fodder for something closer to thought experiments on the nature of form itself. What are the consequences when form does not serve its intended function? What happens if one prioritizes social norms with such singlemindedness that the form eclipses the social intercourse it is meant to facilitate? Do normalized behaviors merely serve social relations, or can they generate relations of their own? These problems open onto fundamental questions about the relationship between form and substance, performance and agency.

"Never Let Your Guard Down on a Swift Horse" (Fudan kokorogake no hayauma) exemplifies this aspect of the collection, featuring a samurai's over-the-top response to a seemingly trivial matter of form gone awry. As a result, the story presents an inquiry into the ironies that attend an overly strict adherence to form and becomes a meditation on form itself: on its violence and dangers, but also on its generative qualities and capacity for surprise.

The narrative opens with a deceptively simple social practice: a greeting. Minbu, a high-ranking retainer of the lord of Sado Island, rushing on horseback through the castle town in response to the lord's summons, passes the lower-ranking samurai Han'emon, who is on foot: "Minbu called out to him as he passed, 'Han'emon, I beg your pardon. I have removed my feet from the stirrups.' But nothing could be done about the fact that Han'emon did not hear his greeting."[41] It was generally permissible for a samurai on horseback to pass another (excepting the domain's highest-ranking figures) without dismounting, provided that he greet the other samurai and perform the symbolic courtesy of removing his feet from the stirrups.[42] Such formalities were designed to preserve relations; but ironically, if an expected formality was bungled or misread, the effect could exacerbate the damage. Minbu performs the greeting precisely, but Han'emon does not hear the greeting: a failure of form. Han'emon, whose domain stipend is a mere 300 *koku* compared with Minbu's 3,000 *koku*, interprets the perceived slight as an act of condescension. His household members remonstrate with him: it is not in Minbu's character to have neglected the proper greeting. But Han'emon is adamant: "Even if Minbu *did* make the greeting, nothing alters the fact [*shiawase*] that I did not hear it. It's unpardonable!"[43] He issues a letter of challenge to Minbu, who accepts it without hesitation, replying, "I removed my feet from the stirrups and performed the proper apology, but there is no use making such excuses now. I understand you wish to settle things at sword point tomorrow evening in the grove of pines at Chōrin Temple. I will meet you there at the Hour of the Rooster [5:00–7:00 p.m.], and I will not waste our time with conversation."[44] From an apparently small misunderstanding, the story quickly escalates to a duel to the death, and already we glimpse the shared character of Minbu and Han'emon: for both, the legibility of form itself takes precedence over the ambiguities of intentions, circumstances, or excuses. Minbu instantly acknowledges the legitimacy of Han'emon's resentment, and his succinct reply twice negates the worth of talk in favor of action. The duel substitutes one (destructive) form for another: as the greeting was intended to do, it will clarify their relationship beyond doubt.

Before they face each other, however, word reaches the lord, who summons them:

> The two of you exemplify the principles of the warrior. Minbu removed his feet from the stirrups and made the proper greeting, but when the time came, he did not dwell on such excuses but intended to throw his life away: truly admirable! And Han'emon, who might have simply shown forbearance, not having heard the greeting, instead proposed to sacrifice his life. This, too, is commendable! Since there was never any malice to begin with, henceforth let no grudge [*ikon*] come between you.[45]

The lord attempts to realign form and substance: there was no antipathy in the first place, so the miscommunicated form should not be allowed to generate it. A story by Issetsu might end here, with an authority figure's affirmation of the exemplary qualities of the two protagonists and a nonviolent resolution of their rift: a fitting paean to the warriors of a peaceful age.

But instead, the story gets stranger. The two samurai respectfully withdraw, and that night, Minbu departs Sado with his wife and child for the mainland, abandoning his high-ranking position without a word to his lord. The family settles in ramshackle lodgings in the Asakusa neighborhood of Edo, where Minbu prominently hangs a sign bearing his name and lives in impoverished freedom while he awaits Han'emon's arrival. Before long, Han'emon, too, takes leave of Sado with his family and arrives at Minbu's door:

> The two dissolved in tears. "There is nothing so inescapable [*zehi naki*] as warrior principles [*giri*]. Our end comes not from any grudge. Ashamed at what the world will think of us, we throw our lives away and depart as companions on the dream road [to the other world].

Well, then, it being our last night. . . ." With good feeling, they exchanged cups of sake to bid farewell to this floating world. Their wives joined them. The two women had never known each other back home, but, unexpectedly brought together here, they talked over the past and lamented the present.[46]

Minbu has a teenage daughter; Han'emon's son is two years older. They decide to marry them: a celebration amid the tears. The two wives then shave their heads as nuns, and the families walk to a nearby temple and spread a mat on the grass. The men kneel, contemplating their final moments. Then, "each grasped the other's left hand, and with a cry of 'Hail!' as signal, they struck each other with their swords. Leaving behind not a trace [of rancor] in their hearts, their souls departed and, just like that, became the same smoke rising from a pyre. They are models for posterity."[47]

It is easy to see why scholars have interpreted this story as a satire of samurai principles pushed to absurd limits. Taniwaki Masachika characterizes the entire collection as a "camouflaged" satire of contemporary samurai culture, particularly of samurai who had become urban-based bureaucrats even as they maintained the cultural trappings and prerogatives of battle-ready warriors. He reads the two men's lament about warrior principles and shame as a critique of the degeneration of those principles during the peaceful seventeenth century, from a set of organic values to an assortment of hollow, pro forma behaviors performed solely for the eyes of others.[48]

We needn't deny the possibility of this reading to recognize that there is, nonetheless, more at play in this story. For once the men have committed their lives—and deaths—to each other, a relationship is established between them that is as generative as it is destructive. This connection, rooted in an unarticulated but shared understanding, is so powerful as to outweigh even the vertical relationship between vassal and lord and, synecdochally, the hierarchical warrior society that relationship represents. That vertical order, represented by the tenfold difference in stipend between the two men (and underscored by the initial contrast between Minbu on horseback above Han'emon on foot), triggers their seeming antagonism. But by the story's end, the defining feature of their relationship is equality. Both have renounced their positions. Their families have come together in friendship and marriage. And even the depiction of their death—no longer a duel, but a joint suicide—is characterized by symmetry: from their clasped hands, to their unified cry of "Hail," to the way the smoke from their pyres, likened to their souls, becomes undifferentiable as it rises. As Someya Tomoyuki has noted, even their final exclamation about grudges, shame, and the world's opinion is ambiguous. It can be read in Taniwaki's terms to mean that the men sacrifice their lives solely from a fear of public opinion; but, read another way, it suggests that their sole fear is for the public to *misunderstand* their act as the product of ill will.[49] On that second reading, the commitment to form is anything but rigid or hollow for these characters. It is a medium of connection, the mark of a meaningful relationship. Taken to the point of absolute fidelity as a mutual responsibility that must be fulfilled, form becomes more than the sum of its parts.

And where, in all of this, is revenge proper? A revenge plot intersects the men's story while Minbu is waiting in Asakusa for Han'emon's arrival. Minbu's life there is characterized by penurious freedom: "The woven bamboo fence was shabby, the rain leaked through the rafters, the moon shone in coldly, the wall was completely covered with ivy, and the rough winds blew right in, but he did not begrudge the discomfort, gave no thought to the world, and passed each day just as his heart wished, exhausting all forms of amusement."[50] One frosty autumn night, as he delights in listening to his wife and daughter play music together, a commotion breaks out in the street before their door: a blood revenge, launched by a young woman, her "frail" husband, and his teenage brother against "three tough men" responsible for the murder of the woman's father.[51] Having tracked down their enemies after a three-year search, the avengers fight "as though they were prepared for their lives to end here and now."[52] Minbu rushes to aid them, but his wife holds him back: "Is your life not reserved for another?" She joins the fray instead while Minbu calls out instructions ("Sweep the leg!") to the avengers from atop a wall, and together they succeed in defeating the killers. While the avengers, ecstatic, thank Minbu and his wife, Minbu alludes to his own behavior: "It was not a matter of cowardice that I held back and did not fight alongside you when even my woman lent her strength. You will understand my behavior in days to come."[53]

This interpolated revenge scene operates as a foil in the story of Minbu and Han'emon: an example of moral and formal clarity set against the ambiguity of the two men's relationship. Among the many messy retributions in *Inheritance of the Martial Way*, this one adheres perfectly to the revenge form, exemplifying vengeance as a self-sacrificial act, rooted in genuine feeling, performed on behalf of a superior, in a way that counters threat with exemplarity. The enemies are imposing thugs; the avengers, delicate and inexperienced but fully committed. The way this antagonistic difference is written into their very bodies contrasts with the general movement in "Never Let Your Guard Down on a Swift Horse" toward symmetry between Minbu and Han'emon. The revenge form also serves its proper purpose: it affords a structure that contains acrimony and channels it into moral exemplarity. Minbu and Han'emon's situation is the inverse: the only publicly validated form that can accommodate their mutual respect at this point is a destructive one, a duel. Even as they commit to that form, they *deform* it in the way they "fight" it, without the contestation that would produce a winner and a loser, thereby contradicting its socially accepted meaning and demonstrating instead what it represents for *them*: reciprocal equality and the absence of rancor.

Ultimately, the revenge episode underscores the question of how social forms shape the rewards—whether tangible or ephemeral—garnered from the profound act of committing one's life to another human being. The avengers stake their lives on behalf of the dead, but in so doing they will earn reintegration and reward when they return home. Minbu, by contrast, must restrain himself because his life is "reserved for another." But even if his life is "reserved" for a death that holds no promise of broader social reward, the trust and shared feeling that the commitment exemplifies grants Minbu, in the meantime, the spiritual freedom to live with "no thought to the world, . . . pass[ing] each day just as his heart wished," as he is doing when the revenge arrives on his doorstep.

Perhaps the greatest irony of Minbu and Han'emon's relationship emerges when we consider it as an example of the type of violence that the revenge form aims to counter: private violence staked on personal reputation and carried out without sanction. Many of the revenges in *Inheritance of the Martial Way*—including the one inserted into this story—aim to rectify just such circumstances: a personal dispute that erupts into killing. Yet, far from the rampaging *ashura* decried by Issetsu, Minbu and Han'emon exemplify the qualities of self-control, patience, and circumspection that he associates with the ideal avenger. They are embodiments of disruption *and* order, reciprocity *and* equality, destruction *and* generation, death *and* life. And perhaps that is what makes their relationship so difficult to fit into any neat category of satire, critique, or valorization: they are exemplars, but of a relationship that exceeds categories, that has no proper place—a relationship without a name.

The Nameless Woman

If "A Woman's *Shakuhachi*, Played with Feeling" dresses transgressive murder in the clothes of the revenge form, and "Never Let Your Guard Down on a Swift Horse" treats the normative stature of blood revenge as the foil to a relationship no form can fully capture, "Vying Over Smoke at the Field Altar" (Nozukue no keburi kurabe), by contrast, keeps the proper revenge form front and center. It focuses on a wholly appropriate vengeance, perfectly executed, following years of arduous searching, by the filial sons of a murdered samurai. And its beginning, middle, and end map neatly onto the revenge form's rhythm of killing, exile, counterkilling, and reintegration. But this tale, too, is laden with ironies. By widening the focus *beyond* the revenge form's conventional ingredients such that the story exceeds them, the narrative suggests that revenge can mask other, messier violences that precise attention to formal perfection can fail to disclose. And in so doing, it questions how the ethical exchanges that structure revenge proper measure up when situated in a world of burgeoning capitalist exchange.

Read one way, "Vying over Smoke at the Field Altar" adheres perfectly to the revenge form. The murder at its outset stems from two young samurais' antagonism over which of them will offer incense first at the funeral of their lord (and former lover): an instance of personal grievance threatening the cohesion of communal order, represented here by the strictly regimented funeral scene with which the story opens. One kills the other and flees, and the dead man's sons, aged only eleven and seven, having "set their childish hearts on killing their father's enemy," tearfully bid their mother farewell and embark on the search once they come of age.[54] Nine long years pass before they catch word that their enemy is hiding in the northern castle town of Shōnai. Casing the outskirts disguised as a peddler, the younger brother, Toranosuke, becomes involved with a woman who knows the heavily fortified manor where their target is ensconced. With her help, the brothers succeed in ambushing and killing the man when he slips out in disguise to visit a local temple. The key elements are all here: disorder and restitution, exile and reintegration, precarity and exemplarity.

Yet the story reads as anything but a conventional revenge tale, for set into collision within it are other hierarchies and relationships that are rooted in tangled monetary, moral, and affective economies. At the center of them all is the woman who helps Toranosuke locate and overcome his enemy. She represents a socially liminal figure who emerged in the late seventeenth century: the independent working woman, making her way on the urban periphery through contract labor and sex work. The growth of large cities in the seventeenth century provided new opportunities for female labor, particularly as domestic servants.[55] The increase in cotton production from the sixteenth century on, meanwhile, with its multiple, specialized steps of processing, fostered an urban textile industry that employed women on a subcontractual basis. As the labor historian Yokota Fuyuhiko emphasizes, "This 'women's work,' instead of being done by wives to maintain their families' self-sufficiency, now integrated women into the work force, into a social system of production and marketing."[56] That is, it rendered them independent of the household and its watchful eye. But that freedom and the low status of their labor also marked the women in moral and erotic discourse as sexually loose. Yokota notes that the *Great Mirror of the Way of Love* (*Shikidō ōkagami*, 1678), an encyclopedic work on sexual culture by Fujimoto Kizan (1626–1704) that heavily influenced Saikaku's writing, includes a section instructing its male readers on how to seduce various types of urban working women. He concludes that "all women on the list—whether or not they were explicitly engaged in sexual labor as prostitutes—were regarded as sexually loose (prostitute-like) as long as they had contact with the wider society through their work."[57] When Toranosuke first encounters the woman as he ducks into her dwelling to evade a band of drunken swordsmen, a glance at the silk-working tools that lie side by side with sensual *kyara* incense, and at her sash, tied coquettishly in front, reveals her to fit this type.

The woman and Toranosuke begin a romantic dalliance that lives up to the working woman's loose reputation: soon they are engaged in erotic play in broad daylight, unabashed even before the crone who shares the woman's rundown dwelling. But they also begin to speak of their relationship as sharing the "bond of two lifetimes," a term usually restricted to the relationship between spouses. And when she discovers that Toranosuke is not the peddler he seems (while looking through his pack for a sex toy and finding nothing but a sword), her flirtatious language switches to a register of emotional commitment as she insists that he reveal his identity:

"These may seem a woman's useless questions, but having pledged myself to you, however fleetingly, I must hear the details. Above all, I offer up to you my own life."[58] From a sexual liaison, their relationship shifts abruptly into the morally shaded, hierarchical register of husband and wife. Her statement establishes a question of exchange that will ripple throughout the story: What does it mean to offer one's life to another human being? If such a gift is proffered freely, as the woman offers it here, can it also be freely recalled when circumstances change? And how does her pledging of her life intersect with Toranosuke's commitment of his own life to that of his murdered father?

At first, it coincides quite well, for the woman knows, by virtue of her work status, the mansion where Toranosuke's enemy is hiding. She had applied for a job there as a domestic servant, but, intimidated by the heavy security (the mansion is highly guarded against a possible revenge), she refused the position. Now she concocts a plan: "Now that I have formed this mysterious bond with you, I cannot go against my word to offer you my life. Right now, the procuring agent is eager to hire me, so from the fifth of the Third Month, I will go into service there, find a way to lead you in, and then you can cut him down just as your heart desires."[59]

These tight lines reveal the competing forms of relationship suddenly at play: relations of love ("this mysterious bond"), of obligation ("offer you my life"), of filial virtue ("cut him down just as your heart desires"), and of commodity exchange ("the procuring agent is eager to hire me"). Even the woman's economic act of hiring herself out evokes an affective exchange: Toranosuke refers to her plan as an act of "exchanging her body" (*mi o kaete no kokorozashi*) for his. And this exchange, in turn, echoes his staking of his own body against that of the enemy in place of his slain father.[60]

But new forms of relationship and exchange are yet to come. Once the woman enters the household, the enemy, who now goes by the name Muraku, takes a liking to her, and she finds herself serving in his bed as a contracted concubine. Concubines, too, were domestic employees, hired on six-month renewable contracts either for the employer's sexual pleasure or to produce an heir for his household. Thrust into this uncomfortable position between transaction and intimacy, the woman resolves to maintain a distinction between her body (*mi*), which she will treat as "something to be thrown away" for the sake of her lover's revenge, and her heart (*kokoro*), which will remain loyal to Toranosuke. But bodies and hearts are not so easily kept separate:

> Because her body was a woman's, it couldn't be helped: she ended up getting pregnant. While still lost in her thoughts, the months piled up, and she safely delivered a boy. In this midst of all his troubles, the child seemed quite pitiable [to Muraku], who now found it difficult to part with the woman. "From this day forward, you are the lady of the house," he said, and he had all the women [of the household] adjust their speech to her accordingly. Well, this truly was a gesture of kindness impossible to forget. The woman's heart was thrown into confusion. "I could tell Muraku about Toranosuke and have him cut down," she thought, with a woman's fickle heart. "Ah, but how mortifying! Having once pledged myself to Toranosuke, I must not exchange my feelings just because I have come into such favorable circumstances." She stiffened the resolve in her heart.[61]

Impossible to convey in English is the subtle way the narration slips from the woman's perspective to Muraku's, hinting at the growing affection that aligns their perspectives through the child they have created together. The passage also indicates a profound shift in the woman's social status: by insisting that the other women now refer to her as "the lady of the house" (*okusama*), Muraku signals that he considers her his proper wife and the mother of his heir. The morally suspicious working woman finds herself ensconced in a samurai household, the epitome of respectability.

Two very different plot shapes intersect here. Interrupting the revenge form's movement from rupture, to exile, to triumphant reintegration is the new path centered on the woman: from the social periphery into the heart of domestic space and propriety, and from self-oriented independence to other-oriented responsibility. Even the narration subtly moves the woman from an object at the tale's periphery, "read" by Toranosuke from her dress and possessions as sexually available, to the subject at its center: once she enters Muraku's household, the focus moves inward to her "heart," and we become privy to her secret thoughts, as in the quotation. And once the story's center shifts to her, the revenge becomes peripheral, its imperatives relativized, for the real drama now concerns the woman's choice between two identities. Indeed, the revenge no longer rests on Toranosuke's self-sacrifice or filial piety, but on *her*—a figure with no proper connection to it.

The revenge form's assertion of hierarchical relationships and communal values, moreover, looks increasingly tenuous in a narrative in which so many dyads—avenger and enemy, lover and lover, master and servant, husband and wife, mother and child—are revealed as interchangeable. When the woman chooses to remain loyal to Toranosuke, the decision can be read as an act of exemplary fidelity. But it can simultaneously be seen as a perversion. Though the pair had employed conjugal language, their sexual affair possessed no formal social validity, whereas Muraku officially recognizes her as his wife and the mother of his heir. Betraying him is, from that perspective, extraordinarily transgressive. Rather than celebrating the rectification of moral relationships, the story, by aligning our perspective with the woman's, renders moral clarity impossible.

As a result, the story draws attention to the uncomfortable link between violence and justice, for someone will die, whichever option the woman chooses. Indeed, when the revenge goes forward, Muraku is not its only victim. The woman alerts Toranosuke that Muraku will pay a visit to a local temple, hidden in a chest filled with Buddhist implements being delivered to the monks. Toranosuke and his older brother hide their weapons in a cart filled with radishes and then ambush Muraku on the road, killing him without a hitch. In the aftermath, the woman suddenly appears: "She showed no grief over the grievous scene but explained everything from the beginning. Then she said, 'As for this child, mine was only a borrowed womb!' and just like that, she stabbed it to death, and with the same hand took her own life, like a flower falling before everyone's eyes. There was not a single person who was not moved by her actions."[62] The woman disavows her connection to her own son with the words "mine was only a borrowed womb" (*waga hara wa kashimono*), a contemporary expression that affirms her identity as a contractual reproductive laborer with no personal claim to the child or his father. She then turns the weapon on her *own* body, ostensibly to punish herself for her physical unfaithfulness to Toranosuke during her time with Muraku, though perhaps better read as expiation for the many betrayals (including to her child) wrought by her impossible situation.

But this self-destruction is a chilling enactment of an erasure that reverberates through the narrative in other ways. For, though the reader has accompanied the woman to the center of the story and shared her innermost thoughts, from the perspective of the revenge plot *proper*, she remains invisible. It is Toranosuke's older brother, Ryūnosuke—barely a character in the story—who returns home in triumph as a successful avenger, having sought, located, and killed his father's murderer. (Toranosuke himself becomes a monk and prays for the woman's repose.)[63] That Ryūnosuke could not have accomplished the revenge without the sacrifice of his younger brother's lower-class lover—the main driver of action in the story—is, from a public perspective, immaterial. As though to underscore this invisibility, the narrator (who names even the most minor characters throughout *Inheritance of the Martial Way*) keeps her anonymous: with the poignant exception of the moment when Muraku names her "the lady of the house" (*okusama*), she is referred to throughout the story simply as "the woman" (*onna*).

The story probes the limits of the revenge form by maintaining its conventional pieces but decentering them, expanding the narrative frame to reveal the collateral violences masked by the symmetry of killing and counterkilling, and drawing attention to the messy fluidity of the hierarchical relationships that the form would valorize. Indeed, the story questions the nature of reciprocity itself. It not only collides the revenge trajectory with the woman's trajectory, but also mashes up moral exchanges with economic exchanges. A womb is "lent," one "self" (*mi*) is substituted for another, and a contractual relationship grows into bonds of feeling. The narrative unsettles the coherence of morally normative exchanges in a society increasingly colored by the logic of the market. Motifs throughout the story underscore this muddling of the moral and the commercial: a peddler's box is opened to reveal an avenger's sword; the weapons of filial justice are concealed in a cart of radishes; a murderer is hidden in a delivery of Buddhist implements. And ultimately, one story—a woman's economically inflected story of upward social mobility—is exchanged for a man's morally inflected story of revenge, at tremendous personal cost. Far from affirming the power of formalization to contain violence and mediate human relations, "Vying over Smoke at the Field Altar" evokes the blurriness with which moral, commercial, and affective exchanges intersect, exceeding the channels of the idealized forms that seek to contain them, nearly one century into an age of peace.

Conclusion

At the outset of this chapter, we witnessed Issetsu's insistence on the highly idealized "truth" of his revenge stories in *A Mirror of Japanese Warriors*, which he contrasted with the "obscene falsehoods" of Saikaku's tales in *Inheritance of the Martial Way*. Issetsu's concern with truth speaks to an anxiety over the alignment of reality with appearances: "No one will recognize an evergreen if it shows not its color." Reality, that is, can go unrecognized if not performed in a legible way; conversely, empty performances of idealized forms can mask reality. And the exercise of violence was particularly fraught, for while violence properly performed could make legible the moral stature of warriors in a peaceful age, improper indulgence in violence under the cover of warrior prerogatives threatened to inflict damage on the social order—and on the coherence of authenticity itself. Issetsu's collection responds to these ambiguities by showcasing stories of revenge in which proper form and moral character align, each validating the "truth" of the other.

As should be clear by now, the world of Saikaku's *Inheritance of the Martial Way* operates according to a very different order from Issetsu's "truth." Saikaku's tales may dress themselves in a similar language of ideality, but their trickster-like forms reveal the contingent nature of the very terms that Issetsu insists upon. Whereas Issetsu's revenges seek a reassuring closure, the shape of Saikaku's tales can be characterized as "full of beginnings without ends, of initiations, of losses, of transformations and translations, and far more tricks than conflicts, far fewer triumphs than snares and delusions."[64] Ursula K. Le Guin, writing in a very different context, uses these words to advocate a nonlinear approach to science fiction that undercuts the mythical, linear narrative of a "Hero" and his conflict-based quest and transposes it to the plane of realism. "It is a strange realism," Le Guin argues, "but it is a strange reality."[65]

We may see the idiosyncratic formal dynamics of Saikaku's revenge stories as composing their own, distinctly early modern brand of strange realism, a means of accessing the strange reality of a world in which the seeming and the authentic were increasingly difficult to differentiate. It was a world of slippage between signs and referents, characterized by the fluctuating value of currency, the disjuncture between ostensibly firm class boundaries and socially fluid realities, and the exponential growth of printed material purveying diverse "truths" and subject to piracy, plagiarism, and imposture. Rivi Handler-Spitz, writing about China and Europe, identifies these forms of slippage—and the accompanying anxiety over such "mutability and malleability of truth" and the difficulty of "adjudicating between authenticity and falsity"—as characteristic of early modernity well beyond Japan's shores. One way of apprehending this strange reality, she argues, was through recourse to a literary style she calls "bluff," characterized by "self-contradiction, paradox, and irony."[66]

Inheritance of the Martial Way fits squarely into this literary category. It revels in this malleable reality and embraces ironic style, showing up the incapacity of any formalized container, frame, or narrative structure to fix meaning permanently in place. The stories do not depict the historical reality of blood revenge, but their form nevertheless invites readers to "intuit something about the way in which the world is configured": not according to a neat model of everything-in-its-place and normative reciprocity, but in a jumble of exchanges, multiplicities (and duplicities), and voices (*including* the prescriptive language of morality), shot through with the unpredictable pathways of desire.[67] Reality dissembles, and ideality wears guises other than those that readers expect. Acknowledging as much constitutes its own morality, one that resists the dubious premise that violence properly performed can contain other violences without birthing dangerous consequences of its own. Contra Issetsu, Saikaku's book can indeed "serve as a teaching to people"—one far more realistic, albeit bewildering, than the teaching that Issetsu advocates. And it accomplishes that teaching at a formal level, opening up alternate perceptual possibilities through its inversion, deformation, and remixing of the accustomed ingredients and idealized conventions of the revenge form.

As we will see, a concern with the authentic and the false, and with the capacity of form to mediate between them, pervades early modern popular literature well beyond Saikaku's revenge tales. It figures prominently in the next chapter, which explores adultery, punishment, and the power of the theater to transform—through its own formal logic—the perception of reality beyond its walls.

CHAPTER III

The (Un)crucified Lovers

Adultery, Punishment, and the "Truth" of Transgression

On the twenty-second day of the Ninth Month of 1683, a macabre procession wended through the avenues of Kyoto. A man holding aloft a paper banner led the way, accompanied by another hoisting a wooden signboard; both listed the details of a crime and the names and ages of the condemned. Next marched a phalanx of officials and enforcers bearing a motley assortment of weapons, and in their midst, borne on horseback, sat the criminals, bound with ropes: a young woman and a man. The procession made its way through the city's thoroughfares, exposing the doomed couple to the eyes of city dwellers from all walks of life, before veering to its final destination: the execution ground at Awataguchi, in the heavily trafficked area where the Tōkaidō (Eastern Highway) made its last descent over the Eastern Hills and into the city. There, the two were pulled from the horse, bound to posts, and impaled repeatedly with spears. Their bodies would remain on public display for three days and two nights, greeting travelers on their way into or out of the old capital. The wooden signboard, now erected beside them, identified the corpses as Osan, the young wife of Ishun, the city's imperially licensed producer of calendars, and Mohei, one of his clerks. Their capital offense: adultery. Displayed with their bodies was the severed head of Tama, the young maidservant said to have acted as their go-between.

This grim act of penal theater ended the lovers' lives, but it initiated a lengthy afterlife of storytelling about them—and, through them, about sexual transgression and its punishment—that would continue across diverse genres and media throughout the Edo period. Shortly after their demise, Osan and Mohei began to transform into "Osan-Mohei," shorthand for a cluster of texts and performances that took up the doomed lovers' story. Balladeers dressed as ascetic mountain priests sang their tale in the form of "song supplications" (*utazaimon*) on the streets of Kyoto and Osaka. Ihara Saikaku made Osan the subject of the third story in his collection *Five Amorous Women* (*Kōshoku gonin onna*, 1686). And in 1715, Chikamatsu Monzaemon's *jōruri* puppet play *The Calendar-Maker and the Old Calendar* (*Daikyōji mukashigoyomi*) went up at Osaka's Takemoto-za theater. Other versions in kabuki, fiction, and the visual arts followed, making the incident "one of the most frequently treated in the various arts throughout the early modern period."[1]

But the first entry in the texts and performances that make up Osan-Mohei was the execution itself. This was a carefully formalized production with several "acts" and multiple "players." It featured designated protagonists (Osan, Mohei, the maid), a specific audience (Kyoto's populace and those travelers arriving in the city along the Tōkaidō), and the framing of a story (inscribed on the signboard). The first act brought the production to the audience, making sure that as many observers as possible got a good look at the condemned, the details of their crime, and the agents of justice as they paraded through the streets. The second act—the execution itself—was carried out away from public eyes, masking from spectators the gruesome transformation of the condemned from living beings into mutilated bodies.[2] The killing, however, made possible the grisly final tableau: a three-day performance, in deathly stillness, with corpses as puppets, hanging limp by the roadside. Daniel Botsman refers to the displayed corpses of criminals under the Tokugawa as "bodies-as-signs."[3] The corpses and signboard together created a formalized scene intended to be "read" by those who passed by, and they conveyed a multivalent message—about particular people and a particular crime; about sexuality, status, authority, and transgression; about the government's power to maintain control and exercise violence—and a personal message as well: "Do as they did, and this will be *your* fate."

The execution, that is, was more than a punishment; it was a formalized representation of order, and its import extended well beyond this single instance of adultery. The corpses of Osan and Mohei were put on display at a physical crossroads, but they stood at a social crossroads as well:

a site of intersection among the *macrocosm* of the social order, with its deep, communal investments in law, order, hierarchy, and power; the *microcosm* of the household, which mirrored aspects of the larger society in miniature; and the individual *person*, possessed of a discreet body and a complex inner world of desires and emotions. When the authorities transformed Osan and Mohei's bodies into formalized bodies-as-signs, they did so in the service of the macrocosmic social order. The bodies-as-signs of the lovers attested to the authorities' commitment to policing the hierarchical relations and boundaries of status, to enforcing moral standards, to maintaining order, and to exercising violence if it were necessary to do so. They also signaled the authorities' commitment to what Botsman calls the "little kings of everyday life," the hierarchical superiors within the household and other microcosmic social institutions that together made up society at large: figures like the calendar-maker Ishun—Osan's husband and Mohei's employer—to whom their affair was not solely a private, sexual matter but a direct affront to hierarchy and authority.[4] The display of bodies-as-signs demonstrated the shogunate's commitment to preserving these "microlevel power structures," not only underscoring to "servants, children, students, and wives that they should submit to their superiors, [but also reminding] those superiors that their own positions were supported and protected by the power of the shogun."[5] And the calendar-maker was a symbolically potent "little king," for the almanac-like calendars that he produced facilitated the temporal synchronization of the realm and undergirded the legitimacy of those who administered it.

The shogunate's formalized display of bodies-as-signs necessarily denied those bodies voices of their own; Osan's and Mohei's corpses were made to communicate the authorities' intent. But formalization cut two ways. Authority and social consensus might imbue a form with a normative significance, but if the form was rearranged, even slightly, through the remixing or embellishment of its modular components, it could open up alternate perceptions and become the bearer of divergent meanings—including ones that challenged the normative standard. Indeed, as Osan and Mohei's story grew and transformed, it slipped the bonds of the official message. The *basic formal ingredients* did not change: calendars, the calendar-maker's wife, her husband's clerk, the maid, adultery, flight from the capital to Tanba Province, capture, parade through the streets, crucifixion. These constituents are always present in the different versions of Osan-Mohei; they are the modular forms around which the topos coheres. And at play in each version is the same cluster of stakes—sexuality, status, transgression, and authority—signified in the shogunate's bodies-as-signs. But in the way each version animated, remixed, and remade these conventionalized forms, they could translate into very different stories—even different truths—and invoke a different kind of relationship between viewer and sign.

The Osan-Mohei topos thus provides a compelling avenue into the politics involved in innovation among—and deviation from—established forms. Instructive here is the poet and ethnographer Michael Jackson's differentiation between a "true" (in quotation marks) narrative—an official, public, and conservative one told in the interest of communal cohesion and order—as opposed to a "fictional" one, which is private, probing, questioning, and critical:

> At the same time that the . . . legacy of "true" narratives lays down the law, reinforces respect for received values, and draws attention to the foundational principles of the social order, "fictional" narratives persistently address quotidian problems of injustice, revealing the frailty of authority, mocking the foibles of men, and shaming all those who mask their greed and ambition with the language of ideology and the trappings of high office. And while some stories create and sustain dehumanizing divisions between the powerful and the powerless . . . others work to deconstruct such division and redress such imbalances, enabling the powerless to recover a sense of their own will, their own agency, their own consciousness, and their own being.[6]

The version of the Osan-Mohei story that the authorities established with the lovers' crucifixion is a "true" narrative in this sense: one told in the service of reinforcing communal and hierarchical order and values. But that does not mean that we should understand the politics of the reworkings by the *utazaimon* singers, Saikaku, and Chikamatsu as fiercely oppositional to this "true" narrative and what it represents. Rather, these variations occupy points on a spectrum between Jackson's "true" and "fictional." And the "fictional" is best characterized not by opposition to or subversion of authority, but by a shift in focus: it peers beneath the veneer of communal values, probes the way order can be invoked to serve private ends, and attends to the experiences of individuals on the receiving end of authority's judgments. The figure of the adulteress, in particular, lights up different points on this spectrum, for while a married woman's sexual behavior may have had a foundation in personal desire, her sexuality was embroiled as well in communal expectations, anxieties, prohibitions, and investments. And her body, whether as a living, sexual body or as a punished corpse, held implications for the health of the larger social bodies of which she was part—including the body politic. Her body was therefore a particularly potent medium for the negotiation between "true" and "fictional" narratives.

What makes Osan-Mohei remarkable is that its various texts and performances do not simply exist along a continuum between these poles of the "true" and the "fictional," but seem actively to reflect on it, to make the interrelationship between these two poles their subject matter. In quite different ways, the *utazaimon*, Saikaku's story, and Chikamatsu's play ask what it means to have one's person interpreted as a form by a larger community—whether the microcosm of the household, the umbrella of state authority, or community in the broadest, most amorphous sense. And they are particularly attuned to the ways in which seemingly transparent forms—not only literary tropes but bodies and behaviors—can signify in alternate, or even contesting, ways. In the process, these works meditate on the intersubjective nature of identity, which does not involve a pure subject juxtaposed to objective "society," but instead comprises a constant relational interplay between individual agents and the various overlapping collectives—vast or intimate—that are constituted of them *and* exercise their own claims on them.[7] The Osan-Mohei topos enables us to probe the role of literature and theater in mediating the borderlands between the person as a subjective agent and as a communal signifier, and in the process to consider how a shogunal "true" narrative could be changed from within into a "fictional" one that comes at the same subject matter from a very different angle. As Jacques Rancière notes, "all political activity is a conflict aimed at deciding what is speech or mere growl," and in that sense, the stakes involved are inherently political, for in imputing different meanings to the lovers condemned and silenced in the official "true" version, the retellings restore to them voices of their own.[8] And they implicitly address themselves to a community in which those voices can be heard.

In this chapter I am therefore interested less in the transgressive nature of adultery itself than in the transformative potential of formal remixing, in its capacity to remake the import of signs and to foster new perceptions and feelings about what they represent. This dynamic looms over Saikaku's

Osan, who performs the role of adulteress with such commitment that she transforms the import of her crucifixion. And the dynamic is particularly charged for Chikamatsu's play, my primary focus in the chapter. The play not only cultivates sympathy for Osan and Mohei, but, in a climactic twist, delivers them from crucifixion altogether—in defiance of historical fact, three decades of convention, and the would-be executioners on the stage. It is an ending that formally reworks the significance of the calendar itself, and in doing so, it pushes us to weigh the powers that the play lays claim to: not only over its audience, but over the order of the world beyond the theater's walls.

Adultery and Bodies Sexual and Textual

To apprehend the dynamics of the Osan-Mohei topos, we first need to understand the simultaneously public and private dimensions of adultery in the early modern period and grasp how male concern with female sexuality turned women's bodies (and not only crucified ones) into interpretable forms. Adultery occupied a fraught position in Tokugawa Japan. It not only constituted a personal transgression against a spouse for the sake of sexual or emotional fulfillment, but it also threatened authority and lineal continuity within the fundamental social unit, the household (*ie*), and presented, in turn, an affront to the hierarchical and status-bound norms that governed the social order at large. That said, not all infidelities counted as "adultery." Adultery (*fugi* [unrighteousness] or *mittsū* [illicit liaison]), in the sense of an illicit act and legal offense, depended on the gender and status differentials between the parties involved. A married, male household head, for example, did not court censure or punishment for pursuing an affair with an unmarried housemaid (or concubine, or prostitute)—indeed, such behavior was largely expected and taken for granted.[9] But for those infidelities that most egregiously transgressed lines of status—such as a man's affair with a married woman, particularly one of superior status or, most heinous of all, the mistress of the household in which he was employed—adultery was considered an outrage against the social order severe enough to merit death.[10]

Punishments for adultery, which had not yet been standardized in the seventeenth century, ranged from confiscation of property to banishment to various forms of execution. In general, the more severely the affair transgressed differentials of status and hierarchy, the more stringent the penalty was.[11] An affair between a married woman and her husband's servant incurred execution for both parties. But for other iterations, the accused man and woman were sometimes punished differently from each other, and not all punishments were carried out by the legal authorities; the head of a household frequently had a say in the punishment of his household inferiors, particularly in the fate of the female party. Samurai, meanwhile, retained the prerogative to cut down an adulterous wife and her lover, a practice known as wife revenge (*megatakiuchi*)—though, as Eiko Ikegami notes, the scrutiny that an affair would bring to a samurai's control over his household (or lack thereof), and the resulting damage to his reputation, meant that in practice many samurai preferred to keep a wife's affair secret.[12] Among commoners as well, Amy Stanley has shown that locally or internally mediated reconciliation in the wake of an affair was often preferred to state involvement and violent punishment.[13]

Concern with adultery—and with wifely fidelity, in particular—grew in tandem with the entrenchment of the patriarchal stem-family household structure. This structure emerged among warriors in the medieval period, but the late seventeenth century marked a new inflection point, as it was around that time that the household achieved near-universal adoption by non-samurai, becoming the basic organizing unit for society at large and the government's primary unit for population registration, taxation, and surveillance.[14] The household, typically overseen by a male head, was a corporate enterprise devoted, above all else, to its own continuity, and the headship customarily devolved upon a male heir. While women—the patriarch's mother and wife, in particular—could exercise considerable managerial authority within the household, a wife's foremost duty was to produce an heir.[15] She was also expected to avoid behavior that challenged the authority of the head (or, if they were still living, that of his parents) or that otherwise disrupted the household's smooth functioning. A married woman's adultery presented a crisis on all these fronts, risking the continuity of the lineage, the clout of the patriarch, and the harmony of the household. Exacerbating these concerns was the fact that the household included not only kin, but staff who often lived on-site. A large merchant household, such as that of Osan's husband, the calendar-maker, included male clerks and servants as well as female housemaids, which meant that the wife shared sometimes tight quarters with men other than her husband.

The consolidation of the household in the seventeenth century coincided with the explosion in commercial print. The abundance of educational and admonitory reading material addressed to female readers—particularly those of the samurai and upper-townsman classes—reinforced the principle that a married woman's primary responsibilities involved serving her husband and in-laws and producing an heir. It placed a strong onus, in particular, on a woman's management of her body and her emotions. Print culture facilitated new, detailed regimes of self-care (*yōjō*) for men and women alike, encouraging them to direct a "managerial and strategic gaze" (*kanriteki de senryakuteki na manazashi*) at their own bodies—a charged site for a society in which status and identity were displayed through codified forms of dress, hairstyle, and accessories.[16] But the stakes differed markedly by sex. A work like Kaibara Ekiken's *Instructions for Cultivating Life* (*Yōjōkun*, 1713) posits a man's mastery of the techniques of self-care as a responsibility to his progenitors and to the larger natural regime ("heaven and earth") that gave him life; but it was also a responsibility to himself, for only through a long, healthy life could he fully realize the blessing (*megumi*) of having been born human.[17] A married woman, by contrast, needed to maintain her health not for her own flourishing, but in order to produce a healthy *heir*, and that entailed protecting herself not only from outside afflictions to her body, but from the danger of her own inner states.[18] Women's conduct manuals warned their readers repeatedly of the threat posed by their own anger, jealousy, and excessive sexual desire.[19] These manuals targeted unchecked libido, which might draw a woman to men other than her husband, but they particularly castigated jealousy (*rinki*)—specifically, jealousy of her husband's dalliances with other women—as a uniquely feminine vice with the capacity to wreak havoc on household harmony.

Such "inner desires" (*naiyoku*) or "inner injuries" (*naishō*) endangered the health of both women and the children they carried in their wombs; but because they were interior states, they could be externally confirmed only by reading the outward form of a woman's body and that of her child. *The Mirror for Women: A Book of Secret Transmissions* (*Omuna kagami hidensho*, 1650), for example, advises a woman to remain compassionate, gentle, and honest if she wishes to give birth to an "intelligent, dignified, knowledgeable, and healthy" child. But if a woman behaves just as she likes (*jiyū ni*), "the child will grow large, and the birth, when the time comes, will be difficult [*kurushiki*]."[20] As Susan Burns has argued, such injunctions to emotional and sexual self-control rendered the bodies of mother and child "incarnate texts upon which was inscribed the success or failure of the woman's ability to control and restrain the actions, desires, and responses of her body. Pregnancy and birth were understood not only as biological events, but as moments of judgment in which the woman's place within a[n] ethically ordered world was determined and made known."[21] Like the body of an executed criminal, the body of a woman—an "incarnate text"— could thus be made to signify beyond her intentions, its form communicating to the household community whether she had succeeded in keeping her emotions and impulses in check for the sake of serving the communal good.

And yet the late seventeenth century also witnessed a profusion of discourse treating the female body as an object of male desire, which textualized her body in a different way. This discourse emphasized the female body not as a site of reproduction, but of male pleasure; while it treated the professional courtesan as its pinnacle object, it did not limit the desiring male gaze to her alone.[22] *The Great Mirror of the Way of Love* (*Shikidō ōkagami*, 1678), an encyclopedic compendium I mention in chapter 2, explicates for a male readership the convoluted culture, social structure, and protocols of the licensed quarters, but it expands outward in book 14 to discuss the seduction of various categories of women beyond the licensed sex trade, including household maids, wandering nuns, daughters, widows, divorcées, nursemaids, seamstresses, women encountered on the road, and bathhouse and teahouse girls.[23] The discussion begins with wives, and while it opens by examining the ways a wife and her jealous nature inhibit her husband's sexual freedom, it also appraises the attractiveness of townswomen in comparison with courtesans.[24] Within the *Great Mirror*'s pages, the female body is placed into a different formal regime from that posited by conduct manuals: one in which it can be read to evaluate its desirability and accessibility—as well as the risks of attempting to access it—for a male subject.

Married women's sexuality was thus highly overdetermined in popular discourse: it was crucial for the sustaining purpose of reproduction, but it also courted danger—whether to lineal continuity through adultery, or to the health of child and home if willfully indulged in as pleasure. And a woman's sexuality was linked to her outward form: whether she maintained a firm grip over these dangers could be read by others from her comportment and physical appearance—and even from the health of her child. But her body was also a text from which desirous men could attempt to discern her lustfulness and availability. And because the "ethically ordered world" for which her sexuality carried implications was made up of the microworlds of households, wifely sexuality was a source of patriarchal anxiety, reverberating from the household to the level of the domain and the regime, each of which was organized as a patriarchal house and invested in reinforcing the authority of the lesser patriarchs below—Botsman's "little kings of everyday life."

Utazaimon: Osan and Mohei as a Cautionary Tale

The story of Osan and Mohei—with its setting in a high-profile household, its lovers' transgression of strict social boundaries, and their spectacular public punishment—seems made for the exploration of this tangle of anxiety about and surveillance of the sexuality of married women. And indeed, writers, balladeers, and the general populace soon began to retell and transform the story to explore the implications of adultery and its punishment. They did so not through wild flights of imagination, but by adopting the contours and the formal ingredients of the "true" version instantiated by the authorities and then adapting, embellishing, and remixing them to new ends.

The tale of Osan and Mohei quickly became fodder for the street performance of *utazaimon*. These rhythmical narrative ballads had a distant origin in formal appeals to deities, buddhas, and departed spirits during the Heian period. They were initially performed in the seventeenth century by singers dressed as ascetic mountain priests, who sang them for coppers from house to house, keeping time by shaking the metal rings on the staffs they carried and occasionally blowing on a conch shell. In time, they dropped the priestly attire, added stringed accompaniment, and performed on stages at sites popular for public entertainments, like the Kamo riverbed at Shijō in Kyoto and the Ikutama Shrine in Osaka. By the turn of the eighteenth century, the subject matter approached tabloid status, with a focus on celebrated love affairs, love suicides, criminals, requiem-like paeans to recently deceased actors, and (for good measure) the occasional work of religious edification.[25] The performers often sold cheap broadsheet versions of the lyrics, which is how these texts have come down to us.

At least two *utazaimon* versions of the story of Osan and Mohei took shape in the years following the lovers' deaths: "The Calendar-Maker's Osan and Mohei" (Daikyōji Osan Mohei) and "The *Utazaimon* of 'The Calendar-Maker's Osan'" (Utazaimon daikyōji Osan).[26] These two texts—each just a few pages long—are largely identical, with the second slightly expanding the depiction of the adulterers' first lovemaking and tweaking the message of the final line. One might expect a tale narrated by mendicant storytellers who lived on society's margins to have a subversive thrust. But both are quite conservative, treating the lovers' story as a lurid cautionary tale about transgressive male predation, wifely susceptibility, and female lust. Indeed, the city streets where the *utazaimon* were performed—an exposed, public setting, open to all and sundry—were perhaps most amenable to versions of the adulterous tale that reinforced communally sanctioned values: the "true" version of the story. In both *utazaimon*, the events begin while Osan's husband, the calendar-maker Ishun, is away in Edo on long-term business. Mohei, his clerk, enlists the aid of the housemaid, Tama, "who, in the way of any young person, had little thought for consequences [*tenpo mamayo*]."[27] She finds a moment when Osan looks particularly lonely and slips her Mohei's love letter, claiming that she found it on the street and (being illiterate) wondered what it says. Osan is astounded to discover that it is intended for her: a confession of unbearable desire, written by Mohei in language coded in technical calendrical terms. Osan is horrified. She scolds Tama, who replies, "Your anger is justified, but be that as it may, Mohei has made up his mind: if your reply is poor, today or the next day he'll hang himself and die. To save this one man is an act of goodness deeper than the sea. Please think it through once more and grant him your pity [*nasake*]."[28] Osan, with "a woman's foolishness," asks, astonished, does he *really* mean to die? She agrees to let him come to her bed for one night only. Mohei is overjoyed, and they make love all night long. In the morning, however, the gravity of their wrongdoing weighs on him. To atone for the sin of deceiving his master and bedding his wife, he resolves to shave his head and take vows. But Osan's feelings have changed, too—from pity to lust. "It's worth worrying about the dew only *before* you get wet," she tells him: having crossed the line, there is no reason to stop now.[29] Their affair continues for months, by which time Osan finds herself pregnant, and she and Mohei—together with Tama—flee for the mountains of Tanba Province. When word reaches the calendar-maker, he sends people to search throughout the provinces. The lovers are apprehended and hauled back to Kyoto: "Ah, how pitiful! Osan, as a warning for ages to come, was paraded through one after another of the capital's neighborhoods. Her man, for his atrocious adultery [*fugi*], met with bitter punishment at Awataguchi. They were finished off by the waters of Keage, and though their corpses rotted, their names linger on. . . . Their story is one of a pathos rare in the world, a tale of desire's dark road [*renbo no yamiji*]."[30]

The second version concludes with a line even more stark: an insistence that the world should never again see such a "catastrophe of madness" (*kurui no sainan*).[31]

These ballads pitch themselves directly to the place where titillation intersects anxiety. They may have evoked in audiences a transgressive pleasure in listening to the step-by-step unfolding of a seduction, but it is a pleasure tinged with horror, for the *utazaimon* point to the many sexual vulnerabilities of Osan's household: an absent husband, a maid too young to consider consequences, a lustful live-in clerk, and a wife whose compassion is her downfall. This last is the most ironic danger, for Osan's sense of sympathy or pity (*nasake*)—as opposed to selfishness and envy—was characterized as a wifely virtue in popular discourse.[32] But Osan's capacity for feeling is a liability, one that the servants can prey on in the master's absence—and it transforms in an instant from a compassionate opening *to* the other, to a consuming desire *for* the other. "The Calendar-Maker's Osan and Mohei" and "The *Utazaimon* of 'The Calendar-Maker's Osan'" may underscore the sorrow of the lovers' tale, but they leave no ambiguity about the place of such behavior in the world. Osan's pregnancy is referred to as a "repugnant" (*utomashiki*) turn of events, and her brutal punishment—a "warning for ages to come"—is depicted as wholly appropriate for her having courted such a "catastrophe of madness." Even after the body-as-sign of her crucified corpse has rotted away, the song itself continues to do its work, warning the world of the dangers that threaten wives and of the punishments that await those who give in to them.

Saikaku's Osan: Public Perception and Personal Defiance

Were this the only way Osan and Mohei's story was recounted, it would amount to little more than an example of conventional popular morality. Three years after their deaths, however, the writer Ihara Saikaku took up the formal ingredients of the lovers' story and remixed them into something much stranger and more self-reflexive. Osan is the third heroine of his book *Five Amorous Women*, which tells five stories, all modeled on real incidents, of transgressive love and (with one exception) punishment—from the adultery and violent death of the barrel-maker's wife Osen, to Oshichi, the Edo greengrocer's daughter who was burned at the stake after committing arson for the sake of a rendezvous with her lover.[33]

"A Tale of the Calendar-Maker, Seen in the Middle Section" (Chūdan ni miru koyomiya monogatari), Saikaku's version of Osan's story, plays with the idea of the body as a legible form: an object of both surveillance and desire, subject to a public gaze that can shape the meaning of a woman's life beyond her intentions.[34] And it does so not by dramatically rewriting the story, but by embellishing the fundamental formal ingredients and plotline already present in the historical incident and the *utazaimon* in a way that opens up new perceptual possibilities and alters the story's import. The story opens with four wealthy playboys, known as the "Four Heavenly Kings" for their flashy fashion and sexual carousing, sitting at a Kyoto teahouse. Noticing the attractiveness of the city's women returning along the avenue from wisteria viewing, they devise a viewing contest to judge the best looking. There is a transgressive thrill to appraising these "local women" (*ji onna*)—women who belong to proper households, as opposed to the sexually available courtesans with whom the Four Heavenly Kings usually frolic. The men engage in a close reading of each passing woman: careful inspection of her dress, carriage, and body reveals to them information about her age, background, marital status, sensitivity, and sensuousness. They examine women in their teens, twenties, and thirties, each the embodiment of a different category of attractiveness. Yet each is found to possess a flaw that abruptly cools the men's desire: a missing tooth, a facial scar, tattered clothes, a trailing brood of young children. The fifth woman, however, brings them up short: an exquisite teenager, impeccably dressed and adorned with wisteria blossoms, she is the undisputed winner. And this is how we meet Osan—mediated by the gaze of men.[35]

But more powerful than the scrutiny of women by specific men in Saikaku's story is the way society in a less differentiated sense—what contemporary readers knew as "the world" (*seken*)—reads a woman and her actions. The tale evokes the *seken* by presenting Kyoto as a city of rumor, where eyes are always watching and tongues are constantly wagging. The clerk (whose name Saikaku discreetly alters from Mohei to Moemon) is not a lecher in this version; he is a finicky workaholic with no designs on Osan—or any other woman.[36] But when the housemaid falls in love with him, Osan helps her craft letters to win him over, finally enticing him to the maid's bed. A mix-up in the dark, however, leads him to the bed in which Osan lies sleeping, and, each mistaking the other's identity, they unwittingly make love. Ashamed though she feels when she realizes what has happened, Osan is resolute: "There is no way this will have gone unnoticed. All I can do now is throw myself away, devote my life to making a scandalous reputation, and travel together with Moemon on the road to the mountains of death."[37] This is a drastic shift in character for a woman who has thus far been characterized as an exemplary townsman's wife.[38] Abrupt swerves in character, mood, and plotting are typical of Saikaku's style (see chapter 2). Here, the shift underscores the narrative's concern with gazes and perception: even if her encounter with Moemon was purely accidental, Osan's reaction emphasizes that because it possessed the *form* of an act of intentional adultery, it will be *perceived* as such. And once the story is in the hands of society at large—the *seken*—it will be completely beyond the control of its subjects. The power of Saikaku's Osan—far cannier than her *utazaimon* alter ego—is that she is presented as grasping this dynamic and opting to embrace rather than resist the role that rumor will shape for her. Becoming a true-to-form adulteress before social perception can make her one is her sole way of maintaining some degree of ownership over herself and her story.

The degree of her resolve contrasts with that of Moemon, who follows her lead but feels the sting of the control that the *seken* maintains over his story. The two ultimately flee Kyoto, fake their deaths, and, in keeping with the historical incident, go into hiding in the depths of Tanba Province. But Moemon finds himself longing for Kyoto, and he pays a visit to the city in disguise. Eavesdropping on some young men near his old neighborhood, he discovers that they are discussing *him*. One envies his supposed seduction of the beautiful Osan, but another lambastes him as "less than human" for having transgressed against his own master. Moemon recognizes the man's voice: "'Why, that's the voice of Kisuke from the Daimonjiya house. He really has no feeling, to spit out such vile talk! I once lent him eighty *monme* of silver on a promissory note. I think right now I'll take repayment, even if I have to strangle it out of him!' He gnashed his teeth and got to his feet—but, as someone hiding from the world, there was ultimately nothing he could do but bear it in chagrined silence."[39] The conversation about the lovers continues, and Moemon ends up so confounded by the stories told about him—and by his inability to intervene and correct them—that he is a wreck by the time he returns to Tanba, swearing off Kyoto forever. Osan, by contrast, never wavers. Even when Monjushiri (Mañjuśrī), the bodhisattva of wisdom, appears in a dream, warning her of the dangers of her sin and advising her to become a nun, she tells him off:

> "Don't concern yourself over me, whatever may happen in the end. Me, I like what I'm doing, and I've committed myself to unfaithfulness [*wakigokoro*] all the way. Monju, you understand only the love between men and boys. You don't have a clue about the way of women." Just as the words seemed to leave her lips, she awoke from the unpleasant dream. The wind blew through the pines along the sandbar at Hashidate. "It's a world of dust," she said, and after that she did not change her ways at all.[40]

Osan's retort asserts a perverse steadfastness: now that social perception has foreclosed to her the role of faithful wife, she commits herself to being a faithful adulteress. She literally tells Monjushiri that she has traded her "self" (*mi ni kaete*) for the role of faithless wife, an expression that signals her readiness to sacrifice her life for that commitment, with a resolution firm enough to tell off a bodhisattva to his face. Osan taunts Monjushiri that he does not understand "the way of women" (*nyodō*): a reference to sexual proclivities for a bodhisattva associated with pederasty.[41] But here the term suggests as well something like "a woman's way." He is just one more man, her rejoinder suggests, telling her who she is and how she should live—to which she replies that she has chosen to live (and, implicitly, die) on her own terms. The fact that the bodhisattva vanishes when confronted by her riposte suggests the power of this stance. But it also brings into relief the deep solitude that attends it, underscored by the lonely sound of the wind in the pines in the wake of his disappearance and by her pronouncement: "It's a world of dust" (*chiri no yo ja mono*), words that evoke both defiance and resignation, strength and desolation.

Having characterized Osan in this way, Saikaku's depiction of the execution scene takes on a very different significance from that in the *utazaimon*—and pointedly different from the meanings intended by the shogunate's formalized bodies-as-signs. The scene is sketched with Saikaku's compact economy:

> Judgment was handed down after thorough investigation. They were paraded through the streets together with Tama, the housemaid who had served as their go-between, and they vanished like dew on the grasses at Awataguchi. Their lives faded like a dream at dawn on the twenty-second of the Ninth Month, but the impeccable grace with which they met death was spoken of by all. As vivid as the pale-blue robe she wore that day—which even now I see as though it were before my eyes—Osan's name lives on.[42]

The passage harkens back to the scene of the Four Heavenly Kings and the contest of beauties with which the story opens. Once more, an audience close-reads Osan, appraising and interpreting her appearance as she proceeds down the avenues of the old capital. And though the body the onlookers read this time is that of a condemned criminal, they do not glean from it the shogunate's "true" message about transgression, punishment, and order. Instead, they read in it a character of grace and poise—even fashion, in the figure of her pale-blue robe. As in the *utazaimon*, Osan's name lives on (*na wa nokorishi*), but this ingredient is transformed, now serving not as a "warning for ages to come," but as the embodiment of self-possession. *This* version of Osan, the ending suggests, will become the collective property of the *seken*, passed along on the city's gossiping lips (*yogatari to wa narinu*). Herein lies the power of Saikaku's version of the adulteress: recognizing the capacity of popular perception to determine her identity, she embraces that identity and adopts its form with such conviction that, at the bitter end, it is she who exerts a power over the gazing eyes of the populace, retaining possession over how they see and remember her—over what she signifies. The onlooker-narrator's sympathetic response to her execution drives home this complex politics of gazing and signification. His words convey a sense of satisfaction: he sees in Osan's end not a grim warning, but a part played to perfection.

Together, Saikaku's tale and the *utazaimon* versions of Osan and Mohei's story show that transgressors and their punished bodies—even for a crime, like adultery, that touched on the deepest anxieties of the order of status and households—were not fixed signs at the turn of the eighteenth century.

They were a field where meanings and emotions vied and were contested, shaped and channeled by the stories told about them, their forms adaptable to different significations. The body of a punished criminal could be made a locus not just of respect for communal values and the authorities who policed them, as in the *utazaimon*, but of sympathy, subjectivity, even awe. "A Tale of the Calendar-Maker, Seen in the Middle Section" is startling for the double move it makes. It first draws attention through its protagonist to the ways in which identities are mediated by communal gossip, gazes, appraisals, and punishments—what Arthur Kleinman calls "the violences of everyday life," whereby "social formations are not just replicated, but the ordinary lives of individuals are also shaped, and all-too-often twisted, bent, even broken." It then invites readers to sympathize with that protagonist, to view the politics of identity through her eyes, and to feel moved by her defiant ownership of the role that society assigns her.[43] There is a subversive current to this telling of Osan's story, for it returns subjectivity to [a] body the authorities would reduce to a sign and displaces the meanings that the sign was intended to signify.

If Saikaku's story suggests that subjective identification with the adulteress can alter the intersubjective dynamic, transforming the communal values that her execution is intended to enforce, Chikamatsu's play elevates the stakes of this intersubjective alchemy, remixing the modular ingredients of the Osan-Mohei topos in a way that makes affective affiliation with the adulteress the basis for a critical, possibly transgressive, yet deeply moral renewal of social values.

The Calendar-Maker and the Old Calendar

Cat's Play and Domestic Politics

The Calendar-Maker and the Old Calendar is a *jōruri* puppet play; in performance, a chanter (*tayū*) recited the play's libretto, accompanied by a shamisen player who sat beside him at the side of the stage on which puppeteers manipulated the puppets representing the play's characters. Chikamatsu had dramatically broadened the subject matter of the puppet theater when he began writing "contemporary life plays" (*sewamono*) in 1703, starting with *The Love Suicides at Sonezaki* (*Sonezaki shinjū*). These plays broke from the puppet theater's long-standing focus on power struggles set in the past, the topic of "history plays" (*jidaimono*).[44] Andrew Gerstle characterizes the different dynamic between these two types of play: "Conflict in *jidaimono* was depicted as the struggle between the demands of the state (meaning some political entity such as a fief or court) and the family. In contrast, the new *sewamono* focused on conflict between the family unit (which was the "world") and the individual."[45] These conflicts in *sewamono* have conventionally been characterized as involving an opposition between personal feelings or emotions (*ninjō*) and communal mores and responsibilities (*giri*)—an opposition that, in most of Chikamatsu's *sewamono*, can be resolved only tragically, often through suicide.[46]

The Calendar-Maker and the Old Calendar, however, does not quite fit the mold of the playwright's best-known *sewamono*. Its central conflict does not revolve around the clash of feeling and responsibility. Instead, the play's central irony is that Osan and Mohei are *not* adulterous lovers. Their single act of intercourse, as in Saikaku's story, is unintentional: a matter of mistaken identities in the dark. But, unlike in Saikaku's version, that mistake does not initiate a real affair. Instead, even as they flee the wrath of the law and Osan's vengeful husband, Ishun, the pair steadfastly maintains the proper forms of relationship between a clerk and his master's wife. We are told that they "never thought of loving one another even in their dreams," and Osan continues to profess her emotional loyalty to her husband, despite his own philandering, his unpleasant character, and his determination to see her punished.[47] If anything, Osan and Mohei are presented as exemplary figures whose personal feelings remain largely aligned with their sense of social obligation, even in the face of unforeseen and unsought hardship. The source of trouble in the play comes instead when the structures of communal authority entrusted with policing behavior, adjudicating transgressions, and enforcing order—the agents of public "truth" existing in the microcosm of the patriarchal household all the way to the macrocosm of the state—*fail to recognize* Osan and Mohei's innocence and exemplarity.[48] And the fallibility of these structures is not necessarily innocent. As we will see, authority can be abused by its agents, whose personal desires corrupt their ability to enforce moral order. But even when the instruments of order are well intentioned, their vision remains limited to the signs available to them—and those signs can signify imperfectly. The play thus stages the tragedy of individuals caught in the dynamics of social structures that cannot, or will not, read them correctly and thus recognize them for what they really are. And it asks whether there is an alternative form of authority—one not rooted in hierarchy or proscriptive law—that can perceive lucidly and in a way that restores subjectivity to those who risk being relegated to objects.[49]

The play begins by problematizing any easy assumptions about what transgression looks like within the complicated social terrain of a household. It does so by presenting the calendar-maker's household as a site where a hierarchical organization does not equate to a just order; instead, it is a messy field of sexual politics where desire, power differentials, and registers of expression and violence collide and intertwine. Inverting the import of the *utazaimon*, here it is not the household's underlings who pose a threat to order. Rather, the more dangerous figures are the representatives of household authority—the calendar-maker, Ishun, and his head clerk, Sukeemon—who can invoke their prerogative to preserve order as a cover to indulge their private desires, or to punish those whom they perceive as threats. The play's first act, which takes place entirely within this household, brings into relief the politics of language and signification: the question of who is allowed to say what, whose speech can be heard, how words or actions can be misread to serve inappropriate ends, and how different registers of expression can modulate the convoluted erotic energies that flow through the household community. It thereby invites the members of the audience to recalibrate their expectations of what an accusation of "adultery" really means.

To give shape to these politics of sexuality and expression, the play imports a new formal ingredient, one absent in the other Osan-Mohei variations but well-established from other texts involving transgressive sexuality: the household cat. Cats and adultery had been linked in the literary imagination since *The Tale of Genji*, in which a cat plays a crucial role in the illicit affair between Kashiwagi and the Third Princess.[50] More recently, "cat's love" (*neko no koi*)—the motif of cats disappearing while in heat, crying heartrendingly, and returning home haggard—had become an established topos in *haikai*, where it evoked a brazen freedom in lovemaking that was foreclosed to humans, especially women.[51] And in contemporary moral discourse, a woman who engaged in improper sexual relations was said to have fallen from a human level to that of a "beast" (*chikushō*), like a cat or a dog that takes multiple partners.[52] The cat was thus an overdetermined form in its own right, and the play draws upon its various affordances to bring into focus the sexual dynamics of Ishun's household.

In the first scenes, the household's cat serves as a projection ground: the different ways that household members talk about the cat begin to reveal the larger household politics of authority, impunity, desire, and the threat of violence. As the play opens, the calendar-maker's clerks are working furiously to prepare calendars for sale and for delivery to other parts of the country in time for the New Year. The prideful head clerk, Sukeemon—the master's top delegate of managerial authority over the household and its staff—is ranting. He complains that the clerk Mohei has not returned yet, chides Osan for playing with the cat, and enumerates an absurdly lengthy list of chores for the housemaid Tama to attend to. Then he pauses, directing his attention back to the cat and Osan: "And as for that troublesome cat, its only ability is to cry out, 'Meow, meow!' It never catches a single mouse. But it behaves loosely if it spots a tom. It's always up on the roof or in the hedge! If I catch it mating up on the roof again, I'll bind its four legs and toss it into the stream along Nishinotōin!"[53]

Sukeemon's threat is striking not only for its abrupt brutality, but for its seemingly unprovoked fixation on sexuality. The narrator even interjects here to note that the cat is an "irrelevant" (*kake mo kamai mo nashi*) target, suggesting that Sukeemon's vitriol is in fact oriented toward a different object. We later learn that indeed it is: in the past, Sukeemon had made secret advances on Osan that were quietly stymied. René Girard has emphasized the close connections between sexuality and violence, both of which tend to "fasten upon surrogate objects" if their original objects remain out of reach, erupt more chaotically if repressed, and easily substitute for each other with a "shift from violence to sexuality and from sexuality to violence."[54] Here, deflecting onto the cat his sexual frustration over the inaccessibility of his master's wife, Sukeemon's words warp the real dynamic, demonizing his female object—who has always remained faithful to her husband—as promiscuous and deserving of sadistic punishment at his hands. As in the *utazaimon*, the household contains a lascivious clerk; in the play, however, the danger lies not in his lustfulness but in his authority, which affords him violent, retaliatory channels into which he can redirect his licentious energies.

If Sukeemon's coded language about the cat suggests how his authoritative gaze combines surveillance with erotic appraisal of the household's women, when the women invoke the cat, they do so to give protective cover to their conversations about the household's men. After Sukeemon leaves the room, Osan teasingly asks the housemaid Tama, who is unmarried, whether Sukeemon is the type of man she is attracted to. Tama answers that she much prefers the calm and gentle manner of the clerk Mohei, who is friendly and never loses his temper. Osan replies:

> Now that you say it, you're right. Among cats as well as humans, the forces that unite couples are mysterious [*ai'en ki'en*]. The red cat of the rouge merchant next door is so gentle in appearance, and when he calls out to this little calico, he makes his voice so plaintive and looks almost ashamed. He's the kind of man [*otoko*] I'd like for her. But the gray cat at the silk starcher's across the street looks so hateful and ungainly. He's completely unashamed, and he calls out to our calico from the roof in a horrid voice that sounds like someone berating a packhorse.... Listen, kitty. Don't find yourself a bad man. If that gray cat makes advances to you, you shake him off right from the start. That's what's important.[55]

When the little calico meows, however, the voices of male cats echo from throughout the neighborhood, and she tries to run out to them. "Oh, what a fickle thing you are!" Osan says. "If you're going to have a man, it should be only one. If you take a lover, you'll be crucified. Don't you know a girl's proper modesty?"[56]

That Osan's speech to the calico is really about humans, not cats, is hinted at by her reference to "men" (*otoko*) throughout, reverting to the feline-specific "male cat" (*oneko*) only at the end. The speech provides a veiled commentary on the men of the household, yet these feminine appraisals can be voiced only obliquely, accompanied by a keen recognition of the limitations—and threat of punishment—that attend them. The circumlocution of Osan's speech also leaves the precise referent of her criticism of the nasty gray cat unclear. She appears to be giving advice to Tama, by way of the little calico, about the appeal of Mohei (the red cat) and the maliciousness of Sukeemon (the gray cat). But by the end, she seems to speak to the calico from a more personal perspective. She may be alluding to the advances that, we later learn, Sukeemon has made on her in the past. But when we meet her husband, Ishun, the calendar-maker, we discover that he, too, conforms to the image of the nasty gray cat: loud, pushy, impolite, oversexed, and completely inconsiderate of his wife's feelings. The switch into the language of cats can be read as a safely ambiguous means for Osan to voice her wish that her husband would behave differently. As a whole, her metaphorical language brings into relief the asymmetric relationship between the sexes in the household, in which men have greater freedom to impose their desires on women, while the stakes are very different for women in how they respond to those advances—and in how they express themselves.

These differences are driven home by the way Ishun, the pinnacle of household authority, employs language. When Ishun sexually harasses the maid Tama, he speaks in code words as well. But his codes are crassly transparent: rather than veiling his meaning, they highlight his impunity over those under his control. Sneaking up on Tama, Ishun reaches his arms around her from behind and fondles her breast, saying, "Ah, what a lovely cat I've caught."[57] Drawing on legends about the precious jewel (*tama*) kept in the Dragon King's palace at the bottom of the sea, he refers to drawing his "sharp sword" (*riken*) and plunging into the sea's depths; a few lines later, he employs wordplay about shellfish, a thinly veiled reference to female genitalia. The consequences for such behavior present a stark contrast with the threat of crucifixion alluded to by Osan. "This is the last time," Tama tells her master as she holds him at bay. "I'll tell the mistress and have her pinch you all over until you're completely purple. Oh, what a nuisance!" Ishun, undeterred, presses on. "Hold on! I'm not letting you go. Wives and jealousy go together like *udon* noodles and pepper. It doesn't bother me at all. Purple is nothing—she can bruise my whole body till it's dark brown for all I care, so long as it's for you."[58] Whereas Osan warns the female cat about the danger of crucifixion, pinching is the worst punishment to confront the lecherous calendar-maker.

Heaven, the Empathetic Audience

These differentials in the ways language maps onto authority and sexual agency in the household relativize the impact when accusations of "adultery" begin to be made, and they transform the import of the punishment that accompanies those accusations. Indeed, the play's first climax revolves around the question of who can speak and who can be heard in the household, and it reveals how authoritatively "true" narratives, in Jackson's sense, about transgression and punishment can be rooted in willful, self-serving misreadings of form by those in positions of power.

The trouble begins when Osan asks the clerk Mohei to quietly lend her parents a single silver piece from the household's coffers to cover the financial straits in which her natal household finds itself. That household is of long-standing good repute, but its financial troubles, if revealed, will place Osan's parents in legal jeopardy and bring scandal-by-association upon the calendar-maker; yet her parents dare not ask their wealthy son-in-law for assistance directly.[59] Mohei understands the situation and readily agrees to procure a silver piece from the household treasury discreetly. To do so, he must sneak his master's seal from its pouch and imprint it on a piece of blank paper, which he will then fill in as a note to obtain the silver from the household stores.

These are actions, however well-intended, that match the form of a clerk's petty embezzlement, and they lead to a series of misreadings by the household's authority figures. The pitiless head clerk, Sukeemon, catches Mohei just as he removes the seal from its pouch and imprints it on the paper, and he rouses the household and the master, who instructs Sukeemon to beat Mohei ferociously until he explains his actions. Mohei, however, refuses to implicate the lady of the house or her parents, prompting the housemaid Tama to rush to his defense. She claims that it was she who begged him for the money in order to save her destitute uncle, a samurai on the verge of suicide over unpayable debts. Rather than placating Ishun, however, Tama's "admission" enrages him: "So, you two have been having an affair [*mittsū*]! I am the calendar-maker, a servant of the imperial court, a townsman with the standing of a samurai! To commit adultery [*fugi*] and top it off with the theft of your master's seal is a heinous crime."[60] He orders that Mohei be locked up in the vacant house next door and promises a thorough investigation the following day. Tama's words give no indication of any personal relationship with Mohei. And, indeed, there is none; though she is attracted to him, he has never reciprocated her affection. But the calendar-maker's immediate reaction is to slap on them the labels *mittsū* and *fugi*—both legalistic terms for the crime of adultery.

The preceding scenes have prepared the audience to recognize this leap from monetary to sexual crime as grounded in the master's own sexual designs on Tama. He jealously misreads paltry signs, conjuring up a punishable affair where none exists. And his inflated characterization of his position augments this sense of authority being twisted to inappropriate ends. The role of calendar-maker was indeed an important one, with connections to exalted political institutions, including the shogunate and the imperial court, but his status was that of a townsman. By arrogating to himself a status equivalent to that of a samurai, Ishun authorizes himself to inflict harsh punishments, as illicit sexual relationships among the staff of samurai households were considered severe transgressions.[61] Here, the danger underlying the household's uneven language politics becomes frighteningly apparent. Ishun can invoke his prerogative to punish Tama and Mohei in the name of enforcing communal order precisely because that hierarchically differentiated order affords them no safe recourse for protest or reprisal; the clerk and housemaid are safe objects for the redirection of their master's stymied sexual energies into violence. To phrase it in Jackson's terms, the characters, reduced to objects, are afforded no recourse to expose the falsity of the "true" narrative that the calendar-maker imposes on them.

But the play as a whole is an example of Jackson's "fictional" narrative, oriented to "shaming all those who mask their greed and ambition with the language of ideology and the trappings of high office," and returning to the powerless "their own will, their own agency, their own consciousness, and their own being."[62] It accomplishes this move by appealing to a power beyond conventional hierarchical authority—one imbued with the capacity to recognize the truth behind warped or misleading forms. Mohei is the first to invoke this power, when he agrees to procure the silver piece to aid Osan's parents:

> Everything will be resolved if I perform a momentary impropriety. Which is to say, it is not theft, merely the concealment of something from others' eyes. And even if we call it theft, Heaven will see clearly that I do not act from personal desire. You are my master as well, and a parent's shame is a daughter's shame, a father-in-law's shame is the shame of his son-in-law. To save my masters from shame is, in the end, an act of service to my master.[63]

Central to this quotation is Mohei's invocation of Heaven (*tendō*) as an all-seeing arbiter. Sneaking his master's seal to procure the silver piece (a paltry sum for the wealthy calendar-maker) may resemble a clerk's petty theft. But, Mohei clarifies, his act should properly be understood as a form of service for his master's—and the household's—greater good. Only Heaven, an authority unhampered by blind spots and biases, can read the relationship between form and substance *correctly* and thus perceive the full complexity of the murky situation and the justice of Mohei's actions. When Ishun tries to get him to explain why he pilfered the seal and thus tells Sukeemon to beat Mohei in front of the assembled household and Osan's mother, Mohei again invokes Heaven:

> [Sukeemon] grabbed him by the topknot and knocked him twenty, thirty times with fists tough as turban shells. "Well, then, still won't spit it out?" He glared at Mohei. Mohei's hair had come wildly undone. "That's it! Beat me! Beat me again! Give me a good stomping. I've done an outrageous thing, stealing my master's seal! And yet, to this day, never once have I stopped off at a teahouse while on the job. I have no idea how to play cards. I have a change of clothes, the same as anyone, and I'm not fettered with a wife and kids [to support]. What do I lack that could prompt me to act so selfishly? Even if my body is beaten to dust, I won't utter an excuse. Mistress Osan, Madame, if you try to intercede, I'll resent it into the world to come. Oh, Sukeemon! If Heaven could talk, it would be I who beat *you* across the face until you cried, 'Forgive me, Mohei!' What a shame that I can't make you grovel. Oh, what regret!" He gnashed his teeth, dropped his head, and wept.[64]

Mohei's cries suggest the ease with which a community will, like the *seken* in Saikaku's story, leap to conclusions on the basis of superficial signs, and how quickly a "true" narrative that serves communal authority can impose itself upon an assortment of signs in a way that victimizes the innocent. A servant who pilfers his master's seal *must* be up to no good—but here, concluding as much means ignoring other signs that do not add up. Mohei lists these conflicting pieces of evidence, which collectively present a picture of an upstanding clerk with no history of or motive for misbehavior. But the household's power differentials force him to assert his innocence only obliquely for fear of creating trouble for Osan. Again, only Heaven—all-seeing, but mute—can perceive truth in all its complexity.

And in this sense, "Heaven" resembles the audience watching the play: all-seeing observers, invisible to the characters onstage, initiated throughout the opening scenes into the tangled domestic politics of the household, and invited to appraise the behavior of the characters in ways that resist the facile ascriptions of conventional values. The audience is bidden to open itself to alternative ways of reading ostensibly legible forms: here, a clerk's pilfering and household members' "adultery"—and, later, a real instance of sexual transgression and its ultimate punishment. And it is invited to do so with a strong emotional response. From Mohei's appeals to common sense (even as he goads Sukeemon to beat him harder), to his refusal to implicate Osan or her mother (who must watch him suffer to protect them), to his tears (not of pain, but of frustration that his position prevents him from bringing punishment down upon the genuinely corrupt Sukeemon), the scene is designed to elicit sympathetic tears from members of the audience who perceive Mohei's innocence clearly but are powerless to intervene. As his statements on his philosophy of playwrighting make clear, Chikamatsu was deeply concerned with the question of how to facilitate the flow of emotion between a play and those who watch it.[65] His avowed strategy was to arrange the circumstances such that the audience could not help but experience the desired feeling. When he discusses the depiction of "sadness" (*urei*), for example, he says that it is not enough—or even appropriate—for the chanter to recite the lines in an overly sorrowful style or to interject comments like, "Ah, how moving!" (*aware nari*): "My 'sadness' rests entirely on reason [*giri*]. The various elements of the play's artistry [*gei*] all converge in a logical way [*giri ni tsumarite*] to evoke sadness, and so the chanting and expressions are all the more moving for being constrained [*kittoshitaru*]."[66] In *The Calendar-Maker and the Old Calendar*, the revelation of the gap that exists between the facts and the "true" version asserted by the household's authority figures works to evoke an outflow of sympathy and moral outrage at the suffering that version inflicts.

This effect carries a political valence relevant beyond this scene, and even beyond the play. Suffering, as David B. Morris argues, "is not a raw datum, a natural phenomenon we can identify and measure, but a social status that we extend or withhold. We extend or withhold it depending largely on whether the sufferer falls within our moral community." One crucial function of literature, he posits, is to "expand the borders of the moral community and force us to acknowledge suffering where we normally do not see it."[67] Chikamatsu's audiences were diverse; they comprised men and women from different status groups and walks of life.[68] Yet within the space of the theater, beholding Mohei's beating—and, later, the other travails of the innocent but condemned protagonists—*The Calendar-Maker and the Old Calendar* bade them to cohere into an undifferentiated "moral community" rooted in shared feeling. And it calibrated that community's moral compass not to the "true" narratives of official, public morality, but to the ostensible transgressors whose voices those narratives coopted and whose suffering they discounted. Even when Osan and Mohei are silenced on Chikamatsu's stage, the play enables the Heaven-like audience to hear them, restoring them as subjects, even as it demonstrates the impunity with which they could be transformed into objects.

Form and Feeling

That Chikamatsu's treatment of feeling (*ninjō*) carries an ethical charge has long been recognized.[69] But there is also a critical, political edge to empathy in *The Calendar-Maker and the Old Calendar*, as it asks the audience to register—at a subjective, emotional level—the ethical failures, or at least vulnerabilities, of an authoritarian social system. The shogunate itself was aware of the emotional volatility of a witnessing crowd, which may explain why the government's regime of bodies-as-signs publicly displayed the results of crucifixion but generally kept the *act* of execution hidden from the eyes of the populace. Public executions, notes Botsman, were "potentially unstable and destabilizing events" in which spectators could turn against the authorities "if they did not approve of an execution, or if they sensed that the basic rights of a condemned person had been violated."[70] This dynamic of violation pervades the play, brought to a fever pitch at moments of punishment such as Mohei's beating, but present at every instance in which the failures of those in authority result in the infliction of suffering on the powerless figures beneath them. And those failures reliably follow from misrecognition—willful or otherwise.

The play's ensuing scenes repeatedly ask the audience to bear witness both to the subjective experiences of the protagonists *and* to the ways in which various levels of authority fail to perceive them accurately. These misrecognitions emerge from an overreliance on outward forms; they are faulty because they take appearance as truth, without considering the varieties of truth carried by subjective experience and intent. The greatest misrecognition of all is the perception that Osan and Mohei are adulterers. Their offense is, in fact, a pure mistake that emerges from the scene of Mohei's beating. Tama's intercession on his behalf awakens Mohei's feelings for her, and he escapes his confinement and slips into her room later that night. Tama, meanwhile, has confessed to Osan that the calendar-maker has been attempting to seduce her each night in her bedroom; she explains that his violent treatment of her and Mohei is rooted in his jealousy and frustration at her resistance. Osan, incensed, convinces Tama to let her take the young maid's place for the night; Osan, acting as Tama under cover of darkness, will acquiesce to Ishun's advances and then shame him for his behavior when day breaks. But the calendar-maker is kept out late that night. He never comes to Tama's room; Mohei does. Only in the early morning, when Sukeemon opens the door to rouse the housemaid for the day's work, do the clerk and his master's wife discover that they have spent the night in each other's arms. Their act of "transgression" is not a transgression at all. But Sukeemon sees only a pair of adulterers, and when the two flee the household in a panic, their action seems to confirm their guilt.

The ensuing scenes hinge on the difficulty of achieving accurate perception—which requires recourse to the heart—when all one has access to is outward form. Even as they flee into the depths of the countryside, Osan and Mohei strive to maintain the proper forms that should prevail between the lady of the house and an employee. But they acknowledge that outward appearances alone are not enough. It is their inner state that matters, but inner states cannot be conveyed to those who remain empathetically unreceptive. Osan, who stays emotionally faithful to the calendar-maker, tearfully laments to Mohei that there is no way to make the inner state of her heart outwardly visible to her husband: "And poor Ishun, whom I have known since we were children. I only wish I could explain to him, before I die, that your heart and mine have remained unsullied in the least."[71] Instead, Osan's and Mohei's bodies and gestures continue to signify beyond their intent: at another climax, when the pair leans, sobbing, against two pillars, the shadows they cast ominously resemble bodies bound to crucifixion posts.[72] Meanwhile, the only characters capable of recognizing them as human subjects rather than abject transgressors are those who already possess a deep emotional attachment to them. In a poignant scene, Osan's father must wrestle between the social imperative to reject Osan as a subhuman "beast" (*chikushō*) and his deeply felt desire to care for her as his daughter.[73] He speaks in a kind of doublespeak, envisioning Osan's body within the same sentence as that of a crucified criminal impaled with spears—a body-as-sign—*and* as that of the daughter on whom he had lavished care and affection as she grew up.[74] Affection wins this emotional tussle; later, at the execution ground, Osan's parents will offer themselves to die in the pair's stead.[75]

These scenes of emotional reckoning, in which characters must wrestle with their own hearts as they weigh their appraisal of Osan and Mohei, have the effect of revealing the weaknesses of powerful systems in which the heart is not involved. Most striking is the depiction of the shogunate's instruments of justice, who, unlike the calendar-maker and his head clerk, are portrayed as well intentioned and unbiased, but nonetheless limited in their ability to perceive the full truth of the situation. At the moment of the pair's arrest, Tama's uncle Bairyū, an imposing, unemployed samurai with a formidable moral character, appears on the scene bearing Tama's severed head. Bairyū explains that Osan and Mohei's seeming adultery was the result of a series of unintended errors that all sprouted from Tama's words to Osan about her husband. As the housemaid was the origin of the problem, he says, she has submitted to her punishment: "Let the lives of these two be spared!"[76] But the officials admonish Bairyū, for his act has condemned the very people he intended to save:

> Ah, Bairyū, you have acted rashly! The truth or fiction of these prisoners' crimes had not been established. Had Tama, the [accused] go-between, been investigated as a witness in Kyoto, the real circumstances would have become clear, and the lives of all three would have been saved. But you have beheaded the key witness, the lynchpin—what kind of evidence could an investigation now reveal? You've left us nothing to go on. What a shame, what a shame! The investigation of these two is now settled![77]

Tama's severed head, they announce, intended as a sign that affirms the innocence of Osan and Mohei, will now be displayed with their crucified bodies as a sign that confirms their guilt. The authorities' job is to enforce law (*hō*), and they do so in a way that prioritizes rational order, relying on procedure, investigation, evidence, and trial. From their perspective, Tama's death has removed a key source of information. But the process of rational, evidence-based investigation is here presented as already internally impaired, for by relying exclusively on analysis of forms, it cuts off access to deeper understanding. Tama's sacrifice may be rash and dramatic, but the audience, watching the play with the all-seeing eyes of Heaven, knows that it is the fruit of deep empathy. In an earlier scene, when the housemaid and her uncle first discuss the possibility of such a sacrifice, they motivate themselves by imagining themselves into the experiences of Osan, Mohei, and Osan's parents:

> [Tama wondered], "How must Mohei be faring now? And the really pitiable one is Mistress Osan. Where can she be, and how must she be coping? I know her heart, always frail and honest, and my feelings go out to her so!" She wept bitterly, and Bairyū, too, spoke. "Ah, you pity Madame Osan. But my feelings are for her parents at Shimoda-chiuri, and how they must grieve!" Within the house, uncle and niece continued talking it over and weeping.[78]

Tama's death is not a servant's obligatory act of self-sacrifice to protect her master; it is only in opening their hearts to the affective experiences of others that Tama and Bairyū arouse a great urge to help them. That current of feeling may itself be fatally misdirected into self-destructive ends, but it remains completely illegible to the shogunate's officers, who therefore misappropriate the form of Tama's sacrifice and make it stand for the opposite of its intent.

Un-crucifixion and the Renewal of Order

These examples of the ways in which even the realm's highest agents of order and justice fail to rise to the level of all-seeing Heaven reach a climax when the time comes for the protagonists to confront their crucifixion. And it is here that *The Calendar-Maker and the Old Calendar* makes its most breathtaking move. Having displayed for an empathetic audience the ways in which the normative structures of authority have failed to protect the fundamentally innocent Osan and Mohei, the play overrides those structures and protects them by fiat. The accused lovers are arrested, bound, paraded through the city, and brought to the execution ground when, in a deus ex machina twist, a monk—the priest of Osan's family temple at Kurodani—rushes onto the scene, throws his robe over the pair, and takes them into his care, defying the shogunate's executioners and saving their lives.

To grasp the implications of this surprise ending, we must recall that the Osan-Mohei topos relied upon the remixing of established formal ingredients: the calendar-maker's household, a lustful clerk, a maid as go-between, flight to Tanba, crucifixion for the lovers and beheading for the maid. Here, the problems of the play are settled by formally reworking an ingredient that was central to all versions of the crucified lovers' story: the calendar. The calendar (*koyomi*) was not simply a chart of days; like an almanac, it predicted cosmological events and included horoscope-like information about auspicious and unpropitious days for various activities. Agriculture, officialdom, and commerce all depended on its predictions and its uniformity. And political legitimacy was at stake at an ideological level as well, for, as Peter Kornicki notes, "The calendar was not simply a matter of computing the length of the year and dividing up time. It was also, in Confucian thought, a reflection of the harmony that was supposed to lie between the heavens and the governance of the state."[79] The calendar was therefore a highly sensitive political document, one that enabled state and society to function smoothly and that signified the shogunate's legitimacy to rule and maintain order.[80] Japan's calendrical system, however, had been adopted from Tang China in 862 and had not been updated since; its predictive capacities were increasingly imprecise. The old calendar was finally abandoned in 1684, the year after Osan's and Mohei's crucifixions, and the new "Jōkyō Calendar" (Jōkyōreki), named for the current era name, came into use in 1685. Saikaku's decision to make the calendar-maker's wife the heroine of the central story in *Five Amorous Women*, published in 1686, quite possibly drew on public interest not only in the scandal and crucifixion, but in the major event of calendrical renewal.[81]

And, indeed, aspects of calendrical language and layout became indispensable ingredients of the Osan-Mohei topos. In the *utazaimon*, Mohei's letter of seduction to Osan is coded in a vocabulary of double entendre that relies on specialized calendrical terms, as in the following lines: "*Masaru ten ichi tenjō no / gosui hassen mabi mo nashi / Kakaru kokoro no jūnichi o / semete gogen ni kuchi tokan to / iroiro kannichi megurasete / mata mata au yo kanoesaru.*"[82] Mohei is lamenting that he has not been able to express his feelings directly to Osan. The gist translates roughly as: "Heaven has not given me its protection, and I have not been able to act at liberty. I want at least to express directly to you what is in my heart, but I have met only obstacles. There has still not been a night when I could meet you." But the lines are constructed almost wholly from calendrical terms. Some involve homophonic play: *kokoro no jūnichi* conveys "what is in my heart" (*kokoro no chū*) by punning on *jūnichi*, the word for a day on which fortunes, good or ill, would be doubled, while *kanoesaru*, one of the signs of the calendrical sexagenary cycle (*eto*), doubles as *kanaezaru* (to fail to bring to fruition). Others, like *hassen mabi* and *kannichi* evoke Mohei's inability to act as he wishes by using terms related to directional taboos and inauspicious dates. Employing the unique vocabulary of the calendrical lexicon is likely part of what made the *utazaimon* entertaining in performance: one can imagine the pleasure of listening to a skilled singer play up the linguistic twists that transform calendrical terms into words of seduction.

The *Calendar-Maker and the Old Calendar* returns to this trick of the *utazaimon*, now transforming it from within: instead of serving up a jaunty seduction, the calendrical language punctuates Osan and Mohei's parading to the killing ground. The printed version of the play titles this scene "The Calendar Song of Osan and Mohei" (Osan Mohei koyomiuta), and the notation specifies that the chanter should sing key parts of it in the style of an *utazaimon*.[83] Osan turns to Mohei to apologize to him and to encourage him to remain strong to the end. The final words of her address parallel those in Mohei's letter to Osan in the *utazaimon*: "*Omoeba ten ichi tenjō no / gosui hassen mabi mo nashi. / Tada nanigoto mo kannichi to / koe mo namida ni kakikururu.*"[84] No longer referring to a stymied would-be lover, through these lines Osan now speaks of the ill fortune of the condemned, "abandoned by Heaven, fated to die as even heavenly beings must, never granted a day of reprieve, meeting only with days of poor fortune," before trailing off into tears. This recasting of the *utazaimon* lines encapsulates the dynamic of the play as a whole: reworking an established form from within, it transforms Osan and Mohei from transgressive lovers into tragic figures tossed about by forces beyond their control. And while the allusion to Heaven here is to a calendrical deity (*ten'ichijin* or *nakagami*) whose periodic ascent to the heavens leaves humans without protection, the wording recalls as well Mohei's earlier appeals to Heaven in the broader sense of *tendō*, as the one entity capable of seeing the protagonists as they really are: a position in which the audience once again finds itself, now wishing ardently for the pair's reprieve.

When the play, a few lines later, grants that reprieve, it again employs references to the calendar, but now in a way that evokes the calendar's association with symbolic authority over time and order, suggesting the invocation of a superior form of authority—and the instantiation of a new order of time. When the monk of Osan's family temple throws his robe over the pair and claims their lives as his own, the official overseeing the execution is incensed: "Monk, your claim to aid prisoners whose guilt has been established makes light of those in authority above [*kami*]. Impossible, impossible! Tear off that robe!" But the priest does not budge:

> "The principle of salvation is a robe of blessing that spans past, present, and future [*sanze*]. If my wish is granted and the lives of these two are spared, then with my robe I save them in the present. Even if they have committed sin, I will make them my disciples and so save them for the future. Whether future or present, salvation is one and the same. I have saved them!" he cried, and a heartfelt shout went up from those assembled. [Osan's parents] raised their voices in joy, and such a joyful sound will resound through calendars of ten thousand years, through calendars old and calendars new, and into the calendar of this very year, opening with great auspiciousness.[85]

The play itself premiered at a temporal crossroads. It marked thirty-two years since Osan's and Mohei's executions—a symbolically charged anniversary in Buddhist mourning practices—and it has been understood as a requiem work, intended to bring solace to their spirits.[86] It was also a New Year performance, as suggested by the felicitous nature of its closing words. But that wording is undeniably defiant. The monk's blessings override the agents of "those in authority above," whether the shogunate's executioners or the "little kings of everyday life" represented by Osan's husband. And they do so by means of the monk's robe, which he likens to the "principle of salvation"—literally, "the obligation to help" (*tasukuru to iu giri*). That obligation, which requires an empathetic turning toward the subjective experience of another, is the principle that underlies the dynamic of the entire play. The play fosters in its audience the wish to see the protagonists saved, likens that wish to the position of Heaven, and then sees to it that Heaven's will be done. And with its auspicious wording and the responsive shouts of joy, it suggests that such a compassionate opening to the other not only has the capacity to counteract the shogunate's regime of bodies-as-signs by returning subjectivity to those it would reduce to objects, but also possesses a superior power to achieve the shogunate's own agenda of maintaining a healthy and well-ordered body politic, revitalizing the values of the official "true" narrative through its own fiction. Casting its own robe of compassion over characters and spectators alike, the play lays claim to the power to set right time that is out of joint.[87]

This does not mean that *The Calendar-Maker and the Old Calendar* should be understood as fundamentally at odds with how the dynamics of power and authority structured early modern life in Japan. Its new order of time proffers renewal, not revolution. The play is, in fact, deeply invested in an ideologically orthodox vision of every person in his or her proper station. Its antagonists are figures like the calendar-maker, Ishun, and the clerk Sukeemon, who liken themselves to samurai in order to lay claim to privileges reserved for those above them, and whose personal ambitions lead them to neglect the moral obligations incumbent on their authority over others. It valorizes Tama's uncle Bairyū, a tough old samurai who hews faithfully to samurai ideals, even as that fidelity relegates him to the impoverished life of a *rōnin*. And it repeatedly highlights the ways that money—the lack of it or the lust for it—distorts human relationships and hierarchical order, leading the narrator at one point to declare money the protagonists' true enemy.[88] Nor does the play take the truly radical step of making Osan a *willing* adulteress and then absolving her: that scenario seems to lie beyond the play's horizon of possibility. Instead, the play, by reworking the modular ingredients of Osan-Mohei to foster experiences of shared emotionality, aims to renew to health an intersubjective dynamic it takes for granted: one in which individual personhood will always be inextricable from the hierarchically ordered, nested boxes of community that collectively make up its very terrain.

Conclusion

"Art," Chikamatsu famously asserts in his statements on playwrighting, "lies between the skin and the flesh of truth and falsehood" (*Gei to iu mono wa jitsu to uso to no aida ni aru mono nari*).[89] His words refer specifically to the matter of realism in the theater—to the necessity for a certain degree of artifice in order for the performance to bring aspects of reality into presence. But the Osan-Mohei variations demonstrate how the navigation of truth and falsehood could itself become art's subject matter. In their remixing of the formal ingredients of the Osan-Mohei topos, the different versions reflect on the relationship between form, fiction, and truth. Even as the versions imbue Osan and Mohei's story with wildly different meanings, they probe *how* forms signify, how they can symbolize or even instantiate truths, and how they can go astray (or be led astray) and thus obscure reality. They reflect as well upon the question of how form and truth might be realigned and proper perception thus restored.

Despite their conservative message, even the *utazaimon* present a slightly different "truth" from that of the shogunate's crucified bodies. Whereas those bodies conveyed a message about power and order, the *utazaimon* probe at the vulnerability of the household's patriarchal structure to transgression, locating danger even in the laudable moral quality of a wife's compassion. Saikaku's retelling demonstrates the extent to which popular "truth" comes down to the collective perception of outward forms, and it then shows how the import of those forms could be transformed from within to enact an alternate, empowering reality. And in Chikamatsu's play, the theater, as a space of contact between truth and fiction, reveals itself as not simply a reflection of the world, but an agent within it: a site wherein the social order could be recalibrated by pushing outward the boundaries of moral community to encompass even the casualties of normatively "true" narratives. Through its reworking of the established forms of Osan-Mohei, the play returns the role of the heart—the affective opening to others—to the operations of the social order and suggests that doing so can avert the potential for violence inherent in the misreading (willful or otherwise) of outward forms.

Concern over how to distinguish the seeming from the real, however, did not stop at the story of Osan and Mohei. If anything, the question of how to access the true and authentic intensified during the eighteenth century, reaching beyond popular fiction and theater and into the scholarly world of "study of the country" (*kokugaku*), a body of discourses concerned with the nature of Japanese community across time and text. In the next chapter I trace the attempts of a *kokugaku* scholar and writer to convey authentically the truth of an unusual murder, an endeavor that required him to wrestle with the relationship between truth and fiction in unprecedented ways—ways that confronted the potential violence of literary form itself.

CHAPTER IV

Ueda Akinari and the Form of Fiction

In Which a Brother Is Celebrated for Beheading His Sister

On an early summer day in 1806, the writer and scholar Ueda Akinari (1734–1809)—by then an aged, semi-impoverished writer-scholar who had spent the better part of his life thinking about the bonds between the living and the dead, the entanglement of reality and fiction, and the question of what held together "Japan" as a community across time and space—came face to face with a killer.

It was the death anniversary of Tokugawa Ieyasu, the founder of the Tokugawa shogunate. Akinari had walked from his humble dwelling in the shadow of Kyoto's Nanzenji temple to Ichijōji village, on the capital's northern outskirts, for the commemorative ceremonies at a temple called Enkōji. Ieyasu had founded the temple, and its grounds included a shrine to his spirit. Akinari was then over seventy years old, widowed, with failing eyesight and little money. Although best known today for the ghostly narratives collected in *Tales of Moonlight and Rain* (*Ugetsu monogatari*, 1776), his written works spanned a vast range of subject matter and styles: satirical fiction, scholarly studies of ancient Japanese myth and poetry, commentaries on Heian-period prose and fiction, treatises on *sencha* tea, and copious *haikai, waka*, and *kyōka* poetry. Above all, the intellectual endeavors of his mature years had been deeply connected with *kokugaku* (study of the country), a diverse body of discourses concerned with the bonds—emotional, historical, cultural, textual—that gave, or could give, coherence to "Japan" as a transhistorical community.[1]

When the festivities at Enkōji were complete, the abbot invited Akinari and other attendees to join him for some saké. Among those assembled, Akinari was quite taken by an elderly gentleman of the vicinity:

> He had passed sixty in years, yet he had a boyish face and looked quite dignified. He liked saké, and his manner as he spoke was tremendously frank and refreshing [*kawaraka nari*]. There was a time when this man's actions had resounded throughout the world, but since then forty years had passed, and I now thought it little more than an old tale—no one realizes that he is still living in the world like this. At that time, I, too, had heard of those astonishing events and had thought to myself, "[To think that] such a *masurao* exists, even in this world!" That I have lived long enough to meet him in person makes me grateful for my aged years.[2]

The man's name was Watanabe Genta. Nearly thirty-nine years earlier, on a winter day in early 1768, this villager of samurai descent had carried out a "resounding" deed, causing a stir that reached all the way to the shogun's Judicial Council (*Hyōjōsho*): Genta, who was then twenty-six, had killed his younger sister, Yae, at the home of their neighbor Watanabe Danji. Danji was a distant kinsman with whose son Yae had been romantically involved. Genta had brought her to his house that day in a last attempt to urge Danji to let the young lovers marry. But as before, the much wealthier Danji refused, and he hurled abuse at Genta and his sister. This time, Genta did not withdraw. He drew his sword and, before the astonished eyes of Danji's household, beheaded his sister. As the house erupted in panic, he then calmly seated himself to await arrest.

Why should Akinari have felt delight at meeting such a man? He even refers to him with the archaic term *masurao*—the word, which roughly translates as "valiant man," had become associated in certain *kokugaku* circles with the idealized character of primordial Japanese society. And Akinari was not alone in being affected by Genta's act. After Genta was taken into custody, the authorities in Kyoto received multiple petitions requesting clemency for him.[3] A kabuki play partially inspired by the murder opened in Kyoto a mere seven weeks after the beheading and enjoyed a successful two-month run.[4] And just a few weeks after that, the writer Takebe Ayatari (1719–1774)—himself deeply influenced by *kokugaku* thought—published a fictionalized version of the killing titled *A Tale of* the Western Hills (*Nishiyama monogatari*). The work is considered an early example of the erudite fiction known as *yomihon* (reading books), of which Akinari would come to be recognized as an exemplary author.

The authorities, meanwhile, were not certain what to make of Genta's act. It resembled a patriarchal honor killing, and yet it was like no such killing in the shogunate's records. As an act of unauthorized violence, it unquestioningly deserved punishment; but the officials had a difficult time deciding who was at fault and how best to apportion penalties. Kyoto ultimately sent the case to Edo for review by the shogun's Judicial Council, which delivered a verdict that largely absolved Genta of guilt—but did so by downplaying the aspects of the murder that made it formally unusual.

Yet it was the very unusualness of the killing that appears to have captured Akinari's attention. Where the authorities opted to see a conventional honor killing, Akinari identified the behavior of a *masurao* and traces of the archaic Japanese spirit. Following his encounter with the aged Genta, Akinari composed two works inspired by the killing: an essay that came to be known as "The Tale of a *Masurao*" (Masurao monogatari, 1807), and a short story titled "The Smile of the Severed Head" (Shikubi no egao). The latter is one of the ten narratives in Akinari's last great *yomihon* collection, *Tales of the Spring Rain* (Harusame monogatari, 1808).

These two works make a confounding pair. In "The Tale of a *Masurao*," Akinari purports to present the unadulterated "truth" (*masashigoto*) of the incident, and he denounces those who would fictionalize it, singling out Ayatari's *Tale of the Western Hills* as a work that "does injury to a good man." Yet in "The Smile of the Severed Head," written the following year, Akinari overtly fictionalizes the incident himself. And—ironically—prominent modern critics have judged his "factual" essay superior to his fictional story, which they characterized as exaggerated, inconsistent, and unpolished.[5] The scholar Morita Kirō even contended that Akinari's "truthful" essay ultimately makes a better tale (*monogatari*) than his explicitly fictional version.[6]

But the formal strangeness of "The Smile of the Severed Head" echoes the stylistic enigmas that make *Tales of the Spring Rain* as a whole so extraordinary. Although composed in the last two years of Akinari's life, this collection marked a new departure. Like a crucible, he poured into it questions of fact, fiction, history, knowledge, and form that had long weighed on him, and forged from them an experimental new approach to fiction, one that *performs* a set of arguments about these questions, often at the level of form and style. Kazama Seishi calls *Tales of the Spring Rain* an unusual "piece" that cannot easily be fitted into the edifice of early modern literary history, adding, "We can label it a 'difficult work' [*nankai na shōsetsu*]; but how it is 'difficult' and what about it is 'difficult' are themselves 'difficult' questions."[7] And yet its stylistic peculiarities have also been recognized—particularly by modern authors—as pointing to formal possibilities largely unexplored elsewhere in Edo-period letters. The writer Ishikawa Jun (1899–1987) went so far as to assert that, had other writers carried on what Akinari began with *Tales of the Spring Rain*, Japan might not have been shocked by the arrival of European literature in the Meiji period.[8]

In this chapter, I take Akinari's doubled treatment of Genta's beheading of his sister as an entry point into this larger tangle of the writer's late experimentation with fiction—and with the question of fictionality itself. Violence is central to this exploration, for Akinari was deeply sensitive to the violent potential of fiction. He characterized the composition of fiction as an act rooted in writerly "rage" (*ikidōri*), and he noted the potential of fiction to inflict "injury" in the world beyond the page. But he also saw fiction, which he likened to allegory, as a form of cover: a way for a writer to express his rage obliquely, without incurring the wrath of the powerful. From the perspective of Akinari's *kokugaku* studies, the writing of fiction was in this sense a symptom of a degraded world that had lost the direct expressivity of the primeval past. In Genta's act, however, Akinari recognized traces of that ancient expressivity—the *masurao* spirit—living on in his own world.

Akinari's two versions of the "Genta disturbance" thus represent more than attempts to depict a murder in words. They are a site of process wherein we observe Akinari working out a set of propositions about form, fictionality, and the work that writing performs in the world. Far from unpolished, "The Smile of the Severed Head," I suggest, marks the culmination of this process: a renewed commitment—in the wake of a failed attempt to articulate truth plainly in "The Tale of a *Masurao*"—to the obliqueness of fictional form, which may, ultimately, perform work in the world more powerful than truth telling. Testing the bounds of narrative form, the story's exaggerations, elisions, and ambiguities mark a bold attempt to make perceptible, to a world caught in a state of normalized distortion, the fact of distortion itself.

Through an examination of one writer's attempts to write about a peculiar murder, this chapter thus delves into the relationship between fiction and *kokugaku* thought and returns us, via a new avenue, to the charged early modern relationship among truth, fictionality, and form. I begin by exploring the shogunate's own attempts to make the murder fit an acceptable narrative form in its judgments. I then turn to the *kokugaku* scholar Kamo no Mabuchi's conceptualization of the *masurao*, which shaped Akinari's view of that archaic figure, before diving into a close examination of "The Tale of a *Masurao*" and "The Smile of the Severed Head," respectively.

The Facts, Fiction, and Form of the Case

It may be tempting to think that the authorities' judgments on the Genta disturbance will help us to grasp what "really" happened on that winter day in 1768. But a close look at the records reveals that those who adjudicated the case carried their own set of formal and narrative concerns. Their deliberations, in fact, help us to recognize the formal strangeness of the killing—a strangeness that would open the door for *kokugaku*-inspired writers like Ayatari and Akinari to present interpretations of the murder that diverged significantly from the framework resorted to by those in power.

Officers of the Kyoto city magistrate took Genta into custody and interrogated the other figures involved in the affair. When two months had passed without a decision, they released Genta. Nearly ten months after the murder, they sent a request to Edo begging for assistance, and the shogun's Judicial Council finally pronounced its decisions just over a year after Yae's death. Their judgments list the preliminary conclusions submitted by the Kyoto magistrate's office alongside the Judicial Council's responses, affording us a glimpse not just of the facts as the authorities understood them, but of a narrative process, whereby they tried out different approaches for making those unusual facts fit into a conventional moral box.[9]

The general sequence of events agreed on by the authorities follows: Genta and his mother, Tsuya, had been dimly aware that Yae was romantically involved with Unai, a twenty-year-old neighbor and distant relative who recently had inherited the title of village headman (*shōya*) from his wealthy father, Danji. As unsavory rumors about the affair spread in the village, Genta's mother instructed him to consult Danji about marrying the lovers. Danji, however, not only rejected the proposal, but met it with insults. And he punished his son. He demanded that Unai break things off immediately, threatened to revoke his status as headman, and sent him to stay with relatives. Through a go-between, Unai attempted to make a clean break with Yae, but the go-between did a poor job of communicating between the lovers. When Yae demanded, in defiance of her mother and older brother, to meet with Unai one last time to hear his feelings directly and express her own, they came to feel that she was irredeemably unfilial. Tsuya instructed Genta to take Yae with him to Danji's house once more to see if a marriage agreement could be reached; if they again met with a refusal, Genta was to end things by taking Yae's life.[10]

The officials of the Judicial Council felt that they were in uncharted territory because of the peculiar aspects of the case. "We have not identified precedents for the punishment of the murder of a younger sister under circumstances such as these," they stated plainly.[11] By "precedents for the punishment" (otogame no rei), the officials meant that no penalty for such a case existed in the *Rules for Determining Legal Matters* (*Kujikata osadamegaki*), a two-volume book of legal codes, precedents, and punishments in 184 articles, compiled on the order of the shogun Tokugawa Yoshimune (1684–1751, r. 1716–1745) between 1720 and 1754.[12] The *Rules* was intended to serve as a guide for judicial officers' adjudications. The second volume, also known as the *Hundred Articles* (*Hyakkajō*), consisted of 103 examples of crimes and their appropriate punishments, but it contained none that mapped neatly onto the peculiarities of the Genta case. Nonetheless, the officials endeavored to identify familiar frameworks into which they could fit the incident. Most conspicuously, they opted to view the case primarily through the lens of the well-worn frameworks of licentiousness (*hōratsu*), illicit sexual conduct (*mittsū*), and unfilial behavior (*fukō*).[13] The officials in Kyoto already had framed the incident in these terms in the preliminary judgment on Genta that they forwarded to the Judicial Council:

> The younger sister, Yae, behaved with loose morals [*mimochi hōratsu*] and pursued an illicit affair [*mittsū*] with Unai. Her mother Tsuya and older brother Genta repeatedly admonished her, but to no avail. Her behavior toward her mother was inexcusably unfilial [*fukō no dan furachi ni zonji*]. Furthermore, Danji's manner of response [to the marriage proposal] was highly inappropriate, and so the mother, Tsuya, tasked her son [*nin mōshitsuke*], instructing him to kill Yae. For the

household heir to commit murder in a situation that called instead for discrete handling was outrageous [*futodoki*]. However, as the source of the trouble was Yae's licentiousness, we request your opinion on whether it is appropriate to banish [Genta] to a distant isle.[14]

The charge that Yae's affair with Unai was illicit (*mittsū*) refers not to sex out of wedlock, but to the fact that the household did not condone her behavior.[15] In response to Kyoto's query, the Judicial Council reaffirmed the framework of licentiousness and unfilial behavior. But in so doing, they found Genta *less* culpable:

> According to the *Rules for Determining Legal Matters*, the punishment for the rash murder of a younger sibling, nephew, or niece is banishment to a distant isle. In this case, no rashness was involved. The younger sister, Yae, behaved licentiously, paid no heed to [her family's] repeated admonishments, and behaved unfilially to her mother, Tsuya. Tsuya instructed her son to take action [*nin mōshitsuke*], and the outcome was a murder. Had the same circumstances obtained when the father of the household was still living, and had he taken [his daughter's] life himself, there would be no need to discuss punishment. The same point pertains even in the case of a mother or older brother.[16]

The Judicial Council's judgment treats Yae's murder as the inappropriately violent but justified punishment of a licentious daughter on behalf of the household: a patriarchal honor killing. The council's observation that there would be no need for deliberations had Yae been killed by her *father* underscores the framework of patriarchal values and household authority through which the legal authorities made sense of the case. In their reading, Tsuya took up her dead husband's mantle of household authority, and Genta—a filial son—served as the household's instrument of punishment. They deemed the deepest responsibility to lie with the murdered Yae herself; or, in Blake Morgan Young's words: "In effect, Yae was placed on trial for her own murder and found guilty."[17] As Genta was following his mother's directions rather than acting "rashly," a stern reprimand would suffice as punishment rather than banishment—and since he already had spent sixty days under arrest, the Judicial Council essentially sentenced him to time served. Similarly, while Kyoto had inquired whether banishment from the province was appropriate for his mother (following the stipulation in the *Hundred Articles* of that punishment for an accomplice to murder), the Judicial Council ruled that Tsuya be exonerated for the same reasons as Genta.[18]

Yet, as Moriyama Shigeo notes, emphasizing Yae's guilt and her household's recourse to private punishment sidesteps the odd fact that Yae's murder was carried out not privately, but in the household of Danji and Unai.[19] The setting suggests that Genta and Tsuya understood the killing not as an internal household matter, but as aimed in some way at Danji's household: perhaps a prideful response to Danji's vituperative reception of their marriage proposal. In that case, however, the killing would no longer fit neatly into the box of "honor killing," and the impetus would lie not with a teen-age daughter's dissolute and unfilial behavior, but in a more complicated interfamily dynamic. Indeed, Moriyama suggests that the act can be read as a *household* undertaking—one in which Genta, Tsuya, and Yae were all complicit; he even suggests that the impetus may have been Yae's herself.[20] And the authorities did recognize that Danji and Unai bore some responsibility: they stripped Unai of his headman title and sentenced him to thirty days in manacles for seducing Yae; and they ordered that Danji be confined to his home for fifty days for ineffectively policing his son's behavior, for behaving in a way unbecoming for one of his stature, for failing to intervene in the beheading, and for temporarily sending Unai—the village headman—out of the village.[21] These punishments did not contradict the "illicit love" narrative, and they reinforced the values of moral behavior, vertical authority, and social order that appear to have shaped the authorities' interpretation of the case. Collectively, however, they did not resolve the question of why the killing took such an unusual form. But the authorities' narrative was not the only way of reading the murder.

Kokugaku and the *Masurao* Ideal

When Ueda Akinari—a *kokugaku* scholar in the lineage of Kamo no Mabuchi (1697–1769)—looked at the Genta disturbance, he recognized in its unconventional pieces not a scandalous daughter and a patriarchal killing, but traces of the *masurao*: a figure celebrated by Mabuchi and his disciples as the embodiment of the archaic Japanese spirit. This figure exemplified sincerity of heart and direct expressivity: values cherished and fiercely debated in the eighteenth century, well beyond *kokugaku* circles. The Genta disturbance, with its formal oddity and elusive truth, stood in complex relation to these values. And for Akinari, so did the writing of fiction—which may explain why the incident held such allure for him. But to understand Akinari's engagement with the *masurao*, we must first understand the symbolic weight that this figure was made to bear in the thought of Mabuchi and his school.

Akinari never studied with Mabuchi directly; the master died shortly after Akinari turned to *kokugaku*. After an abortive attempt to begin his *kokugaku* studies with Takebe Ayatari, whom he apparently found lacking in erudition, he became a devoted student of Katō Umaki (1721–1777), a shogunal retainer and one of Mabuchi's leading disciples.[22] Akinari steeped himself in Mabuchi's scholarship and was instrumental in disseminating his work, preparing published editions of Mabuchi's lectures and scholarship on the *Kokin wakashū* (*Collection of Ancient and Modern Poems*, early tenth century) and *Tales of Ise* (*Ise monogatari*, ca. ninth-tenth centuries).[23] He also arranged the publication of two collections of Mabuchi's poetry.[24]

The modern reception of *kokugaku* sometimes treats it as a largely linear progress of (primarily political) thought, but it is better understood as a convoluted tangle of branches.[25] Not all of those branches engaged in the same way with the philological studies that formed the bedrock of much *kokugaku* thought, and not all of them were explicitly concerned with political questions.[26] But for all its diversity of method and lineage, *kokugaku* was largely defined by a fundamental set of questions, summarized by Susan Burns: "What is 'Japan'? How did it emerge and how is it maintained? What binds those within it together?"[27]

These questions partook of a wider intellectual current of seeking models of communal harmony in the texts of the distant past. A range of scholars began to look to the archaic past—whether of China or Japan—in search of a "lost wholeness" that they imagined as having existed in an idealized, primordial polity.[28] Confucians such as Itō Jinsai (1627–1705) and Ogyū Sorai (1666–1728) looked to ancient China, seeking access to authentic language and genuine human emotionality in the earliest Confucian texts (particularly the ancient *Classic of Poetry* [*Shijing*, compiled after the seventh century BCE]), and rejecting the later, orthodox Neo-Confucian emphasis on metaphysical abstraction and rational principle (*ri*). *Kokugaku* scholars drew on aspects of these innovations, but they made their focus ancient Japan. They imagined the archaic "divine age" as a harmonious natural polity, as yet uncorrupted by the importation of Chinese writing and concepts of governance.

Three interlinked elements ran through these intellectual developments. The first was a sense of historical transformation: a keen awareness that life and politics had been different in the past and that seemingly transcendent concepts and values were historically contingent. The second, connected, element recognized texts as the products of unique historical contexts, and that careful study of those texts could afford access to moments of past time now lost. And third, Confucian and *kokugaku* innovators alike emphasized the importance of emotion to the recuperation of "lost wholeness." In a world where surface appearances increasingly seemed artificial and deceptive, emotion offered access to the raw authentic: a point of shared connection that could enable mutual understanding and communal cohesion. It could even leap the chasm of time: to many thinkers, the study of old texts, particularly poetry, offered a channel to the emotional lives of the vanished ancients.

Kamo no Mabuchi rose to prominence in part because he synthesized these three elements in a novel way, creating a coherent narrative—told with arresting metaphors—of Japan's "divine age" past and its corruption by Chinese models of writing and governance. For Mabuchi, Chinese culture—in particular, Confucianism—presented rigid, artificial frameworks for apprehending the world, distorting a primordial Japanese character that was instinctively spontaneous, supple, and attuned to the variegated and harmonious patterns of nature. In his essay "On the Meaning of Our Country" (Kokuikō, 1765), he characterizes the Chinese obsession with formalized principles as "square-like" (*ketani*), defined by rigid lines that artificially—and dangerously—force organic diversity into fixed molds.[29] By contrast, ancient Japanese culture was "round and even, in accordance with heaven and earth."[30] This roundness mirrored the roundness found in the natural world—like the sun and moon—and, therefore, it responded to circumstances harmoniously, just as when "a dewdrop rests on an indented leaf, it accordingly adopts an unusual shape, but when it is returned to an even surface, it returns to its original roundness."[31] In ancient Japan, he argues, there was no need for such inflexible categories as Confucianism's celebrated "five constants": humaneness, righteousness, propriety, knowledge, and integrity. Virtue was implicitly understood, which made it far more agile and sincere.[32]

For Mabuchi, culture emerged spontaneously from the naturally aligned "true heart" (*magokoro*), rather than from externally imposed frameworks.

This "true heart" did not discriminate artificially between ethical statuses or affective experiences and was therefore deeply receptive to emotions—negative as well as positive. Governance, likewise, was rooted in sincerity and natural patterns, ensuring a peaceable polity. The "divine age" did not lack evil; human hearts being naturally diverse, there were those who plotted malicious acts. But because their actions, too, originated from the "true heart," their evil could not be hidden, and thus could easily be addressed and defused.[33] The key quality of the ancients was their straightforward (*naoshi*) nature; but, as Peter Flueckiger summarizes, "that straightforwardness [was] not an absolute moral perfection. Instead, [Mabuchi saw] it as defined by a complete transparency, in which people are exactly what they seem to be."[34] By contrast, Mabuchi claims, political machinations had always plagued Chinese politics, leading to the succession of dynasty upon dynasty. And, following the adoption of Chinese models of governance, similar features of scheming and antagonism began to infect Japanese politics as well.[35]

Language plays a central role in Mabuchi's conceptualization of the dynamics of the "divine age." In contrast to the thousands of complicated (and, again, square-shaped) Chinese characters, which make expression unnecessarily complicated, Mabuchi argues that the fifty sounds of the Japanese language conform organically to the sounds of heaven and earth.[36] This language most profoundly manifested the spirit of the ancients, he contends, when they expressed themselves in poetry, which retained its primordial sense of "song" (*uta*). Ancient song-poetry encapsulates all that Mabuchi idealizes about the past. He characterizes it as natural, spontaneous, and sincere: the outward manifestation of an internal emotional state without distortion or pretense.[37] And this manifestation, articulated in natural tones, in turn aligned with the rhythms and patterns of heaven and earth. Through this unadulterated expression, humans could know one another without suspicion or artifice, and thus live in a state of integral community.[38]

According to Mabuchi, this ancient poetry possessed a distinctive style that emblematized the ancient culture: he calls it the "*masurao* style" (*masuraoburi*), and he locates its greatest expression in the eighth-century anthology *Man'yōshū* (*Collection of Ten Thousand Leaves*).[39] An archaic term meaning, roughly, "valiant man," *masurao* appears throughout the *Man'yōshū*.[40] In the *Man'yōshū*, it typically denotes a man of courtier status but in possession of a robust masculinity—possibly derived from the martial legacy of the early Japanese nobility.[41] Accordingly, Mabuchi defines the *masurao* style as possessing "a lofty and straightforward spirit. Within this loftiness exists elegance; within this straightforwardness exists a spirit of gallant manliness."[42] For Mabuchi, the *masurao* is both the idealized ancient person *and* the ancient form of expression: straightforward, elegant, masculine, and harmonized with the modulations of the natural world. He singles out particular poets such as Kakinomoto no Hitomaro and Takechi no Kurohito as *masurao*, but he clearly understood the *masurao* spirit as defining ancient Japanese culture as a whole. As he asserts in "New Learning" (Niimanabi, 1765): "Looking now at the form [*sama*] of the tones [*shirabe*] [of ancient poems], we learn that Yamato was a country of *masurao*, and in ancient times even women were *masurao*."[43] Hara Masako argues that Mabuchi's conception of the *masurao* in fact exemplifies a profound *balance* between a bold, rough-hewn exterior and a capacious, more vulnerable emotional life—one that has ample space for a less masculine, even effeminate, range of affects, including ardor and heartache.[44] Mabuchi celebrates the *masurao*'s ability to live at the point of equilibrium between these "wild" and "gentle" spirits: the mark of harmony with the larger natural and human orders.[45]

But the *masurao* had vanished from the archipelago by Mabuchi's day—as had the ancient culture he epitomized. Just as continental doctrines corrupted politics, argues Mabuchi, so did they come to infect language and expression: "Thoughts and language from babbling China and the lands where the sun sets came and mingled [with our culture] and made everything unsettled. People's hearts, which had been straight and true, became warped like the wind that whips around corners; their words became chaotic like the dust of the crossroads, numberless and diverse."[46] The symptoms of this infection carried into poetic style. Following the establishment of the Heian capital, the *masurao* style of poetry gave way to a feminine style (*taoyameburi*), exemplified by the poetry of the *Kokin wakashū*, which prized cleverness of expression over straightforwardness.[47] And by his own time, Mabuchi laments, poetry—mediated by a superstructure of tradition and convention—had become completely artificial: a matter of "following old traces, without giving voice to one's own heart."[48] As in poetry, so in politics: in each, directness, sincerity, and loftiness had vanished, replaced by superficiality and artifice.

But all was not lost, for in Mabuchi's account, composition itself could point the way back to wholeness. We encounter a distinctly formal aspect of his project as articulated in his "Thoughts on the Meaning of Poetry" (Ka'ikō, 1760–1764):

> Let us face each morning the mirror of the past, mingle with its boundless shade and blossoms, and compose poetry and prose with the aim of resembling [that of the past] in form and color. Because we are fundamentally the same in body as the people of ancient times, striving in this way our hearts will become polished mirrors and our words will emerge from the thickets and wastes and transform into mountain blossoms in full flower.[49]

Here, the composition of poetry and prose in the style of the ancients becomes a corridor to the spirit of the lost past. For just as ancient poetry directly expressed the archaic "true heart," naturally aligned with the patterns of heaven and earth, the act of reading and composing in the manner of the ancients could bring one's *own* heart into alignment, shedding the artifice of latter-day culture and recovering sincerity. As Flueckiger summarizes, Mabuchi's injunction to imitate derived from "a belief that the spirit of ancient Japan was connected to specific literary and linguistic forms that people of the present must reconnect with in order to create a harmonious society. . . . It was only by copying the forms of ancient language and literature, Mabuchi believed, and allowing them to permeate and transform one's heart, that it was possible to recover the Ancient Way and reenact it in the present."[50]

Mabuchi practiced what he preached. He composed his essays in a neoarchaic style that shunned Sinitic constructions and embraced grammatical features of Nara-period Japanese writing. And his poetry, which he forged in a robust style that defied the thematic restrictions of "proper" *waka*, aspired to the lofty elegance that he found in the *Man'yōshū*. By composing like a *masurao*, Mabuchi suggested, one could become a *masurao* and thus restore the *masurao* spirit to a culture that had lost its way.

Genta as a *Masurao*

The *masurao* not only loomed large in Mabuchi's thought, but influenced the thought of his followers, including Akinari's teachers Takebe Ayatari and Katō Umaki, and, of course, Akinari himself.[51] And both Ayatari and

Akinari equated Genta with the *masurao* in their writing.[52] Although neither author spelled out the logic behind this identification, we can draw some plausible conclusions. It seems likely that it was precisely the formal strangeness of the killing—the same strangeness that flummoxed the authorities—that made it stand out to these *kokugaku* writers. First, the sheer brazenness of it: the beheading had contrasted starkly with the culture of calculation and contrivance that for Mabuchi and his school characterized their present era. Genta appeared to have acted without hesitation, negotiation, or concern for the consequences he would face. Second, that Genta had committed the act before the assembled household of his antagonistic kinsman suggested that the killing was not (only) a private punishment for Yae (which would properly have been carried out behind the walls of her home), but it was in some way directed at Danji. This hint that Genta had channeled negative feeling into decisive action mapped well onto the *masurao* as a figure united in emotion and deed. And third, the killing clearly had not been the wild outburst of a madman: Genta's reported self-control in the commission of the act and his composure in its wake suggested the equilibrium that Mabuchi identified in the *masurao*—the balance point between a rough exterior and a quiescent inner life. Even the fact that he had not attacked Danji directly—which would have been flagrantly illegal—yet nonetheless inflicted damage upon him, suggested a figure poised between action and restraint, intense feeling and self-control. For thinkers steeped in a particular imagination of ancient Japanese culture, Genta must have seemed a striking fit.

Accordingly, Ayatari and Akinari wrote about the Genta disturbance in ways that built on Mabuchi's conceptual foundations. But they adopted strikingly different approaches. Ayatari saw in Genta an opportunity to expand—into the realm of fiction—Mabuchi's project of formal alignment with the past through absorption in archaic language and style. Ayatari had for a time been an enrolled student in Mabuchi's school, but, like Akinari, he was not primarily a *kokugaku* scholar; he was more a synthesizer who dabbled in multiple arts and schools of thought, combining them in idiosyncratic ways. (Mabuchi appears to have thought poorly of him, at one point advising another disciple to steer clear of him.)[53] Building on Mabuchi's project of immersion in archaic literary forms, Ayatari tried to revitalize the ancient *katauta* verse form, with its distinctive 5-7-7 syllabic rhythm, which appears in the *Kojiki* (*Record of Ancient Matters*, 712) and *Nihon shoki* (*Chronicles of Japan*, 720). Ayatari argued that these antique origins made *katauta* a channel to the spirit of the ancients and that it was, therefore, superior to the *haikai* linked verse that flourished in his own time.[54] His revival was a failure, but a similar logic undergirds his fictionalization of the Genta incident, *A Tale of the Western Hills*.

Linguistically, *A Tale of the Western Hills* is a very peculiar text. Although it is modeled on the Genta disturbance and ambiguously set in what appears to be the Muromachi period, Ayatari composed it in a pseudoarchaic style that incorporates language from much older texts. Each time he employs an archaic usage, he cites in interlinear notes the meaning and—not always correctly—the textual source. The first three pages alone cite linguistic constructions adopted from the Nara-period *Kojiki*, *Nihon shoki*, and *Man'yōshū* and the Heian-period *Tale of the Bamboo Cutter* (*Taketori monogatari*), *Tales of Ise*, and *Classified and Annotated Japanese Names* (*Wamyō ruijū shō*, a Sino-Japanese dictionary). If we imagine an English romance written in the eighteenth century but set in the Middle Ages and composed by weaving in vocabulary from texts ranging from *Beowulf* to *The Canterbury Tales*, with regular interruptions to cite and explain each instance, that might approximate the experience of reading *A Tale of the Western Hills*.

The preface, written by the *kanshi* poet Kinryū Keiyū (1712–1782), suggests the work's resonance with Mabuchi's project to restore the Japanese "true heart" through immersion in old linguistic forms. The preface opens: "That which is shared between present and past is human feeling. That which differs between past and present is language."[55] Keiyū likens Ayatari's rewriting of a "recent event" (*jiji*) in archaic language to a manual for students that teaches, in narrative form, a technique (*jutsu*) for "taking control of the present by means of the past and achieving the elegant by adhering to the vulgar."[56] That is, by dressing the story of a present-day *masurao* in language evoking Mabuchi's "*masurao* style," Ayatari aims to reopen a passage to the archaic ways and to reintroduce the elevated heart of ancient Japan into the latter-day, "vulgar" world.

The linguistic form of Ayatari's narrative is, in this sense, rather radical, but its narrative form is more conventional. The plot reads like a novelization of a kabuki play, with a melodramatic love story, a cursed sword, ghostly visitations, and the climactic revelation of hidden moral debts running beneath apparent antagonisms.[57] Whereas Genta's beheading of Yae seems to have resulted from genuine antipathy between Genta and Danji, Danji's stand-in in *A Tale of the Western Hills* is merely playacting when he berates the Genta-inspired character; his refusal of the marriage offer is a ploy to avert the deadly fate that a soothsayer has predicted for the lovers if they are permitted to wed. He tearfully explains this background in a grand reveal while cradling the young woman's corpse in his arms. Ayatari even altered the culminating deed itself: rather than behead the young woman, her brother stabs her in the chest—no less violent an act, yet less extravagant than decapitating her.[58] And, following her death, the young woman appears to her lover in ghostly form and pledges her affection from the world beyond. If "human emotion" remains unchanged between past and present in Ayatari's story, it appears more aligned with the tear-jerking sensibilities of eighteenth-century theater than with the robust emotional world of the long-vanished past.

When Ueda Akinari wrote "The Tale of a *Masurao*" in the wake of his encounter with the elderly Genta, he castigated *A Tale of the Western Hills* as "a worthless piece of writing that does injury to a good man."[59] And his own versions—"The Tale of a *Masurao*" and "The Smile of the Severed Head"—depict the event in terms that differ starkly from Ayatari's linguistic and narrative strategies (and from each other). To understand Akinari's critique of Ayatari, and the formal moves he made in writing the Genta story (and in writing it *twice*), we must step away from the framework of Mabuchi's *kokugaku* project to examine the ways in which Akinari—a writer as much as a scholar—theorized the writing of fiction. This detour, however, will lead us back to *kokugaku* and the *masurao*.

A Writer's Rage: Akinari and the Allegorical Nature of Fiction

Akinari's opinions on fiction appear in scattershot fashion, showing up both in his fictional works (typically in their prefaces) and in his scholarship on classical fiction. Throughout, he gravitates to three questions: Why do authors write fiction? What is the relationship between fiction and truth? What work should fiction be understood as performing in the world beyond the page? These concerns appear already in his earliest fiction, written before he turned to scholarship in earnest, in the *ukiyozōshi* (books of the floating world) style of Ihara Saikaku and his successors. Akinari playfully teases the relationship between truth and fiction in the opening lines of his first work, *Worldly Monkeys with Ears for All Ways* (*Shodō kikimimi sekenzaru*, 1766): "Among the precepts of that ancient group of sages, a rule held that one might speak the truth in a manner resembling lies, but one must never tell a lie stinking of truth. Shakyamuni's Tripitaka and Zhuangzi's *Classic of Southern Florescence* are lying truths and truthful lies, and the thoughts one voices from one's heart alter as they pass along from one mouth to another, changing quickly from a marten into a weasel."[60] The style is deliberately mock-serious in its invocation of ancient sages and Buddhist and Daoist classics.[61] And Akinari quickly ties the question of truth versus fiction to the matter of gossip, which informs the satirical portraits that follow. But the questions he poses—whether truth can take the guise of fiction, and whether there are lines separating lies from truth that should never be crossed—would concern him with greater seriousness as his career continued.

By the time he published *Tales of Moonlight and Rain* in 1776, a work deeply informed by his *kokugaku* scholarship and by his erudition with Chinese and Japanese texts, Akinari had moved beyond satire and wordplay and was able to articulate a sense of fiction's power—and specifically, its danger. His preface begins:

> Master Luo authored *The Water Margin*, and his descendants were born mute for three generations; Lady Murasaki wrote the *Tale of Genji* and plunged for a time into the evil realms. Truly, this was none other than recompense for the karma [incurred by their writings]. Indeed, when one examines their works, they depict all sorts of spectacles. Their sounds and silences evoke reality, and their styles peak and plummet, tumble and roll along smoothly. They summon a deep resonance within the hearts of readers.[62]

According to Akinari, then, the skill exhibited by Luo Guanzhong in crafting the Chinese historical romance *The Water Margin* (Ch. *Shuihu zhuan*, J. *Suikoden*, fourteenth century) and by Murasaki Shikibu in creating *The Tale of Genji* (*Genji monogatari*, eleventh century)—works that summon engrossing fictional worlds out of mere words—caused the authors to suffer painful fates into their afterlives, whether in hell or through disabled progeny.[63] Concern with fiction's negative power possessed a long history, both in Buddhist thought, where some held that an entrancing story deepened worldly attachments, and in Confucian thinking, which asserted that fiction was of value only if it served morally edifying ends. It was legends emerging from these traditions that had condemned Luo and Murasaki to the fates that Akinari references.⁶⁴

As Akinari came to theorize fiction more comprehensively, however, he rejected the Neo-Confucian proposition that literature should serve a sociopolitical moral purpose, canonically articulated by Zhu Xi (1130–1200) as "rewarding virtue and castigating vice" (*kanzen chōaku*). He was not alone. As we have seen, eighteenth-century Confucian and *kokugaku* thinkers had begun to detach literature from abstract moral frameworks and to connect it to emotional expression. And Akinari came to view fiction as rooted in the emotions—particularly the *negative* emotions—of the author. In a commentary on *The Tale of Genji* titled "The Scroll of Darkness" (*Nubatama no maki*), written in 1779 (though likely revised in the late 1790s), the spirit of the ancient poet Hitomaro (d. ca. 708) visits a Confucian scholar and criticizes him for prizing *The Tale of Genji* as a book of moral instruction, which is how it had been read for much of the medieval period:

> Just what do you think tales [*monogatari*] are? Over in China they produce this kind of writing as well, and the main idea is that it's all falsehoods [*soragoto*] ᵃˡˡᵉᵍᵒʳʸ [*gūgen*]. Although we say that it has no real substance, however, it is without question [shaped by] what the author's thoughts dwell upon, whether lamenting the lasciviousness of the world's ways or grieving over the decline of the state. But, thinking of the inadvisability of pushing against the times, and fearing the wrath of those of high stature, the author sets his material in the past and only hints at the reality of the present, writing about it in a hazy way.⁶⁵

According to this characterization, the purpose of a work like *Genji* is not to promote socially edifying morals. But that does not render it meaningless. Akinari characterizes fiction as made up of falsehoods (literally, "empty words" [*soragoto*]), but he glosses this with the word "allegory" (*gūgen*). The latter term (literally, "stand-in words" and alternatively translatable as "fable" or "parable") derives from the ancient Chinese text *Zhuangzi*, which relies heavily on fanciful stories, exaggerations, and jokes—often featuring illustrious mouthpieces, such as Confucius or the god of the Yellow River—to communicate its Daoist vision of reality. In a chapter titled with this latter term (Ch. *yuyan*), the *Zhuangzi*'s narrator explains that he places his words in the mouths of others, or claims they are citations from authoritative texts, as a means of increasing the words' effectiveness while evading blame from those who don't agree. He then calls into question the value of authority itself and the idea that words can possess a fixed meaning, proclaiming that his words pour forth in a stream of endless transformations that itself approximates nonspeech.[66]

Akinari does not follow Zhuangzi to the radical ends of his Daoist vision, but he is quite taken with the idea that fiction's artifice can provide the writer cover to speak about the real. His allusion to *gūgen* partakes of a broader eighteenth-century Japanese rediscovery of *Zhuangzi* and the other great ancient Daoist text *Laozi*. From this rediscovery emerged a discourse that linked *gūgen* to fiction, understanding it to mean, as Nakano Mitsutoshi summarizes, "the explication of the real [*jitsu*] by means of the false [*kyo*]."[67] In the quotation from "The Scroll of Darkness," Akinari suggests that the writer of fiction feels the impetus to write about the world *as he sees it*—in particular, its negative or politically fraught aspects. But in a gesture of self-protection, he obscures his criticisms by fictionalizing them and setting them in the past to avoid the wrath of the powerful. Akinari fleshes out this writerly posture in "The Good and the Bad" (*Yoshiya ashiya*, 1793), a commentary on the *Tales of Ise*:

> When people of knowledge and talent do not align with the times, they either [console themselves] . . . and recite the poem likening themselves to an undiscovered pearl, or their writing turns to rage [*ikidōri ni naru*]. The hearts of the people of Japan and China do not differ in this respect. There, they call them romances and novels [*engi shōsetsu*]; here, we call them tales [*monogatari*]. The hearts of those who write them, lamenting over their own lack of fortune, feel enraged at the world and long affectionately for the past. They look at the way the present age flourishes with the glow of blossoming flowers, and they think of how those flowers will eventually fade. Or they speculate about the future fortunes of the prosperous and secretly scoff at them. Or they admonish that everything ultimately goes up in smoke even if one prays for unprecedented longevity, and they heap scorn upon those fools who wander about in pursuit of rare treasures. But, fearing for their reputation in the present world, they write it all up as a seemingly harmless tale rooted in the baseless happenings of long, long ago. That is the real heart and tone of this kind of writing.[68]

In Akinari's characterization, fiction blossoms from the bitter seed of negative emotions: rage, resentment, pessimism, and fear. The writer, finding no formal outlet for his talents in a socially and politically warped world, channels his critical energies into his writing.[69] But even as rage impels his writing, fear restrains it, obscuring its critical bite within a haze of fictional story and setting. Fiction is rage, distorted by caution. Akinari invokes rage in "The Scroll of Darkness" as well: "When the realm flourishes and people's hearts run only to extravagance, things are done with skill and words are used with technique, bound this way and twisted that way, and everything is done on conflicting bases; then writing emerges from rage."[70]

A twisted social order, distorted expression, and truth bent into fiction: for Akinari, the modern writer is far removed from Mabuchi's celebration of ancient directness, emotional sincerity, and patterned harmony! The *masurao* ideal celebrated a figure who gave expression to emotions freely, whether positive or negative, leaving nothing hidden. Akinari's fiction writer, by contrast, expressing himself only slantwise, stands as a symptom of his degraded times.

Truth, Fiction, and the "Tale" of a *Masurao*

These issues sit at the forefront of "The Tale of a *Masurao*," which we can read as Akinari's attempt to write *like* a *masurao*: directly, without fictionalization, stating things as they are. Akinari wrote it shortly after his encounter with the aged Genta, and in it he claims to have learned the "true version of events" (*masashigoto*) through his disciple Ōzawa Shunsaku, a close acquaintance of Genta.[71] He situates his essay in opposition to Ayatari's *A Tale of the Western Hills*, which he criticizes severely for its fictionalization of the incident, suggesting that fiction, handled poorly, inflicts a form of violence on the real. Yet what makes "The Tale of a *Masurao*" fascinating is that Akinari's own attempt to escape fictionality fails—and the writer appears to recognize this failure within the essay. A work that sets out to establish a clear difference between truth and fiction thus transforms, by its end, into a meditation on whether the two are separable at all—and about what consequences this question holds for a writer seeking to escape fiction's distortions and violence.

The essay's dueling titles reflect its hazy position between fact and fiction. Akinari appears to have left the work untitled; on his autograph copy, an unidentified hand has labeled it "An Account of Master Akinari's Pilgrimage to Ichijōji" (Akinari-ō Ichijōji mōde no ki)—a title that suggests its generic status as a factual record.[72] But when the essay was published in 1919 as part of an anthology of Akinari's manuscripts, the scholar Fujii Otoo retitled it "The Tale of a *Masurao*" (Masurao monogatari), by which it has been known since.[73] And the essay has been praised for its storytelling qualities, as in Morita Kirō's aforementioned assessment that this ostensible "true record" (*jitsuroku*) makes a superior "tale" (*monogatari*) to Akinari's later, fictional version of the Genta disturbance.[74] The essay's structure compounds these tensions, for its tale-like retelling of the "resounding" deed is nested within a first-person account of Akinari's own visit to Ichijōji and his encounter with the elderly Genta, recorded, as Uchimura Katsushi notes, in a style that suggests an essay of personal observations (*zuihitsu*) or a travelogue (*kikōbun*).[75]

At the outset, however, Akinari insists that his aim is to convey the truth of the Genta disturbance, and he couches this aim in a critique of Takebe Ayatari that suggests the potential of writing to inflict violence:

> The version of this event written up as *A Tale of the Western Hills* by a half-baked wit is a worthless piece of writing that does injury to a good man [*yoki hito o ayamatsu itazurabumi*]. Whether the romances of China or the tales of this country live on in the world or quickly vanish without a trace depends entirely upon the wisdom or foolishness of their authors; the point is so evident that it hardly bears repeating. We can clearly number this work among those that quickly perish. Now then, though it is unbefitting to write down the truth [*masashigoto*] of this case with brushstrokes as coarse [*orosogenaru*] [as mine], it is my hope that by writing without lies [*itsuwari naranu*] my version will be passed down for a long time to come. Readers, judge for yourselves which parts are an old man's grumblings and continue to tell the story and pass it on.[76]

When Akinari criticizes Ayatari's tale for doing "injury to a good man," he uses the verb *ayamatsu*. This word can suggest a relatively innocuous mistake or misjudgment, or the weightier sense of committing an injustice or turning one's back on the proper path. But it also connotes the infliction of a *physical* injury—especially a death blow. We can presume that Akinari means that *A Tale of the Western Hills* does a disservice to Genta's reputation by twisting his story into something fanciful. But the violent nuance of *ayamatsu* resonates both with the violence of the incident itself and with Akinari's broader concern with the real-world harm that writing can cause, evinced in his preface to *Tales of Moonlight and Rain*. There, he alludes to the otherworldly punishments suffered by consummate writers for the influence their superior fiction exerts on the nonfictional world. Here, punishment befalls the text itself, which suffers an attenuated afterlife for the crime of crudely—and thus injuriously—wrenching the truth into a fictional form.

Akinari proposes that his own text will be different. It will recount the "truth" (*masashigoto*) of the case "without lies" (*itsuwari naranu*), even if the writing must be "coarse" (*orosogenaru*). It is as though Akinari, inspired by the *masurao* Genta, has challenged himself to set aside his own writerly inclinations to embellish and allegorize, and has resolved instead to simply tell the story plainly. The power of direct, truthful expression, he hopes, will grant his account a long afterlife, regardless of any infelicities of form. His intent echoes Mabuchi's project of formal alignment with the texts of the past; writing *about* a *masurao* with the unadorned straightforwardness *of* a *masurao*, he might leave behind the distortions and indirection of his fiction and write in harmony with the world as it is.

Yet for all his claims to write directly, Akinari freights the essay with allegorical gestures and fictional tropes. He does so even in the record-like frame of his encounter with the aged Genta. At the outset, as he describes his arrival at Enkōji's shrine to Tokugawa Ieyasu's spirit, for example, he highlights details that resonate with his understanding of the thematics of the Genta disturbance—directness, virility, the aura of Japan's divine past:

> The grove of trees grew deep and rampant, the pond's heart was spacious, and the sound of the trickling stream, faint as it was, stirred the feelings [*aware nari*]. The god's shrine sat atop a tall hill. When, with another's help, I finally managed to reach the top and look about, I was surprised to discover such a simple structure for this most illustrious spirit; but its simplicity made me feel its dignity all the more as I made obeisance. A portrait [of Ieyasu] hung inside, flanked to left and right by his "Sixteen Horsemen" in full battle dress.... Although I wondered which campaign it might have been, out of deference I dared not ask. When the votive offerings were taken

down to be shared, the head priest began to offer us [saké] in earthenware cups. Among those gathered was an elderly man who had arrived early. His name was Watanabe Genta.[77]

Akinari totters out of the mundane world and into the elevated realm of the sacred: a domain of rampant, heart-stirring nature, of ostentation-shunning architecture, of a deified man enshrined not as a politician but as a warrior, equipped in his portrait for the rigors of a campaign. The emphasis on simplicity and masculine vigor evokes the spirit of the ancient past idealized by Mabuchi and his followers, but Akinari has come across it on the outskirts of contemporary Kyoto. And there at the center, like the object of a pilgrimage, sits Genta: "He had passed sixty in years, yet he had a boyish face [*warawagao*] and looked quite dignified. He liked saké, and his manner as he spoke was tremendously frank and refreshing [*kawaraka nari*]."[78] Akinari refers to Genta using the word *okina*—literally, "old man," but also the name of the mask worn to represent gods of felicitation in the *nō* theater. Like the *okina* mask, Genta looks both elderly and youthful, at ease and yet dignified—and he possesses a god's taste for saké. It is as though Akinari has met a visitor from the "divine age."

When Akinari commences his "true" account of Genta's story, it becomes even more difficult to disentangle fact from literary embellishment. The first line of his retelling already adopts the language of a classical tale: "Was it perhaps in the days of the aged [Genta's] own aged ancestors, that in this village a family of illustrious pedigree and impressive reputation fell from favor with the times and came to live in poverty?"[79] The posture of questioning the temporal origins of a narrative harkens back most famously to *The Tale of Genji*'s opening line, "In which reign might it have been . . . ?" As Konoe Noriko has noted, Akinari employs vocabulary from *Genji* throughout "The Tale of a *Masurao*." He also incorporates language and motifs from "The House Overgrown with Grasses" (Asaji ga yado) and "The Kibitsu Cauldron" (Kibitsu no kama), two of his own stories from *Tales of Moonlight and Rain* that foreground powerful feminine emotions and tragic love. Those stories, too, adopt language from *Genji*, which Akinari apparently considered a key intertext for these themes. Konoe speculates that he was not consciously trying to draw connections to *Genji* in "The Tale of a *Masurao*," but that *Genji*'s, language had become part of his lexicon for evoking heartbreak and the atmosphere of classical elegance, both of which he emphasizes in his retelling.[80] Even as he attempts to recount the truth plainly, Akinari resorts—consciously or not—to the legacy and devices of classical fiction.

He unfolds his story as a tale of two households, related by ancestry but unalike in stature and character. Genta's household, of good lineage but poor, is managed firmly by his mother. Danji's household is wealthy, but—Genta's mother explains to her children—the wealth has warped Danji, giving him a "devilish" (*onionishi*) character and souring relations between the two households after generations of mutual support. And, she adds, Danji deserves no credit for his wealth; most of it was inherited. She speculates that Kichijōten, the goddess of good fortune, long ago took up residence in Danji's branch of the family, bringing it great wealth, while the inauspicious Kokuanten, consort of the god of death, settled in Genta's house and brought its fortunes low.[81] She criticizes Danji for his "barbarian heart" (*ebisugokoro*) and later calls him a "wild barbarian" (*araebisu*), whereas the text refers to Genta throughout simply as "the *masurao*." Akinari thus characterizes the conflict between the two households as emblematizing a more elaborate set of oppositions: between traditional ways and the logic of money, between a *masurao* and a "barbarian," between a warrior and a demon—even between the goddess of fortune and the goddess of death. Already, allegorical significance has begun to weave its way into his account, casting the opposition between the two families as that between an archaic Japanese simplicity and the warped dynamics of foreign culture and a commercial economy.

When Danji's gentle son Unai and Genta's sister, Yae, fall in love, Danji rejects Genta's proposal of marriage with sharp insults about the family's poverty and forbids Unai to see Yae anymore. Unai, brokenhearted, obeys. Yae's mother admonishes her about the impossibility of the match and the grave consequences—in this world and beyond—of opposing the will of one's parent. After some time, however, Yae approaches and kneels before her mother:

> Your repeated admonishments have sunk into my flesh and bones. But the devilish heart of that man has set my thoughts ablaze, instructing me to die. My breast feels crushed, and I can hardly tell what is real. I thought to become a nun, but that is not a road to embark upon by going against the will of my mother and brother. Oh, I feel I have reached the limit of my life, and I would like your permission to take leave of this world. But what is most hateful is the heart of a

man. [Unai] said that if his father did not give his permission, then he would run off with me to hide someplace and await the day when we could live openly in the world together. But wasn't that just a lie [*itsuwari*] to humor me? It was only yesterday that he said to me, "Dying is easy. [Instead,] put your trust in me." I will die first. I'm not going to wait around for word from a coward.[82]

Yae's defiance may at first glance resemble the willful, unfilial behavior identified in the shogunate's verdict on the events. But her rancor—aimed at both Unai and his father—reveals a more complex dynamic. She repeats the earlier characterization of Danji as "devilish" and suggests that his words have aroused her will to die, as though her death will constitute a riposte to his insults. And in a tale that Akinari claims to recount "without lies," Yae invokes precisely that term—*itsuwari*—to characterize the words of comfort that Unai offered her. Uncertain what is true and what is a lie, she feels that she is losing her hold on reality (*utsutsu naku zo haberu*). Dying, as she presents it, represents a way of reasserting control over the boundary between truth and fiction through recourse to the stark fact of death.

Her mother's response likewise reflects a more complex set of concerns than a patriarchal honor killing would suggest: "Her mother watched her closely, then called her brother. 'This child is possessed [*mono no tsukitaru zo*]. But to let her carry on like a dog or a cat and fall into the Hell of Beasts is too pitiful [*itōshi*]. [Danji's] heart will remain the same as always, and Unai is hopeless. Whether we look after her or cast her off I leave up to you. Take her to their house and bring things to some kind of resolution.'"[83] The mother's reaction gives voice to the enmity that exists between the two houses, one strong enough to "possess" the daughter with a rancorous will to die. It also expresses a mother's concern for a "pitiful" child who is slipping beyond her aid, and, at the same time, a determination to resolve a seemingly impossible situation through decisive action. In Akinari's telling, therefore, the killing takes shape not as the punishment of a wayward daughter, but as a family's collective action against Danji's household: one fueled by the daughter's resentment, authorized by her mother, and orchestrated by her brother. Like a collective *masurao*, the family embraces the negative emotions that the situation arouses and, rather than repressing them and bowing to the social superiority of Danji's family, seeks to express them with the directness of action.

That Yae's beheading is a family endeavor intended as a response to Danji and Unai comes into sharp focus at the denouement. In the morning, Genta leads Yae to Danji's house in a bride's white robes. The household assembles at their unexpected arrival, and the pair kneels in the courtyard. Genta explains their intrusion in a way that heaps scorn upon Danji's family and underscores Yae's resolve. Having pledged her chastity to Unai, he says, she would now rather "shatter as a jewel than preserve herself as a tile." But rather than hang or drown herself, she and her family feel it fitting that she end her life in a dignified way (*migurushikaranu sama*) in the courtyard of the man who is the source of her anguish—with or without permission. Genta calls out: "Where is Unai? Do you think you can use obedience to your parent as an excuse to treat another's child like a cat or a dog? Come out here and let us hear you make a formal break with her. After that, we'll resolve things as we see fit."[84] But Unai is nowhere to be seen, and Danji claims that he has run off—into Yae's arms, he had presumed. He laces into Genta: "And what is this conduct of yours? You're imitating theater actors in order to threaten me. Your poverty has warped your hearts—despicable! Begone from here, quickly."[85] Danji likens Genta and Yae to *sarugaku* performers, suggesting that they are putting on empty theatrics in order to get at his wealth. Earlier, Genta's mother suggests that wealth has "twisted" (*higaminejiku*) Danji; here, his distorted view prompts him to apply a related word to the brother and sister, characterizing their hearts as "warped" (*higahigashi*). Pretense versus sincerity, fiction versus truth, twistedness versus directness: these are the very terms by which Akinari had characterized the role of fiction in a corrupted society. The story's allegorical undertones intensify.

The climactic moment of the retelling becomes a celebration of directness and the sting of the real over pretense and empty performance. Genta turns back to his sister. "What would you like to do now?" he asks. Yae answers:

"No doubt, [Unai] has gone off somewhere with the intention of dying. I don't want to fall behind, even for a moment. If I am not to die by your hand, I can still make a noble death of it with my personal dagger. All I ask is that it be here, and that it be now." [Genta] replied: "That is precisely why Mother told me to accompany you. Let us sully this place. Whether he gives us his leave or not." Thinking that they would not possibly go through with it, [Danji] said, "Go ahead, wherever you like." "In that case, come over here before the Buddha image." Genta positioned Yae before the flowers and incense of the family altar. She brought her palms together and sat with a poignant beauty. Her brother stood behind her and unsheathed his sword. At the sight, [the household] was shocked and thrown into confusion. Danji attempted to stop him, but two of his fingers were cut, and he was gripped with fear. As he turned and fled to the rear, the young maiden's head tumbled down into her lap.[86]

The members of Danji's household, fearing that Genta will kill them next, flee in confusion, but Genta calmly places Yae's head before the family altar and seats himself to await arrest: "The expression on his face had not changed in the least. He requested some breakfast and finished it off with evident relish."[87]

The moment when the blade slices Danji's fingers can be seen as the moment when a different reality pierces the skein of meanings that he has wound out of differences of income and class. Earlier, he dismisses Yae as no better than a "chapped-footed" housemaid, and he calls her a "cursed talisman" (*majichi*) who would destroy his fortunes if she were allowed to marry into the family.[88] Here, Genta and Yae employ his own terms to strike back at him: Yae's fierce resolve belies his dismissive appraisal, and the siblings' determination to "sully" (*kegasu*) his courtyard with blood makes brutally literal the metaphorical danger that he projected onto the young woman. Akinari represents the killing as resentment honed to a fine point of self-control: a seemingly self-destructive act turned into a weapon that inflicts maximum damage on their target without veering into the wild disorder of a physical attack on him.

And yet this denouement remains shaded by metaphor and allegory. When the village headman rushes to Genta's house to inform his mother of the events, he finds her seated at her loom. She responds to his frantic report calmly: "'So, is that what happened? What can one do? It's a pitiful business.' The sound of her weaving reed did not falter in the least, throwing the headman further into fear and confusion. 'In the old tales, the warrior Watanabe is said to have grappled with demons. Truly, demons are no match for those of his clan!' he said, and quickly took his leave."[89] The headman refers to the warrior Watanabe no Tsuna (953–1025), celebrated for his demon-quelling activities in medieval anecdotes, the *Taiheiki* (*Chronicle of Great Peace*, late fourteenth century), and the *nō* play *Rashōmon* (ca. late fifteenth century). Genta's family traced its origins to the same warrior family. Akinari's "true" account in this way subtly adopts the hues of a classic demon-quelling narrative, with the *masurao* warrior family subduing the "devilish" Danji, who has been wreaking havoc on the social health of the village. This motif, combined with other motifs that Akinari employs—the juxtaposition of the two "goddesses," Danji's suggestion that Yae is a "cursed talisman," the characterization of Yae by her mother as "possessed," and Genta's invitation to Yae to "defile" Danji's house—suggest a shadow narrative behind the killing, evoked in ghostly but grand terms.

Here it is helpful to recall the perception that Akinari posited as animating writers of fiction with "rage": "They look at the way the present age flourishes with the glow of blossoming flowers, and they think of how those flowers will eventually fade. Or they speculate about the future fortunes of the prosperous and secretly scoff at them. Or they admonish that everything ultimately goes up in smoke even if one prays for unprecedented longevity, and they heap scorn upon those fools who wander about in pursuit of rare treasures."[90] Danji, in his insistence on the superiority afforded him by his wealth, his demand that his son marry up, and his crass disparagement of Yae and her family, precisely embodies the system of values that enrages Akinari's writer of fiction: one in which avarice blinds the fortunate to the ephemerality of prosperity, warps their sense of obligation to bonds of mutual succor, and upends the distinctions between reality and illusion. Akinari's account of Yae's beheading reads as a fable in which personifications of the ancient Japanese way channel their rage at this dynamic, not into the obfuscations of allegory but into action that breaks the demon's spell and eviscerates his power.

The irony is that Akinari, while claiming to relate the story of the Genta disturbance with a similar directness, has ended up crafting an allegory of his own. And, indeed, as he draws his retelling to a close, Akinari betrays doubts about his attempt to convey the "truth" of the incident. He concludes his account with apparent confidence: "Meeting the elder [Genta] today, and witnessing his lightheartedness and congeniality, I feel that, truly, he must have been just that way in the past." The statement expresses confidence; but it also concedes that the writer remains at a remove from the events, and that he has, in fact, fabricated his own Genta from imagination. As though suddenly recognizing these facts, his tone abruptly changes: "I will omit further details. With the faltering brushstrokes of an old man, I will likely inflict further injury [*kizutsuke ya suramu*], in which case [this essay] would amount to insipid slander."[91] Whereas earlier, in his critique of *A Tale of the Western Hills*, Akinari chose the verb *ayamatsu*, with its whiff of physical violence, here he uses the even stronger verb *kizutsuku*, which strongly suggests the infliction of bodily harm. His only recourse is to stop telling the story, lest he cause greater injury—under the pretense of "truth"—than the overtly fictionalized *Tale of the Western Hills*.[92]

But he does not end "The Tale of a *Masurao*" here. Instead, in a coda, he describes an encounter that occurred as he departed Ichijōji village, giving his meditations on truth and fiction a final, enigmatic twist. It was the same day on which the god of the Lower Kamo Shrine was taken out in procession. The route passed through Ichijōji, and Akinari crossed its path on his way home, dropping to his knees in the roadside grasses and touching his brow to the earth. Among the procession was a horse with a silk parasol held aloft over its saddle: the mount of the god. Akinari admired the glinting of the horse's trappings in the light of the setting sun and was overcome with feeling: "I had paid my respects to the god before. But to encounter the deity so unexpectedly here in this mountain village is, to my eyes, a most wondrous event. As I looked across the landscape as far as my eyes could see, the sight of the procession wending through the broad fields made me think of the poem, 'The past Age of the Gods . . .' That may have been a more splendid sight. But now it's no more than a fiction [*esoragoto*], this."[93] And there the essay ends. The poem that Akinari cites appears in the *Tales of Ise*, where it is attributed to Ariwara no Narihira (825–880), who is said to have recited it when accompanying an empress's pilgrimage to Ōhara, not far from Ichijōji:

Ōhara ya Oshio no yama mo kyō koso wa kamiyo no koto mo omoiizurame
At Oshio Hill in Ōhara, today of all days the deity must fondly
    recall the past Age of the Gods.[94]

Narihira's poem emphasizes the continuity between the present day and the "divine age"; Akinari, citing it, likewise feels moved by elements of the mythic past that are alive in the landscape before him. But, in a twist, he concludes the essay by invoking "fiction," throwing into deeper question his claim to disclose the "truth" through the essay. In Japanese, the final passage reads *ima wa esoragoto nari, kore wa*, ending with a demonstrative pronoun (*kore*) of unclear referent. *Kore* means "this," but its referent's proximity may be physical, temporal, or psychological; without clarification, "this" is supremely ambiguous. In a deft reading, Uchimura Katsushi shows that *kore* may refer to the Age of the Gods, to the procession before Akinari's eyes, or to the very tale that Akinari has just told.[95] *Kore* as easily refers, I would add, to the episode from the *Tales of Ise* in which the poem appears. But Uchimura's point holds: whatever *kore* refers to, Akinari characterizes it as a fiction (*esoragoto*). But by leaving the referent unclear—following the topic marker *wa* with silence—he closes his essay with a performance of the questions that run through it: What is fiction? What separates it from the true? Can something be both fictional and true (this and also *this*) at the same time? The image of the Kamo deity—an empty space between a horse's saddle and a silk parasol—resonates here: a presence unseen, apprehensible only by the accoutrements that surround it, but believed in. *Real.* And it harkens back to the first glimpse of Genta: a flesh-and-blood man who seems, somehow, simultaneously to be a god. Having aspired to represent the "truth," and having run up against the difficulty of doing so without recourse to the forms of fiction, Akinari ends the essay in a way that suggests he is finding his way back to the truth *within* fiction—and to the power of form to create truth of its own.

Generative Fiction: "The Smile of the Severed Head"

Something changed for Akinari between the writing of "The Tale of a *Masurao*" in 1807 and the composition of his final collection of stories, *Tales of the Spring Rain* (*Harusame monogatari*) in 1808. Akinari himself highlighted this interval as a turning point, symbolized for him by a dramatic act in late 1807: "Last autumn, I had a sudden inspiration. I gathered the books from my library and many of my own writings, put them into five bundles, and dumped them into the old well of my hermitage. A refreshing coolness came to my heart."[96] Akinari came to refer to the well as his "well of dreams" (*yume no i*).[97] Nagashima Hiroaki argues that his disposal of his writings was a watershed moment for the writer; the writings that followed evince a turn away from proper scholarly forms and the pursuit of verifiable truth and display a freer embrace of fictionality, even in writings that engage scholarly subject matter.[98] Whatever the act signified, it was followed by a burst of late creativity. The year 1808 saw him publish a collection of letters, produce new scholarship on the *Kojiki* and *Nihon shoki* and an essay on *sencha* tea, draft the miscellany *A Record of Boldness and Caution* (*Tandai shōshin roku*), assemble a collection of his poetry and poetic prose, and compose the ten elusive narratives—some of them closer to essays than "tales"—that *Tales of the Spring Rain* comprises.[99] He died early the following year.

Tales of the Spring Rain marks a bold turn in Akinari's long-standing grapple with the relationship between truth and fiction. He foregrounds this relationship in the preface, composed in the compressed, enigmatic style that characterizes the entire collection:

> How many days has the spring rain been falling, so tranquil and agreeable? As usual, I reach for my brush and inkstone, but think as I might, I have nothing to say. To imitate the style of classical tales would be something new. But in my condition, as lacking in cultivation as a mountain rustic, what could I possibly have to tell? In [reading about] the affairs of past and present, I have been deceived by others and have ended up writing lies [*itsuwari*] of my own. Enough, enough. There are those who go on telling fictions [*soragoto*] and press people to accept them [as real]. And so, I go on talking. And the spring rain keeps falling and falling.[100]

A concern with lies pervades *Spring Rain*; the word *itsuwari* shows up in seven of the collection's ten narratives.[101] But the preface's meditation on truth and lies gestures not to a final resolution, but to a resistance to closure that characterizes the whole collection. The preface takes the form of a dialogue the writer carries on with himself, punctuated by concessive particles and vacillations.[102] Inspired by the spring rain, he first thinks to compose a verse on this long-standing poetic topic. Unable to conceive of one, he next considers writing a tale but ends up second-guessing himself on that count. He then identifies the real crux: texts taken as "true" (likely a reference to official histories) themselves contain falsehoods—and in passing them on as true in his other writings, he has ended up lying and deceiving others, contrary to his intent. What is one to do? But then he notes that there are others who blithely present fictions as truth all the time—so why make such a fuss about it? Despite all this, the preface does not arrive at a resolution. It finishes where it began, with falling rains and an old man mumbling to himself: "And so, I go on talking. And the spring rain keeps falling and falling."

This voice differs markedly from the one that set out to present the "truth" of the Genta disturbance in "The Tale of a *Masurao*." But neither is it the voice of one who has dispensed with truth altogether. Kazama Seishi locates the ethical heart of the preface in the phrase *mono iitsuzuku* (to go on talking), identifying the "sincerity" (that charged *kokugaku* value) of a writer who acknowledges his own doubts and recognizes his limits but, rather than seek solace in a transcendent ideal (in the manner of Akinari's intellectual antagonist, Motoori Norinaga) or fall silent, continues to speak from a position of doubt. And the fruit of this act of speaking, Kazama suggests, is *Tales of the Spring Rain* itself: a work that blurs the distinction between scholarship and tale.[103] Indeed, I propose that the preface signals a newfound recognition of the generative power of doubt. Wrestling with the fraught dialectic between fictionality and truth can propel speech and thus be a creative force—as affecting and life-giving as the spring rains. Such wrestling is not without discomfort; the preface's hesitations and second-guessing underscore the disquiet that attends the hazy border between truth and deception. But part of what makes *Tales of the Spring Rain* so arresting is the way that Akinari translates that discomfort directly into the form of the stories, imbuing them with unsettling affects, eschewing the solace of consistency or closure, and embracing multiplicity, repetition, oddity, and mutation.

The collection's material form echoes these qualities. It is unclear whether Akinari had intended it ever to be published; it exists only in a few drafts and copies in his hand and in additional manuscript copies made from these, with considerable differences among the extant variants. ("The Smile of the Severed Head" exists only in the last and most complete of these versions, the so-called Bunka 5 variant.) In the Edo period, *Tales of the Spring Rain* already had acquired a near-mythical status among book aficionados for its quality and rarity, and it came to public notice only in the twentieth century as scholars began to publish fragments and attempt to reconstruct a "whole" version of the text.[104] But in the latter part of the century, scholars began to question this endeavor and instead recognize the text's multiplicity as one of its most salient features—and one that resonates with Akinari's reformulated approach to the idea of "truth." Satō Miyuki takes this line of interpretation to the most radical level, arguing that *Spring Rain* represents both Akinari's growing skepticism about the reliability of written documents and his emergent understanding of historical truth as a matter of flux, something cocreated between texts and readers in an ongoing process of historical change. He gave form to that understanding, argues Satō, by embracing a type of "variant anarchism" (*ihon anakizumu*), not only declining to give *Spring Rain* a final form through publication, but sharing out different versions of the text and drawing no meaningful distinction between forgeries or copies (*gisho*) and originals.[105]

Whether or not we locate such clear-cut intent behind the text's multiple versions, the stories do reflect a posture of resistance to recoverable truths.[106] As Susan Burns has argued, *Spring Rain* embodies Akinari's late conviction that the ethical response to the past was to "play" in it—rather than attempt to recover it—through forms that united historical scholarship with fictional invention.[107] The first three narratives in *Spring Rain*, for example, are set in the milieu of the classical Heian court, and they draw strongly on Akinari's historical and philological scholarship. Yet they are formally enigmatic. They resist narrative satisfaction, blurring at times into something closer to treatises; but they eschew legible morals and proffer symbolically charged images—a bloodstained robe that never dries, for example—without offering interpretive guidance to their significance. Akinari extended these qualities of formally challenging "play" to each narrative in the collection, making *Spring Rain*, in all its plurality, a difficult work of "tales" that raises the question of what it means to write fiction.

"The Smile of the Severed Head" exemplifies this question. Akinari did precisely what he criticized Ayatari for doing in "The Tale of a *Masurao*": he wrote a blatantly fictionalized version of the Genta disturbance. He altered the setting, names, and characterizations, as well as some fundamental details. Yet the basic plotline remains unchanged. A young woman and her neighbor fall in love, but the man's miserly father refuses to let them marry. The rebuff devastates the young woman—in this case, sending her into a life-threatening love sickness—and prompts her family to make one final marriage request. Met with abuse upon this second attempt, the woman's brother beheads her before her lover's household and is arrested; the authorities, however, ultimately deem the greater fault to lie with the miserly father and his son.

Whereas "The Tale of a *Masurao*" insists on trying to capture the truth of the historical incident in words, "The Smile of the Severed Head" instead draws attention to the nature of fiction itself: fiction not necessarily as a category of writing but as a part of life, a fundamental mode by which people apprehend and navigate their world, and a quality that can therefore emerge even from well-intended sincerity. Fictionality, the story suggests, is inescapable, and the self-awareness with which one meets this fact is more important than any attempt to hew strictly to truth. It is ultimately self-possession, more than sincerity or directness, that makes the *masurao*. I argue that the narrative is generally (if somewhat obscurely) structured around this allegorical import. But more important than an abstractable meaning is the text's form, for its style strains against any attempt to reduce the narrative to an allegorical takeaway. Blunt, spare, exaggerated in some respects and elliptical in others, lacking a reliable narratorial viewpoint: these formal aspects, which led earlier commentators to deem the tale unpolished and inconsistent, mark Akinari's turn away from "truth" as the value that can bring closure to a text. Instead, they place the onus on readers to activate their own self-possession in engaging the work, to resist the lure of narrative guidance and to undertake their own continued speaking with a text that proffers significance with one hand while withholding it with the other. This dynamic comes together most strikingly in the titular figure of the severed head's smile.

In certain respects, "The Smile of the Severed Head" appears to wear its allegory on its sleeve. As it introduces the characters who correspond to Danji and Unai, we are told that in the village of Unago in Ubara district, the household of a man named Gosōji has made a great fortune as saké brewers:

> [Gosōji] had one child. He was called Gozō. He did not resemble his father but was by nature [cultured like] a person of the Capital. He wrote with a good hand, and he liked and studied poetry and [fine] prose. When he took up a bow, he could shoot down a bird on the wing, and he possessed a stout heart that belied his [gentle] countenance. But even so, he always thought of what he could do for others, and he was polite in all of his interactions. He felt pity for the poor and strove to lend them his strength. And so, people called the devilish [*onionishi*] father "Demon Sōji," and but they honored his son as "Buddha Gozō."[108]

Where "The Tale of a *Masurao*" elegantly interweaves hints of an allegorical demon-quelling narrative, here the miserly father is explicitly called

Demon Sōji from the beginning. There are moments when he physically embodies a demon's wildness ("Demon Sōji stamped his feet, threw up his hands, and wailed—a sight hideous to behold"), and when he prepares to unleash his torrent of verbal abuse, he "open[s] his demon's mouth as wide as it would go."[109] The earlier narrative alludes to possession and pollution, but here it is Demon Sōji who seems possessed: he is obsessed with propitiating what he calls his "god of fortune" (*fuku no kami*), he abhors monetary waste of any kind (at one point instructing his son to sell his books because the "god of fortune" detests the wastefulness of using lamp oil to read them at night), and he is so terrified of the pollutive danger of his neighbor's poverty that he insists on cleaning and purifying his house in the wake of the first proposal of marriage. His son, Buddha Gozō, meanwhile, is depicted as a conventional ideal protagonist: attractive, erudite, skilled in the martial ways, and possessed of a pure and sympathetic heart. The narrative, that is, overtly adopts the stereotypical characterizations of a moral fable: demon versus buddha. But the text also marks these character labels as emerging from village discourse. They are projections by means of which the villagers make sense of the contrastive temperaments of father and son, but the narrative need not adhere to that framework. Instead, much of the story's trouble stems from the "exemplary" behavior of Buddha Gozō.

The Genta-inspired character, Motosuke, meanwhile, is once again described as a *masurao*—but beyond that, his characterization remains highly abstract. Unlike "The Tale of a *Masurao*," which affords some insight into Genta's attitude, motivations, and concerns, "The Smile of the Severed Head" offers only fleeting glimpses of Motosuke's gestures and words. When, following Demon Sōji's refusal to allow the two young people to marry, Gozō visits and pledges himself once more to Motosuke's lovesick sister, Mune, inspiring her to rise from her sickbed, "her mother was overjoyed. Her brother simply acted as though he didn't notice [*usobukite nomi*]."[110] The verb *usobuku* suggests feigned indifference, but the narration offers no guidance to parsing the significance of Motosuke's studied nonchalance. Is it meant simply to contrast a masculine self-control with the effusiveness of his mother and sister? Or should it be read as signaling a mistrust of Gozō and his reliability? Or perhaps it simply marks him as a young man uninterested in lovers' affairs. So minimal is the characterization of Motosuke that some commentators have seen in the story a shift by Akinari away from fascination with the *masurao*, instead placing Mune or

Buddha Gozō at the story's center.¹¹¹ But the portrayal of Gozō is equally perplexing.

Gozō is depicted as utterly sincere. No matter the role—faithful lover, filial son—he performs it to the utmost. When he is with Mune, he insists on his love for her and promises that he will marry her, even if it means opposing his father and leaving his household. When he is with his father, he embraces the role of filial son and follows his father's instructions to cut off relations with Mune. As Kazama Seishi has noted, he seems not to be willfully deceptive; rather, he is presented as a sincere lover *and* a sincere filial son who can never resolve to forsake one of these roles for the other.¹¹² The result is that his sincerity becomes a type of falsehood. And it is most dangerous when it takes the form of a narrative. (Indeed, the text marks both Gozō and Mune as avid readers of classical tales.)¹¹³ When Demon Sōji rejects the first marriage proposal and forbids his son from seeing Mune, the young woman begins to waste away from lovesickness. Her mother summons Gozō, who reaffirms his commitment to her: "Even if I must oppose my father, I will not deviate from the words I once [shared with you]. Let us hide ourselves away somewhere deep in the mountains. Think how joyful it will be to face each other each day."¹¹⁴ He crafts a narrative about what will happen after they run off: his wealthy family will adopt an heir, forget all about him, and thrive, leaving the two lovers morally unburdened to pursue a life together. It is no more than a fiction; but so powerful is this story of a future together that it motivates Mune to rise from her sickbed, dress herself, and insist that she is perfectly well. She prepares for Gozō a fish that he has brought—appropriately—from Akashi, a site deeply associated with *The Tale of Genji* and the setting of Akinari's own meditation on fiction, "The Scroll of Darkness."

But such fictions evaporate when Gozō is with his father. When he returns home the next morning, Demon Sōji berates him and threatens to disown him for seeing the young woman. Gozō immediately repents: "'There is nothing I can say. Young as I am, I don't think much about the choice between life and death, and I don't begrudge my life. I have no desire for riches. But thinking of how leaving home and refusing to serve my parents goes against the proper way of things, I resolve, right now, to reform myself. Please, forgive my transgression.' His face as he spoke was sincere [*makoto nari*]."¹¹⁵ As sincere as he was with Mune on her sickbed, he is now equally sincere in his filial devotion to his parents. He again cuts off all contact with Mune and throws himself into his work for his household. When Demon Sōji makes him dispose of his beloved books, Gozō's sole reply is: "From now on, I will abide by everything you say."[116] But the effect of his abandonment on Mune is so strong that she weakens until she is on her deathbed, and when her family secretly summons Gozō, he comes at once. Yet again, he pledges himself to her, addressing her family:

> "We don't know whether the afterlife is just a lie [*itsuwari*], so we cannot rely on it. All I ask is that you send her to my house tomorrow morning. Whether for ages upon ages or just for a fleeting moment, we are husband and wife. My one desire is that we be married before my father and mother. Brother, I rely on you to arrange things." Motosuke replied with a happy face, "I shall do everything just as you say. Prepare your household and wait for us." His mother said, "Long had I awaited the day, wondering when she would leave our home [as a bride]. Hearing that it will be tomorrow, my heart is finally at peace."[117]

Gozō and Mune drink saké together as a formal marriage rite, and Gozō returns home. But this pledge is just one more fiction. When Motosuke, as promised, brings Mune to Gozō's home in a palanquin the next morning, it is evident that Gozō has not broached the topic with his parents; no one is expecting her arrival.

Gozō's sincerity breeds fictions so naturally that it is difficult to tell where sincerity ends and lying begins. A similar dynamic operates in Akinari's narrative style. The narration is presented in a spare, generally straightforward but often elliptical manner; yet at moments the reader can no longer tell what is meant to be "real." Mune's illness exemplifies this dynamic. When her family summons Gozō to her side, the narrator describes Mune as so ill that she is expected to die as soon as "today or tomorrow."[118] Yet suddenly, she is to be brought in a palanquin to Gozō's house the next morning, as his bride. The family's apparent joy at the prospect of presenting their critically ill daughter at the home of Demon Sōji, who has treated the relationship all along with disgust, appears baffling. Mune's mother dresses her and combs her hair the following morning. She recalls the happiness of her own marriage and imparts advice to her daughter, counseling her to do her best to win over her devilish father-in-law and to trust in the care of her mother-in-law. Motosuke, dressed in formal wear with his sword at his side, reminds his mother that Mune will, in accordance with tradition, return home for a visit in five days. Mune smiles broadly and says, "I will return before long." At the front gate her mother sees her off in apparent happiness (*ureshige nari*). They behave as though Mune is in good health and as though they expect her to be welcomed by Gozō's household.

Here the reader must overlook the earlier depiction of Mune as deathly ill (and Demon Sōji as adamantly opposed to the match), assume that the marriage promise has somehow restored her health, or (as several modern scholars have done) write off the discrepancy as the sign of sloppy writing. It is only when the palanquin bearers mutter at the unnatural character of the "wedding" that the reader begins to register that all is not, in fact, well. And when Gozō's household expresses astonishment at the critically ill young woman being delivered to the house in a palanquin ("Who is this sick person being brought here?"), we realize that Mune's family has been performing a collective fiction of health and felicitation. In contrast to "The Tale of a *Masurao*," however, which details the family's distaste for its arrogant neighbor, the daughter's rancorous possession, and the mother's instructions to "bring things to some kind of resolution," the family's motives in "The Smile of the Severed Head" remain obscure. Only in the wake of the ensuing violence will it become clear that Mune's family has anticipated bloodshed all along.

In the *masurao* family's going through the motions of a happy wedding, we receive a clue to the allegorical import of "The Smile of the Severed Head." For if Gozō embodies sincerity so unmoored that it transforms into its opposite, the family of *masurao* temporarily embraces fiction with such commitment that it will break Gozō's circular spell and restore the real to his empty promises. They do so by treating his latest promise as absolutely, fatally true. When Motosuke and Mune are met with the rage of Demon Sōji, Motosuke repeatedly insists that they are simply following Gozō's instructions, though his words suggest a rebuke of Gozō's behavior: "[Mune] grew ill as the months and days passed while [Gozō] insisted that he wanted to marry her quickly. But he requested that she at least enter the grounds of his home to die, and so I have brought her in accordance with his wish. Let her die here, and then bury her alongside the tombs of this house."[119] Motosuke insists that Gozō follow his promise through to its conclusion, enabling Mune to die and be interred as a member of his household. Such behavior necessarily provokes Demon Sōji, and Motosuke does not hide his disdain for him. But unlike in "The Tale of a *Masurao*," where the climax centers on the *masurao* siblings' direction of self-controlled rancor at the demonic father, in "The Smile of the Severed Head" the tension coalesces around the question of what Gozō will do. By committing to one of his fictions as though it is real, the *masurao* family has *made* it real, forcing Gozō, for the first time in the narrative, to choose between the objects of his sincerity.

The choice that Gozō makes has led several commentators to regard him as the story's main protagonist. Nakamura Hiroyasu even characterizes the narrative's plot in terms of Gozō's transformation into a *masurao*, with Motosuke serving only as a secondary character.[120] Motosuke, however, is central to the way in which Gozō's choice—and Mune's death—take shape. Enraged at Motosuke's words, Sōji summons Gozō, threatens to disown him, and kicks him into the courtyard. But, for the first time, Gozō openly defies his father:

> "Do as you will. This woman is my wife. I had long thought that if you drove me out, I would take her by the hand and leave here together with her. This morning, it happens just as I had thought. Come." And, so saying, he took her hand and made to depart. Her brother spoke: "If she takes one step, she'll collapse. She is your wife. She should die in this house." He drew his sword and cut off his sister's head. Gozō picked it up, wrapped it in his sleeves, and without a single tear made to leave through the gate. His father, shocked, leaped onto a horse. "You, where do you think you're going with that head? I won't let you place it among the graves of my ancestors!"[121]

Demon Sōji rides off to alert the village headman, and we do not learn what Gozō does next. But the (jarringly) spare depiction of Mune's beheading belies the complicated dynamic at play in the passage. For while Gozō does, at last, defy his father, he does so by telling a new story—this time, about his determination to run off with Mune. This story, however, conflicts with the one that he told Mune's family the previous night about his intention to marry her before his parents and welcome her into his household. The discrepancy appears crucial to Motosuke's act, for in his insistence just before he beheads her—"She is your wife. She should die in this house"—he demands that Gozō remain faithful to the story that he told the night before, the story that Motosuke and his family have embraced to bring matters to a conclusion.

And so, in "The Smile of the Severed Head," the beheading becomes not the punishment of a licentious daughter, or a form of rancorous retribution, but an act of violence that transforms fiction into truth. And it does so through an *embrace* of fiction so committed that it makes the fiction true. In contrast to "The Tale of a *Masurao*," which posits a clear cleavage between truth and fiction and then witnesses its collapse, in this tale sharp distinctions between the real and the false prove less important than the posture one adopts in the face of their blurring. Gozō's example demonstrates that even the prized *kokugaku* value of sincerity can prove a fount of falsehood if it remains unwedded to self-awareness, whereas the example of the *masurao* family attests that for the self-possessed, falsehood can itself be a pathway to truth if one is willing to accept the sacrifices that commitment to that pathway entails.[122]

Indeed, self-possession and its power runs as a theme throughout *Tales of the Spring Rain*. Some of the collection's most complex characters are those, like Gozō and Emperor Heizei in the opening story, "The Bloodstained Robe" (Chikatabira), who have a fundamentally good nature but lack self-awareness and self-control, causing their goodness, ultimately, to effect grave injury. And the collection also features characters whose cultivation of mastery imbues them with tremendous power. The pliant Kodenji in "Suteishimaru," for example, is forced by the authorities to seek revenge for the apparent murder of his father, though he knows the death to have been of natural causes. Yet he commits so fully to the role of avenger that he ultimately gains the power to toss aside revenge, responsibility, and social expectations altogether and to live a life of profound freedom. The collection's final and longest story, "Hankai," depicts a man of brute strength and wild disposition who, over the course of a career as a highwayman, gradually learns to channel his outsized power into self-awareness and mastery, ultimately becoming a respected Zen monk. Requested by his disciples on his deathbed to leave them with a final verse (*ige*) that will summarize his spiritual insight, he coolly dismisses this venerable Zen convention:

"Deathbed verses are all lies [*itsuwari*]. I will end my life telling you something true [*makoto no koto*]. I was born in the province of Hōki and was a bandit who did such and such. I had a sudden realization, and now I have reached the present day. The Buddha, Bodhidharma, and I share the same heart: completely unclouded." And with that, they say, he died. This Hankai embodied the expression, "Master the heart, and anyone can be a buddha. Leave the heart unrestrained and become a monster."[123]

Invoking "truth" and "lies" once more, Hankai's final words, which come at the close of *Tales of the Spring Rain*, harken back to the collection's preface and its vacillations over the impossibility of evading lies altogether. There, the author's voice reveals a commitment to "go on talking" in the face of the reality that truth and lies can never be cleanly uncoupled. Here, Hankai rejects the idea of a single expression that can summarize ultimate truth—the very idea is itself, he asserts, a lie. The "something true" that he offers in its place is not a final word, but a story—in fact, a *retold* story, the story of his own life, which is the story of "Hankai" itself, a fiction, the very fiction in which the retelling occurs. *Tales of the Spring Rain* sets aside the concern with the dividing line between truth and fiction and suggests that what matters most is the attitude with which one faces up to the fact that a final, absolute differentiation between the two is not possible. Better to be a Motosuke, who knowingly embraces a fiction as though it were true and thereby imbues it with truth, than a Gozō, who can hardly differentiate truth from fiction. For a writer, better to keep telling one's stories with a heart that has made peace with their fictionality; perhaps in that way, their fiction will channel truth.

What does this stance mean for Akinari the writer? The answer, it seems to me, lies in the story's style—in what modern commentators critiqued as its lack of polish, its inconsistencies. The story jolts. It confuses. It withholds. Its brusque sentences leave out what we most want to know, while tendering details that confuse as much as they clarify—like the contrast it draws between "Buddha" Gozō and "Demon" Sōji. Akinari lards the story with allegorical hints, comparisons, and contrasts, but without drawing their significance into the light. The narrator likens Motosuke's mother to the weaving goddess, Takuhatachijihime, without elaboration (though, like the goddess, she uses a loom); in another instance, the village headman refers to her as a demon. Akinari sets the story in Ubara, a site associated in legend with the "Ubara maiden," who kills herself rather than choose between two lovers, who then follow her in death. The legend vaguely resonates with the themes of doomed love and male antagonism in Akinari's story, but without mapping onto it neatly. (And in some versions of the legend, the woman is named Unai—the name of Yae's lover in the actual incident. So is the setting a meaningful allusion or an authorial in-joke?) Meanwhile, how ill *is* Mune? Is she aware of the fate that awaits her? How does the family feel about the sacrifice of the daughter? And what does Gozō *really* think? (On this point, even the authorities who interrogate him in the aftermath are flummoxed: "Gozō's heart is very enigmatic [*ito ayashi*].")[124] When Gozō and his father depart for banishment in the killing's aftermath, Sōji, blaming it all on Gozō, throws his son to the ground and thrashes him until the blood flows. "[Beat me] to your heart's content," says Gozō, and offers no resistance. Is it a sign of the inner strength that he has found in having once defied his father? A mark of his continued passivity? An acceptance of his culpability? The answers to these questions are left to the reader's imagination.

And that is the point. Akinari now recognizes the writer's role as to "go on talking," without fussing over the way his reader reads. Whereas in "The Tale of a *Masurao*" he tries (and fails) to embody the *masurao* ideal by writing only the "truth," now he writes like a *masurao* by simply *writing*—directly, and without a net. As the preface to *Tales of the Spring Rain* makes clear, even the best of intentions won't keep truth and fiction from getting muddled, so why fret? For if it is mastery over one's own heart that separates clarity from delusion, then responsibility for the effects of fiction rests as much with the reader as with the writer. And so, it is incumbent on the reader to *read*.

Nothing embodies the challenge of such reading more than the story's titular figure: the smile of the severed head. The smile appears only in the tale's last line, after arrests have been made and punishments apportioned: "People told and passed down how dauntless [*takedakeshi*] appeared the smile that remained upon the young woman's severed head."[125] There the story ends, with an image that generates questions in place of closure. What does Mune's smile signify? The title suggests that the answer will reflect something central to the narrative as a whole—but what? The modifier *takedakeshi* (I have translated it as "dauntless," but other possibilities include "ferocious," "determined," "bold," "valiant," "courageous," and "strong") intimates a warrior-like quality. And the image echoes legends of warriors so self-possessed that they could perform a last action—such as biting at the enemy—even after their heads had been severed. So in this way, Mune's smile reinforces the celebration of self-possession that runs through *Tales of the Spring Rain*. It draws a contrast with Gozō's fecklessness and Sōji's unruliness and suggests a quality that characterizes the *masurao* family. But her smile also suggests pleasure. Pleasure that she and her lover are united at last? That his promise has been made true before his father, even at the cost of her own life? Or, in a more bitter vein, that the contrast between their commitments has been made humiliatingly clear? That his arrogant father has at last been shaken? Because we know Mune only through fleeting glimpses throughout the story, it is easier to generate such questions than to answer them. And then there is the line's framing in the language of legend: "People told and passed down . . ." In a collection that probes the relationship between truth and fiction, and a story inspired by an incident of debated facts, the wording raises the question of whether Mune's uncanny smile should be understood as a legendary embellishment that accrued to the incident in its telling and retelling by the community.[126]

Mune's smile makes the perfect end to a story that embraces uncertainty in place of truth, within a collection that emphasizes not closure but continued speaking. The severed head's smile does not summarize; it generates. It places the onus on readers to read, not simply receive. It resonates with Satō Miyuki's characterization of *Tales of the Spring Rain* as an "apparatus" (*sōchi*) constructed of "facing mirrors," in which questions rebound without end, ever generating new interpretations: "By setting its mechanism in motion, readers can go beyond the authorial intentions assumed to lie at its origin point and themselves pursue the construction of future-facing interpretations."[127] And therein lies the moral import of the enigmatic style of *Tales of the Spring Rain*. To write—and read—like a *masurao* means not to nail down the truth, but to embrace generation—like the natural patterns of heaven and earth, creating infinitely, beyond strict intentions. If one can enter into this process, whether as writer or as reader, with heart "unclouded," in embrace of uncertainty, then concern with the formal boundaries of truth and fiction will give way to the clarity of perception and the boundlessness of creation.

Conclusion

From the messiness of an unusual murder, we thus witness the complexity of thinking not only about form, but with and through form, and of finding answers *in* form. And we see how enmeshed form was with questions about the relationship between truth and fiction. For the authorities who adjudicated Genta's case, the process was one of fitting formally unusual details, however artificially, into the grooves of precedent until unruly form matched established form and thus created an officially palatable "truth." For Akinari, the engagement with form was one of process: a process of first attempting to pin truth down, like a preserved butterfly, before recognizing that the formal pins he employed in his writing were not stable entities but themselves quivered and flitted like a butterfly's wings, always in motion, charting unpredictable and vagabond pathways rather than holding anything fast. The only solution was to stop trying to hold things still and instead to seek an open, unsettled style that would enable a full range of motion.

Akinari's writing exemplifies the inextricability of form from formation—a dynamic that Tom Eyers calls "the formativeness of form."[128] This formativeness can take many shapes. Akinari took it to the level of an experimental style, one that steps off the more well-trodden paths of didacticism and entertainment. As I show in the next chapter, however, even a more conventionally commercial engagement with form, one that is much more formulaic, could possess an arresting formative power. And it could engage, with startling complexity, questions that animated Akinari—questions concerning Japan as a community, its health, and what held it together—but from beyond the *kokugaku* frame.

CHAPTER V

Frontier Violence

Late Yomihon *Form and the Bodies and Bounds of the Realm*

A paradox lies at the heart of the early modern imagination of "Japan." On the one hand, a keen sense of differences and their boundaries permeated the early modern polity. A "taxonomic consciousness"—propounded in the pages of the encyclopedias, gazetteers, and other informational texts of the flourishing print market—posited a highly formalized vision of each person in his or her place. Early modern Japanese were differentiated from one another by dress, hairstyle, and comportment; fell into clearly delineated communities of status (*mibun*) and rank (*kakushiki*); and clearly distinguished themselves from both the "proximate Others" of East Asia (Chinese and Koreans on the continent, as well as Ainu to the north and Ryūkyūans to the south) and the Europeans who had first appeared in Japanese waters in the mid-sixteenth century.[1] Commercial maps represented the formal geography of the realm as crisscrossed by the boundary lines of provinces that had been established by the imperial court in the hoary past, and the administration of the realm remained divided between the shogunal house and semi-independent domains that possessed their own laws, governing structures, and ruling lords, and that actively asserted their differences from one another. Superseding these internal subdivisions, meanwhile, the realm as a whole, ringed by the border of the sea, could appear to be a "natural region"—a geographic fait accompli.[2] And the fact that in the early seventeenth century the shogunate had closed all ports but Nagasaki to foreign trade, limited the trade at

Nagasaki to only the Chinese and the Dutch, and forbidden Japanese from traveling beyond the realm's shores reinforced the sense of the archipelago as a "closed country" (*sakoku*), locked tight against the otherness of the outside world.

On the other hand, the differentiation of spaces, boundaries, and Others—and even of the cultural and geographic shape of "Japan" itself—remained strikingly ambiguous throughout most of the Tokugawa period. None of the inhabitants of the archipelago questioned the existence of the shared entity of Japan (albeit called by a variety of names); but the questions of just where this entity began and ended, and who properly belonged within it, remained open-ended. In early modern maps—both those of the mind and those inscribed on paper—the polity possessed what Ronald P. Toby has characterized as "ragged edges."[3] Its borders remained hazy. Maps sometimes incorporated the island of Ezo (present-day Hokkaido) to the north and those of Ryūkyū (Okinawa) to the south, but often left them out, and encyclopedic works evinced a similar ambiguity about the boundaries of the realm.[4] Many aspects of Japanese culture, from dress and comportment to written languages, were highly standardized (sometimes by law), but the realm also comprised an astonishing cultural and linguistic diversity. Even the familiar image of the "closed country" has proved misleading, for through the port of Nagasaki flowed not only foreign goods but a vast range of foreign books—East Asian and European alike—and, with them, information and ideas from the wider world that took on their own elaborate lives within the archipelago. As Marcia Yonemoto summarizes, "'Japan' was at the same time both a thoroughly mapped and narrated space *and* a profoundly elusive and impressionistic amalgamation of places and peoples."[5] And, we might add, of ideas.

However malleable the space and identities of early modern Japan may have been, identity—whether at the micro or the macro level—was recognized by means of what Tessa Morris-Suzuki has called a "logic of difference," defined always within a dialectic of similarity and dissimilarity, Self and Other.[6] This was not necessarily a dialectic of strict, essentialized binaries (though it could seem fixed in any given instantiation), but an ever-shifting relationality fitted to an ever-changing jumble of contexts. And form was crucial to its navigation. Whether in the two swords worn at the waist that distinguished even the most impoverished samurai from men of other statuses; in the emphasis placed on the facial hair of foreign peoples when differentiating them from the clean-shaven (and shaven-pated)

Japanese; or in the staged performance of "Ainu" ceremonies before Japanese officials in the far north to demarcate a civilizational boundary in diplomatic encounters with the indigenous people of Ezo, the formal marking of difference was crucial to the establishment of identity.[7]

Questions of difference, and of the coherence of Japan as a shared culture and a bounded geography, however, took on a new urgency beginning in the late eighteenth century, as the world beyond the waters hove abruptly into more threatening view. The Russian Empire had reached the shores of the Pacific, and the increasing—sometimes antagonistic—encounters with Russian trappers and traders around the Kuril Islands alarmed Japanese officials and raised fears of larger clashes, or even a Russian invasion.[8] Direct Russian requests to open trade, and the increasing appearance of ships of other nations in the waters around the archipelago, drew attention to the vulnerability of the polity's "ragged edges" to foreign aggression. At the same time, the threat of danger from abroad propelled new thinking about the identity of "Japan," not only geographically, but culturally. Timon Screech, for example, characterizes the decades of the late eighteenth and early nineteenth centuries as defined by the "reification of 'Japanese culture' . . . to counter a belligerent Other," emphasizing that this reification was "fear-led."[9] And the work of delineating a comprehensible cultural identity was necessarily tied to the demarcation of formal boundaries and the pinpointing of difference.[10]

In this chapter, I ask what role popular fiction—particularly the representation of violence therein—played in this process of marking boundaries and constructing "Japan." My genre of choice is late *yomihon* (alternatively known as Edo *yomihon* or *haishimono yomihon*), a genre that emerged in the city of Edo at the turn of the nineteenth century, precisely in the midst of this new confrontation with foreign Others—and of a series of domestic disturbances that called into question the social integrity of the realm. Although they share the name *yomihon* (literally, "reading books") with the earlier texts from the Kamigata region discussed in chapter 4, early and late *yomihon* are distinct genres. The earlier form, composed primarily by writers in the Kyoto–Osaka area, drew heavily on adaptation of Chinese vernacular fiction and primarily took the shape of short-story collections. But late *yomihon*, composed by a new generation of commercial literary stars based in Edo, such as Santō Kyōden (1761–1816) and Kyokutei Bakin (1767–1848), took the form of sprawling (sometimes gargantuan) historical romances, often incorporating a heady dose of the supernatural.

Although partially inspired by Chinese vernacular fiction in form and style, in content late *yomihon* are concerned largely with native history, lore, and cultural practices: potent material for probing the coherence of Japanese geographic and cultural space. Here I focus on one of the foundational works of the late *yomihon* genre, Kyōden's *Revenge and Strange Tales: The Asaka Marsh* (*Fukushū kidan Asaka no numa*, 1803), which helped to lay the groundwork for the genre's form and style and which explicitly considers the cultural and spatial frontiers of "Japan." As a revenge story that sees its avenging protagonist set out from the cultural and political heartland of the realm into the outland of northern Honshu in search of his enemy, *The Asaka Marsh* evokes cultural frontiers—including the far northern frontier between Japanese and Ainu lands—in sophisticated, provocative ways that have received surprisingly scant attention in scholarship.

In exploring the text's play with the concept of spatial and cultural frontiers, I am guided by Michel de Certeau's meditations on the relationship between stories and space, particularly on the role of story in structuring space by partitioning it. This partitioning takes many forms: "From the distinction that separates a subject from its exteriority to the distinctions that localize objects, from the home (constituted on the basis of the wall) to the journey (constituted on the basis of a geographical 'elsewhere' or a cosmological 'beyond'), from the functioning of the urban network to that of the rural landscape, there is no spatiality that is not organized by the determination of frontiers."[11]

This "culturally creative act" of establishing spaces through narrative, however, is not a simple matter of drawing a line in the metaphorical sand and excluding everything beyond it; as Certeau notes, the establishment of a limit sets in motion as well the possibility of its transgression or transcendence, making "the story a sort of 'crossword' decoding stencil (a dynamic partitioning of space) whose essential narrative figures seem to be the *frontier* and the *bridge*."[12] In contradictory fashion, these two figures are inseparable, for the drawing of distinctions itself constitutes a type of encounter. A frontier is both a point of differentiation and a point of contact; indeed, differentiation can happen only *through* contact.[13] Similarly, the bridge "alternately welds together and opposes insularities." It marks a point of departure and return, a place where one crosses over to an alien "other side," a "bewildering exteriority" independent of the laws and limits that obtain on this side. But it is also an opening to that other side, such that "in recrossing the bridge and coming back within the enclosure the traveler henceforth finds there the exteriority that he had first sought by going outside and then fled by returning. Within the frontiers, the alien is already there, an exoticism or sabbath of the memory, a disquieting familiarity. It is as though delimitation itself were the bridge that opens the inside to the other."[14]

The Asaka Marsh is precisely such a story of departure and return, one that moves through the shadowlands of the archipelago's "ragged edges" and—seemingly—seeks to affirm legible cultural boundaries, boundaries that it maps onto differences of body and of relationship to space. These boundaries are linked to the exercise of violence: certain types of bodies evince a propensity to immoral violence, and the outland of northern Honshu serves as a staging ground for murders of different varieties, building to a spectacularly brutal denouement. But just as a frontier shares qualities with a bridge, the clear lines that the text initially purports to establish reveal themselves, in its latter half, as blurrier than they first appear. The outland is shown to possess disturbingly intimate links to the heartland; different bodies prove to be less differentiable than they initially seem; iconography imported from beyond the seas is made to underscore occult similarities between Selves and Others; and the murderous danger of the "ragged edges" is found to be lying in wait, already, in the diseased heart of the body politic.

Late *yomihon* have been treated largely as a genre of high fantasy and rigid morality, exemplifications of the Confucian dynamic of "rewarding virtue and castigating vice" (*kanzen chōaku*). In literary history, they hold a place as the last great narrative genre of Japan's early modernity before the doors of the "closed country" flew open, letting in European concepts of emotional realism and national literature and dramatically transforming Japanese approaches to fiction. Indeed, in seminal works like Tsubouchi Shōyō's (1859–1935) *The Essence of the Novel* (*Shōsetsu shinzui*, 1885–1886), the modern Japanese novel is explicitly theorized against *yomihon*, which are recast as the fanciful, didactic products of a feudal age.[15] But the kind of attention I bring to *The Asaka Marsh* reveals a different side. This, I argue, is a book deeply involved in imagining, and *problematizing*, Japan as a shared and bounded cultural geography—what Thongchai Winichakul has called a "geo-body"—well before Commodore Matthew Perry's black ships and the Meiji Restoration thrust the archipelago into the global order of nations.[16] The crises of the late eighteenth century have long been seen as precipitating new forms of proto-national discourse, prefiguring motifs of the Japanese nationalism that would come into full, deadly flower in the late nineteenth and early twentieth centuries. But unlike these discourses, which essentialized Japanese cultural and geographic difference, *The Asaka Marsh*, even as it evokes Japan as a shared, intimately interconnected body, does so *critically*, depicting that body as internally sick and corrupted—even autophagic. And it unsettles any reassurance that the bounds of cultural or geographic distance are as clear-cut and protective as they may appear. The text does so through a formal system that does indeed differ from the mimetic realism and psychological depth of the modern novel, relying instead upon typological characters, narrative modularity, and intertextual play with both literary tradition and contemporary texts and images. But it is precisely the affordances of this literary formal system that enable the text to theorize the amalgamation of geographic and bodily forms into a coherent geo-body. In so doing, it invites us to rethink the relationship between the formal elements of early modern popular fiction and the emergence of a modern conception of Japan.

Northern Frontier, Northern Outland

From the perspective of Edo, the "north" was actually a diverse series of peripheries. The most dynamic of these—a site where Japanese political authority, trade, and cultural influence directly interacted with a cultural Other—was the island now called Hokkaido, known at the time as Ezo and containing on its southern peninsula an area of Japanese settlement: the Wajinchi. The parts of Ezo beyond the Wajinchi were subsumed within the larger, less clearly defined space of Ezochi, which included the Kuril Islands and Sakhalin and was populated by the indigenous Ainu people. The boundary between the Wajinchi and the Ezochi was a clearly demarcated political border, but it was also a "civilizational boundary between the Ainu and the Japanese, articulated through the medium of customs."[17] This civilizational boundary partook of a model borrowed from China, the "ka-i system" (*ka-i chitsujo*), whereby "the known, settled, orderly center (*ka*) was surrounded by boundless circles of increasing strangeness, disorder, and barbarism (*i*)."[18] As Tessa Morris-Suzuki notes, the difference between the "civilized" center and the "barbarian" periphery in this model was marked, in particular, through "appearance and etiquette: hairstyles and clothing, footwear and tattoos, diet and housing, festivals and ceremonies were the parameters which defined the foreign."[19] The strangeness of civilizational Others had been imagined in terms of bodies, dress, and customs since well before the Edo period. In the late medieval tale *Yoshitsune Crosses the Isles* (*Onzōshi shimawatari*), for example, the warrior Minamoto no Yoshitsune (1159–1189) journeys into the waters north of Honshu in search of a precious scroll of military strategy, visiting along the way islands populated by tiny people, giants, naked people, cannibalistic women, and human–animal hybrids.[20] But with the establishment of the line between the Wajinchi and the Ezochi as a political boundary under the Tokugawa settlement, the *formalized performance* of difference came to play an important role in northern cross-border relations through formalized ceremonies and dress. David L. Howell has shown the role of Japanese administrators from Matsumae Domain, which administered the Wajinchi, in manipulating and reinventing traditional Ainu ceremonies in which the Ainu ritually demonstrated their submission; he argues that these rituals "were not directed primarily toward the Ainu, but rather were designed to reassure the Japanese themselves of their own legitimacy" by highlighting Japanese civilizational difference from, and political authority over, a tributary barbarian population.[21]

The line separating the "civilized" Japanese polity from the "barbaric" outside, however, was not the only periphery to the north of Edo. Between the Wajinchi and the shogun's capital lay the vast expanse of northern Honshu, best known today as Tōhoku, but called at the time by a range of names: Michinoku, Oku, Ōu, Ōshū, Ushū. Kawanishi Hidemichi has argued that while northern Honshu unlike Ezo, was considered part of the Japanese polity for centuries, it was perceived by those from Edo and parts farther west as an outland, situated between the center and the Ezo periphery. Thus, as Kawanishi explains, Honshu was in some ways regarded as cruder and more backward than the Japanese settlements in Ezo, and in the popular imagination of the center it was "related to the historical world of the Ainu" and treated as hierarchically inferior to Edo and Kamigata.[22] In earlier times, northern Honshu had in fact been a frontier region, the site of battles during the eighth century between the expansive Yamato state and a people they called the Emishi, and later a region only nominally under the direct control of the court.[23] This frontier legacy lived on into the Edo period through poetic memory. The Shirakawa Barrier, for example, which had marked the boundary between the archaic state and the Emishi frontier from at least the Nara period to the Kamakura period, remained an important topos in *waka* poetry as a site where one crossed from a culturally familiar center into the outland.[24]

And, indeed, though northern Honshu was a rough backwater to those from the inner provinces, it abounded in long-standing poetic associations and classical lore, its geography a tissue of poetic sites (*utamakura*) reaching back to the poetry of the ancient anthology *Man'yōshū* (*Collection of Ten Thousand Leaves*, after 759). Mount Asaka, for example, in present-day Fukushima Prefecture, was associated with a legendary encounter between Prince Kazuraki (Tachibana no Moroe, 684–757) and the elegant daughter of the local governor, who cheered the visiting prince with a poem:

Asakayama kage sae miyuru yamanoi no asaki kokoro o waga omowanaku ni.
Mount Asaka: its reflection clear in the shallow heart of the
    mountain spring. Not shallow at all are my own heart's thoughts
    of you.[25]

The *kana* preface to the seminal *waka* anthology *Kokin wakashū* (*Collection of Ancient and Modern Poems*, early tenth century) cites this verse, together with another known as the "Port of Naniwa" poem, as one of the "parents" (*chichi haha*) of classical verse; both poems, as the preface notes, were copied by students at the start of their study of *kana* handwriting.[26] Other northern *utamakura* included Mount Shinobu and Sue no Matsuyama. Elegant motifs employed in *waka* poetry, such as bogwood (*umoregi*) and brocade staffs (*nishikigi*), were associated with northern Honshu as well. The great *haikai* poet Matsuo Bashō (1644–1694) based *The Narrow Road to the Interior* (*Oku no hosomichi*, published 1702) on his journey through this poetic landscape in 1689; his renowned narrative is less a realistic depiction of contemporary northern Honshu (though it includes many realistic touches) than an account of a *haikai* poet's experience of communing with and contributing to a textual territory composed of centuries of poetic compositions, associations, and legends. When Bashō crosses the Shirakawa Barrier, he experiences it entirely through the lens of older poems, and he claims to be so overwhelmed that initially he cannot compose a verse of his own.[27]

A series of events and transformations in the late eighteenth century, however, focused popular and political attention on the north in new ways. The Russian Empire had established an outpost on the Pacific at Okhotsk by the mid-seventeenth century, and encounters with Russian trappers and traders around the Kuril Islands became more frequent beginning in the mid-eighteenth century, prompting concerns that Russia's expanding empire posed a threat to Japanese defense.[28] The Russian interest in Japan became explicit in 1792 with the arrival in Ezo of the Russian envoy Adam Laxman (1766–1803?), dispatched by Catherine the Great (1729–1796) to return the castaway Daikokuya Kōdayū (1751–1828) to Japan and to seek the opening of trade relations.[29] In 1793, Laxman met directly with shogunal representatives at Hakodate, but the shogunate denied his request to travel deeper into Japan and ultimately sent him away without a firm trade agreement.[30] In response to the perceived Russian threat, from 1799 to 1821 the shogunate assumed direct control of Ezo, which had until then been administered by the lords of Matsumae Domain.

The economy of Ezo also developed dramatically in the late eighteenth century, as *konbu* seaweed and fertilizer made from the herring caught off its coasts became major commodities, transforming the diet and agriculture of the Japanese islands to the south. Because its colder climate differed from that of the rest of the Japanese archipelago, the flora and fauna of Ezo also became important commodities sold to the central provinces, particularly as pharmaceuticals. So important did these northern products become that in 1799, "the practice of surveying for medicinal plant and animal products, many of which were associated with Ainu medical culture, became shogunal policy; and subsequently many Ainu medicines were integrated into the culture of gift giving that delineated hierarchical relations and cemented personal alliances in the early-modern Japanese state."[31] Japanese physicians traveled to the far north to catalogue materia medica. One of them was Tachibana Nankei (1753–1805), who journeyed extensively in northern Honshu in 1785 and 1786 and who published a highly readable, sometimes embellished account of his travels as *Journey to the East* (*Tōyūki*, 1795). The book was so popular that it went through multiple printings and inspired Nankei to publish a sequel two years later.[32]

Even as northern pharmaceuticals brought promises of health to the Japanese islands, however, and even as fertilizer from Ezo helped to grow the crops that fed their populations, the Great Tenmei Famine—the worst famine of the Edo period—devastated northern Honshu in the 1780s. Frigid rains, floods, and the eruptions of Mount Iwaki and Mount Asama in 1783 contributed to the failure of harvests in the north, and a condition of chronic famine gripped the region throughout the decade. Riots and uprisings broke out, and refugees flooded into Edo, bringing northern Honshu before the eyes of the shogun's capital in the most negative way. Rumors of cannibalism emerged from the northern provinces gripped by starvation; hunger and illness are estimated to have killed as many as 300,000 in northern Honshu.[33]

Pausing here, we can recognize that the northern reaches of the Japanese polity at the turn of the nineteenth century represented more than a verifiable geography apprehensible on a map; layered onto them were multiple histories, peoples, events, subgeographies, desires, fears, products, routes of circulation, and texts (old and new) that a skillful story could combine, set in opposition, differentiate, and navigate among. And the strategies whereby a story set these diverse elements in motion had the potential to stitch together this entity as a legible whole, to position its relationship to the political and cultural heart of the polity, and to establish a sense of boundary between the realm's interior and its exterior, and between a culturally coherent Japanese identity and a (possibly barbarian) Other. A particularly sophisticated story might even show itself cognizant of the dialectical relationship between such categories, attending not only to the partitioning of inside from outside and Self from Other, but to the bridges, blurrings, and crossings-over that existed between them.

Late *Yomihon* and Cultural Geography

Questions of space and cultural identity had been integral to the *yomihon* genre since the early form's inception in the Kamigata region in the mid-eighteenth century. Early *yomihon* were heavily influenced by—and often directly modeled on—Chinese vernacular works. The act of writing involved transposing Chinese cultural situations and geographies into Japanese cultural and geographic settings, a process that entailed weighing the nature of civilizational similarity and difference. Such questions remained foregrounded in *yomihon* as it developed into an Edo-based genre at the turn of the nineteenth century. This new form is now typically known as late *yomihon* or *haishimono* (petty history) *yomihon*. The term "petty history" (*haishi*, Ch. *baishi*) derives from the ancient Chinese practice of sending officials to collect "anecdotes, stories, and rumors circulating among the common people" as supplements to official histories. Later, it came to refer to vernacular fiction with a historical bent, as in works like the Ming dynasty novel *The Water Margin* (Ch. *Shuihu zhuan*, J. *Suikoden*), which creatively elaborates accounts of outlaw resistance during the latter years of the Song dynasty into a sweeping, morally complex romance.[34] Late *yomihon* took up this posture of fantastic historical fiction: they are typically set in the past and often incorporate their authors' research into historical lore, cultural practices, and anecdotes; but they also are intricately plotted for suspense and surprise and include a generous admixture of fantasy and magic. Unlike the early *yomihon* of Kamigata, many of which take the form of short stories within collections, late *yomihon* are closer to modern novels in length—and sometimes, as in the case of Kyokutei Bakin's monumental *Eight Dog Chronicle* (*Nansō Satomi hakkenden*, 1814–1842), significantly longer.

Late *yomihon* are generally recognized as having reached their apex under Bakin, but their first pioneer was Bakin's mentor, friend, and sometime rival, Santō Kyōden. Kyōden was arguably the most versatile innovator within the body of Edo-based commercial genres collectively known as *gesaku* (literally, "frivolous writings"). A prodigy who began illustrating and writing witty illustrated fiction (*kibyōshi*) while still in his teens, he became a best-selling author who left an indelible mark on *kibyōshi*, as well as on their lengthier and more plot-driven successor genre, "bound books" (*gōkan*), and "wit and fashion books" (*sharebon*, works depicting the interactions between patrons and courtesans in the licensed quarters). Although these genres contain varying amounts of cultural—and sometimes political—satire, none of them bear any pretentions to seriousness as literature; *gesaku* fell at the decidedly low end of the contemporary genre hierarchy, written to entertain and to turn a profit. *Yomihon*, too, are a *gesaku* genre. But their posture is one of greater (though never total) weightiness: the sober uncle to the flippant *kibyōshi*. They are physically larger than other *gesaku* genres, and they are longer and prosier; the name *yomihon* (reading book) draws an explicit contrast with illustration-heavy genres like *kibyōshi* and *gōkan*.[35] Kyōden also turned to writing *yomihon* at a moment when circumstances had coincided to dampen the wit and satire that had defined *gesaku* at the start of his career. New censorship protocols in the 1790s had driven politically suggestive material from the market and had even landed Kyōden himself in manacles in 1791.[36] And an expansion in readership and sales in the late 1790s had spawned a new demand for plot-driven works—particularly revenge stories.

Kyōden's first *yomihon*, published in two parts in 1799 and 1801, drew on this confluence of circumstances and explicitly foregrounds the dynamic intersection between Chinese and Japanese substance and style. As its title suggests, *The Water Margin of the Loyal Retainers* (*Chūshin suikoden*) mashes up the plot and characters of *The Water Margin* with those of the celebrated *jōruri* revenge play *The Treasury of Loyal Retainers* (*Kanadehon chūshingura*, 1748). The book ingeniously interweaves aspects of the Chinese novel and its cultural world with the world of the Japanese play to produce an effect that William C. Hedberg has identified as a classic example of *mitate*, the early modern aesthetic of double exposure in which "signifiers from different periods, texts, or cultures are superimposed upon one another and viewed as one."[37] In Kyōden's book, the *mitate* effect brilliantly exemplifies the intricateness with which culturally Japanese fiction could be produced using the forms of Chinese source material. But *The Water Margin of the Loyal Retainers* also represents the departure of late *yomihon* from certain highbrow aspects of early *yomihon*. While Kyōden, a great admirer of the early *yomihon* master Ueda Akinari (see chapter 4), appears to have modeled the first installment of his book on the style of Kamigata *yomihon*, writing for a presumed audience of well-read, sophisticated readers who possessed at least some familiarity with the world of vernacular Chinese fiction, the second volume evinces a shift toward greater accessibility. In the first installment, Kyōden had drawn on the stiff, Sinified style of a recent Japanese translation of *The Water Margin* (*Tsūzoku chūgi suikoden*, 1790), and he had plundered an earlier Japanese printing of the Chinese text (*Chūgi suikoden*, 1728) for vernacular Chinese vocabulary, turns of phrase, and stylistic devices.[38] But in the second installment, he modulated the style to make it much more accessible, in what Inoue Keiji recognizes as an attempt to accommodate the growing interest of mainstream readers.[39]

The Asaka Marsh is Kyōden's second *yomihon*, and its relationship to the style of Chinese vernacular fiction and to the geographic space of the Japanese islands marks a distinctly new inflection. Gone is the double-exposure *mitate* effect: rather than building the book on a Chinese source text, Kyōden structured it around a classic Japanese revenge plot of the type so popular in other *gesaku* genres at the time, with a murder at the opening, a long and arduous search in the middle, and a revenge killing at the end. But by setting the avenger's peregrinations in the outland of northern Honshu, and by playing with ideas of cultural, geographic, and physical difference—including working in subtle allusions to the Ezo frontier—Kyōden kept the dynamic of cultural interplay in the foreground. China has not vanished from this text; we will see how he invoked Chinese legends and spaces in strategic ways in constructing northern Honshu as a region of uncanny cultural and geographic difference. Instead, China is now but one ingredient in a work that navigates among multiple aspects of civilizational similarity and difference, across boundaries foreign and domestic, spatial and cultural.

Kyōden also opened up a new, spatial dimension of the revenge plot, linking it to the exploration of cultural geography. According to revenge convention, the murderer flees into hiding after killing the protagonist's senior relative (typically his father), and the avenger then spends much of the narrative undergoing various hardships as he travels through the realm in search of the killer. In the first decade of the nineteenth century, writers began to treat this period of pursuit as an opportunity to add interest to a largely formulaic plot structure by choosing interesting geographic settings for the quest and by weaving into their stories aspects of local information, from historical and literary references to folklore and cultural practices. *The Asaka Marsh* was one of the first books to foreground this relationship between revenge and the particularity of provincial locales. Kyōden had immersed himself in cultural and antiquarian research beginning in the 1790s, and he incorporated into *The Asaka Marsh* elements of his reading on classical customs associated with the north as well as information derived from recent travel narratives such as Nankei's *Journey to the East*. In 1804 (the year following the publication of *The Asaka Marsh*), Kyōden published *Thoughts on the Wondrous Traces of Recent Ages* (*Kinsei kiseki kō*), a five-volume book of research into the customs, arts, and lore of the early Edo period—the temporal setting of *The Asaka Marsh*—and he continued to incorporate the fruits of this kind of study into the narratives of the journeys of the avengers in his many revenge works. In his revenge *kibyōshi* and *gōkan*, aspects of this research might be written right into the title: in *The Women of Okazaki: A Revenge* (*Katakiuchi Okazaki joroshu*, 1807), for example, by the time the villain meets his end, the reader has learned the purported origins of a song, popular in the seventeenth century, associated with the prostitutes of the Okazaki post station on the Tōkaidō.[40] Other writers followed his lead, and in this way, revenge fiction began to resemble a violent subgenre of travel literature. *The Asaka Marsh* can be seen as a foundational text in establishing this relationship between revenge fiction and the exploration of the spatial and cultural diversity of the Japanese islands.

The Asaka Marsh has also been recognized as foundational in setting the style and structure of late *yomihon* as a genre more broadly. Ōtaka Yōji identifies *The Asaka Marsh*, together with *The Water Margin of the Loyal Retainers* and Kyōden's third *yomihon*, *The Tale of the Udumbara Flower* (*Udonge monogatari*, 1804), as crucial to the development of what he terms the "*yomihon* framework" (*yomihonteki wakugumi*), which came to structure all *yomihon* to follow.[41] In this formulation, the plot of a *yomihon* requires the early introduction of a number of "people, animals, objects, and words," which then—overtly or implicitly—make their presence felt throughout the ensuing scenes as the story develops. Only at the conclusion are the relationships among all of them made clear: a stolen object returned to its proper place, the meaning behind a riddle revealed, the spirit of a rancorous ghost pacified, the predictions of a mysterious mendicant fulfilled, and so on.[42] The presentation of these various pieces at the outset, and the convoluted paths to their ultimate destinations and resolutions at the conclusion, helped to structure the *yomihon* as a plot-driven book of significant length. Because Kyōden's (and Bakin's) first *yomihon* were revenge stories, the development of the *yomihon* framework served to add twists, suspense, and texture to what was otherwise a rather basic tale of murder and countermurder.[43] *The Asaka Marsh*, for example, tells the story of the young, impoverished samurai Yamanoi Hamon's quest for vengeance against the man who murdered his family. But interwoven with this basic plot are Hamon's early betrothal to a beautiful young woman and their ensuing separation (they are reunited in an unexpected circumstance at the end); a riddling prediction offered to the hero by an enigmatic wandering nun (the riddle's significance unfolds with the plot, finally becoming clear by the book's conclusion); and a second plot about the murder of a cuckolded kabuki actor and his ghostly revenge on his killer (who happens to be the brother of the killer of Hamon's family, the avenger's and the ghost's stories intersecting at various points throughout the narrative).

This *yomihon* framework has prompted scholars to understand late *yomihon* as a genre in which composition involved switching in and out different possibilities within established structural forms. Hamada Keisuke, for example, building on Ōtaka's conception of the *yomihon* framework, discusses the structural components of *yomihon* as *kata*: patterned "forms" akin to those of traditional martial and performing arts. The composition of a *yomihon* was a matter of putting its structural forms into practice in an inventive way, which involved selecting from an array of literary precedents and possible structures for any given plot piece: a love story, a riddle, a stolen object, a murder.[44] Seen this way, the genre might resemble little more than a formulaic, combinatory game, in which composition consists primarily of arranging modular pieces into compelling patterns for the purposes of constructing novel plots. The danger of understanding the genre's modular structure solely in these practical and prosaic terms, however, is that one risks overlooking the idiosyncrasy with which the formal ingredients could be selected and arranged, as well as the unexpected connections and surprising perceptions that their juxtaposition could produce about the world beyond the page. That is, one risks losing sight of the possibility that the text has a deeper import.

The very nature of the *yomihon* framework itself, in fact, seems to imply something important about the world. It presents "people, animals, objects, and words" as all connected to and exerting a force on one another, albeit often in obscure or implicit ways that are made fully legible only at the end. At the level of plot, this interconnectedness manifests in extraordinary coincidences; even in the vast hinterland of northern Honshu, the characters in *The Asaka Marsh* have a habit of running across one another and affecting one another's fate, whether intentionally or not. The effect makes for sudden twists and surprises, to be sure; but it also suggests that different people, from various walks of life and all corners of the realm, are stitched together in uncanny ways. It posits a vision of society defined by interrelationships, even among strangers who possess no knowledge of one another. One's fate is never wholly one's own, and the teeming streets of Edo are implicated even within events that take place at the remote cultural peripheries of the realm, and vice versa. No act is isolatable— particularly not an act of violence.

Even as *The Asaka Marsh* contributed to the conventions that would govern all future *yomihon*, its development of these features opened toward a set of questions oriented to the imagination of Japanese community: questions not only of spatial and cultural difference, but also of the nature of interrelationship among all those who made up the early modern polity. In this text's vision, no danger can be assumed to lie safely on the far side of a border.

The Asaka Marsh

Strange Bodies and Textual Spaces
(or, Otter Skin Beards and Eagle Eyes)

The dynamic of the traditional *ka-i* vision of civilization and barbarity is very much at play in *The Asaka Marsh*, operating at various levels and to diverse narrative ends. The idea of a civilized, Japanese center, marked not only by cultural knowledge but by normative bodies, fading out into an increasingly uncivilized periphery of cultural and bodily strangeness, underlies the narrative's presentation of character and geography. Even the outland of northern Honshu takes shape in a kind of multiple exposure, simultaneously marked by civilization and by otherness, depending on the nature of the character who perceives it. By closely reading the text's formal treatment of bodies and geography, we can begin to recognize the complicated way the narrative ties together character, culture, ethics, and otherness—a process that involves both setting and blurring boundaries.

Yamanoi Hamon is the young, handsome, talented son of a once-illustrious samurai family fallen into poverty. When he learns that his family has been murdered in cold blood by a man they trusted, and that the killer has made off with an heirloom sword, the household's one tangible link to its former glory, he sets off to seek revenge. As in most revenge fiction, however, he has few clues to go on: in this case, no more than a vague rumor that his enemy, an unemployed samurai named Todoroki Unpei, has absconded into the "broad country" (*hiroki kuni*) of Michinoku—the classical name for northern Honshu.[45] In the absence of further information, Hamon decides to settle in one location for the time being, in disguise, to see what he can uncover about his enemy's whereabouts.

The Michinoku in which Hamon finds himself is a complicated amalgam. It is constructed not only from the real geography of the region, but also through allusions to sites and lore made famous in classical *waka* poetry. The village that Hamon first lodges in, called Kyō (written with the characters for "narrow cloth" 狭布), is in fact not a real location at all, but an imaginary space derived from a *waka* trope. In the Nara and Heian periods, the word *kyō* had referred to a white hempen cloth of narrow width that was submitted to the capital as tax from Michinoku. The cloth came to figure as a motif in *waka* poetry for its homophony with "today" (*kyō*) and for the idea that the narrow fabric's ends would not meet if someone tried to make it into a garment, which enabled wordplay on the futility of meeting. A poem by Nōin (Tachibana no Nagayasu, b. 988), anthologized in the *Goshūi wakashū* (*Later Collection of Poetic Gleanings*, 1086), served to establish the latter trope:

> *Nishikigi wa tatenagara koso kuchinikere kyō no hosonuno mune awaji to ya.*
> My brocade staffs, just where I stood them, have rotted away. The ends of the slender cloth called *kyō* cannot meet across the breast—will we not meet, either?[46]

The poem draws on another *waka* trope derived from the ancient culture of Michinoku. Local youths were said to set a "brocade staff"—a stick, about one foot long and decorated with five colors—before the doors of the young women they courted. If the woman took in the staff, it signaled her acceptance of the young man; but if the man planted one thousand staffs before her door and none was accepted, it meant he must abandon his pursuit. Nōin's poem inspired many more on brocade staffs and the "slender cloth called *kyō*." But at some point, this construction came to be understood as the "slender cloth *from* Kyō," with Kyō now taken as a place-name. It is in this completely fictional village, fashioned from the centuries-long transformation of the semantics of a *waka* expression—but where, we are told, the women still practice the antique craft of weaving narrow cloth—that Hamon rents a house and keeps his ears open for word of his enemy. And the environs of Kyō, too, are constructed largely from poetic references. Various sites mentioned as "close" to Kyō in fact reach from present-day Aomori, at the northern tip of Honshu, down to present-day Fukushima, the traditional "gateway" to Michinoku at its southern end. This is the Michinoku of such classical poetic sites as Asaka Marsh, Mount Shinobu, the bogwood (*umoregi*) of the Natori River, and the "brocade staff mound" (*nishikigi zuka*) of Kominato: less a differentiated assortment of geographic locales than one great poetic space.

Yet we can perceive a different Michinoku coexisting with this poetic landscape. The wealthiest man in Kyō, for example, is a merchant who trades in the specialized products of the region, through the "nearby" port of Aomori. His goods include elegant products such as "Shinobu print silk" (*Shinobuzuri no kinu*)—long famous from its role in the opening narrative of the *Tales of Ise* (*Ise monogatari*, ca. ninth–tenth centuries)—and other items that possess the patina of classical culture, including, of course, narrow cloth. But he also sells such items as pongee (*tsumugi*) and Michinoku paper (*Michinokugami*), still very much actively traded goods in the late Edo period. Some of the merchandise, like ten-strand sedge mats (*tofu no sugagomo*), had once been presented to the central court as tax payment from the region; Bashō, in *The Narrow Road to the Interior*, notes that the mats remain so.[47] But the emphasis here is less on ancient taxation than on modern business. The description of the merchant's trade serves to evoke the far north as a site of commerce, its goods (exotic or elegant though they may be) bound into the modern economy of the realm through the connection points of ports and the circulation of capital.

Far more striking in this sense is the depiction of the denizens of the region, who are constructed from yet another register of northern references. Kyōden depicts the young men of the area as "crude roughs of frightening disposition, with hair on their heads that could be mistaken for minced *konbu*, beards that look like masks made of otter skin, and eyes that gaze like fur seals: a bunch as fierce as Ezo eagles."[48] None of the products or creatures referenced in these lines can be found in the elegant vocabulary of the poetic classics. Instead, the text crafts the bodies of these Michinoku men from commodities—specifically, commodities from still farther north, from Ezo—that traveled through northern Honshu to reach Edo and points farther south. With the development of the Wajinchi in Ezo and the establishment of regular shipping routes, *konbu* seaweed, which thrived in the frigid waters off Ezo's shores, had increasingly become part of the Japanese diet, while the more exotic pelts and feathers were prominent in high-level trade exchanges between the Ainu and the Japanese authorities.[49]

Not only do the exotic bodies of these men not fit into the elegant landscape of poetic Michinoku, but they mark the men as Other in complicated—and possibly conflicted—ways. The *ka-i* worldview presumed that the model human body was that of the civilized center, and that (possibly monstrous) bodily difference from the norm would become more prevalent the farther one moved into the periphery. The hybrid nature of the northern men's bodies, which seem to be a mix of the human and the animal, accord with that tradition, serving as a register of the civilizational distance that Hamon has traveled from the heartland of the realm. But something is different. When the warrior Yoshitsune, for example, encounters human-animal hybrids among the strange bodies of the far north in the late medieval tale "Yoshitsune Crosses the Isles," the moral lesson written into their bodies is perfectly legible. In a manuscript version of the tale that dates to the mid-seventeenth century, a race of half-horse, half-human people explains their origin to Yoshitsune: "A human and a horse made love and were exiled to this island from Japan, and since neither the form of the human nor the shape of the horse died out [in their offspring], this place is called Horse-Man Island (*mumahito shima*)."[50] A bestial transgression and an exile from the center: in their physical difference, the horse-men serve to instantiate both the physical and the moral norms of Yoshitsune's civilized homeland. But the men whom Hamon encounters are not true hybrids: their bodies *resemble* those of animals—and, with their beards, the "barbarian" Ainu as well—but they remain, unquestionably, human. The fact that they are likened to goods consumed in the center, moreover, differentiates them from deviants who had sex with sea otters.

The ambiguity of bodily difference and consumption is one we will return to, for it intensifies in the latter half of *The Asaka Marsh*. But when Hamon first meets these men, the emphasis remains one of difference, for Hamon's body has been characterized from the outset as a pinnacle of perfection. We first encounter him at the narrative's opening, in fact, as pure bodily form: a portrait of a beautiful young man (*bishōnen*), painted by the famed artist Hishikawa Moronobu (d. 1694) with such exquisite care that his visage seems to "mock jewels and make flowers ashamed."[51] This painting of Hamon is so attractive that the daughter of the man who purchases it falls in love with the image and begins to waste away; only when her father, fearing for her life, tracks down the painting's model do we first meet Hamon as a character. The contrast between this exquisitely beautiful young man and the animal-like young men of Michinoku quickly descends into a relationship of antagonism and violence, but the terms on which it does so have much to do with the contrast between Michinoku as an outland of cultural difference, on the one hand, and as a classically integral poetic space, on the other.

The source of trouble between Hamon and the local men is a woman: O-Aki, the daughter of the village's wealthy merchant trader. O-Aki is physically situated within the northern outland, but culturally, she is a young woman of the Japanese cultural heartland:

> Already sixteen years old, she was a rarity for one born in the countryside: the elegance of her appearance was like a pear blossom washed

with rain, like a pearl imbued with fragrance. What was more, she wrote a flawless hand and had also given her heart to some study of poetry. Because her mother was originally from the capital, she had some memory of such niceties, and had trained her daughter, including having her learn the language of the capital, so that O-Aki's voice bore no trace of the accent of the provinces, but resembled instead the beautiful cry of a warbler [*uguisu*].[52]

So deeply steeped is O-Aki in the culture of the center that she even speaks in Kyoto dialect, the idiom of the classical locus of elite Japanese culture, and her voice resembles that of the most celebrated songbird of classical poetry. A "warbler" among "Ezo eagles," she is desired by the rough youths of her village but disdains them. When Hamon moves in next door, however, she is instantly captivated by the sight of such a "beautiful man" (*binan*). From her second-floor window, she watches him engage in his favorite pastime of reading, and she swoons at his elegance and sophistication. When she falls in love with him, her love is mediated by the tropes of classical Michinoku. The narration slips into elegant wordplay, as in the following sentence, which in the Japanese weaves in puns on Michinoku, Mount Shinobu, Iwate, and Ezo, and makes a reference to the Courtyard Stele (Tsubo no ishibumi), another famous northern *utamakura*: "Her thoughts of him **filled** [*michinoku*] her breast, but because she kept them **secret** [*shinobu*] and **spoke them not** [*iwade*], there was **no way** for him to know [*e zo shiranu*]. Even if it took a letter as wordy as the Courtyard Stele, she longed to convey to him even a hint of what was in her heart."[53] She sends Hamon letters, one thousand of them, like the brocade staffs of yore; but Hamon, intent on his revenge, ignores these advances from a local woman, and the narrator likens the letters to the hidden bogwood of the Abukuma River—another *utamakura*. The text continues to evoke the turmoil of O-Aki's subjective state through wordplay that incorporates poetic references to Mount Iwate, the Broken Thread Bridge (Odae no hashi), and the far northern sea (Oku no umi).

Her attempts unavailing, O-Aki, heartsick, finally determines to end her life; but she manages to throw one final letter—inscribed in blood on Shinobu print silk—through Hamon's window. Reading it at last, Hamon is startled to discover that the writer is as sophisticated as he. O-Aki pours out her heart, again in Michinoku-specific imagery, and concludes with the famous Mount Asaka poem:

Asakayama kage sae miyuru yamanoi no asaki kokoro o waga omowanaku ni.
Mount Asaka: its reflection clear in the shallow heart of the
   mountain spring. Not shallow at all are my own heart's thoughts
   of you.

Hamon recounts the *Man'yōshū*'s report of the circumstances of the poem's inscription—the expression of love by a local woman of courtly elegance to a Japanese prince journeying through the northern outland—and deduces the messages O-Aki implies with the medium and the poem. The choice of Shinobu silk suggests the feelings that O-Aki has been struggling to bear (*shinobu*) in her heart, and the phrase *yamanoi no asaki* hints at "Yamanoi no Aki:" "Aki who belongs to Yamanoi Hamon." Hamon is smitten: "I had heard that it is rare even to meet a person who can read *kana* in this area, where there are places that rely upon calendars with pictures in place of words. What a rare depth of heart for a person of the rustic wilds!"[54] Deeply moved, he and O-Aki begin a secret affair.

In this way, through the skillful arrangement of forms borrowed from literature and life, the text seems to establish two versions of northern Honshu that appear to be layered on each other; but the classical, poetic version is perceptible only to those who partake in some way of the civilized culture of the center, whether by birth (Hamon) or by upbringing (O-Aki). For these initiates, the local landscape and its poetic legacy become a shared medium through which they can establish a relationship with each other. It is telling that Kyōden depicts O-Aki's (and later, Hamon's) subjective state in the language of poetic allusions and *utamakura*, which suggests that classical Michinoku is as much a state of mind, or a civilized lens through which to apprehend one person's inner geography and to access the subjective experience of another, as it is a geography locatable on a map.

Conversely, a lack of sensitivity to the classical landscape reveals a defect of character—or worse: for those most blind to the landscape evince the greatest proclivity for illicit violence. This point holds true even for those who hail from the center, as does Adachi Sakurō, a native of Edo and one of the narrative's villains. The younger brother of Todoroki Unpei, the *rōnin* who murdered Hamon's family, Sakurō himself is intent on murder when he enters Michinoku; he is looking to kill his lover's husband, a struggling kabuki actor who is on a provincial tour in the north. Sakurō rushes into the northland with nothing but murder on his mind: "He traveled alone through night and day. Unfeeling as he was, he looked upon the

Wanderer's Willow and the pure waters by the roadside without interest, and he crossed the Shirakawa Barrier and the Abukuma River without sparing a thought. Not shrinking from traveling at night, he passed the Ghostly Jizō [Bake Jizō] of the Odagawa post town and soon approached Husband-and-Wife Slope [Fūfu-zaka]."[55]

The "pure waters" and "Wanderer's Willow" find their origin in a poem by the poet-monk Saigyō (1118–1190):

> Michinobe ni shimizu nagaruru yanagikage shibashi tote koso tachidomaritsure.
> By the roadside, where the pure waters flow, in the shade of a willow I thought to rest for only a moment; but I ended up lingering.[56]

This willow entered into literary legend, and it became associated with a particular willow along the main highway into the north.[57] Bashō stops there in *The Narrow Road to the Interior*, just before reaching the Shirakawa Barrier, and composes this *hokku*:

> Ta ichimai uete tachisaru yanagi kana.
> A full paddy of rice planted before I take my leave of the willow tree.[58]

The willow thus came to represent not just space—a marker, like the Shirakawa Barrier, of entry to the northern reaches—but time: a departure from the rush of the civilizational center and an adjustment to more archaic and agricultural, but also introspective, rhythms. The willow's shade captures the poet and holds him in the landscape until he loses himself in it and loses his sense of time's passage. When the unfeeling (*kokoronak[i]* [literally, "heartless"]) Sakurō rushes past the willow (and the Shirakawa Barrier and the Abukuma River) without sparing a thought, his lack of receptiveness to their power points to a deficit in his character, one that keeps his heart closed and permits him to kill in cold blood. Whereas the poetic northern landscape becomes an affective bridge that helps Hamon to see O-Aki and her suffering and draws him close to her, Sakurō speeds right past landscape features—Husband-and-Wife Slope and the Ghostly Jizō—that foreshadow his own fate: for the husband he seeks to murder will later become a ghost and bring Sakurō's own life to a ghastly end.

Classical Michinoku remains invisible to the locals—specifically, the *konbu*-haired young men of Kyō—even though they live their lives within the storied landscape of northern Honshu. As a result, their character resembles that of Sakurō. Blind to the poetic landscape around them, they lack any common ground on which to establish a positive relationship with Hamon. Instead, their stance toward him remains purely antagonistic. When O-Aki is later found raped and murdered in her own bedroom, the local men, aware of Hamon's secret relationship with her, see an opportunity to take revenge against the interloper. They cook up a story to frame Hamon and gleefully urge the local shogunal deputy (*daikan*) to use torture to force the truth out of him before punishing him. The deputy, however, is (quite literally) a figure of the center: a representative of the central government. Like recognizes like. The deputy reflects: "Looking over Hamon, his appearance is beautiful [*katachi bi ni shite*)], and by birth he possesses a gentle character. I see no sign that he could have murdered someone."[59] The deputy ensnares the real killer—a local mendicant—and lets Hamon go free; he has those who framed Hamon beaten and banished from the district. When the men ambush and attempt to kill Hamon at night on his way out of Kyō, he defeats them with ease, tossing them off a bridge and into the raging torrent below. The murder of the cultured and beautiful O-Aki is treated as a major crime. But the narrator emphasizes that the local men, violent and subhuman, are lamented by no one; no deputy will concoct a scheme to locate their killer. They are disposable, like the very commodities they resemble.

While the antagonism between Hamon and the youths of Kyō seems to exemplify the classic geographic consciousness that distinguished the civilized center from the barbarian periphery, however, the Michinoku of this portion of the narrative ultimately resists easy categorization. Viewed in terms of the rich layers of archaic poetic association with which Hamon and O-Aki engage, it seems coextensive with the Japanese cultural heartland; but this aspect of it rests uneasily with its simultaneous characterization as a site of murder and aggression, of exotic commerce, and of not-quite-human bodies. Indeed, the allusions to the market and to the circulation of goods implicitly complicate the idea of static civilizational boundaries. Readers in Edo could find on their own dinner trays (and in their own bellies) the minced *konbu* that the narrator likens to the youths' hair; the otter skins, seal pelts, and eagle feathers invoked to characterize their rough frontier bodies were also to be found in the shogun's capital—as luxury goods, in the clothing and quivers of the ruling samurai themselves. It is no coincidence that O-Aki, living in a Kyoto-esque bubble deep in the heart of Michinoku, is the daughter of a merchant. The flows of commerce jumble the signs of center and frontier, rendering dividing lines more porous and supple than they may appear on the surface. The antagonism between Hamon and the wild locals may be a stark one, but the treatment of the space of Michinoku itself—simultaneously of and not of the center, a site of transit and exchange between wilder Ezo and the realm's ancient heartlands—implicitly calls into question where and how borders are to be drawn: a question that comes grotesquely to the fore in the latter half of *The Asaka Marsh*.

Bad Medicine and the Body Politic

The second part of Hamon's quest further muddies any facile dichotomies of center and periphery, even as it increasingly foregrounds northern Honshu as a frontier where a recognizably Japanese cultural space shades into realms of civilizational and spatial otherness: parts of a larger world. It has now been three years since Hamon set off in search of his family's killer, and he is running low on funds, when he receives a fortunate invitation. A doctor named Makita Honchū has earned a reputation for remarkable skill in healing even the most extraordinary medical afflictions using special, expensive, secret medicines. Only the richest can afford his high prices, which must be paid in advance of treatment, but the medicines are so effective that Honchū's practice flourishes and he has grown quite wealthy. He has built for himself a secluded mansion—beautiful and highly fortified—facing the ocean, at the base of a sheer cliff in a remote place called Ojikayama. Catching word that Hamon is a skilled painter, Honchū commissions him to stay with him at the mansion and adorn its walls with paintings.

Ojikayama, unlike Kyō, is a real place. Known properly as the Ogayama or Oga Peninsula—though really a set of mountainous islands joined to one another and to Honshu by sandbars—its rocky shores and steep sea cliffs jut out into the Sea of Japan from the coast of present-day Akita Prefecture.[60] Kyōden's description of the site is lifted, nearly verbatim, from the description of the area in *Journey to the East*, the aforementioned, immensely popular travel account written by the Confucian scholar, poet, and innovative physician Tachibana Nankei.[61] As part of his medical studies, he had traveled through northern Honshu; *Journey to the East*, his somewhat embroidered narrative about various places he had visited, emphasizes accounts of the strange.[62] The entry on Ogayama in *Journey to the East* is titled "The So Bu Shrine." So Bu is the Japanese reading of Su Wu (ca. 140–60 BCE), the famous Han dynasty minister said to have spent nineteen years in exile among the Xiongnu, the nomadic northerly antagonists of the Han. In legend, Su Wu remained faithful to his homeland even as he married a Xiongnu woman and took up the nomads' shepherding lifestyle, ultimately abandoning his wife and children when the opportunity arose to return home. Nankei explains, in language directly plagiarized by Kyōden in *The Asaka Marsh*, that atop Mount Sekishin on the Ogayama Peninsula sit five shrines; one is dedicated to the Han emperor Wu (156–87 BCE), one to Su Wu, and the other three to native Japanese gods. The reason given for the presence of shrines to the Chinese statesman and his emperor is that the mainland across the Sea of Japan from the site corresponds to the old Xiongnu lands, and Ogayama is said to be the actual location of Su Wu's exile. Nankei dismisses this as impossible, but he concedes that the exotic geography and climate of the area certainly have the *feel* of the Xiongnu frontier. Kyōden's narrator, however, simply lets the assertion stand, underscoring the sense of the peninsula as a site simultaneously within and beyond the bounds of the realm, a liminal space halfway between the native and the foreign, a Japanese frontier that is also somehow a Chinese frontier—quite different from the poetically inflected Kyō.[63] This in-between quality is reflected in the geography itself; though attached to the mainland, when viewed from afar the peninsula looks, both texts state, like a separate island. Its terrain is so forbidding, in fact, that to access it one must cross by boat, as though leaving Honshu behind.

Hamon does so, in a skiff rowed by one of Honchū's servants on a beautifully calm day. As he looks about, taking in the splendid view, an osprey flying over drops something into the boat. Hamon is startled to discover that it is a clump of human hair, with the flesh of the scalp still attached. The servant laughs and reassures him: there was a recent drowning; no doubt, the osprey discovered the corpse and mistook its flesh for fish. After this unsettling crossing, Hamon arrives at Honchū's spectacular, isolated mansion, where the physician welcomes and entertains him and has him produce paintings to decorate the manor. Even once the work is finished, however, Honchū insists that he stay longer, and Hamon, unable to say no, remains for a few days. Soon it is the night of the early-autumn full moon, and Hamon sets out on a midnight walk. He wanders about the garden, but then notices, in an obscure corner, a little gate that happens to be open. A long, winding path finally leads him to a promontory from which he takes in an awe-inspiring vista of the moon, craggy cliffs, and the wild ocean. The prose style turns heavily Sinified, underscoring the foreign feel of the landscape, but Hamon muses that it compares favorably with Matsushima and Kisakata, other famous northern coastlines celebrated as *utamakura* in *waka* poetry. Just then, however, a putrid stink assaults his nose, and he hears the cries of human beings, as faint and plaintive as the hum of a mosquito. Uneasy, he follows the trail farther until he discovers a hut in a thick cluster of trees. He peers through a window:

> In an earthen-floored room were more than ten people arranged in a row, their necks and feet bound in stocks and fetters. Wondering if this was some kind of prison, he looked closer and saw that they were men, women, and small children, all mixed together, and all of them missing parts of their bodies. Some had had their ears or noses sliced off, their eyes gouged out, or their tongues removed. Others had had their fingers and toes chopped off. All seemed half-dead and half-alive, and the cries they raised in their unbearable suffering were deeply pitiable. Off to one side, white bones were stacked in a pile, and hunks of cut flesh were scattered about. There were women with bellies ripped open, and the skinned bodies of young children. Six or seven pairs of human thighs hung from the rafters, and ripped-out organs and bowels had been piled up on a block. Fresh blood flowed like a shallow river, and the stench that assailed Hamon's nose was difficult to bear. Even bold Hamon, looking at the scene, felt his hair stand on end.[64]

Feeling as though he has walked straight into the depths of hell, Hamon attempts to calm himself. He asks the people who they are and why they are being made to suffer such hideous punishment. One replies:

> All of us have been kidnapped from distant provinces. We were procured for that villainous doctor Honchū, and made to suffer like this so that we can be turned into medicine. He brings his closest followers here and has them butcher us for the parts he wishes to use. Others

and those working in his household know nothing of this. That's why he has chosen a place so distant from the world to live. A foreign barbarian [*banjin*] once gave him a book of secret methods. All human physical ailments can be miraculously treated by using the same body parts of other people.[65]

Honchū has his victims kidnapped, we learn, because for the medicines to work, the bodies from which they are made must be perfect. His henchmen, therefore, scour the realm, seeking attractive, healthy victims who will be good matches for his ailing, wealthy patients. That is why the doctor has pressed Hamon to stay: he plans to make use of his beautiful body for his nefarious purposes.

In the vicinity of Kyō, we saw local inhabitants of the frontier who physically resembled the exotic commodities being traded from the periphery into the center. The implications of this scene, however, are more complex. Recall that northern Honshu and Ezo—with their climate, flora, and fauna so different from those of the central provinces—had become the object of medicinal investigation in the early modern period. Ezo, in particular, became a site of tremendous interest by the shogunal authorities in the island's materia medica, which, in a grotesque twist of fate, became more visible to the Japanese as the Ainu used native pharmaceuticals to try to stave off pathogens introduced by Japanese traders and settlers.[66] Kyōden takes that association of the northern frontier with powerful, exotic pharmaceuticals and transforms it into a platform for a darkly grotesque commentary not only on the culture—and health—of the Japanese heartland, but even on the interconnected ways in which the Japanese realm cohered into a whole, separate from foreign otherness. The evil physician is revealed to have sought out an ambiguous outland, a site attached to and yet somehow separate from the mainland, not for its proximity to exotic medicines, but because there he can hide from his patients and the authorities the true nature of his dark healing arts. The "medicines" ultimately originate not from the frontier, but from the heartland itself, and they are made not from herbs and animals, but from humans—specifically, the weak and defenseless, who are unwittingly preyed on by the wealthy and powerful. During the horrific Great Tenmei Famine, there had been rumors of cannibalism in northern Honshu, and Kyōden possibly draws on that association to underscore the horror of this climax.[67] But he reverses the power dynamic: in *The Asaka Marsh*, it is not the starving but the well-fed who are the cannibals—a daring depiction at a moment when disparities of wealth and poverty had grown more severe, leading to greater social unrest from the late eighteenth century and to the imposition of strict social and economic reforms in the century's last decade.

The doctor's obsession with perfect bodies, meanwhile, inserts an unsettling twist into the earlier celebration of Hamon's ideal attractiveness, which had marked his cultural and moral superiority in the eyes of the shogunal deputy in Kyō. Now it is not difference that threatens, but sameness: to possess body parts that resemble those of other Japanese—or that exemplify, indeed, the perfect Japanese body—marks one as a target. And the image of kidnappers circulating throughout the realm, identifying similar bodies and snatching them up to be processed in the hinterland and reintroduced to the center as grim commodities, posits not only a chilling vision of economic circulation, but a negative inversion of protonational social cohesion. In this view, "Japan" coheres as a realm where sameness can be found among bodies inhabiting even distant geographic corners; the occult connections of identity are there, even if they remain invisible to most eyes.

In yet another twist, the novel brings this unsettling sameness to the fore by invoking a highly ambiguous foreignness. The claim that Honchū learned his devious medicinal arts from a "foreign barbarian" points to yet another kind of frontier and another kind of commodity—scientific information—on which Kyōden draws here. Kyōden was fascinated by the field of Dutch studies (*Rangaku*).[68] Scholars of Dutch studies attempted to learn the Dutch language in order to read the Dutch books—specifically, scientific and medical books—brought into Japan through the port of Nagasaki, with the primary aim of learning Western medicine. One of the Dutch studies scholars' most monumental accomplishments had been the publication, in 1774, of the *New Book of Anatomy* (*Kaitai shinsho*), a translation into Japanese of the Dutch book *Ontleedkundige Tafelen*, which was itself a translation of a German book of human anatomy. A quick glance through the pages of the *New Book of Anatomy* reveals depictions of the human body that are echoed in the description of the miserable victims in Honchū's hut of horrors: severed and dissected body parts, gouged-out eyes, peeled-away skin, exposed viscera. This is not the only instance of Kyōden drawing on the treatment of the human body in Western science to macabre effect. The Dutch studies scholars who produced the *New Book of Anatomy* are said to have been convinced of the Dutch book's value when they conducted the dissection of the corpse of a recently executed woman at the execution ground at Kozukappara in Edo in 1771 and discovered that the representations in the book were strikingly accurate.[69] We find this scene grotesquely reimagined in one of the illustrations in Kyōden's *yomihon An Old Tale with a Thunderbolt Cover* (*Mukashigatari inazuma byōshi*, 1806). And that work's sequel, *Complete Biographies of the Drunken Bodhisattvas of Our Realm* (*Honchō suibodai zenden*, 1809), features a clever frontispiece of an attractive young woman. The image is printed on a semiattached piece of paper, which, when lifted, reveals beneath it the woman's skeleton. The skeleton is a direct copy of the illustration of a child's skeleton in the *New Book of Anatomy*.[70]

Even as Kyōden's hut of horrors highlights the negative sameness of Japanese bodies, his employment of imagery from the *New Book of Anatomy* in the scene complicates that sameness and further muddies the lines of early modern Japan's "ragged edges." The dissected bodies that Kyōden observed in the anatomy book's pages and transformed into the hacked-apart bodies of the victims in *The Asaka Marsh* were originally European; imported within the pages of books at the port of Nagasaki and visually translated into Japanese bodies in the *New Book of Anatomy*, they too circulated throughout the realm as intellectual commodities, intimately linked to the science of healing. And yet the anatomy book reveals that when the skin is pulled aside and the bones and viscera are revealed, there is ultimately little to differentiate a European body from a Japanese body, or from any other human body. Honchū's kidnapping operation may point to the likeness to be found among Japanese bodies throughout the realm, but the scene of the result of the dismemberment of those bodies—and the apparent influence of the *New Book of Anatomy* on that depiction—suggests the uncanny foreign likeness hiding just beneath the skin of any Japanese body. The description of the hut of horrors not only affords a dark commentary on the dysfunctional disparities of the Japanese heartland, where the wealthy few prosper by (wittingly or otherwise) preying on the struggling victims of a volatile economy and an ineffectual administration, but also, ultimately, undercuts any reassurance that the idea of a boundary may offer, by suggesting a vision of amorphous borders and bridges: between civilization and barbarity, center and periphery, familiar and foreign, and ultimately—in the exchange of body parts and the consumption of bodies by other bodies—between Self and Other.

Conclusion

Late *yomihon* have been regarded as one of the last premodern genres of Japanese fiction. When Tsubouchi Shōyō wrote *The Essence of the Novel*, celebrated as the first theorization of a modern Japanese novel grounded in European conceptions of emotional realism, he explicitly defined the genre against the example of *yomihon*, which—with their rigid moral framework, fantastic elements, and modular structure—appeared to be antithetical to his new model of a proper national literature.[71] And, indeed, aspects of *The Asaka Marsh* fit Shōyō's characterization. Hamon serendipitously discovers his fiancée among the kidnap victims in the butchery hut and rescues her; he locates his family's murderer among Honchū's henchmen and takes his revenge with his family's heirloom sword, which he retrieves from the killer's possession. The doctor is captured and punished. The hero and heroine marry and flourish. The various modular threads of the *yomihon* framework coalesce in a fantastic climax of virtue triumphant and vice punished.

And yet to write off *The Asaka Marsh* as an entertaining, formulaic hodge-podge is to miss both its critical bite and the sophistication with which it probes the relationship among the Japanese heartland, the realm's "ragged edges," and the world of difference beyond. As I have suggested, it is possible to read *The Asaka Marsh* itself as a protonational work: one that responds to the late eighteenth-century moment of threat from abroad by questioning what holds together the Japanese realm internally, as a geography and a culture apart from others. What emerges is a vision of Japan that pulls simultaneously in two directions: inward, to a portrayal of the realm as (disturbingly) interconnected; and outward, to a sense that an embrace of strict boundaries—cultural or geographic—will provide little protection against dangers that threaten the polity from within.

The modularity and formulas of the *yomihon* framework are crucial to this questioning. Indeed, the text's disturbing vision emerges precisely from within its premodern mode of storytelling, which remixes and mashes up preexisting forms—some of archaic standing—in novel ways. By juxtaposing well-established poetic tropes with allusions to modern commodities and visions of bodily difference, the text foregrounds the messy dialectic of classical elegance, contemporary backwardness, and flowing commerce that defined the Japanese heartland's relationship to its peripheries. And by integrating ancient Chinese legends with local geography and the forms of foreign anatomical science, the text turns the sense of threat from beyond the seas to one emerging from the polity's diseased heart. The structure of dispersed elements that uncannily intersect and reconnect across the temporal and spatial unfolding of the plot, also posited by the *yomihon* framework, evokes the sense of a community held together—for better or worse—by invisible threads. *The Asaka Marsh* has been criticized for the poor integration of its two major plotlines—Hamon's proper revenge quest, and the ghostly revenge of a murdered kabuki actor—but the way the storylines repeatedly brush up against and exert an invisible force on each other underscores this sense of a shared community that is more than the sum of its parts, one in which an individual's fate may be sent askew by the interconnected fates of other people.[72] And the ghost plot serves to remind us as well that no point within the realm is separate from the influence of other points, near or far. The actor's antagonist brutally drowns him in the shallow waters of the Asaka Marsh, deep in the northern hinterland; but when his ghost wreaks its revenge, it re-inflicts every form of pain that was inflicted on his body in life, down to the slightest detail, in the very heart of the shogun's sprawling capital. The murderer ultimately drowns in Shinobazu Pond, one of Edo's most famous bodies of water, on the grounds of the funeral temple of the shogunal house, a stone's throw from the shogunal graves. As in a double exposure, this urban geography of power appears to meld uncannily with the landscape of the hinterland, linked each to each by a thread of violence.

If there is one thread that holds together the entire work, however, it is the motif of sickness. The portrait of the beautiful Hamon casts the young woman who gazes on it into a state of life-threatening love sickness. Hamon's upright, impoverished samurai family is devastated when illness strikes, causing them to take extreme measures to procure medicine that they cannot afford and thus allowing the *rōnin* who will ultimately take their lives to begin preying on them. And, of course, Honchū's dissection hut brings the theme of sickness to a horrifying climax. But the motif of illness first shows up in the preface, in which Kyōden, in a register that cleverly mimics vernacular Chinese, offers a firsthand account of the book's inception: "In the Fifth Month of the Monkey year of the Kansei era, I, Kyōden, suffering from a slight affliction, donned my woven sandals and straw traveling cloak and went alone to take the waters of the hot springs at Atami."[73] While recuperating at the hot springs, he encounters an elegant female guest, a prodigious reader, who delights in discussing books with him. She ultimately deduces his identity as the famous writer Santō Kyōden, however, and begins to chastise him for his unserious style of writing. She charges him with caring only for making an empty name for himself, for wasting paper and ink with useless books, and for neglecting the truth that books lacking in practical value invite disaster. In language that equates him with a doctor and his writing with medicine, she accuses him: "You understand the medical treatment of only small afflictions; you do not know how to treat great afflictions."[74] Invoking the power of language to effect change and the capacity of writing to instruct and edify, she admonishes him to take his writing seriously and to produce a work that will be of genuine benefit to others. Ashamed, Kyōden promises to follow her advice. *The Asaka Marsh*, he explains, is the result.

The scene is almost certainly fictional, but Kyōden presents it at his book's outset to signal the seriousness of his new approach to *yomihon*. It is possible to read the woman's admonishments as pointing to the didactic and moralizing elements that modern critics would later highlight as signs of late *yomihon*'s feudal premodernity—and therefore, ironically, as an indication of its unworthiness to be taken seriously. But the preface's invocation of the language of sickness, and the complex ways in which the theme resurfaces in the book to evoke a disturbing vision of a society preying on itself, suggests the importance of returning to the *yomihon* genre with fresh eyes, reappraising the import of its formal system, and weighing the work it performed in offering a coherent, critical vision of "Japan" that was more than a reification. In *The Asaka Marsh*, Kyōden points to the power of fiction to do more than entertain or edify: he suggests that it can help diagnose the affliction gnawing at the heart of the body politic.

Epilogue

Forms in Context, Forms Beyond Context

Among the portraits of warriors in Tsukioka Yoshitoshi's (1839–1892) print series *One Hundred Selected Portraits of Those Who Dash Ahead* (*Kaidai hyakusensō*, 1868–1869), produced in the first years of the Meiji period, there is one that always makes me catch my breath. It is a portrait of Komagine Hachibyōe (d. 1638?), a legendary marksman, framed against a plain dark background.[1] He is a samurai; his two swords, sheathed, are tucked into his obi at his side. But his real weapon, held cocked and ready to fire, is a gun. His entire form concentrates around the weapon's barrel as he steadies it. His shoulders hunch; he holds his arms close to his body and the barrel level with his eyes. A bandana keeps back his hair, though a few locks peek out, antic in the wind. His face is still. His brows furrow; he bites his lower lip as he takes aim with piercing, concentrated eyes. The eyes, like the gun's barrel, aim directly at us. We are his target.

That weapon and those eyes followed me throughout the writing of this book. They seem to emblematize the questions I was trying to answer. How seriously should we take the claims made on us by early modern works? How should we understand the relationship between what is on the page and what was in the world beyond it? How should we tease out meanings from early modern forms? How should we make sense of the violence that is so prominent in the early modern arts? Staring down the barrel of Hachibyōe's flintlock, pointed out of his world and into mine, made me feel the urgency of answering these questions.

Figure 6.1 "Komagine Hachibyōe," from Tsukioka Yoshitoshi's woodblock print series *One Hundred Selected Portraits of Those Who Dash Ahead* (*Kaidai hyakusensō*, 1868–1869)
Source: National Diet Library Digital Collections

A close examination of Hachibyōe's portrait can encapsulate the answers I posit to these questions throughout *Writing Violence*. But our attention to the reception history of the series in which this print appears can also point us to a new question, one beyond the immediate scope of this book but no less crucial to the study of early modern forms: What becomes of those forms when they move beyond the cultural context that initially gave them meaning?

Throughout this book I have argued for the importance of taking early modern forms seriously, including—indeed, *above all*—those aspects that appear modular, derivative, or formulaic. For it is in the variations introduced into familiar formal units, I believe, that new perceptual possibilities become available, enabling different voices to be heard, altering long-standing assumptions, opening up alternative understandings of the constitution of the world, and even remaking the shape of time and space. In the preceding pages, we have witnessed the capacity of sometimes banal forms—stock characters, conventionalized plots, rehashed tropes, calendrical boilerplate—to transform the significance of disaster, upend the moral guarantees of revenge proper, remix the import of adultery and its punishment, probe the relationship between truth and fiction, and evoke a terrifying vision of Japan as a self-consuming geo-body. The politics of early modern Japanese literature, I contend, inhere in such perceptual transformations.

And these dynamics extend beyond the commercial fiction I have largely focused on in this book. One can find them at play in the early modern visual arts as well. Indeed, arresting as the print of Hachibyōe is in its gestalt, a similar formal reading of its details can help us to unpack the politics of the marksman and his threatening firearm. For the print, like so many early modern works, is composed from an admixture of preexisting formal ingredients. It relies on the familiar early modern dynamic of doubleness, aligning some of those ingredients so that they can signify more than one thing at once. The doubling is there, already, in the title of the series: *Kaidai hyakusensō* 魁題百撰相. The characters' literal meaning, "One Hundred Selected Portraits of Those Who Dash Ahead," suggests the theme: portraits of dauntless Japanese warriors from the fourteenth through the early seventeenth century (some of the most volatile years in the archipelago's history).[2] But its first character also appears in one of Yoshitoshi's sobriquets, so we can also read it as "Yoshitoshi's One Hundred Selected Portraits." Or, reading the word *kaidai* homophonously, we get "One

Hundred Selected Portraits with Explanatory Notes"—another good descriptor of this series, in which each image is inscribed with a prose account of the warrior and his exploits. But if we read the entire title aloud, it sounds like "One Hundred Wars Within the Realm."[3] And this last reading indicates that the profiles in the series refer as much to Yoshitoshi's contemporary moment as to the past.

For warfare had returned to the archipelago. Multiple rebellions, riots, acts of violence against foreigners, and punitive bombardments by Western powers had gripped the country in the years following the arrival of American "black ships" in 1853 and the subsequent opening of the realm to the outside world. Even after the last shogun stepped down in 1867, conflict between those who remained loyal to the shogun and those who rallied around the figure of the emperor came to a head in the Boshin War (1868–1869). The country had not experienced fighting on such a scale since the early seventeenth century. This time, the violence reached even into the streets of Edo, Yoshitoshi's hometown. At the Battle of Ueno, fought in the city in 1868, a unit of shogunal loyalists called the Shōgitai (League to Demonstrate Righteousness) met their downfall at the hands of imperial troops from the western domains of Satsuma and Chōshū. Yoshitoshi's series began to appear two months later. According to his stepdaughter, he had run to the battlefield in the immediate aftermath of the violence, shirtless in the summer heat and carrying a lunchbox, to sketch directly from the corpses of the slain.[4] Carnage and gore mark many of the prints in *One Hundred Selected Portraits*. Blood drips from the mouths of warriors, coughed up or sipped from the severed necks of enemies. Impalings and eviscerations abound; guts tumble frothily from slit-open bellies.

In these images of gruesome death, a viewer could recognize the battlefield corpses, gibbeted heads, and other horrors of the world beyond their windows. But, true to early modern practice, the series is also deeply intertextual and rooted in earlier visual models. Yoshitoshi and his collaborators who composed the inscriptions drew on a wide range of texts in selecting and characterizing the historical figures.[5] The sources include war chronicles such as the *Taiheiki* (*Chronicle of Great Peace*, late fourteenth century), *The Naniwa War Record* (*Naniwa senki*, 1672), and *Jōzan's Talks on History* (*Jōzan kidan*, 1739). They relied as well on a series of books by the *senryū* poet Ryokutei Senryū (Mizutani Ryokutei, 1787–1858), starting with *Heroes: One Hundred Verses* (*Eiyū hyakushu*, 1844), that feature short biographies of eminent warriors accompanied by their most famous poems.[6]

And the formal style of *One Hundred Selected Portraits* builds on models from Yoshitoshi's teacher, Utagawa Kuniyoshi (1797–1861). The portraits' general structure—close-ups set against a dark background—derives from Kuniyoshi's depictions of warriors in the series *Portraits of Loyal Retainers* (*Seichū gishi shōzō*, 1852).[7] But Yoshitoshi incorporated into this model unusual angles in portraying its subjects' faces—the dead-on gaze, for example, of the marksman Hachibyōe. Here, too, he appears to have been inspired by a work of Kuniyoshi's: *True to Life: A Compendium of One Hundred Faces* (*Shōutsushi hyakumen sō*, 1841).[8] This book explores the human face in all its variety, particularly in moments of unusual expression (mid-sneeze; tongue stuck out for the doctor; reacting to a foul stench) and viewed from unaccustomed angles. Kuniyoshi, for example, depicted a man's head tilted straight up as a whirlwind snatches a clutch of papers into the air above him. Yoshitoshi reworked this pattern in his portrait of the warrior Shigeno (Sanada) Yozaemon (d. 1615), who was killed in the siege of Osaka Castle.[9] With a similarly sharp tilt of his head, Yozaemon gazes up—not at swirling papers, but at the fireball of a detonating bomb. Kuniyoshi created a playful typology of the human face in fleeting moments of quotidian life; Yoshitoshi reworked his master's conceits to evoke the psychic intensity and physical grotesquerie of battle.[10]

The artist left ample clues that encouraged viewers to discover in the prints not only the past, but also the present. Indeed, scholars agree that *One Hundred Selected Portraits* was intended as a grand *mitate* that depicts the antagonists of the Boshin War, with a particular emphasis on the Shōgitai and other doomed supporters of the shogunate. (One likeness, ostensibly portraying a sixteenth-century Ashikaga shogun, subtly evokes Tokugawa Yoshinobu [1837–1913, r. 1866–1867], the last Tokugawa shogun himself.) Some of the hints are obvious even to our eyes: the sixteenth-century generals, for example, who sport nineteenth-century brass-buttoned overcoats. Others are less evident. A print depicting the medieval Prince Moriyoshi (1308–1335) making his escape from the battlefield at Kasagiyama in 1331 offers little to suggest a modern warrior. But the Meiji-period novelist and critic Aeba Kōson (1855–1922) recalled the great popularity of this print among Edo viewers, who could recognize from clues in the inscription that they were to read this scene as Prince Kitashirakawa Yoshihisa (1847–1895), a leader of the Shōgitai, evading the victors at the Battle of Ueno: "Edoites one and all understood. Their tears welled up and they wailed aloud."[11]

So, too, does the portrait of Hachibyōe layer the present into the past, beginning with the inscription in the rectangular plaque that hovers just behind him:

> Komagine Hachibyōe. He allied himself with the local populace, holed up in a besieged castle, treated the western domains as enemy, and never once showed any cowardice. His acts may resemble those of a treasonous rebel, but his intent [*kokorozashi*] was to respond to the favor of his deceased lord and avenge an old hatred. He also acquired a remarkable skill with gunnery and could hit the target one hundred times out of one hundred without the slightest blunder. When already ensconced in the castle, he took aim at the commander of the enemy forces and killed him, earning a matchless reputation that has been passed down to later generations.[12]

Hachibyōe's actions at the "besieged castle" refer to his participation in the Shimabara Rebellion (1637–1638), when masterless samurai and disaffected peasants, including many Catholics, rebelled against the Matsukura clan in Kyushu in response to oppressive taxation policies and the persecution of Christians. The rebellion, which culminated in the siege of Hara Castle by 125,000 troops, marked the last major outbreak of warfare under the Tokugawa until the turmoil of Yoshitoshi's day. Correspondences between the 1630s and the 1860s abounded: a rebellion against the shogunate, the crucial role of firearms, and the involvement of foreigners. American, French, British, and Dutch ships bombarded various Japanese targets during the 1860s, just as a Dutch ship had shelled Hara Castle in 1638 at the shogunate's request. A contemporary viewer, reading that Hachibyōe had "allied himself with the local populace, holed up in a besieged castle, [and] treated the western domains as enemy," could identify not only the marksman of yore but a member of the Shōgitai, holed up in Kan'eiji Temple on Ueno Hill, defending the populace of Edo from the imperial forces from the western domains of Satsuma and Chōshū.

In this way, the conflagration that marked the beginning of the Tokugawa Great Peace and the violence that was now bringing that peace to an end are formally melded in one image. The result is a transformed perception of time and of history. We saw in chapter 1 that the early modern conception of time had flattened out the medieval entanglement of past, present, and future. It weakened the primacy of the past and emphasized an eternal present that would stretch into an unchanging future: a model promoted in Tokugawa ideology, which foregrounded the everlastingness of a peaceful reign. Through its formal double exposure, the portrait of Komagine Hachibyōe bends this model of time. It pegs the present back into the past and curtails the ageless future. Together with the images in the rest of the series, it reveals history as a process of repetition with variations. Sugawara Mayumi has noted that a sizable subset of the prints in *One Hundred Selected Portraits* depict figures who were involved in the warfare that accompanied the establishment and consolidation of the Tokugawa shogunate, including nine warriors who participated in the Battle of Sekigahara (1600) and twelve who were involved in the siege of Osaka Castle (1614–1615). The emphasis is on those who perished in that process, making the series a funereal "homage to the obliterated."[13] Here, those historical figures are formally fused with the Tokugawa loyalists who were falling on the contemporary battlefield. The erstwhile victors double as the latter-day victims. The Tokugawa merge with the likes of their old adversaries, the Toyotomi.[14] They become just one more instance in a history defined by a pattern of rises and falls. Between Hachibyōe and his modern shadow stretches a new historical consciousness of the Tokugawa Great Peace as an epoch with an end.

But the print's formal complexity does not end there, for Hachibyōe's unusual, direct gaze and his aimed weapon implicate the viewer in the new age just dawning. The marksman may target his firearm at an invisible enemy from the 1630s, but he trains it as well on whomever happens to gaze at the print. We may speculate about the effect of the print and its inscription on a viewer in 1868, the inaugural year of the new Meiji era: "His acts may resemble those of a treasonous rebel, but his intent was to respond to the favor of his deceased lord and avenge an old hatred." In a moment of blurred lines between friend and foe, hero and villain, loyalist and traitor, the print proffers an ironic promise of moral legibility, portraying Hachibyōe the rebel as an exemplar who lived up to an ethical code of loyalty and sincerity—but in the same gesture, it places the viewer at the opposite end of his gun barrel. The print's form offers no resolution to the social disorder of its moment, but it crystallizes the moment's dilemma. The violent actors of 1868 could be motivated by profoundly moral impulses and be worthy of appreciation or even celebration; but that did not make them any less dangerous if one got in their way, and the chaos could catch anyone in its claws. Such were the capricious wages of a world in which violence had been loosed from its fetters. With lines, color, and a few words, the print marks the demise of an era; encapsulates the emotion, ambiguity, and danger of a new world taking shape; and, pinning the viewers to the age just dawning, demands that they contemplate their own place within it.

The image of Hachibyōe thus easily joins the texts I have examined throughout this book as a work that encodes a perceptual politics—evoking a complex conceptualization of the world beyond its frame—through a nuanced manipulation of precedents and forms. But his portrait stands as the coda to this book not simply to offer another instance of my method, and not (only) for the felicitous fact that the print was produced at the very moment of the collapse of the Tokugawa shogunate.

Rather, the immediacy with which the marksman continues to aim his weapon at the viewer, long after the moment of the print's production, serves as a caveat to the arguments I have made in this book. It reminds us that works of art and literature continue to train their sights on the world long *after* their moment of creation—and even after the formal dynamics that informed them have become less intelligible. Forms are uncanny in their capacity to travel, to continue speaking beyond their moment. Hachibyōe's portrait retains its arresting power even for a viewer who knows nothing about the Shimabara Rebellion, the political circumstances of the 1860s, the Battle of Ueno, or the Shōgitai. And it is striking how Yoshitoshi's print series, and others like it, could evoke utterly new modes of perception from within the perspective of a modern, imperial, and then post-imperial Japan.

I have argued that early modern forms drew close to the lived world because they shared with it a cultural grammar that relied heavily on formalization. But the mystery novelist and critic Edogawa Ranpo (1894–1965), writing in 1936, when much of that grammar had long since fallen away, identified a different cultural logic underlying what he called Yoshitoshi's "cruelty pictures" (*muzan-e*), including those from *One Hundred Selected Portraits*.[15] He called it "nostalgia for brutality" (*zangyaku e no kyōshū*): the longing for an archaic, atavistic human cruelty that had been rendered taboo by the processes of civilization. The only places where the taboo could be violated (each in its own way) were warfare and art. Ranpo located Yoshitoshi's pictures alongside other works that offered channels to this repressed, primeval impulse. He imagined the works piled high in a phantasmic red "room of cruelties:" myths, ancient legends, the biblical story of Abraham's sacrifice of Isaac, Sophocles's *Oedipus Rex*, the "clownish" cruelty of *Don Quixote*.[16] Whereas in 1868 Yoshitoshi's prints could summon tears from an Edoite who recognized in their doubled forms the recently slaughtered Shōgitai, the resemblances that Ranpo found in them seventy years later were more thematic and impressionistic, joining the prints to works far-flung in time and place—but taken primarily from the Western canon. The prints spoke to Ranpo not of the 1860s, or of the curtailed time-space of the Tokugawa age, but of questions relevant to the highly modernized and increasingly militarized Japan of the 1930s, a time of political terror and military excess. They invited for him questions about the correlations among civilization, modernity, and barbarism, and about the relationship of imperial Japan to the cultural legacy of the imperial West.

Ranpo's was not the only possible modern reading. The novelist Mishima Yukio (1925–1970) located new meaning in Yoshitoshi's violent prints a full century after they had been produced. Writing, in the centennial year of the Meiji Restoration, about the artist's prints of the mid-1860s in an essay on decadent art, he characterized them as "blood-smeared pictures" (*chimidoro-e*), and he read them as reflections of Yoshitoshi's "insatiable bloodlust" (*akunaki chi no shiyoku*). He respected them for the way they "joined [the artist's] own physiology with the agitated nerve endings of his era, in a happy unity in which we can witness the shuddering of his soul." Such an approach, Mishima commented, one that unites the artist's visceral sense with the nervous atmosphere of his times, is "the one narrow path by which decadent art can come to possess a diabolical power [*demōnisshu na chikara*]."[17] Two years later, Mishima killed himself in a sensational death by *seppuku*—a cultural form that by 1970 had come to seem profoundly anachronistic. Four months after his death, his words about Yoshitoshi were excerpted and reprinted as the foreword to the first modern compendium of Yoshitoshi's prints, a collection with the suggestive title *Banquet of Blood: The Art of Taisō Yoshitoshi* (*Chi no bansan: Taisō Yoshitoshi no geijutsu*).[18] Mishima's high appraisal of Yoshitoshi had the effect of resurrecting the printmaker's dormant reputation. But it recast him as a bloodthirsty decadent, and it foregrounded in his prints some of Mishima's own obsessions: the human physique, the contortions of the psyche (individual and collective), and the fetishization of violence. The publication of *Banquet of Blood*, so soon after Mishima's suicide, made it difficult to read the prints independently of the author's own grisly death by an archaic, violent practice. The renewed attention to Yoshitoshi instigated by Mishima's interest was characterized for years by a psychologizing focus on blood and madness in his art—concerns that obscured the early modern formal dynamics that had structured the prints and imbued them with meaning in their moment of creation.[19]

I mention the reception of Yoshitoshi's prints by Ranpo and Mishima as a reminder that forms have eerie lives of their own. Legible in one moment, their meaning can turn opaque in another—or take on a new significance that was unimaginable in their time of inception. They may go into hibernation for years—even centuries—only to reactivate later. And Mishima's death by the outmoded form of *seppuku* reminds us that these principles apply to cultural as well as artistic forms.

Herein lies another significance of Hachibyōe's pointed gun, and the ultimate reason why it stands as this book's closing image. When he aims his weapon beyond the frame of the print, he points it at *us*, in our moment, in our world. He meets *our* gaze. I still find it difficult to look at the print without a frisson of tension. I tilt my head, just slightly, to dodge the invisible bullet. My mind conjures up similar, unconnected images that came into the world only many years later: Justus D. Barnes firing his pistol directly at the camera in the silent film *The Great Train Robbery* (1903); Luke Skywalker leaping forward, blaster in hand, in the poster for *Star Wars* (1977) that adorned my childhood bedroom wall. Perhaps these images are what drew me to Yoshitoshi's print in the first place. Too, I cannot view Hachibyōe's portrait without thinking of the mass shootings that continue to plague my country. The print prompts me to contemplate what it would feel like to find myself staring down a gun barrel—not in 1860s Japan, but today in the United States, where I write these words. Form's capacity to float free of context and nonetheless remain vital alerts us to the limitations of a strict positivism or historicism. It reminds us why literature and art are not mere subfields of history. Good formal work does not ignore literary history, sociopolitical context, or the insights that can be gleaned through attention to the material qualities of books. But neither does it cede to these the locus of all meaning. And it certainly does not pretend that we are not implicated in the process of meaning-making or that texts are strictly time-bound. Forms are vagabond, texts are strange, and reading is endless.

I have sought to make intelligible some of the more daunting formal dynamics of early modern fiction and to do justice to the complexity with which early modern works propose their arrangements of the world and its horizon of possibilities. I do not intend my readings of the texts in this book to provide a final word, but to help open new possibilities for reading them. I encourage others to return to them—and to other texts of the Edo period—with a sense of fresh possibility and an appetite for surprise. I hope that this book will serve as a counterbalance to the impulse to subordinate early modern texts, in all their particularity and eccentricity, to broader historical narratives. Those narratives are important, too; but there is so much to be discovered by letting texts lure us from the path.

Formalism (together with its attendant practice of close reading) has become a dirty word in some domains of scholarship, suggestive of a fusty exercise that fetishizes the surfaces of texts while ignoring matters of juicier critical import. But a capacious formalism—one that works from the ground up, attends to idiosyncrasy, embraces arbitrariness, apprehends text and context as collaborators, attends to forms' time-traveling capacities, and does not discount the appeal they make not just to our intellects but to our bodies, feelings, and spirits—has the happy outcome of renewing texts' capacity to astonish. Formalism of this kind enables us to hear anew the cacophonous diversity of the addresses they make to the world. It demands, however, that we commit to "the slow, hard tussle of reading works closely,"[20] and that we cede some agency to the texts and let them lead the way. The endeavor requires making ourselves vulnerable to the places where their specificities trip us up and leave us bewildered. But doing so promises to renew our understanding of their world. And, by awakening us to new perceptual possibilities, it may even help to renew our understanding of our own. All it asks is that we afford texts the gift of our deep, sustained attention, and then bring to bear every faculty at our disposal to help others hear what they have to say.

Notes

The following abbreviations are used in the notes and bibliography.

NKBT   *Nihon koten bungaku taikei.* Tokyo: Iwanami shoten, 1957–1967.
NKBZ   *Nihon koten bungaku zenshū.* Tokyo: Shōgakukan, 1970–1976.
SNKBT *Shin Nihon koten bungaku taikei.* Tokyo: Iwanami shoten, 1989–2005.
SNKBZ *Shinpen Nihon koten bungaku zenshū.* Tokyo: Shōgakukan, 1994–2002.
SNKS   *Shinchō Nihon koten shūsei.* Tokyo: Shinchōsha, 1976–1989.

Introduction

1. Alex Woloch, *The One vs. the Many: Minor Characters and the Space of the Protagonist in the Novel* (Princeton, NJ: Princeton University Press, 2003), 19.
2. Kyokutei Bakin, *Geppyō kien*, in *Kyokutei Bakin shū*, Kindai Nihon bungaku taikei 15 (Tokyo: Kokumin tosho kabushiki gaisha, 1927), 1:1–107. Bakin published the book in 1803 with the Osaka publisher Kawachi Yatasuke after visiting Osaka the year before. By his own account, it was a great commercial success, selling over 1,000 copies in Osaka and Edo: "After this, *yomihon* gradually grew in popularity and eventually became all the rage." See Kyokutei Bakin, *Kinsei mononohon Edo sakusha burui*, ed. Tokuda Takeshi (Tokyo: Iwanami shoten, 2014), 212.
3. Kyokutei Bakin, *Geppyō kien*, 6–8.

[221]

4. Kyokutei Bakin, *Geppyō kien*, 67.
5. Chikamatsu Monzaemon, *Tsu no kuni meoto ike*, in *Chikamatsu jōrurishū*, ed. Matsuzaki Hitoshi, Hara Michio, Iguchi Hiroshi, and Ōhashi Tadayoshi, SNKBT 92 (Tokyo: Iwanami shoten, 1995), 2:81–164. For an English translation, see Chikamatsu Monzaemon, *Lovers Pond in Settsu Province*, in *Chikamatsu: Five Late Plays*, trans. and ann. C. Andrew Gerstle (New York: Columbia University Press, 2001), 118–201.
6. See, for example, Donald H. Shively, "Bakufu Versus Kabuki," *Harvard Journal of Asiatic Studies* 18, nos. 3–4 (1955): 326–356; Taniwaki Masachika, "Saikaku no jishu kisei to kamufurāju: ichiou no sōkatsu to kongo no kadai," in *Saikaku to ukiyozōshi kenkyū*, vol. 1, *Media*, ed. Nakajima Takashi and Shinohara Susumu (Tokyo: Kasama shoin, 2006), 117–131; and Katsuya Hirano, *The Politics of Dialogic Imagination: Power and Popular Culture in Early Modern Japan* (Chicago: University of Chicago Press, 2014), 3–4.
7. Nakano Mitsutoshi adopts the term "art for art's sake" (*geijutsu no tame no geijutsu*) from Nakamura Yukihiko, who employs it to characterize an approach to literature and the arts that emerged from eighteenth-century *kokugaku* and literati (*bunjin*) culture and came to characterize the body of writing known as *gesaku* (frivolous writings). (See Nakamura Yukihiko, *Gesaku ron*, vol. 8 of *Nakamura Yukihiko chojutsushū* [Tokyo: Chūō kōronsha, 1982], 62–66.) But in contrast to Nakamura's more limited usage, Nakano stretches *gesaku*—as an apolitical, primarily expressive body of writings—to encompass *all* early modern popular prose: see Nakano Mitsutoshi, "Saikaku gesakusha setsu saikō: Edo no manako to gendai no manako no motsu imi," *Bungaku* 15, no. 1 (2014): 150–151, 154, 157. For Nakano, the three key principles of early modern popular fiction are humor (*kokkei*), moral edification (*kyōkun*), and newness (*atarashisa*), none of which, he claims, entail politics or critique because they never call into question the dominant values and political structure of the age. See Nakano Mitsutoshi, "Jūnana seiki no shōsetsushi: watakushi no gesakuron josetsu," in "Saikaku chōhatsu suru tekisuto," ed. Kigoshi Osamu, special issue, *Kokubungaku kaishaku to kanshō* (March 2005): 19–27. I am grateful to Thomas Gaubatz for drawing my attention to these articles. For a precis of Nakano's stance in English, see Nakano Mitsutoshi, "The Role of Traditional Aesthetics," trans. Maria Flutsch, in *18th Century Japan: Culture and Society*, ed. C. Andrew Gerstle (Sydney: Allen & Unwin, 1989), 124–131.
8. I point this out not to discount the value of these approaches, which indeed have much to teach us. For an example of a highly rewarding volume on seventeenth-century commercial literature that takes Nakano's interventions as a point of reference and generally emphasizes historical, material, and practical considerations over interpretive and ideological questions, see Laura

Moretti, *Pleasure in Profit: Popular Prose in Seventeenth-Century Japan* (New York: Columbia University Press, 2020). See also Michael Emmerich's nuanced book-historical approach to the early modern genre *gōkan*, in which he engages deeply with materiality, form, and the reading experience but largely stops short of tying these to broader ideological questions about the perception of the world beyond the page: Michael Emmerich, The Tale of Genji: *Translation, Canonization, and World Literature* (New York: Columbia University Press, 2013), 47–170.

9. I am influenced here by Jacques Rancière: "The role of the critic . . . is to draw the outlines of the kind of common world that the work is producing or a kind of common world of which the work is a product. For me, the role of the critic is to say, 'this is the world that this work proposes.' It is to try to explain the forms—as well as the possible shifts in the forms—of perception, description, and interpretation of a world that are inherent in the work." Jacques Rancière, *The Politics of Aesthetics: The Distribution of the Sensible*, ed. and trans. Gabriel Rockhill (London: Continuum, 2006; repr., London: Bloomsbury Academic, 2013), 80.

10. Rancière, *Politics of Aesthetics*, 8.

11. On the constructive qualities of literary form, see Anna Kornbluh, *The Order of Forms: Realism, Formalism, and Social Space* (Chicago: University of Chicago Press, 2019), 1–7, on form and building; and Tom Eyers, *Speculative Formalism: Literature, Theory, and the Critical Present* (Evanston, IL: Northwestern University Press, 2017), 1–6, on the "formativeness of form."

12. Herman Ooms, "Forms and Norms in Edo Arts and Society," in *Edo: Art in Japan, 1615–1868*, ed. Robert T. Singer (Washington, DC: National Gallery of Art, 1998), 25–26. On the military and state origins of early modern taxonomic consciousness, see Mary Elizabeth Berry, *Japan in Print: Information and Nation in the Early Modern Period* (Berkeley: University of California Press, 2006), 33–35, 38–45.

13. Ilya Kliger, "Dynamic Archaeology or Distant Reading: Literary Study Between Two Formalisms," *Russian Literature* 122–123 (2021): 15.

14. Sianne Ngai, "Interview with Sianne Ngai," by Kevin Brazil, *White Review*, October 2020, https://www.thewhitereview.org/feature/interview-with-sianne-ngai/.

15. Raymond Williams, *Marxism and Literature* (Oxford: Oxford University Press, 1977), 186.

16. Williams, *Marxism and Literature*, 187.

17. Kliger, "Dynamic Archaeology," 11–13. Kliger's characterizations of form in relation to material and flow derive from the writings of the Russian Formalists of the Society for the Study of Poetic Language (OPOIAZ), particularly Boris Eikhenbaum and Iurii Tynianov.

18. As its role in the traditional arts suggests, *kata* is not a modern approximation of an imported concept of "form." It can be found already in works as old as the *Man'yōshū* (*Collection of Ten Thousand Leaves*, after 759) and *The Tale of Genji* (eleventh century).
19. Caroline Levine, *Forms: Whole, Rhythm, Hierarchy, Network* (Princeton, NJ: Princeton University Press, 2015), 3.
20. Levine, *Forms*, 6–11.
21. I place my primary focus in this project on narrative fiction, which I understand as including highly textual theatrical forms like the puppet theater, the libretti of which were read by a chanter onstage and consumed by the public as books. The highly modular formal politics I describe were operative in the kabuki theater as well, and forms derived from kabuki, including characters, plots, and staging, permeated narrative fiction and its illustrations. But the highly iterative nature of kabuki from performance to performance and the relative dearth of scripts places kabuki performance beyond the scope of this study, which methodologically relies upon specificity of instance. On the challenges of reconstructing kabuki performances, see Satoko Shimazaki, *Edo Kabuki in Transition: From the Worlds of the Samurai to the Vengeful Female Ghost* (New York: Columbia University Press, 2016), 1–17.
22. Peter Haidu, *The Subject of Violence: The "Song of Roland" and the Birth of the State* (Bloomington: Indiana University Press, 1993), 3.
23. Leo Bersani and Ulysse Dutoit, "The Forms of Violence," *October* 8 (1979), 21. See this essay and its expanded version, *The Forms of Violence: Narrative in Assyrian Art and Modern Culture* (New York: Schocken Books, 1985), on the role of visual, narrative, and cultural forms in shaping perceptions of violence and thereby opening and foreclosing different possibilities for the nature of its harm.
24. Viktor Shklovsky, "Art as Device," in *On the Theory of Prose*, trans. Shushan Avagyan (Dallas and Dublin: Dalkey Archive Press, 2021), 13. Shklovsky's key term is "estrangement" (*ostranenie*), which he treats as the fundamental aim of literature and art: a matter of enabling readers to perceive that which they mindlessly pass over in life ("to make the stone stony"), and thus to "restore the sensation of life" (11–12).
25. I discuss the formalization of blood revenge in chap. 2.
26. Social categorization largely centered on status (*mibun*), which was closely tied to occupation. Status should not be confused with the rigid, hierarchical model of the "four estates" of samurai, farmer, craftsman, and merchant (*shi-nō-kō-shō*), an ideological construct rooted in Confucian discourse that had little relation to the highly diverse and fluid status categories operative in real life. On the complexity of the status system and its relationship to taxonomic thinking, see David L. Howell, *Geographies of Identity in*

Nineteenth-Century Japan (Berkeley: University of California Press, 2005), 24–44.

27. See, for example, *Kokin wakashū* (*Collection of Ancient and Modern Poems*, early tenth century), poem no. 828, which concludes the anthology's volumes on love: "As the Yoshino River flows between Mount Imo and Mount Se, so as a wife and husband live on, dissatisfaction comes between them: ah, such is the way of this world" (*Nagarete wa Imose no yama no naka ni otsuru Yoshino no kawa no yoshiya yo no naka*). *Kokin wakashū*, ed. Ozawa Masao and Matsuda Shigeho, SNKBZ 11 (Tokyo: Shōgakukan, 1994), 312.

28. Chikamatsu lays his scene at Meoto (Wife-Husband) Pond, north of Osaka: a site far less celebrated than Imoseyama, and one that affords neither the emphasis on separateness nor the linguistic ambiguity of "Sister-Brother" / "Wife-Husband" made possible by Bakin's setting. Too, Imoseyama enabled Bakin to incorporate elements of the popular *jōruri* play *Imoseyama and the Women's Cultivation Manual* (*Imoseyama onna teikin*, 1771), cowritten by Chikamatsu Hanji (1725–1783), Matsuda Baku, Sakai Zenpei, Chikamatsu Tōnan, and Miyoshi Shōraku, but I omit discussion of these aspects here for the sake of concision.

29. Howell, *Geographies of Identity*, 32–33.

30. Howell, *Geographies of Identity*, 32–33. See also Maren A. Ehlers, *Give and Take: Poverty and the Status Order in Early Modern Japan* (Cambridge, MA: Harvard University Asia Center, 2018), 1–13.

31. Howell, *Geographies of Identity*, 33.

32. Howell, *Geographies of Identity*, 36, drawing on Sasaki Junnosuke, *Bakuhansei kokkaron* (Tokyo: Tokyo daigaku shuppankai, 1984), 1: 109–341, as well as other works by Sasaki.

33. Ooms, "Forms and Norms in Edo Arts and Society," 25.

34. Berry, *Japan in Print*, 23.

35. *Jinrin kinmō zui*, ed. Asakura Haruhiko (Tokyo: Heibonsha, 1990).

36. Translation by Laura Moretti of the entry "How to eat broth [*suimono*]," from the etiquette manual *One Hundred Points of the Ogasawara School* (*Ogasawara hyakka jō*, 1632), in Moretti, *Pleasure in Profit*, 143.

37. Moretti, *Pleasure in Profit*, 142.

38. Hino Tatsuo, "Engi suru shijintachi," in *Edo no jugaku*, vol. 1 of *Hino Tatsuo chosakushū* (Tokyo: Perikansha, 2005), 219–220.

39. Hino Tatsuo, "Engi suru shijintachi," 220–221.

40. Hino Tatsuo, "Engi suru shijintachi," 220. Our knowledge of *The Rōnin's Saké Cup* comes from the summary provided by the playwright Tominaga Heibei (active ca. 1673–1704) in his short treatise "Mirror of Art" (Gei kagami), collected in the anthology of early kabuki treatises *The Actors' Analects* (*Yakusha rongo*, 1776). For Heibei's summary in both English and

Japanese, see *The Actors' Analects*, ed. and trans. Charles J. Dunn and Bunzō Torigoe (New York: Columbia University Press, 1969), 38–40, 296–299.
41. Luke S. Roberts, *Performing the Great Peace: Political Space and Open Secrets in Tokugawa Japan* (Honolulu: University of Hawai'i Press, 2012), 3.
42. Roberts, *Performing the Great Peace*, 7.
43. Roberts, *Performing the Great Peace*, 5–6.
44. On the "correlations between the relative stability of forms, institutions, and social systems," see Williams, *Marxism and Literature*, 189.
45. Nakamura Yukihiko, "Kata no bunshō," in *Nakamura Yukihiko chojutsushū* (Tokyo: Chūō kōronsha, 1982), 2:149.
46. Nakamura, "Kata no bunshō," 150.
47. Nakamura, "Kata no bunshō," 149.
48. Nakamura, "Kata no bunshō," 152.
49. Nakamura ("Kata no bunshō," 149, 151) singles out Ōta Nanpo (1749–1823) as an exemplar of literary virtuosity.
50. Suwa Haruo, "Edo bungaku to wa nanika," in *Edo bungaku no hōhō* (Tokyo: Benseisha, 1997), 5.
51. Suwa, "Edo bungaku," 24–26. Both, he argues, displaced the medieval period's prioritization of sacred over secular authority.
52. Suwa, "Edo bungaku," 3.
53. Suwa, "Edo bungaku," 2–3. The first known text to style Chikamatsu as *sakusha no ujigami* is *A Chronology of the Puppet Theater* (*Imamukashi ayatsuri nendaiki*, 1727). See Chikamatsu Monzaemon, *Chikamatsu*, 430n8.
54. Shimazaki, *Edo Kabuki in Transition*, 68–69.
55. Nakamura, *Gesaku ron*, 142.
56. For a thorough overview of the *shukō*, with a particular emphasis on its role in *gesaku* fiction, see Nakamura, *Gesaku ron*, 142–178. In English, see Haruko Iwasaki, "The Literature of Wit and Humor in Late-Eighteenth-Century Edo," in *The Floating World Revisited*, ed. Donald Jenkins (Portland, OR: Portland Art Museum; Honolulu: University of Hawai'i Press, 1993), 51–53; and Adam L. Kern, *Manga from the Floating World: Comicbook Culture and the Kibyōshi of Edo Japan*, 2nd ed. (Cambridge, MA: Harvard University Asia Center, 2019), 123–128.
57. Haruo Shirane, *Traces of Dreams: Landscape, Cultural Memory, and the Poetry of Bashō* (Stanford, CA: Stanford University Press, 1998), 12–15.
58. On *fukiyose* and *naimaze*, see Nakamura, *Gesaku ron*, 186–190. Nakamura emphasizes the necessity of formal models for these techniques' success, defining *fukiyose*, for example, as "fitting a variety of different elements into a single form [*keishiki*] in which they do not belong and stretching the incongruity as far as it can go" (186).
59. Devin Griffiths, "The Ecology of Form," *Critical Inquiry* 48, no. 1 (2021): 70–71.

60. Ōgimachi Machiko, *Matsukage nikki*, ed. Ueno Yōzō (Tokyo: Iwanami shoten, 2005). For an English translation, see Ōgimachi Machiko, *In the Shelter of the Pine: A Memoir of Yanagisawa Yoshiyasu and Tokugawa Japan*, trans. G. G. Rowley (New York: Columbia University Press, 2021).
61. G. G. Rowley, introduction to Ōgimachi Machiko, *In the Shelter of the Pine*, xix–xxiii.
62. In this, *The Treasury of Loyal Retainers* follows the example set by Chikamatsu Monzaemon's play *The Chronicle of Great Peace Played Out on a Go Board* (*Goban Taiheiki*, 1710), the first theatrical treatment of the *rōnins*' revenge to set it in the world of *The Chronicle of Great Peace*.
63. Miyazawa Seiichi, *Akō rōshi: tsumugidasareru Chūshingura* (Tokyo: Sanseidō, 1999), 65–69, 102–103, 148–150.
64. Taniguchi Shinko, "Akō rōshi ni miru bushidō to 'ie' no meiyo," *Nihon rekishi* 650 (2002): 50–51; Henry D. Smith II, "The Capacity of Chūshingura: Three Hundred Years of Chūshingura," *Monumenta Nipponica* 58, no. 1 (2003): 12–16.
65. Ooms, "Forms and Norms in Edo Arts and Society," 34.
66. Santō Kyōden, *Katakiuchi ato no matsuri*, in *Santō Kyōden zenshū*, ed. Santō Kyōden zenshū henshū iinkai (Tokyo: Perikansha, 1992), 1:369–370.
67. Takeda Izumo II, Miyoshi Shōraku, and Namiki Senryū, *Kanadehon chūshingura*, in *Jōruri shū*, ed. Torigoe Bunzō et al., SNKBZ 77. Tokyo: Shōgakukan, 2002, 107.
68. Griffiths, "Ecology of Form," 83–84.
69. Ellen Rooney, "Form and Contentment," in *Reading for Form*, ed. Susan J. Wolfson and Marshall Brown (Seattle: University of Washington Press, 2006), 47.

1. Creative Destruction

1. (Epigraph source: *Taiheki*, ed. Gotō Tanji and Kamada Kisaburō, NKBT 34 [Tokyo: Iwanami shoten, 1960], 1: 82–83.) Ishihara Shintarō, quoted in "'Daishinsai wa tenbatsu:' 'Tsunami de gayoku o araiotose' Ishihara tochiji," *Asahi Shimbun*, March 14, 2011, http://www.asahi.com/special/tokyo/TKY201103140356.html, accessed December 3, 2018.
2. Anthony Oliver-Smith, "Theorizing Disasters: Nature, Power, and Culture," in *Catastrophe and Culture: The Anthropology of Disaster*, ed. Susanna M. Hoffman and Anthony Oliver-Smith (Santa Fe, NM: School of American Research Press, 2002), 25–26.
3. Alan G. Grapard, "Religious Practices," in *Heian Japan*, ed. Donald H. Shively and William H. McCullough, *The Cambridge History of Japan*, vol. 2 (Cambridge: Cambridge University Press, 1999), 562.

4. The status of disaster as a genre convention in medieval *gunkimono* complicates the work of modern seismologists, who have relied on such accounts as sources of historical geophysical data. See Sybil A. Thornton, "*Meitokuki*: Earthquakes and Literary Fabrication in the *Gunki Monogatari*," *Japan Review* 28 (2015): 225–234.
5. On the differences between *onryō* and the similar term *goryō* (honored spirit), see Grapard, "Religious Practices," 559–560.
6. *Heike monogatari*, ed. Ichiko Teiji, SNKBZ 46 (Tokyo: Shōgakukan, 1994), 2:442.
7. Laura Moretti, "The Japanese Early-Modern Publishing Market Unveiled: A Survey of Edo-Period Booksellers' Catalogues," *East Asian Publishing and Society* 2 (2012): 200.
8. Literary historiography has sometimes treated *kanazōshi* as a genre, but it is better understood as a medium that facilitated the consumption of a diverse range of genres. See Laura Moretti, "Kanazōshi Revisited: The Beginnings of Japanese Popular Literature in Print," *Monumenta Nipponica* 65, no. 2 (2010): 297–356.
9. In the preface to his miscellany *Essays in Hindsight* (*Nochimigusa*, 1787), the physician and scholar Sugita Genpaku (1733–1817) notes the continued popularity of *Stirrups of Musashi*. Sugita Genpaku, *Nochimigusa*, in *Kikin akueki*, ed. Mori Kahei and Tanigawa Ken'ichi, Nihon shomin seikatsu shiryō shūsei 7 (Tokyo: San'ichi shobō, 1970), 57.
10. On the illustrations in *Stirrups of Mushashi* as early examples of ukiyo-e, see David G. Chibbett, *The History of Japanese Printing and Book Illustration* (Tokyo: Kodansha International, 1977), 126–127.
11. Mary Elizabeth Berry, *Japan in Print: Information and Nation in the Early Modern Period* (Berkeley: University of California Press, 2006), esp. 13–53.
12. See, for example, Mizue Renko, "Kanazōshi no kirokusei: *Musashi abumi* to Meireki no taika," *Nihon rekishi* 291 (1972): 87–100; Sakamaki Kōta and Kuroki Takashi, "Asai Ryōi to *Musashi abumi*," in Asai Ryōi, *"Musashi abumi" kōchū to kenkyū*, ed. Sakamaki Kōta and Kuroki Takashi (Tokyo: Ōfūsha, 1988), 109–150; and Ogawa Takehiko, "Kanazōshi yonhen ni miru tenzai jihen no bungeisei to kirokusei," in *Kinsei bungei ronsō*, ed. Teruoka Yasutaka (Tokyo: Chūō kōronsha, 1978), 61–76. In a recent study of seventeenth-century disaster narratives, Laura Moretti introduces new layers of nuance, expanding the "informational" aspects of *Stirrups of Musashi* to encompass not only facts about the disaster but also reflections on the nature of trauma and the confusion humans can experience in the face of unexpected catastrophe. The reporting of factual and practical information remains, however, her primary focus, and she does not address the ideological and political elements I foreground here. Laura Moretti, *Pleasure in Profit: Popular Prose*

in Seventeenth-Century Japan (New York: Columbia University Press, 2020), 233–253. An exception to the informational emphasis is Peter Kornicki, who argues for the importance of reading *Stirrups of Musashi* as a literary work, in "Narrative of a Catastrophe: *Musashi abumi* and the Meireki Fire," *Japan Forum* 21, no. 3 (2010): 347–361. I take inspiration from his call to attention, though his interpretation of the text differs significantly from my own.

13. I borrow the term "symbolic intentionality" from Robert Appelbaum, who claims that while we can speak of a "violent" accident, storm, or earthquake, "we cannot really say that the accident or the natural disaster is itself violence. For neither has symbolic intentionality"—a claim problematized by comments such as Ishihara's. Robert Appelbaum, "Notes Toward an Aesthetics of Violence," *Studia Neophilologica* 85, no. 2 (2013): 121.

14. Matsuda Osamu, "Chūsei kara kinsei e: jikū ishiki to bungaku ishiki," in *Edo itan bungaku nōto* (Tokyo: Seidosha, 1993), 17–20.

15. For Matsuda, this interaction can be found even in the "allusive variation" (*honkadori*) that dominates medieval poetics, in which the newness of a poem emerges from the way it interacts with and builds on an older base poem.

16. Takahashi Masaaki, "Yōwa no kikin, Genryaku no jishin to Kamo no Chōmei," *Bungaku* 13, no. 2 (2012): 48.

17. Eric Hayot, *On Literary Worlds* (Oxford: Oxford University Press, 2016), 55–60.

18. Hayot, *On Literary Worlds*, 60.

19. On these categories, see Laura Moretti, "A Forest of Books: Seventeenth-Century Kamigata Commercial Prose," in *The Cambridge History of Japanese Literature*, ed. Haruo Shirane, Tomi Suzuki, and David Lurie (Cambridge: Cambridge University Press, 2015), 396.

20. Berry, *Japan in Print*, 16.

21. Noda Hisao discerns in the characterization of Rakuami, the protagonist of this work, traces of Chikusai, the quack doctor at the center of the earlier kana booklet *Chikusai* (ca. 1615–1624) and its many variants. Noda Hisao, "*Tōkaidō meishoki* ron," in *Kinsei shoki shōsetsu ron* (Tokyo: Kasama shoin, 1978), 135–136.

22. On Ryōi's biography, see Noma Kōshin, "Ryōi tsuiseki," in *Kinsei sakkaden kō* (Tokyo: Chūō kōronsha, 1985), 105–147. On the range of Ryōi's literary production, see Hōjō Hideo, *Shinshū Asai Ryōi* (Tokyo: Kasama shoin, 1974), 9.

23. Matsuda Osamu, *Nihon kinsei bungaku no seiritsu: itan no keifu*, in *Matsuda Osamu chosakushū* (Tokyo: Yūbun shoin, 2002), 1:399.

24. Sakamaki Kōta, "Kinsei shoki ni okeru sakusha shoshi dokusha no isō: sakusha Asai Ryōi shoshi Kawano Michikiyo o jiku ni," *Nihon bungaku* 43, no. 10 (1994): 6–8. On p. 8, Sakamaki also notes that roughly 80 percent of the

information in *Stirrups of Musashi* is accurate, suggesting the thoroughness of Ryōi's research.

25. These were not guidebooks intended for practical use but for armchair travelers, as pointed out in Noda Hisao, "*Tōkaidō meishoki* ron," 129.
26. Akira Naitō, *Edo, the City That Became Tokyo: An Illustrated History*, trans. H. Mack Horton (Tokyo: Kodansha International, 2003), 24–25. See also Timon Screech, *Tokyo Before Tokyo: Power and Magic in the Shogun's City of Edo* (London: Reaktion Books, 2020), 38–44.
27. On the origins of the alternate attendance system, see Constantine Nomikos Vaporis, *Tour of Duty: Samurai, Military Service in Edo, and the Culture of Early Modern Japan* (Honolulu: University of Hawai'i Press, 2008), 11–15. See also Naito, *Edo*, 99.
28. A full history of the fire and its aftermath can be found in Kuroki Takashi, *Meireki no taika* (Tokyo: Kōdansha, 1977).
29. Asai Ryōi, "*Musashi abumi*" *kōchū to kenkyū*, ed. Sakamaki Kōta and Kuroki Takashi (Tokyo: Ōfūsha, 1988), 7–8. For a partial translation of *Musashi abumi*, see Asai Ryōi, *Stirrups of Musashi: An Account of the Meireki Fire of 1657*, trans. Henry D. Smith II and Steven Wills, in *A Kamigata Anthology: Literature from Japan's Metropolitan Centers, 1600–1750*, ed. Sumie Jones, Adam L. Kern, and Kenji Watanabe (Honolulu: University of Hawai'i Press, 2020), 410–439.
30. Sakamaki, "Kinsei shoki ni okeru sakusha shoshi dokusha no isō," 2; Mizue, "Kanazōshi no kirokusei," 90.
31. Debate persists over whether some of these seventeenth-century printed examples are newly composed works or adaptations of tales that had circulated orally or in manuscript from the late medieval period; the trope, however, clearly dates from at least the fifteenth century. See Margaret Helen Childs, *Rethinking Sorrow: Revelatory Tales of Late Medieval Japan* (Ann Arbor: Center for Japanese Studies, University of Michigan, 1991), 26–28.
32. Asai Ryōi, *Musashi abumi*, 28.
33. Asai Ryōi, *Musashi abumi*, 54.
34. Asai Ryōi, *Musashi abumi*, 54.
35. Kornicki, "Narrative of a Catastrophe," 357. See also Murakami Manabu, "Nichizō no jigoku meguri: *Dōken jōnin meidoki* to *Kitano Tenjin engi*," *Kokubungaku kaishaku to kanshō* 55, no. 8 (1990): 79–83.
36. Asai Ryōi, *Musashi abumi*, 55.
37. Asai Ryōi, *Musashi abumi*, 8.
38. Asai Ryōi, *Musashi abumi*, 8–9.
39. Asai Ryōi, *Musashi abumi*, 8–9.
40. Asai Ryōi, *Musashi abumi*, 32–33. For the densely inscribed woodblock-printed pages, see Asai Ryōi, *Musashi abumi* (Teramachi Nijō sagarumachi [Kyoto]:

Nakamura Gohei, Manji 4 [1661]), 2:fol. 2a–3a, Waseda Daigaku Sōgō Kotenseki Dētabēsu, https://www.wul.waseda.ac.jp/kotenseki.
41. Berry, *Japan in Print*, 104. Berry discusses these "military mirrors" at length on 104–138.
42. Berry, *Japan in Print*, 107–108.
43. Asai Ryōi, *Musashi abumi*, 59.
44. I am grateful to Keller Kimbrough for pointing me toward consideration of *monozukushi*.
45. *Ryōjin hishō*, in *Kagurauta, Saibara, Ryōjin hishō, Kanginshū*, ed. Usuda Jingorō, SNKBZ 42 (Tokyo: Shōgakukan, 1994), 268. *Imayō uta* (modern style songs) flourished in the late Heian and early Kamakura periods.
46. Suzuki Hideo, "Monozukushi no bungei," *Nihon no bigaku* 32 (2001): 56.
47. Suzuki, "Monozukushi no bungei," 60. *Monozukushi* grew in prominence during the Heian period through the importance to *waka* poetic composition of set poetic topics (*dai*); see p. 56.
48. Suzuki, "Monozukushi no bungei," 59–60.
49. Asai Ryōi, *Musashi abumi*, 17.
50. Asai Ryōi, *Musashi abumi*, 19.
51. The emphasis on the warden's benevolence is particularly striking given the Kodenmachō prison's reputation for torture, overcrowding, and general misery. See Daniel V. Botsman, *Punishment and Power in the Making of Modern Japan* (Princeton, NJ: Princeton University Press, 2005), 61–69.
52. Asai Ryōi, *Musashi abumi*, 38.
53. Asai Ryōi, *Musashi abumi*, 46.
54. Asai Ryōi, *Musashi abumi*, 52.
55. Asai Ryōi, *Musashi abumi*, 59–60.
56. Asai Ryōi, *Musashi abumi*, 60n13.
57. In the wake of the fire, the author of a diary called *Kanmei nikki* noted the uncanny similarity between the twisted faces and corpses of the fire victims and the odd bodily movements of the *shibagaki* dance. See Asai Ryōi, *Musashi abumi*, 60n.13. On *shibagaki*, see also Kuroki, *Meireki no taika*, 6–8.
58. Asai Ryōi, *Musashi abumi*, 60.
59. On Chikusai and his story's diverse adaptations, see Laura Moretti, "Adaptation as a Strategy for Participation: The Chikusai Storyworld in Early Modern Japanese Literature," *Japanese Language and Literature* 54, no. 1 (2020): 67–113.
60. Nishida Kōzō, *Shujinkō no tanjō: chūsei Zen kara kinsei shōsetsu e* (Tokyo: Perikansha, 2007), 12.
61. *Ukiyo monogatari*, in *Kanazōshi shū ukiyozōshi shū*, ed. Jinbō Kazuya et al., NKBZ 37 (Tokyo: Shōgakukan, 1971), 149–150.

62. See, for example, this poem by Priest Saigyō: "At Bell-Deer Mountain I shake off the fetters of the sorrowful world. As the bell rings, what will become of this lone body of mine?" (*Suzuka yama ukiyo o yoso ni furisutete ikani nari yuku waga mi naruran*). See *Shin kokin wakashū*, ed. Minemura Fumito, SNKBZ 43 (Tokyo: Shōgakukan, 1995), poem no. 1613, 468.
63. Taniwaki Masachika, "Ukiyo monogatari," in *Kanazōshi shū ukiyozōshi shū*, ed. Jinbō et al., esp. 29–30. Taniwaki also notes that the emphasis on the moon, snow, blossoms, and autumn leaves itself bears a strong whiff of medieval poetics.
64. Asai Ryōi, *Kanameishi*, in *Kanazōshi shū*, ed. Taniwaki Masachika, Oka Masahito, and Inoue Kazuhito, SNKBZ 64 (Tokyo: Shōgakukan, 1999), 11–83.
65. On these effects of the establishment of the "temple-patron system" (*jidan seido*) in the early Edo period, see Kuroda Toshio, *Kenmitsu taisei ron*, Kuroda Toshio chosakushū 1 (Kyoto: Hōzōkan, 1994), 321–323. I am grateful to Ryuichi Abe for bringing this point to my attention.
66. Suwa Haruo, "Edo bungaku to wa nanika," in *Edo bungaku no hōhō* (Tokyo: Benseisha, 1997), 1–26.
67. Herman Ooms, *Tokugawa Ideology: Early Constructs, 1570–1680* (Princeton, NJ: Princeton University Press, 1985), 151–161.
68. The term "modes of perception" is Gabriel Rockhill's. See Jacques Rancière, *The Politics of Aesthetics: The Distribution of the Sensible*, ed. and trans. Gabriel Rockhill (2006; repr., London: Bloomsbury Academic, 2013), 89.
69. Rancière, *Politics of Aesthetics*, 8.

2. The Vengeance Variations

1. Mukunashi Issetsu, *Nihon bushi kagami*, in *Kanazōshi shūsei*, ed. Asakura Haruhiko (Tokyo: Tōkyōdō shuppan, 2001), 29: 85.
2. Saikaku's new style of fiction, attentive in playful and satirical ways to the contemporary world, quickly spawned imitators, inducing in the market what the book historian Konta Yōzō calls "Saikaku-book shock" (*Saikaku-bon no shōgeki*). See Konta Yōzō, *Edo no hon'yasan: kinsei bunkashi no sokumen* (Tokyo: Heibonsha, 2009), 66–67. By the early eighteenth century, books written in the new style retrospectively came to be called "books of the floating world" (*ukiyozōshi*).
3. Saikaku's works depicting samurai are *Inheritance of the Martial Way* (*Budō denraiki*, 1687), *Tales of Samurai Obligation* (*Buke giri monogatari*, 1688), and *The New Laughable Collection* (*Shin kashōki*, 1688). The first twenty of the forty

tales in *The Great Mirror of Male Love* (*Nanshoku ōkagami*, 1687) also focus on samurai.

4. Several of the stories in *Inheritance of the Martial Way* were embellished from narratives in Issetsu's earlier work *The Mongrel Collection of Things Written and Heard in the Present and the Past* (*Inu kokon chomonjū*, 1684), which may have contributed to his pique.

5. Eiko Ikegami, *The Taming of the Samurai: Honorific Individualism and the Making of Modern Japan* (Cambridge, MA: Harvard University Press, 1995), 241–264.

6. Other authorized violent practices included the samurai prerogative to cut down a commoner for perceived disrespectful behavior (*bureiuchi*) and the right to kill an unfaithful wife and her lover (*megatakiuchi*). Both practices were carefully circumscribed. See Ikegami, *Taming of the Samurai*, 244–247; and Amy Stanley, "Adultery, Punishment, and Reconciliation in Tokugawa Japan," *Journal of Japanese Studies* 33, no. 2 (2007): 312–324.

7. Upon approval of the avengers' request, their names were registered with the Edo town magistrate and they were granted a letter of permission. A follow-up investigation was also typical in the wake of a successful revenge.

8. A list of early modern instances of blood revenge includes 104 entries; however, some of these are poorly documented and possibly apocryphal. For the list, see Hiraide Kōjirō, *Katakiuchi*, Chūkō bunko (Tokyo: Bunshōkaku, 1909; repr., Tokyo: Chūō kōronsha, 1990), 99–106. Page references are to the 1990 edition. For an overview of the blood revenge practice, see D. E. Mills, "Kataki-uchi: The Practice of Blood-Revenge in Pre-Modern Japan," *Modern Asian Studies* 10, no. 4 (1976): 525–542.

9. Mukunashi Issetsu, *Nihon bushi kagami*, 84–85.

10. Some of these arguments focus discretely on *Inheritance of the Martial Way*, while others treat it within broader arguments about Saikaku's so-called warrior works (*bukemono*). See, for example, Kataoka Ryōichi, *Ihara Saikaku* (Tokyo: Shibundō, 1926); Tagawa Kuniko, "'Saikaku no bukemono:' *Nanshoku ōkagami* to *Budō denraiki*," *Nihon bungaku* 19, no. 10 (1970): 1–13; Nakamura Yukihiko, "Saikaku bungaku ni okeru buke," *Kokubungaku kaishaku to kyōzai no kenkyū* 2, no. 6 (1957): 72–76; Taniwaki Masachika, *Saikaku: kenkyū to hihyō* (Tokyo: Wakakusa shobō, 1995), 65–161, and "Shuppan jānarizumu to Saikaku," in *Saikaku kenkyū ronkō* (Tokyo: Shintensha, 1981), 52–53; Yano Kimio, "*Budō denraiki* no sekai: seido ni fūjikomerareta jōnen," in *Saikaku ron* (Tokyo: Wakakusa shobō, 2003), 285–313; Takao Kazuhiko, *Kinsei no shomin bunka* (Tokyo: Iwanami shoten, 1968); and Noma Kōshin, "Saikaku to Saikaku igo," in *Saikaku shin shinkō* (Tokyo: Iwanami shoten, 1981), 65–67. In the first monograph in English on Saikaku, David J. Gundry interprets

Inheritance of the Martial Way as written from a townsman's perspective that "evinces a blend of admiration for the bravery, cultural attainments and style of the samurai with a contrasting frustration with the limits placed on commoners and occasional samurai abuses of power, as well as with contempt for those samurai who do not live up to the ideals of the warrior ethos." David J. Gundry, *Parody, Irony and Ideology in the Fiction of Ihara Saikaku* (Leiden: Brill, 2017), 198.

11. Yano Kimio, "*Budō denraiki*: katakiuchi o gyōshi suru," *Kokubungaku kaishaku to kanshō* 58, no. 8 (1993): 99.

12. The application procedure and regulations for blood revenge were never articulated in formal law under the Tokugawa, but they appear to have built on house laws enacted by various daimyo in the sixteenth century. For a comprehensive overview of the Tokugawa application process, including examples of permission letters from the late Edo period see Hiraide, *Katakiuchi*, 33–43.

13. Ikegami, *Taming of the Samurai*, 251; Hiraide, *Katakiuchi*, 38, 42. Cycles of revenge were also prohibited; the family of a murderer slain by an avenger could not take revenge in turn.

14. Taniguchi Shinko, *Bushidō kō: kenka, katakiuchi, bureiuchi* (Tokyo: Kadokawa gakugei shuppan, 2007), 121–122.

15. *Record of Rites*, in *The Sacred Books of China: The Texts of Confucianism*, trans. James Legge (Oxford: Clarendon Press, 1885; repr. Delhi: Motilal Banarsidass, 1968), 3: 92. For the original, see *Raiki*, ed. Takeuchi Teruo, *Shinshaku kanbun taikei* 27 (Tokyo: Meiji shoin, 1971), 46–47. The *Record of Rites* was compiled during the Former Han dynasty (202 BCE–8 CE) and edited into its most enduring form during the first century CE.

16. See, for example, Yamaga Sokō, "Shidō," in *Yamaga Sokō bunshū*, ed. Mukasa San (Tokyo: Yūhōdō, 1914), 45–48.

17. In practice, blood revenge did not always hew closely to the prescribed model. Not all avengers requested permission in advance; revenge on behalf of a hierarchical junior was not unheard of; and in the latter half of the Edo period, revenge came to be pursued by townsmen and peasants as well as samurai. See Hiraide, *Katakiuchi*, 44–47, 99–106; and Taniguchi, *Bushidō kō*, 120, 125–137.

18. John W. Hall, "Rule by Status in Tokugawa Japan," *Journal of Japanese Studies* 1, no. 1 (1974): 45.

19. Kurachi Katsunao, *Tokugawa shakai no yuragi*, Zenshū Nihon no rekishi 11 (Tokyo: Shōgakukan, 2008), 19–22. See also the discussion of early modern hierarchy and relationality in Watanabe Hiroshi, "'Ōyake' to 'watakushi' no gogi: 'kō' 'shi,' 'public' 'private' to no hikaku ni oite," in *Kō to shi no shisōshi*,

ed. Sasaki Takeshi and Kim T'ae-ch'ang (Tokyo: Tokyo daigaku shuppankai, 2001), 145–154.
20. On dress prescriptions and status, see Herbert Ooms, *Tokugawa Village Practice: Class, Status, Power, Law* (Berkeley: University of California Press, 1996), 177–178.
21. See Constantine Nomikos Vaporis, *Breaking Barriers: Travel and the State in Early Modern Japan* (Cambridge, MA: Harvard University Press, 1994), appendix 2, 267–268.
22. The point that the success or failure of the revenge would reflect back to the honor of the lord was sometimes made explicit in the notice of approval provided to would-be avengers. See Hiraide, *Katakiuchi*, 39; and Taniguchi, *Bushidō kō*, 269–271.
23. Many fictional revenge narratives depict the lord temporarily making the samurai a *rōnin*, with reinstatement contingent on his completion of the revenge. In reality, such a change in status was sometimes only partial, with the avenger's stipend temporarily paid to another household member. See Mills, "Kataki-uchi," 526–527.
24. Aoki Akira, Ikeda Keiko, and Kitagawa Tadahiko, eds., *Manabon Soga monogatari 1*, Tōyō bunko 468 (Tokyo: Heibonsha, 1987); Sasakawa Sachio, Shida Itaru, and Takahashi Kiichi, eds., *Manabon Soga monogatari 2*, Tōyō bunko 486 (Tokyo: Heibonsha, 1988).
25. Konita Seiji, "Adauchi shōsetsu shiron," *Nihon bungaku* 38, no. 5 (1989): 77.
26. On the transformation of the Soga brothers in medieval and early modern theater, see Laurence R. Kominz, *Avatars of Vengeance: Japanese Drama and the Soga Literary Tradition* (Ann Arbor: Center for Japanese Studies, University of Michigan, 1995).
27. Mukunashi Issetsu, *Nihon bushi kagami*, 105.
28. Lewis Hyde, *Trickster Makes This World: Mischief, Myth, and Art* (New York: Farrar, Straus and Giroux, 2010), 7.
29. Hyde, *Trickster Makes This World*, 7.
30. Hirosue Tamotsu, *Saikaku no shōsetsu: jikū ishiki no tenkan o megutte* (Tokyo: Heibonsha, 1982), 10, 36–44. I am grateful to Thomas Gaubatz for bringing this text to my attention.
31. The three characters appear in the stories "Heartstrings Plucked on Lake Biwa" (Shintei o hiku biwa no umi), "A Woman Can Write in a Man's Hand" (Onna no tsukureru otoko moji), and "Vying over Smoke at the Field Altar" (Nozukue no keburi kurabe), respectively. See Ihara Saikaku, *Budō denraiki*, in *Budō denraiki, Saikaku okimiyage, Yorozu no fumihōgu, Saikaku nagori no tomo*, ed. Taniwaki Masachika, Fuji Akio, and Inoue Toshiyuki, SNKBT 77

(Tokyo: Iwanami shoten, 1989), 7–15, 168–174, 230–237. Unless otherwise noted, page references are to this edition.

32. Ihara Saikaku, *Budō denraiki*, 22.
33. In the original woodblock-printed edition, the full narrative is 155 lines long—twelve pages. This "revenge story" makes up eight of those lines: about half a page. See Ihara Saikaku, *Budō denraiki* (Gofukuchō Shinsaibashi sujikado [Osaka]: Okada Saburōemon, 1687), 1:fol. 13a, Waseda Daigaku Sōgō Kotenseki Dētabēsu, https://www.wul.waseda.ac.jp/kotenseki.
34. Ihara Saikaku, *Budō denraiki*, 26.
35. Ihara Saikaku, *Budō denraiki*, 44.
36. Takase Baisei, *Ruisenshū* (Teramachi Nijōagaru machi [Kyoto]: Terada Yoheiji, 1677), 5:fol. 16b, Waseda Daigaku Sōgō Kotenseki Dētabēsu, https://www.wul.waseda.ac.jp/kotenseki; Ihara Saikaku, *Budō denraiki*, 44n4.
37. Ihara Saikaku, *Budō denraiki*, 45.
38. Ihara Saikaku, *Budō denraiki*, 45.
39. I discuss adultery in greater depth in chapter 3.
40. Ihara Saikaku, *Budō denraiki*, 48.
41. Ihara Saikaku, *Budō denraiki*, 151–152.
42. On this practice, see Ihara Saikaku, *Budō denraiki*, ed. Yokoyama Shigeru and Maeda Kingorō, (Tokyo: Iwanami shoten, 1967), 396–397.
43. Ihara Saikaku, *Budō denraiki*, 152.
44. Ihara Saikaku, *Budō denraiki*, 152.
45. Ihara Saikaku, *Budō denraiki*, 152–153.
46. Ihara Saikaku, *Budō denraiki*, 156–57.
47. Ihara Saikaku, *Budō denraiki*, 158.
48. Ihara Saikaku, *Budō denraiki*, 156n6. See also Taniwaki Masachika, "*Budō denraiki* ni okeru fūshi no hōhō: sono ichi sokumen," *Edo bungaku* 1, no. 2 (1990): 34–52.
49. Someya Tomoyuki, "'Fudan kokorogake no hayauma' kō: *Budō denraiki* to shi no yūtopia," in *Saikaku shōsetsu ron: taishōteki kōzō to "Higashi Ajia" e no shikai* (Tokyo: Kanrin shobō, 2005), 384–385.
50. Ihara Saikaku, *Budō denraiki*, 153–154.
51. Ihara Saikaku, *Budō denraiki*, 154.
52. Ihara Saikaku, *Budō denraiki*, 154.
53. Ihara Saikaku, *Budō denraiki*, 156.
54. Ihara Saikaku, *Budō denraiki*, 231.
55. Yokota Fuyuhiko estimates that near the end of the seventeenth century, "between one-quarter and one-half of the female population in various sections of Kyoto and Osaka were servants." Yokota Fuyuhiko, "Imagining Working Women in Early Modern Japan," trans. Mariko Asano Tamanoi, in *Women and Class in Japanese History*, ed. Hitomi Tonomura, Anne Walthall,

and Wakita Haruko (Ann Arbor: Center for Japanese Studies, University of Michigan, 1999), 162.
56. Yokota, "Imagining Working Women in Early Modern Japan," 163.
57. Yokota, "Imagining Working Women in Early Modern Japan," 164. The section he refers to can be found in Fujimoto Kizan, *Shinpan Shikidō ōkagami*, ed. Shinpan Shikidō ōkagami kankōkai (Tokyo: Yagi shoten, 2006), 439–477.
58. Ihara Saikaku, *Budō denraiki*, 234.
59. Ihara Saikaku, *Budō denraiki*, 235.
60. Here Saikaku updates the plot of the late medieval tale *Akimichi*, in which a man instructs his wife to infiltrate the stronghold of the bandit who murdered his father. See *Akimichi*, in *Otogizōshi*, ed. Ichiko Teiji, NKBT 38 (Tokyo: Iwanami shoten, 1958), 394–410.
61. Ihara Saikaku, *Budō denraiki*, 236.
62. Ihara Saikaku, *Budō denraiki*, 237.
63. Toranosuke's dedication of his remaining days to praying for the woman is a gesture that acknowledges her role and maintains the relationship of reciprocity between them.
64. Ursula K. Le Guin, *The Carrier Bag Theory of Fiction* ([London]: Ignota, 2019), 35.
65. Le Guin, *Carrier Bag Theory of Fiction*, 36.
66. Rivi Handler-Spitz, *Symptoms of an Unruly Age: Li Zhi and Cultures of Early Modernity* (Seattle: University of Washington Press, 2017), 3–18; quotations on 5, 7, 10. See also Yuming He's discussion of the "hucksterish" (*baifan*) writing of the late Ming in He, *Home and the World: Editing the "Glorious Ming" in Woodblock-Printed Books of the Sixteenth and Seventeenth Centuries* (Cambridge, MA: Harvard University Asia Center, 2013), 1–16, 140–201.
67. Martin Solares, "How to Draw a Novel," trans. Tanya Huntington, *Literary Hub* (blog), April 8, 2015, https://lithub.com/how-to-draw-a-novel/. The text is a work-in-progress translation of chapter 1 of the Mexican writer's book *Cómo dibujar una novela*.

3. The (Un)crucified Lovers

1. Suwa Haruo, *Chikamatsu sewa jōruri no kenkyū* (Tokyo: Kasama shoin, 1974), 167.
2. Daniel V. Botsman, *Punishment and Power in the Making of Modern Japan* (Princeton, NJ: Princeton University Press, 2005), 18–19.
3. Botsman, *Punishment and Power*, 19.
4. Botsman, *Punishment and Power*, 31–32.
5. Botsman, *Punishment and Power*, 31–32.

6. Michael Jackson, *The Politics of Storytelling: Variations on a Theme by Hannah Arendt*, 2nd ed. (2013; repr., Copenhagen: Museum Tusculanum Press, 2019), 45.
7. My invocation of "intersubjectivity" draws from Jackson, *Politics of Storytelling*, 31–53.
8. Jacques Rancière, *The Politics of Literature*, trans. Julie Rose (Cambridge: Polity, 2011), 4.
9. See, for example, Luke Roberts, "Governing the Samurai Family in the Late Edo Period," in *What Is a Family? Answers from Early Modern Japan*, ed. Mary Elizabeth Berry and Marcia Yonemoto (Oakland: University of California Press, 2019), 154.
10. Amy Stanley, "Adultery, Punishment, and Reconciliation in Tokugawa Japan," *Journal of Japanese Studies* 33, no. 2 (2007): 314.
11. Stanley, "Adultery, Punishment, and Reconciliation," 313–314. My summary of the legal status of adultery in the late seventeenth century is indebted to this article, particularly 312–324. Legal standards for adultery were standardized only in 1742 with the promulgation of the *Rules for Determining Legal Matters* (*Kujikata osadamegaki*), as part of the Kyōhō Reforms of the eighth shogun, Tokugawa Yoshimune (1684–1751, r. 1716–1745). Even then, however, the new regulations were not necessarily adhered to, as Stanley shows.
12. Eiko Ikegami, *The Taming of the Samurai: Honorific Individualism and the Making of Modern Japan* (Cambridge, MA: Harvard University Press, 1995), 246–247. See also Stanley, "Adultery, Punishment, and Reconciliation," 315–316; and Roberts, "Governing the Samurai Family," 157–160, 169–70n.26.
13. Stanley, "Adultery, Punishment, and Reconciliation."
14. Mary Elizabeth Berry and Marcia Yonemoto, "Introduction," in *What Is a Family?*, 4–13.
15. Women's roles in the household, however, varied considerably by status and region, with particularly great variation among farm women, many of whom experienced less differentiation of labor with their husbands than did their urban counterparts. See Anne Walthall, "The Life Cycle of Farm Women in Tokugawa Japan," in *Recreating Japanese Women, 1600–1945*, ed. Gail Lee Bernstein (Berkeley: University of California Press, 1991), 42–43, 52–70. Walthall discusses adultery and the overdetermined aspects of female sexuality within rural communities on 63–64.
16. Matsumura Kōji, "Yōjōronteki na shintai e no manazashi," in *Shintai joseiron*, ed. Edo no shisō henshū iinkai, Edo no shisō 6 (Tokyo: Perikansha, 1997), 114–115.
17. Kaibara Ekiken, *Yōjōkun*, ed. Ishikawa Ken (Tokyo: Iwanami shoten, 1961), 24–25.

18. Matsumura, "Yōjōronteki na shintai," 99. See also Susan L. Burns, "The Body as Text: Confucianism, Reproduction, and Gender in Tokugawa Japan," in *Rethinking Confucianism: Past and Present in China, Japan, Korea, and Vietnam*, ed. Benjamin A. Elman, John B. Duncan, and Herman Ooms (Los Angeles: UCLA Asian Pacific Monograph Series, 2002), 185–186.
19. See, for example, Namura Jōhaku, *Onna chōhōki*, in *Onna chōhōki, Nan chōhōki: Genroku wakamono kokoroe shū*, ed. Nagatomo Chiyoji (Tokyo: Shakai shisōsha, 1993), 20–21.
20. *Omuna kagami*, in *Kanazōshi shūsei*, ed. Asakura Haruhiko and Fukazawa Akio (Tokyo: Tōkyōdō shuppan, 1989), 10:58.
21. Burns, "Body as Text," 188.
22. Books known as "courtesan critiques" (*yūjo hyōbanki*) began to be published in large numbers from around the 1650s. They appraised the attractive qualities of particular courtesans, provided overviews of the various licensed quarters, and instructed male readers in how to comport themselves there.
23. Fujimoto Kizan, *Shinpan Shikidō ōkagami*, ed. Shinpan Shikidō ōkagami kankōkai (Tokyo: Yagi shoten, 2006), 437–477.
24. Fujimoto Kizan, *Shinpan Shikidō ōkagami*, 439–443.
25. On the origin, historical transformations, and subject matter of *utazaimon*, see Suwa Haruo, "Utazaimon no kenkyū," *Kokugo kokubun* 31, no. 10 (1962): 40–57; and Koyama Issei, "Utazaimon ni tsuite," in *Chikamatsu jōruri no kenkyū* (Tokyo: Sōbunsha shuppan, 2000), 125–146.
26. Cheap broadsheet versions of the lyrics were sold by the performers, preserving the texts. Koyama Issei speculates that at least one of them was published in 1686, in "Utazaimon ni tsuite," 132.
27. "Daikyōji Osan Mohei" and "Daikyōji Osan utazaimon," both in *Nihon kayō shūsei*, ed. Takano Tatsuyuki (Tokyo: Shunjūsha, 1928), 8:43, 45. Because the two *utazaimon* versions overlap significantly, I will provide page references for both texts for lines that are identical between them.
28. "Daikyōji Osan Mohei," 44; "Daikyōji Osan utazaimon," 46.
29. "Daikyōji Osan Mohei," 44; "Daikyōji Osan utazaimon," 46.
30. "Daikyōji Osan Mohei," 45. Keage is the name of the area where the Tōkaidō crossed the last pass into the city of Kyoto, in the immediate vicinity of Awataguchi.
31. "Daikyōji Osan utazaimon," 47.
32. So thoughtful is Osan that when Tama presents her with Mohei's love letter, claiming that she found it on the street, Osan's first thought is for the poor messenger who dropped it and how his master will scold him. See "Daikyōji Osan Mohei," 44; and "Daikyōji Osan utazaimon," 45.

33. The collection's fifth story, "The Tale of Gengobei, a Mountain of Love" (Koi no yama Gengobei monogatari), affords a happy ending to the lovers Oman and Gengobei.
34. For a discussion of the title of the tale, see note 81.
35. Ihara Saikaku, *Kōshoku gonin onna*, in *Ihara Saikaku shū*, ed. Teruoka Yasutaka and Higashi Akimasa, SNKBZ 66 (Tokyo: Shōgakukan, 1996), 1:310–315.
36. On Saikaku's likely reasons for changing Mohei's name, see Suwa, *Chikamatsu sewa jōruri no kenkyū*, 167–194.
37. Ihara Saikaku, *Kōshoku gonin onna*, 321–322.
38. Earlier, the text describes Osan's talent with household management and care for her husband—as well as the deep affection between the two—and concludes, "This is the kind of woman a townsman household wants" (Ihara Saikaku, *Kōshoku gonin onna*, 316–317). The abruptness of Osan's shift in this scene from devoted wife to willing adulteress has been recognized as a problem in scholarship on this text. For an overview of attempts to make sense of it, see Minami Yōko, "Sakuhin no kenkyūshi: *Kōshoku gonin onna*," in *Saikaku to ukiyozōshi kenkyū*, vol. 3, *Kinsen*, ed. Taniwaki Masachika, Sugimoto Yoshinobu, and Sugimoto Kazuhiro (Tokyo: Kasama shoin, 2010), 182.
39. Ihara Saikaku, *Kōshoku gonin onna*, 334.
40. Ihara Saikaku, *Kōshoku gonin onna*, 332.
41. "Shiri" in "Monjushiri" is homophonous with "buttocks," which gave the bodhisattva a popular association with male/male sexuality.
42. Ihara Saikaku, *Kōshoku gonin onna*, 336.
43. Arthur Kleinman, "The Violences of Everyday Life: The Multiple Forms and Dynamics of Social Violence," in *Violence and Subjectivity*, ed. Veena Das, Arthur Kleinman, Mamphela Ramphele, and Pamela Reynolds (Berkeley: University of California Press, 1997), 238.
44. Chikamatsu remained a prolific writer of *jidaimono*, which outnumber his twenty-four *sewamono* by more than three to one.
45. C. Andrew Gerstle, "Hero as Murderer in Chikamatsu," *Monumenta Nipponica* 31, no. 3 (1996): 318.
46. Eleven of Chikamatsu's twenty-four *sewamono* are love suicide plays (*shinjūmono*).
47. Chikamatsu Monzaemon, *Daikyōji mukashigoyomi*, in *Chikamatsu Monzaemon shū*, ed. Torigoe Bunzō et al., SNKBZ 75 (Tokyo: Shōgakukan, 1998), 2:556.
48. In these ways, *The Calendar-Maker and the Old Calendar* also differs significantly from Chikamatsu's two other plays on the theme of adultery, with which scholars often group it: *Drum Waves of the Horikawa* (*Horikawa nami no tsuzumi*, 1707) and *Gonza the Lancer* (*Yari no Gonza kasane katabira*, 1717). These two works depict private samurai honor killings (*megatakiuchi*) of wives who wittingly sleep with other men.

49. On the ways in which *The Calendar-Maker and the Old Calendar* exhibits qualities of ethical and interpersonal messiness that characterize Chikamatsu's late plays as a whole, see Suwa, *Chikamatsu sewa jōruri no kenkyū*, 381–394; and Hirosue Tamotsu, *Chikamatsu josetsu: kinsei higeki no kenkyū* (Tokyo: Miraisha, 1963), 199–230.
50. In the play's opening lines, the narrator highlights the similarity between the name of the Third Princess (**Onna san no miya**) and Osan. See Chikamatsu Monzaemon, *Daikyōji*, 531.
51. Matsuzaki Hitoshi, "*Daikyōji mukashigoyomi* no saiginmi," in *Genroku engeki kenkyū* (Tokyo: Tokyo daigaku shuppankai, 1979), 253–254.
52. Later in the play, Osan's father chastises Osan in these terms. See Chikamatsu Monzaemon, *Daikyōji*, 559–560.
53. Chikamatsu Monzaemon, *Daikyōji*, 533.
54. René Girard, *Violence and the Sacred*, trans. Patrick Gregory (London: Continuum, 2005), 36–37.
55. Chikamatsu Monzaemon, *Daikyōji*, 534.
56. Chikamatsu Monzaemon, *Daikyōji*, 534.
57. Chikamatsu Monzaemon, *Daikyōji*, 535.
58. Chikamatsu Monzaemon, *Daikyōji*, 535.
59. Chikamatsu Monzaemon, *Daikyōji*, 536–538.
60. Chikamatsu Monzaemon, *Daikyōji*, 543.
61. Chikamatsu Monzaemon, *Daikyōji*, 543n18.
62. Jackson, *Politics of Storytelling*, 45.
63. Chikamatsu Monzaemon, *Daikyōji*, 539.
64. Chikamatsu Monzaemon, *Daikyōji*, 541.
65. Chikamatsu's statements were preserved by his friend, the Confucian scholar Hozumi Ikan (1692–1769), and later published as the opening to the book of *jōruri* commentary *Souvenirs of Naniwa* (*Naniwa miyage*, 1738). Chikamatsu argues that a play—through text, chanting, music, and puppets—is to produce feeling (*jō*), and the goal is to induce a receptive feeling (*kan*) in the audience. But there are numerous obstacles that can hinder the capacity of feeling to "transfer" (*utsuru*) smoothly from play to audience. Hozumi Ikan, "Chikamatsu no gensetsu: *Naniwa miyage* hottanshō," in *Chikamatsu jōruri shū*, ed. Shuzui Kenji and Ōkubo Tadakuni, NKBT 50 (Tokyo: Iwanami shoten, 1959), 2:355–359.
66. Quoted in Hozumi Ikan, "Chikamatsu no gensetsu," 358. Chikamatsu employs the word *giri* in an idiosyncratic way. Nakamura Yukihiko, drawing on the work of Mori Osamu, suggests that it should be understood to mean something like "natural reason" (*shizen no jōri*) rather than the more familiar sense of "obligation" or "duty." See Nakamura Yukihiko, "Bungaku wa 'ninjō o iu' no setsu," in *Kinsei bungei shichōkō* (Tokyo: Iwanami shoten, 1975), 85.

67. David B. Morris, "About Suffering: Voice, Genre, and Moral Community," in *Social Suffering*, ed. Arthur Kleinman, Veena Das, and Margaret Lock (Berkeley: University of California Press, 1997), 40–41.
68. Chikamatsu himself evokes the mixed nature of *jōruri* audiences in the opening of his play *The Love Suicides and the Two-Page Picture Book* (*Shinjū nimai ezōshi*, 1706), which begins with a scene of the crowds—"old and young," "high and low"—piling into the Takemoto-za theater for the *kaomise* performance that opened the new season. See Chikamatsu Monzaemon, *Shinjū nimai ezōshi*, in *Chikamatsu Monzaemon shū*, ed. Torigoe et al., 2:47.
69. Scholars have identified in Chikamatsu's treatment of feeling (*ninjō*) strong resonances with the thought of the Confucian philosopher Itō Jinsai (1627–1705) and his son Itō Tōgai (1670–1736), who characterized empathetic feeling as providing access to a humanistic truth that supersedes the normative neo-Confucian morality of "rewarding virtue and chastising vice" (*kanzen chōaku*). See Nakamura, "Bungaku wa 'ninjō o iu'" no setsu," 66–76, 81–86.
70. Botsman, *Punishment and Power*, 18–19.
71. Chikamatsu Monzaemon, *Daikyōji*, 570.
72. Chikamatsu Monzaemon, *Daikyōji*, 565.
73. Chikamatsu Monzaemon, *Daikyōji*, 559–561.
74. Chikamatsu Monzaemon, *Daikyōji*, 560.
75. Chikamatsu Monzaemon, *Daikyōji*, 579–580.
76. Chikamatsu Monzaemon, *Daikyōji*, 574.
77. Chikamatsu Monzaemon, *Daikyōji*, 574–575.
78. Chikamatsu Monzaemon, *Daikyōji*, 558.
79. Peter Kornicki, *The Book in Japan: A Cultural History from the Beginnings to the Nineteenth Century* (Honolulu: University of Hawai'i Press, 2001), 356–357.
80. The play periodically underscores the calendar's connection to political authority. At one point, Bairyū comments, "The calendar-maker's household is different from that of ordinary townsmen; it sells the calendars that serve as a mirror of the year for the nation's ruler and his great ministers" (Chikamatsu Monzaemon, *Daikyōji*, 552).
81. Saikaku works calendrical references into the title of his version of Osan's story: "A Tale of the Calendar-Maker, Seen in the Middle Section" (Chūdan ni miru koyomiya monogatari). The title hinges on a pun: "middle section" refers to the story's position within Saikaku's collection—the third of its five narratives—but it is also a calendrical term, referring to the middle register of the calendar's segmented layout. This middle register recorded information about whether the day would bring good or ill fortune. See Ihara Saikaku, *Kōshoku gonin onna*, 310.

82. "Daikyōji Osan Mohei," 44; "Daikyōji Osan utazaimon," 45.
83. Chikamatsu Monzaemon, *Daikyōji*, 576.
84. Chikamatsu Monzaemon, *Daikyōji*, 577.
85. Chikamatsu Monzaemon, *Daikyōji*, 580. There is no evidence that monks ever possessed—much less exercised—such a power to grant sanctuary to condemned criminals. See Okada Morimasa, "Kantsū jōruri *Daikyōji mukashi goyomi* ni tsuite: igai na ketsumatsu ni miru Chikamatsu no sakui," *Aichi shukutoku daigaku kokugo kokubun* 31, no. 3 (2008): 69–84.
86. The thirty-third death anniversary (*sanjūsan kaiki*) was associated with the thirty-three forms attributed to Kannon, the bodhisattva of compassion, in the *Lotus Sutra*. Buddhist death anniversaries in Japan count the year of the death itself as the first year; hence, by the Western count, the thirty-third anniversary is marked thirty-two years after the death it commemorates. In his words on playwrighting, Chikamatsu uses the word *nagusami* to characterize the "diversion" that a play brings to its audience. But as Gerstle emphasizes, *nagusami* also connotes "the additional Buddhistic meaning of calming the spirit and consoling persons as they cope with the suffering inherent in the human condition." C. Andrew Gerstle, "Takemoto Gidayū and the Individualistic Spirit of Osaka Theater," in *Osaka: The Merchants' Capital of Early Modern Japan*, ed. James L. McClain and Wakita Osamu (Ithaca, NY: Cornell University Press, 1999), 121. In Chikamatsu's theater, that is, entertainment and the consolation of both the characters' *and* the spectators' suffering were bound into one.
87. The sense that the play's ending carries a politically sensitive charge is supported by comparison with the version of the play that concurrently went up in Kyoto—the shogunate's administrative center for the region and the seat of the symbolically important imperial court. Renamed *The Old Calendar and the Thirty-third Death Anniversary* (*Mukashigoyomi sanjūsan nenki*) and performed at Kyoto's Ujiza theater, the play excises all references to the title of calendar-maker, discreetly changes Ishun's name to Jishun, and alters references to the imperial court and other sites of traditional authority to vague allusions to "those above." Most importantly, the priest never shows up at the execution ground in the Kyoto version: Osan and Mohei meet their traditional fate of crucifixion. See Takemoto Chitosedayū, "Osan Mohei o tazunete," in *Saikaku to ukiyozōshi kenkyū*. vol. 5, *Geinō*, ed. Hara Michio, Kawai Masumi, and Kurakazu Masae (Tokyo: Kasama shoin, 2011), 215.
88. Chikamatsu Monzaemon, *Daikyōji*, 571.
89. The line appears in *Souvenirs of Naniwa* (see note 65). Hozumi Ikan, "Chikamatsu no gensetsu," 358.

4. Ueda Akinari and the Form of Fiction

1. I am indebted here to Susan L. Burns's characterization of the questions at the heart of *kokugaku*, in *Before the Nation: Kokugaku and the Imagining of Community in Early Modern Japan* (Durham, NC: Duke University Press, 2003), 2.
2. Ueda Akinari, "Masurao monogatari," in *Hanabusa sōshi, Nishiyama monogatari, Ugetsu monogatari, Harusame monogatari*, ed. Nakamura Yukihiko, Takada Mamoru, and Nakamura Hiroyasu, SNKBZ 78 (Tokyo: Shōgakukan, 1995), 623.
3. Noma Kōshin, "Iwayuru Genta sōdō o megutte: Ayatari to Akinari," in *Kinsei sakkaden kō* (Tokyo: Chūō kōronsha, 1985), 309.
4. The play was titled *The Courtesan's Dictionary* (*Keisei setsuyōshū*). See Noma Kōshin, "Iwayuru Genta sōdō o megutte," 323.
5. Nakamura Yukihiko, "Kaisetsu," in *Ueda Akinari shū*, ed. Nakamura Yukihiko, NKBT 56 (Tokyo: Iwanami shoten, 1959), 21–22; Asano Sanpei, "'Shikubi no egao' o megutte: Genta sōdō to Ayatari, Akinari," in *Ueda Akinari no kenkyū* (Tokyo: Ōfūsha, 1985), 605; Nakamura Hiroyasu, "*Harusame monogatari*," in *Hanabusa sōshi, Nishiyama monogatari, Ugetsu monogatari, Harusame monogatari*, ed. Nakamura, Takada, and Nakamura, 617.
6. Morita Kirō, "*Harusame monogatari* no igi," in *Ueda Akinari bungei no kenkyū* (Osaka: Izumi shoin, 2003), 463.
7. Kazama Seishi, "*Harusame monogatari* to wa nanika," in *Harusame monogatari to iu shisō* (Tokyo: Shinwasha, 2011), 15.
8. Ishikawa Jun, "Akinari shiron," *Bungaku* 27, no. 8 (1959): 980. Other modern writers who held *Tales of the Spring Rain* in high regard include Satō Haruo (1892–1964) and Tanizaki Jun'ichirō (1886–1965).
9. Noma Kōshin reproduces the Judicial Council's judgments, including the provisional judgments submitted by the Kyoto magistrate's office, in "Iwayuru Genta sōdō o megutte," 310–317.
10. Noma Kōshin abstracts and summarizes this outline from the official documents in "Iwayuru Genta sōdō o megutte," 319–320.
11. Quoted in Noma Kōshin, "Iwayuru Genta sōdō o megutte," 311.
12. The *Rules* was provisionally completed in 1742 and reached its final form in 1754. For a comprehensive introduction to the *Rules for Determining Legal Matters*, see Dan Fenno Henderson, "Introduction to the *Kujikata Osadamegaki* (1742)," in *Hō to keibatsu no rekishiteki kōsatsu*, ed. Hiramatsu Yoshirō hakushi tsuitō ronbunshū henshū iinkai (Nagoya: Nagoya daigaku shuppankai, 1987), 490–544. I follow the translation of the title of this document in Daniel V. Botsman, *Punishment and Power in the Making of Modern Japan* (Princeton, NJ: Princeton University Press, 2005), 16. On the way in which the

Judicial Council made use of the *Rules*'s precedents and guidelines, see Noma Kōshin, "Iwayuru Genta sōdō o megutte," 310–318.

13. Moriyama Shigeo, "'Masurao monogatari' no seiritsu," in *Gen'yō no bungaku: Ueda Akinari* (Tokyo: San'ichi shobō, 1982), 199, 204–205.
14. Quoted in Noma Kōshin, "Iwayuru Genta sōdō o megutte," 310–311.
15. Moriyama Shigeo, "'Masurao monogatari' no seiritsu," 204.
16. Quoted in Noma Kōshin, "Iwayuru Genta sōdō o megutte," 311.
17. Blake Morgan Young, trans., "A Tale of the Western Hills: Takebe Ayatari's *Nishiyama monogatari*," *Monumenta Nipponica* 37, no. 1 (1982): 79.
18. Noma Kōshin, "Iwayuru Genta sōdō o megutte," 311, 317.
19. Moriyama Shigeo, "'Masurao monogatari' no seiritsu," 202.
20. Moriyama Shigeo, "'Masurao monogatari' no seiritsu," 203.
21. Noma Kōshin, "Iwayuru Genta sōdō o megutte," 312.
22. On Akinari's feelings about Ayatari, see Lawrence E. Marceau, *Takebe Ayatari: A* Bunjin *Bohemian in Early Modern Japan* (Ann Arbor: Center for Japanese Studies, University of Michigan, 2004), 258–260.
23. The editions I refer to are: Kamo no Mabuchi, *Lecture Notes on the* Kokin wakashū (*Kokin wakashū uchigiki*, 1789), and *The Ancient Meaning of* Tales of Ise (*Ise monogatari koi*, 1793). See Peter Flueckiger, "Reflections on the Meaning of Our Country: Kamo no Mabuchi's *Kokuikō*," *Monumenta Nipponica* 63, no. 2 (2008): 230–231.
24. The poetry volumes I refer to are: Kamo no Mabuchi, *Collection of Poems by Agatai* (*Agatai no kashū*) and *Gleanings of Agatai* (*Agatai shūi*), both published in 1790. See Flueckiger, "Reflections on the Meaning of Our Country," 231.
25. This linear-progress model sees *kokugaku* as originating with the philological endeavors of Keichū (1640–1701) and Kada no Azumamaro (1669–1736), taking clearer shape in the *Man'yōshū* studies of Kamo no Mabuchi (1697–1769), reaching its pinnacle in Motoori Norinaga's (1730–1801) study of the *Kojiki*, and then popularized by Hirata Atsutane (1776–1843).
26. The so-called Edo school (*Edo ha*), for example—revolving around Mabuchi's disciples Katō Chikage (1735–1808) and Murata Harumi (1746–1811)—devoted itself to the composition of *waka* poetry, with a strong emphasis on the *Man'yōshū* style.
27. Burns, *Before the Nation*, 2.
28. I borrow the evocative term "lost wholeness" from Peter Flueckiger, *Imagining Harmony: Poetry, Empathy, and Community in Mid-Tokugawa Confucianism and Nativism* (Stanford, CA: Stanford University Press, 2011), 3.
29. Kamo no Mabuchi, "Kokuikō," in *Kinsei shintō ron, zenki kokugaku*, ed. Taira Shigemichi and Abe Akio, Nihon shisō taikei 39 (Tokyo: Iwanami shoten, 1972), 384.
30. Kamo no Mabuchi, "Kokuikō," 384.

31. Kamo no Mabuchi, "Kokuikō," 384.
32. Kamo no Mabuchi, "Kokuikō," 383–384.
33. Kamo no Mabuchi, "Kokuikō," 382, 386.
34. Flueckiger, *Imagining Harmony*, 157–158.
35. Kamo no Mabuchi, "Kokuikō," 376–377.
36. Kamo no Mabuchi, "Kokuikō," 380.
37. Kamo no Mabuchi, "Ka'ikō," in *Kinsei shintō ron, zenki kokugaku*, ed. Taira Shigemichi and Abe Akio, Nihon shisō taikei 39 (Tokyo: Iwanami shoten, 1972), 349.
38. Kamo no Mabuchi, "Kokuikō," 382–383.
39. Although the *Man'yōshū* was compiled in the wake of the court's embrace of continental culture, Mabuchi identifies many of its poems as retaining the ancient style.
40. Although written with a variety of graphs, the etymology of the word *masurao* appears to combine the adjectival stems *masu-* (surpassing, excellent) and *ara-* (rough, wild, unrestrained), and the noun *o* (man). See Paula Doe, *A Warbler's Song in the Dusk: The Life and Work of Ōtomo Yakamochi (718–785)* (Berkeley: University of California Press, 1982), 20.
41. Doe, *Warbler's Song in the Dusk*, 20.
42. Kamo no Mabuchi, "Niimanabi," in *Kinsei shintōron, zenki kokugaku*, ed. Taira Shigemichi and Abe Akio, Nihon shisō taikei 39 (Tokyo: Iwanami shoten, 1972), 358.
43. Kamo no Mabuchi, "Niimanabi," 358.
44. Hara Masako, "Mabuchi no 'masurao' kō," *Edo bungaku* 7 (1991): 114–120.
45. Hara, "Mabuchi no 'masurao' kō," 116.
46. Kamo no Mabuchi, "Ka'ikō," 349.
47. Kamo no Mabuchi, "Niimanabi," 358, 360.
48. Kamo no Mabuchi, "Ka'ikō," 349.
49. Kamo no Mabuchi, "Ka'ikō," 350. Specifically, Mabuchi refers to the "Ya'ata Mirror of the past," likening the poetic forms of the past to the sacred mirror that lured the Sun Goddess out of her cave and returned light to the world in ancient myth.
50. Flueckiger, *Imagining Harmony*, 170–171.
51. Hara, "Mabuchi no 'masurao' kō," 123–126.
52. Takebe Ayatari's *A Tale of the Western Hills* characterizes its Genta-inspired character as "a *masurao* of the present age." Takebe Ayatari, *Nishiyama monogatari*, in *Hanabusa sōshi, Nishiyama monogatari, Ugetsu monogatari, Harusame monogatari*, ed. Nakamura, Takada, and Nakamura, 203.
53. Kamo no Mabuchi, Kamo no Mabuchi to Hōrai Garaku, Meiwa 6 [1769].7.4, in *Takebe Ayatari zenshū*, ed. Takebe Ayatari Chosaku Kankōkai (Tokyo:

Kokusho kankōkai, 1990), 9:181. Marceau translates the relevant passage in *Takebe Ayatari*, 258.
54. On Ayatari's theorization and promotion of *katauta*, see Marceau, *Takebe Ayatari*, 115–131.
55. Kinryū Keiyū, preface to Takebe Ayatari, *Nishiyama monogatari*, 197.
56. Kinryū Keiyū, preface to Takebe Ayatari, *Nishiyama monogatari*, 198.
57. For a note on how the major characters correspond to kabuki stock-character types, see Takada Mamoru, "Nishiyama monogatari," in *Hanabusa sōshi, Nishiyama monogatari, Ugetsu monogatari, Harusame monogatari*, ed. Nakamura, Takada, and Nakamura, 597–598. For a comment on the work's kabuki-esque plot devices, see Nagashima Hiroaki "Akinari no chosho kaiki," *Bungaku* 8, no. 3 (2007): 32.
58. Takebe Ayatari, *Nishiyama monogatari*, 250.
59. Ueda Akinari, "Masurao monogatari," 623.
60. Ueda Akinari, *Shodō kikimimi sekenzaru*, in *Ueda Akinari shoki ukiyozōshi hyōshaku*, ed. Moriyama Shigeo (Tokyo: Kokusho kankōkai, 1977), 27–28.
61. "That ancient group of sages" likely refers to the Seven Sages of the Bamboo Grove of third-century China.
62. Ueda Akinari, *Ugetsu monogatari*, in *Hanabusa sōshi, Nishiyama monogatari, Ugetsu monogatari, Harusame monogatari*, ed. Nakamura Yukihiko, Takada Mamoru, and Nakamura Hiroyasu, SNKBZ 78 (Tokyo: Shōgakukan, 1995), 275–276.
63. Authorship of *The Water Margin* traditionally has been attributed to the fourteenth-century writers Shi Nai'an and Luo Guanzhong, but the biographical details of both men are obscure.
64. The legend of Murasaki Shikibu's condemnation to hell developed in the early medieval period, appearing in such works as *A Sutra for Genji* (*Genji ipponkyō*, ca. 1166), *The Mirror of the Present* (*Ima kagami*, ca. 1170), *Collection of Treasures* (*Hōbutsushū*, ca. 1177–1181), and *Tales of the Present* (*Ima monogatari*, ca. 1239–1240).
65. Ueda Akinari, "Nubatama no maki," in *Ueda Akinari zenshū*, ed. Ueda Akinari zenshū henshū iinkai (Tokyo: Chūō kōronsha, 1992), 5:63. On the essay's dating, see Nakamura Yukihiko, "Ueda Akinari no monogatari kan," in *Nakamura Yukihiko chojutsushū* (Tokyo: Chūō kōronsha, 1982), 1:248.
66. Zhuangzi, *Zhuangzi: The Complete Writings*, trans. Brook Ziporyn (Indianapolis: Hackett, 2020), 225–226.
67. Nakano Mitsutoshi, "Akinari no bungaku kan," in *Jūhasseiki no Edo bungei* (Tokyo: Iwanami shoten, 1999), 275. Nakano discusses the broader eighteenth-century engagement with *gūgen* in "Gūgenron no tenkai: toku ni Akinari no ron to sono haikei," *Kokugo to kokubungaku* 45, no. 10 (1968): 108–113.

68. Ueda Akinari, "Yoshiya ashiya," in *Ueda Akinari zenshū*, ed. Ueda Akinari zenshū henshū iinkai, 5:510–511. Akinari included the essay as a supplement to the published version he prepared of Mabuchi's study *The Ancient Meaning of Tales of Ise*. The "undiscovered pearl" is a reference to *Man'yōshū*, book 6, poem no. 1023.
69. Nakamura Hiroyasu explicitly links Akinari's "rage" to a sense of "self-consciousness" (*jiishiki*) in conflict with an equally strong sense of societal place or social delimitation (*"bundo" no ishiki*), in Nakamura Hiroyasu, "Akinari no bungaku ron," *Nihon bungaku* 13, no. 2 (1964): 13. Similarly, Iikura Yōichi links Akinari's "rage" to the term *fugū*—the obscurity of a talent who does not align with the times—in Iikura Yōichi, "Akinari ni okeru 'ikidōri' no mondai: *Harusame monogatari* e no ichi shiten," in *Akinari kō* (Tokyo: Kanrin shobō, 2005), 31–53.
70. Ueda Akinari, "Nubatama no maki," 66–67.
71. Ueda Akinari, "Masurao monogatari," 623.
72. Nakamura Hiroyasu, "Kaidai," in *Hanabusa sōshi, Nishiyama monogatari, Ugetsu monogatari, Harusame monogatari*, ed. Nakamura, Takada, and Nakamura, 623.
73. Ueda Akinari, *Akinari ibun*, ed. Fujii Otoo (Tokyo: Shūbunkan, 1919), 406–417.
74. Morita Kirō, "*Harusame monogatari* no igi," 463.
75. Uchimura Katsushi, "'Masurao monogatari' ron: 'katari' to sono gaibu," in *Ueda Akinari ron: kokugakuteki sōzōryoku no ken'iki* (Tokyo: Perikansha, 2007), 165–166.
76. Ueda Akinari, "Masurao monogatari," 623–624.
77. Ueda Akinari, "Masurao monogatari," 623.
78. Ueda Akinari, "Masurao monogatari," 623.
79. Ueda Akinari, "Masurao monogatari," 624.
80. Konoe Noriko, "*Genji monogatari* e no manazashi: Akinari no monogatari to monogatari ron," in *Ueda Akinari shinkō: kusemono no bungaku* (Tokyo: Perikansha, 2016), 40–41.
81. Ueda Akinari, "Masurao monogatari," 626.
82. Ueda Akinari, "Masurao monogatari," 627.
83. Ueda Akinari, "Masurao monogatari," 627.
84. Ueda Akinari, "Masurao monogatari," 629.
85. Ueda Akinari, "Masurao monogatari," 629.
86. Ueda Akinari, "Masurao monogatari," 629–630.
87. Ueda Akinari, "Masurao monogatari," 630.
88. Ueda Akinari, "Masurao monogatari," 626.
89. Ueda Akinari, "Masurao monogatari," 630.

90. Ueda Akinari, "Yoshiya ashiya," 510.
91. Ueda Akinari, "Masurao monogatari," 631.
92. Ironically, in saying that he will "omit" (*morashitsu*) further details, he borrows his phrasing directly from *The Tale of Genji*, in which the narrator employs it to abbreviate details of the tale that would otherwise run to great length. See, for example, Murasaki Shikibu, *Genji monogatari*, ed. Abe Akio et al., SNKBZ 20 (Tokyo: Shōgakukan, 1994), 151.
93. Ueda Akinari, "Masurao monogatari," 631.
94. Dan 76 of *Ise monogatari*, in *Taketori monogatari, Ise monogatari, Yamato monogatari, Heichū monogatari*, ed. Katagiri Yōichi et al., SNKBZ 12 (Tokyo: Shōgakukan, 1994), 178.
95. Uchimura, "'Masurao monogatari' ron," 180–184.
96. Ueda Akinari, *Tandai shōshin roku*, in *Ueda Akinari shū*, ed. Nakamura, 310.
97. Iikura Yōichi, *Ueda Akinari: Kizuna toshite no bungei* (Suita-shi: Osaka daigaku shuppankai, 2012), 44–45.
98. Nagashima, "Akinari no chosho kaiki," 26–28. Nagashima argues as well that this shift can help us make sense of Akinari's focus on truth in "The Tale of a *Masurao*" and his turn to fiction in "The Smile of the Severed Head," 31–35.
99. I follow the list provided in Iikura, *Ueda Akinari*, 45–46.
100. Ueda Akinari, *Harusame monogatari: Bunka gonen bon*, in *Ueda Akinari zenshū*, ed. Ueda Akinari zenshū henshū iinkai, 5:147. I have translated the preface as it appears in the Bunka 5 variant, the only variant in which "The Smile of the Severed Head" appears.
101. Iikura, *Ueda Akinari*, 228.
102. Iikura, *Ueda Akinari*, 228–230; Kazama Seishi, "*Harusame monogatari* ron no tame ni: shiteki kenkyūshi to kasetsu, moshiku wa bōsō," in *Harusame monogatari to iu shisō*, 61–63.
103. Kazama, "*Harusame monogatari* ron no tame ni," 62–63.
104. Kyokutei Bakin, *Kinsei mononohon Edo sakusha burui*, ed. Tokuda Takeshi (Tokyo: Iwanami shoten, 2014), 206–207. The late Edo-period writer Kyokutei Bakin (1767–1848) expressed his surprise at learning of the book's existence and noted his desire to access it—as well as the difficulty of doing so. On the complex twentieth-century publishing history of *Tales of the Spring Rain*, see Iikura, *Ueda Akinari*, 214–216; and Kazama, "*Harusame monogatari* to wa nanika," 19–21.
105. Satō Miyuki, "Gisho to ihon," in *Ayatari to Akinari to: Jūhasseiki kokugaku e no hihan* (Nagoya: Nagoya daigaku shuppankai, 1993), 140–145.
106. Satō's thesis remains controversial, and there are other ways to read the existence of the work's multiple manuscript variants. Iikura (in *Ueda Akinari*,

217–226) dwells on the materiality of the manuscript form, noting the many places in which the stories draw attention to their physical inscription, and emphasizes the role of manuscript in early modern literati culture.
107. Burns, *Before the Nation*, 119–129.
108. Ueda Akinari, *Harusame monogatari*, in *Hanabusa sōshi, Nishiyama monogatari, Ugetsu monogatari, Harusame monogatari*, ed. Nakamura, Takada, and Nakamura, 472–473.
109. Ueda Akinari, *Harusame monogatari*, 482, 486.
110. Ueda Akinari, *Harusame monogatari*, 477.
111. Ibi Takashi, "'Shikubi no egao' no shudai," in *Kinsei bungaku no kyōkai: koga to hyōgen no hen'yō* (Tokyo: Iwanami shoten, 2009), 185–200; Asano, "'Shikubi no egao' o megutte," 605; Nakamura, "*Harusame monogatari*," 617.
112. Kazama Seishi, "'Shikubi no egao' shiron," in *Harusame monogatari to iu shisō*, 85–86. He reads this sincerity as an extension of Gozō's stark characterization as a "buddha," whereas I see it as more inscrutable.
113. Ueda Akinari, *Harusame monogatari*, 473, 475.
114. Ueda Akinari, *Harusame monogatari*, 475.
115. Ueda Akinari, *Harusame monogatari*, 478.
116. Ueda Akinari, *Harusame monogatari*, 479.
117. Ueda Akinari, *Harusame monogatari*, 480.
118. Ueda Akinari, *Harusame monogatari*, 480.
119. Ueda Akinari, *Harusame monogatari*, 483.
120. Nakamura, "*Harusame monogatari*," 617.
121. Ueda Akinari, *Harusame monogatari*, 483–484.
122. When the village headman dashes to inform Motosuke's mother of her son's act, she—like the mother in "The Tale of a *Masurao*"—evinces no surprise. For all the smiles and words of marital advice with which she sent off her daughter, she appears to have known that it was a final parting. See Ueda Akinari, *Harusame monogatari*, 484.
123. Ueda Akinari, *Harusame monogatari*, 562.
124. Ueda Akinari, *Harusame monogatari*, 485.
125. Ueda Akinari, *Harusame monogatari*, 487.
126. The mediation of communal retelling is emphasized by both Kazama, "'Shikubi no egao' shiron," 89–90; and Ibi, "'Shikubi no egao' no shudai," 199.
127. Satō Miyuki, "*Harusame monogatari* to iu sōchi," in *Ayatari to Akinari to*, 174–175.
128. Tom Eyers, *Speculative Formalism: Literature, Theory, and the Critical Present* (Evanston, IL: Northwestern University Press, 2017), 5.

5. Frontier Violence

1. Ronald P. Toby, *Engaging the Other: "Japan" and Its Alter Egos, 1550–1850* (Leiden: Brill, 2019), 4.
2. See, for example, a characterization of Japan as a "natural region" with a common culture shaped by a shared geography, in Delmer M. Brown, *Nationalism in Japan: An Introductory Historical Analysis* (Berkeley: University of California Press, 1955), 6–7; and a critique of this position in Tessa Morris-Suzuki, in *Re-inventing Japan: Time, Space, Nation* (Armonk, NY: Sharpe, 1998), 9–10.
3. Toby, *Engaging the Other*, 36.
4. Toby, *Engaging the Other*, 29–45, 48–49.
5. Marcia Yonemoto, *Mapping Early Modern Japan: Space, Place, and Culture in the Tokugawa Period, 1603–1868* (Berkeley: University of California Press, 2003), 5.
6. Morris-Suzuki, *Re-inventing Japan*, 17–20.
7. On the trope of the "hairy barbarian," see Toby, *Engaging the Other*, 190–251; on the role of staged Ainu rituals in Japanese Ezo diplomacy, see David L. Howell, *Geographies of Identity in Nineteenth-Century Japan* (Berkeley: University of California Press, 2005), 119–130.
8. Toby, *Encountering the Other*, 86–87; and Donald Keene, *The Japanese Discovery of Europe: Honda Toshiaki and Other Discoverers, 1720–1798* (New York: Grove Press, 1954), 39–56.
9. Timon Screech, *The Shogun's Painted Culture: Fear and Creativity in the Japanese States, 1760–1829* (London: Reaktion, 2000), 11.
10. Screech, *Shogun's Painted Culture*, 9. Screech, for example, whose book focuses on the role of visual art, in particular, in the establishment of a reified "Japanese culture," characterizes the decades around the turn of the nineteenth century as ones of "building a boundary to construct a center."
11. Michel de Certeau, "Spatial Stories," in *The Practice of Everyday Life*, trans. Steven Rendall (Berkeley: University of California Press, 1984), 123.
12. Certeau, "Spatial Stories," 123.
13. Certeau, "Spatial Stories," 127.
14. Certeau, "Spatial Stories," 128–129.
15. Tsubouchi Shōyō, *Shōsetsu shinzui*, in *Tsubouchi Shōyō shū*, ed. Nakamura Ken and Umezawa Nobuo, Nihon kindai bungaku taikei 3 (Tokyo: Kadokawa shoten, 1974). Shōyō's primary target is Kyokutei Bakin's monumental *Eight Dog Chronicle* (*Nansō Satomi hakkenden*, 1814–1842), widely celebrated as the pinnacle of the genre. For a discussion of the Meiji period reception of this work, and of Shōyō's criticisms in particular, see Glynne Walley, *Good Dogs: Edification, Entertainment, and Kyokutei Bakin's "Nansō Satomi hakkenden"*

(Ithaca, NY: Cornell University East Asia Program, 2017), 1–41. See also Daniel Poch, *Licentious Fictions:* Ninjō *and the Nineteenth-Century Japanese Novel* (New York: Columbia University Press, 2020), 59–86 and 135–139.

16. Thongchai Winichakul, *Siam Mapped: A History of the Geo-Body of a Nation* (Honolulu: University of Hawai'i Press, 1994), 17–18.
17. Howell, *Geographies of Identity*, 110.
18. Tessa Morris-Suzuki, "A Descent into the Past: The Frontier in the Construction of Japanese Identity," in *Multicultural Japan: Paleolithic to Postmodern*, ed. Donald Denoon, Mark Hudson, Gavan McCormack, and Tessa Morris-Suzuki (Cambridge: Cambridge University Press, 1996), 83. See also Katsurajima Nobuhiro, "'Ka'i' shisō no kaitai to kokugakuteki 'jiko' zō no seisei," in *Kokka (jiko) zō no keisei*, ed. Edo no shisō henshū iinkai, Edo no shisō 4 (Tokyo: Perikansha, 1995), 40–59; and Brett L. Walker, *The Conquest of Ainu Lands: Ecology and Culture in Japanese Expansion, 1590–1800* (Berkeley: University of California Press, 2001), 9–10. On Japanese diplomatic recentering of the *ka-i* order from China to the Japanese islands, see Ronald P. Toby, "Contesting the Centre: International Sources of Japanese National Identity," *International History Review* 7, no. 3 (1985): 347–363.
19. Morris-Suzuki, "Descent into the Past," 84.
20. *Onzōshi shimawatari*, in *Muromachi monogatari sōshi shū*, ed. Ōshima Tatehiko and Watari Kōichi, SNKBZ 63 (Tokyo: Shōgakukan, 2002), 91–118.
21. Howell, *Geographies of Identity*, 110–130, 123.
22. Kawanishi Hidemichi, *Tōhoku: Japan's Constructed Outland*, trans. Nanyan Guo and Raquel Hill (Leiden: Brill, 2016), 15–20. In his account of his journey in 1788 through northern Japan, the traveler and geographer Furukawa Koshōken (1726–1807) expresses his astonishment at the architecture, prosperity, and customs of Matsumae, administrative center of the Wajinchi, which he likens to the elegant culture of the Kamigata region, contrasting its "superior" (*jōjō*) qualities to the "remote badlands" (*henpi no akusho*) of northern Honshu. Furukawa Koshōken, *Tōyū zakki*, ed. Ōtō Tokihiko (Tokyo: Tōyō bunko, 1964), 115.
23. The identity of the Emishi, and the question of their possible ethnic relationship to the Ainu or to the Yamato Japanese, remains a matter of dispute. From the perspective of the ancient Yamato state, the people's designation as Emishi (written with characters connoting "barbarian") was political, not ethnically based. See Karl Friday, "Pushing Beyond the Pale: The Yamato Conquest of the Emishi and Northern Japan," *Journal of Japanese Studies* 23, no. 1 (1997): 3–5.
24. See, for example, *Goshūi wakashū*, ed. Kubota Jun and Hirata Yoshinobu, SNKBT 8 (Tokyo: Iwanami shoten, 1994), poem no. 518, 169.

25. *Man'yōshū*, ed. Kojima Nobuyuki, Kinoshita Masatoshi, and Tōno Haruyuki, SNKBZ 9 (Tokyo: Shōgakukan, 1996), poem no. 3807, 4:102–103.
26. *Kokin wakashū*, ed. Ozawa Masao and Matsuda Shigeho, SNKBZ 11 (Tokyo: Shōgakukan, 1994), 19.
27. Matsuo Bashō, *Oku no hosomichi*, in *Bashō bunshū*, ed. Toyama Susumu, SNKS 17 (Tokyo: Shinchōsha, 1978), 116–118.
28. In 1783, Kudō Heisuke (1734–1800) presented to the shogunate's senior councilor Tanuma Okitsugu (1719–1788) his book *Thoughts on the Rumors from Red Ezo* (*Aka Ezo fūsetsu kō*), which advocated for the development of the Ezochi and the opening of trade with the Russians. In *An Illustrated Overview of the Three Countries* (*Sangoku tsūran zusetsu*, 1786) and *Military Talks for a Maritime Country* (*Kaikoku heidan*, 1791), Hayashi Shihei (1738–1793) warned urgently of the threat of Russian advancement into Japanese waters and called for investment in maritime defense and the development of the Ezochi for defensive purposes. On Russian incursions into the Kuril trade and the resulting political fallout, see Walker, *Conquest of Ainu Lands*, 161–172.
29. Daikokuya Kōdayū was the captain of an Ise ship that was blown off course by a storm in 1782. The crew was rescued by Russians, and Kōdayū traveled to Saint Petersburg and received an audience with Catherine the Great before returning to Japan with Laxman in 1792. See Keene, *Japanese Discovery of Europe*, 60–69.
30. Laxman was granted documents stating that one Russian ship would be allowed to dock at Nagasaki, but an attempt to do so nine years later, led by the ambassador Nikolai Rezanov (1764–1807), was rebuffed by the Japanese. See Keene, *Japanese Discovery of Europe*, 65–66, 68.
31. Walker, *Conquest of Ainu Lands*, 194.
32. Itasaka Yōko, *Edo no kikōbun: taihei no yo no tabibitotachi* (Tokyo: Chūō kōron shinsha, 2011), 149–150.
33. Kikuchi Isao, *Kikin kara yomu kinsei shakai* (Tokyo: Azekura shobō, 2003), 55.
34. Walley, *Good Dogs*, 64. Walley discusses various genre frameworks for apprehending the *yomihon*—including *haishi*, *shōsetsu*, novel, and romance—with particular reference to Kyokutei Bakin's *Eight Dog Chronicle* on 61–74.
35. *Yomihon* were printed in a larger size (*hanshibon*) than *kibyōshi* and *gōkan* (*chūhon*) and generally to a higher material standard. They were also published by *shomotsu* publishers, who produced books in such respectable genres as Confucian, Buddhist, and Shinto studies; medical studies; and *waka* poetry. *Kibyōshi* and *gōkan*, however, were published by *jihon* ("local book") publishers, who specialized in lowlier and smaller-format works oriented toward popular entertainment. On the reasons for this difference, see Satō Satoru, "Jihon ron: Edo yomihon wa naze shomotsu na no ka," in *Yomihon kenkyū shinshū*, ed. Yomihon kenkyū no kai (Tokyo: Kanrin shobō, 1998), 1:34–54.

36. For a detailed study of this incident, see Satō Yukiko, *Edo no shuppan tōsei: dan'atsu ni honrō sareta gesakushatachi* (Tokyo: Yoshikawa kōbunkan, 2017), 68–112; and Peter F. Kornicki, "*Nishiki no Ura*: An Instance of Censorship and the Structure of a *Sharebon*," *Monumenta Nipponica* 32, no. 2 (1977): 153–188.
37. William C. Hedberg, *The Japanese Discovery of Chinese Fiction: The Water Margin and the Making of a National Canon* (New York: Columbia University Press, 2020), 88. Hedberg discusses *The Water Margin of the Loyal Retainers* in depth on 85–90.
38. Ōtaka Yōji, *Kyōden to Bakin: "haishimono" yomihon yōshiki no keisei* (Tokyo: Kanrin shobō, 2010), 33–35.
39. Inoue Keiji, *Kyōden kōshōgaku to yomihon no kenkyū* (Tokyo: Shintensha, 1997), 44–45. See also Ōtaka, *Kyōden to Bakin*, 35–36.
40. Santō Kyōden, *Katakiuchi Okazaki joroshu*, in *Santō Kyōden zenshū*, ed. Santō Kyōden zenshū henshū iinkai (Tokyo: Perikansha, 1995), 6:145–187.
41. For a compact summary of his concept of the "*yomihon* framework," see Ōtaka Yōji, "Edo: Kyōden, Bakin to 'haishimono' yomihon no keisei," in *Yomihon jiten: Edo no denki shōsetsu*, ed. Kokubungaku kenkyū shiryōkan and Hachinohe shiritsu toshokan (Tokyo: Kasama shoin, 2008), 51–52. He also identifies *The Asaka Marsh* as a crucial step in the development of the *yomihon*'s style, in Ōtaka, *Kyōden to Bakin*, 81–113. He shows how Kyōden's integration of wording from Ueda Akinari's *Tales of Moonlight and Rain* (*Ugetsu monogatari*, 1776) and Hiraga Gennai's (1728–1779) *Rootless Grasses* (*Nenashigusa*, 1763–1769) helped to give late *yomihon* a written style that mixed elegant and colloquial diction and departed from the "translated" flavor of the style that Kyōden had adopted in *The Water Margin of the Loyal Retainers*.
42. Ōtaka, *Kyōden to Bakin*, 8.
43. Ōtaka, *Kyōden to Bakin*, 8–9.
44. Hamada Keisuke, "Yomihon ni okeru ren'aitan (romansu) no kōzō: yomihon bungaku yōshiki ron no tame ni (jō)," *Bungaku* 6, no. 4 (2005): 186–188, 194. Hamada focuses on the structural genre conventions of love stories within *yomihon*, which he sees as relying on several basic patterns that can be embellished in myriad ways. For an insightful discussion of the way the modularity of the *yomihon* framework played out in the adaptation of textual precedents, see Walley, *Good Dogs*, 149–153. Walley shows how the skillful employment of such precedents could evoke literary seriousness even within a context of structural formulas.
45. Santō Kyōden, *Fukushū kidan Asaka no numa*, in *Santō Kyōden zenshū*, ed. Santō Kyōden zenshū henshū iinkai (Tokyo: Perikansha, 1994), 15:316.
46. *Goshūi wakashū*, poem no. 651, 213.
47. Matsuo Bashō, *Oku no hosomichi*, 125.

48. Santō Kyōden, *Asaka no numa*, 316–317.
49. Walker, *Conquest of Ainu Lands*, 203. Eagle feathers from Ezo had, in fact, been sought by samurai for the purpose of fletching arrows since well before the Edo period.
50. *Onzōshi shimawatari*, 97.
51. Santō Kyōden, *Asaka no numa*, 272.
52. Santō Kyōden, *Asaka no numa*, 316.
53. "Omoi wa mune ni michinoku no, iwade shinobu o e zo shiranu, tsubo no ishibumi kakitsukushite mo kokoro no hodo o chiri bakari tsutaemahoshiku" (Santō Kyōden, *Asaka no numa*, 317).
54. Santō Kyōden, *Asaka no numa*, 320.
55. Santō Kyōden, *Asaka no numa*, 340.
56. *Shin kokin wakashū*, ed. Minemura Fumito, SNKBZ 43 (Tokyo: Shōgakukan, 1995), poem no. 262, 91.
57. In Kanze Nobumitsu's (1450–1516) *nō* play *The Wanderer's Willow* (*Yugyō yanagi*, 1514), for example, a wandering priest encounters an old man in the vicinity of the Shirakawa Barrier who is revealed to be the spirit of the willow tree.
58. Matsuo Bashō, *Oku no hosomichi*, 116.
59. Santō Kyōden, *Asaka no numa*, 331.
60. Kyōden seems to have misread the characters of Oga (男鹿) as Ojika.
61. Tachibana Nankei, *Tōzai yūki*, ed. Munemasa Isoo, Tōyō bunko 248 (Tokyo: Heibonsha, 2003), 11–13.
62. Itasaka, *Edo no kikōbun*, 149–152. On its cover, Nankei's book is subtitled *Strange Tales from Throughout the Provinces* (*Shokoku kidan*).
63. These liminal qualities are underscored as well in the spectacularly overdetermined name of the doctor, Honchū 本冲, written with characters that in various ways suggest "Japan," "China," "center," and "periphery." I am grateful to Irene Pavitt for the question that led me to this observation.
64. Santō Kyōden, *Asaka no numa*, 373.
65. Santō Kyōden, *Asaka no numa*, 373.
66. Walker, *Conquest of Ainu Lands*, 193–194.
67. For a discussion of this aspect of the scene, see Satō Miyuki "Junan suru kodomotachi: Kansei kaikaku go no Santō Kyōden," in *Dokusho to shakaishi*, ed. Edo no shisō henshū iinkai, Edo no shisō 5 (Tokyo: Perikansha, 1995), 73–74.
68. Satō, "Junan suru kodomotachi," 74. I am indebted to Satō for drawing the link between this scene and the dissected bodies of *New Book of Anatomy*.
69. Satō, "Junan suru kodomotachi," 73–74.
70. I was led to both of these examples in Satō, "Junan suru kodomotachi," 73–74.

71. See, for example, his critique of the rigid moral framework and idealized characterization of Bakin's *Eight Dog Chronicle* in Tsubouchi Shōyō, *Shōsetsu shinzui*, 70–71. Shōyō's version of realism, however, retains aspects of Bakin's moralistic "good versus evil" framework, as shown in Poch, *Licentious Fictions*, 135–139.
72. The editors of the *Santō Kyōden zenshū* summarize the "standard reputation" (*teihyō*) of the work among scholars: "From the perspective of structure, the main plot concerning Yamanoi Hamon's vendetta, and the subsidiary plot concerning Koheiji as an angry ghost are not organically linked, and while interesting elements can be found in the approach to each individual section, the overall organization is rather insufficient." Santō Kyōden zenshū henshū iinkai, "Kaidai," in *Santō Kyōden zenshū*, ed. Santō Kyōden zenshū henshū iinkai (Tokyo: Perikansha, 1994), 15:584.
73. Santō Kyōden, *Asaka no numa*, 269.
74. Santō Kyōden, *Asaka no numa*, 269.

Epilogue

1. I follow the pronunciation of his given name as glossed in the print. It would be possible to read the same characters as "Hachibee," and this pronunciation is sometimes given in scholarship about the print.
2. For the complete series with translations and commentary, see Tsukioka Yoshitoshi, *Kaidai hyakusensō*, ed. Machida Shiritsu Kokusai Hanga Bijutsukan, with commentary by Koike Makiko and Ōuchi Mizue, Nazotoki ukiyoe sōsho (Tokyo: Nigensha, 2012). Despite the title (and the series's apparent popularity), only sixty-five prints are known to exist. See Koike Makiko and Ōuchi Mizue, "Yoshitoshi hitsu *Kaidai hyakusensō* no shosō," in *Kaidai hyakusensō*, by Tsukioka Yoshitoshi, 8.
3. Literally, "One Hundred Wars Within the Seas," a reference, in this case, to the Japanese islands as a whole. On the title's multiple meanings, see Koike and Ōuchi, "Yoshitoshi hitsu," 5.
4. Kobayashi Kin, Narasaki Muneshige, Kobayashi Ichitarō, and Takahashi Seiichirō, "Yoshitoshi tsuizen dan (3): Kobayashi Kinjo shi o kakonde," *Ukiyoekai* 5, no. 7 (1940): 23.
5. The inscriptions are attributed to Unpō Sanjin, Katsushika Hatamori, and Seiryū Shika.
6. On the range of the literary and visual sources of *One Hundred Selected Portraits*, see Koike and Ōuchi, "Yoshitoshi hitsu," 7–8.
7. Sugawara Mayumi, *Tsukioka Yoshitoshi den: Bakumatsu Meiji no hazama ni* (Tokyo: Chūō kōron bijutsu shuppan, 2018), 135–137; Koike and Ōuchi, "Yoshitoshi hitsu," 7–8.

8. Utagawa Kuniyoshi, *Shōutsushi hyakumen sō*, in *Edo Meiji hyakumensō ehon hasshu*, ed. Mutō Sadao (Kyoto: Taihei shoya, 1997), 7–31.
9. On Yoshitoshi's use of *True to Life* in this image and throughout the series, see Koike and Ōuchi, "Yoshitoshi hitsu," 7–8. For the image, see Utagawa Kuniyoshi, *Shōutsushi hyakumen sō*, 18.
10. The homophony between *hyakumen sō* (*Compendium of One Hundred Faces*) in Kuniyoshi's title and *hyakusensō* (*One Hundred Wars*) in Yoshitoshi's also suggests the latter's conscious, even playful, reworking of the earlier work.
11. Quoted in Koike and Ōuchi, "Yoshitoshi hitsu," 9.
12. The "commander of the enemy forces" shot down by Hachibyōe is said to have been Itakura Shigemasa (1588–1638), initial commander of the besieging forces. For a modern print version of the inscription with a translation into modern Japanese and a brief commentary, see Tsukioka Yoshitoshi, *Kaidai hyakusensō*, 140.
13. Sugawara, *Tsukioka Yoshitoshi den*, 141.
14. Sugawara, *Tsukioka Yoshitoshi den*, 141.
15. Edogawa Ranpo, "Zangyaku e no kyōshū," in *Edogawa Ranpo*, ed. Nakajima Kawatarō, Sakka no jiden 90 (Tokyo: Nihon tosho sentā, 1999), 94–96.
16. Edogawa, "Zangyaku e no kyōshū," 94–95.
17. Mishima Yukio singles out the series *Twenty-Eight Famous Murders, with Verses*, in "Dekadansu bijutsu," in *Ketteiban Mishima Yukio zenshū* (Tokyo: Shinchōsha, 2003), 35:116.
18. Mishima Yukio, "Jo ni kaete," in *Ketteiban Mishima Yukio zenshū* (Tokyo: Shinchōsha, 2003), 36:395. Taisō is another of Yoshitoshi's sobriquets.
19. In the wake of Mishima's characterization of Yoshitoshi, much was made of Yoshitoshi's bouts of poor mental health, which critics took up as a lens for analyzing the artist's prints as the products of "madness." On Mishima's impact on Yoshitoshi's reception, see Sugawara, *Tsukioka Yoshitoshi den*, 20–26.
20. Eugenie Brinkema, *The Forms of the Affects* (Durham, NC: Duke University Press, 2014), xiv.

Bibliography

The Actors' Analects, ed. and trans. Charles J. Dunn and Bunzō Torigoe. New York: Columbia University Press, 1969.
Akimichi. In *Otogizōshi*, ed. Ichiko Teiji, 394–410. NKBT 38. Tokyo: Iwanami shoten, 1958.
Aoki Akira, Ikeda Keiko, and Kitagawa Tadahiko, eds. *Manabon Soga monogatari 1*. Tōyō bunko 468. Tokyo: Heibonsha, 1987.
Appelbaum, Robert. "Notes Toward an Aesthetics of Violence." *Studia Neophilologica* 85, no. 2 (2013): 119–132.
Asai Ryōi. *Kanameishi*. In *Kanazōshi shū*, ed. Taniwaki Masachika, Oka Masahito, and Inoue Kazuhito, 11–83. SNKBZ 64. Tokyo: Shōgakukan, 1999.
———. *Musashi abumi*. Teramachi Nijō sagarumachi (Kyoto): Nakamura Gohei, Manji 4 [1661]. Waseda Daigaku Sōgō Kotenseki Dētabēsu. https://www.wul.waseda.ac.jp/kotenseki.
———. *"Musashi abumi" kōchū to kenkyū*. Ed. Sakamaki Kōta and Kuroki Takashi. Tokyo: Ōfūsha, 1988.
———. *Stirrups of Musashi: An Account of the Meireki Fire of 1657*. Trans. Henry D. Smith II and Steven Wills. In *A Kamigata Anthology: Literature from Japan's Metropolitan Centers, 1600–1750*, 410–439, ed. Sumie Jones, Adam L. Kern, and Kenji Watanabe. Honolulu: University of Hawai'i Press, 2020.
Asano Sanpei. "'Shikubi no egao' o megutte: Genta sōdō to Ayatari, Akinari." In *Ueda Akinari no kenkyū*, 575–605. Tokyo: Ōfūsha, 1985.
Berry, Mary Elizabeth. *Japan in Print: Information and Nation in the Early Modern Period*. Berkeley: University of California Press, 2006.

Berry, Mary Elizabeth, and Marcia Yonemoto. "Introduction." In *What Is a Family? Answers from Early Modern Japan*, ed. Mary Elizabeth Berry and Marcia Yonemoto, 1–20. Oakland: University of California Press, 2019.

Bersani, Leo and Ulysse Dutoit, "The Forms of Violence." *October* 8 (1979): 17–29.

———. *The Forms of Violence: Narrative in Assyrian Art and Modern Culture*. New York: Schocken Books, 1985.

Botsman, Daniel V. *Punishment and Power in the Making of Modern Japan*. Princeton, NJ: Princeton University Press, 2005.

Brinkema, Eugenie. *The Forms of the Affects*. Durham, NC: Duke University Press, 2014.

Brown, Delmer M. *Nationalism in Japan: An Introductory Historical Analysis*. Berkeley: University of California Press, 1955.

Burns, Susan L. *Before the Nation: Kokugaku and the Imagining of Community in Early Modern Japan*. Durham, NC: Duke University Press, 2003.

———. "The Body as Text: Confucianism, Reproduction, and Gender in Tokugawa Japan." In *Rethinking Confucianism: Past and Present in China, Japan, Korea, and Vietnam*, ed. Benjamin A. Elman, John B. Duncan, and Herman Ooms, 178–219. Los Angeles: UCLA Asian Pacific Monograph Series, 2002.

Certeau, Michel de. "Spatial Stories." In *The Practice of Everyday Life*, trans. Steven Rendall, 115–130. Berkeley: University of California Press, 1988.

Chibbett, David C. *The History of Japanese Printing and Book Illustration*. Tokyo: Kodansha International, 1977.

Chikamatsu Monzaemon. *Chikamatsu: Five Late Plays*. Translated and annotated by C. Andrew Gerstle. New York: Columbia University Press, 2001.

———. *Daikyōji mukashigoyomi*. In *Chikamatsu Monzaemon shū*, ed. Torigoe Bunzō et al., 2:529–581. SNKBZ 75. Tokyo: Shōgakukan, 1998.

———. *Horikawa nami no tsuzumi*. In *Chikamatsu Monzaemon shū*, ed. Torigoe Bunzō et al., 2:485–528. SNKBZ 75. Tokyo: Shōgakukan, 1998.

———. *Lovers Pond in Settsu Province*. In *Chikamatsu: Five Late Plays*, translated and annotated by C. Andrew Gerstle, 118–201. New York: Columbia University Press, 2001.

———. *Shinjū nimai ezōshi*. In *Chikamatsu Monzaemon shū*, ed. Torigoe Bunzō et al., 2:45–81. SNKBZ 75. Tokyo: Shōgakukan, 1998.

———. *Tsu no kuni meoto ike*. In *Chikamatsu jōrurishū*, ed. Matsuzaki Hitoshi, Hara Michio, Iguchi Hiroshi, and Ōhashi Tadayoshi, 2:81–164. SNKBT 92. Tokyo: Iwanami shoten, 1995.

———. *Yari no Gonza kasane katabira*. In *Chikamatsu Monzaemon shū*, ed. Torigoe Bunzō et al., 2:583–637. SNKBZ 75. Tokyo: Shōgakukan, 1998.

Childs, Margaret Helen. *Rethinking Sorrow: Revelatory Tales of Late Medieval Japan*. Ann Arbor: Center for Japanese Studies, University of Michigan, 1991.

"Daikyōji Osan Mohei." In *Nihon kayō shūsei*, ed. Takano Tatsuyuki, 8:43–45. Tokyo: Shunjūsha, 1928.

"Daikyōji Osan utazaimon." In *Nihon kayō shūsei*, ed. Takano Tatsuyuki, 8:45–47. Tokyo: Shunjūsha, 1928.

"'Daishinsai wa tenbatsu:' 'Tsunami de gayoku o araiotose' Ishihara tochiji." *Asahi Shimbun*, March 14, 2011. http://www.asahi.com/special/tokyo/TKY201103 140356.html.

Doe, Paula. *A Warbler's Song in the Dusk: The Life and Work of Ōtomo Yakamochi (718–785)*. Berkeley: University of California Press, 1982.

Edogawa Ranpo. "Zangyaku e no kyōshū." In *Edogawa Ranpo*, ed. Nakajima Kawatarō, 94–96. Sakka no jiden 90. Tokyo: Nihon tosho sentā, 1999.

Ehlers, Maren A. *Give and Take: Poverty and the Status Order in Early Modern Japan*. Cambridge, MA: Harvard University Asia Center, 2018.

Emmerich, Michael. The Tale of Genji: *Translation, Canonization, and World Literature*. New York: Columbia University Press, 2013.

Eyers, Tom. *Speculative Formalism: Literature, Theory, and the Critical Present*. Evanston, IL: Northwestern University Press, 2017.

Friday, Karl. "Pushing Beyond the Pale: The Yamato Conquest of the Emishi and Northern Japan." *Journal of Japanese Studies* 23, no. 1 (1997): 1–24.

Flueckiger, Peter. *Imagining Harmony: Poetry, Empathy, and Community in Mid-Tokugawa Confucianism and Nativism*. Stanford, CA: Stanford University Press, 2011.

———. "Reflections on the Meaning of Our Country: Kamo no Mabuchi's *Kokuikō*." *Monumenta Nipponica* 63, no. 2 (2008): 211–263.

Fujimoto Kizan. *Shinpan Shikidō ōkagami*. Ed. Shinpan Shikidō ōkagami kankōkai. Tokyo: Yagi shoten, 2006.

Furukawa Koshōken. *Tōyū zakki*. Ed. Ōtō Tokihiko. Tokyo: Tōyō bunko, 1964.

Gerstle, C. Andrew. "Hero as Murderer in Chikamatsu." *Monumenta Nipponica* 31, no. 3 (1996): 317–356.

———. "Takemoto Gidayū and the Individualistic Spirit of Osaka Theater." In *Osaka: The Merchants' Capital of Early Modern Japan*, ed. James L. McClain and Wakita Osamu, 104–124. Ithaca, NY: Cornell University Press, 1999.

Girard, René. *Violence and the Sacred*. Trans. Patrick Gregory. London: Continuum, 2005.

Goshūi wakashū. Ed. Kubota Jun and Hirata Yoshinobu. SNKBT 8. Tokyo: Iwanami shoten, 1994.

Grapard, Alan G. "Religious Practices." In *Heian Japan*, ed. Donald H. Shively and William H. McCullough, 517–575. *The Cambridge History of Japan: Volume 2*. Cambridge: Cambridge University Press, 1999.

Griffiths, Devin. "The Ecology of Form." *Critical Inquiry* 48, no. 1 (2021): 68–93.

Gundry, David J. *Parody, Irony and Ideology in the Fiction of Ihara Saikaku*. Leiden: Brill, 2017.

Haidu, Peter. *The Subject of Violence: The "Song of Roland" and the Birth of the State*. Bloomington: Indiana University Press, 1993.

Hall, John W. "Rule by Status in Tokugawa Japan." *Journal of Japanese Studies* 1, no. 1 (1974): 39–49.

Hamada Keisuke. "Yomihon ni okeru ren'aitan (romansu) no kōzō: yomihon bungaku yōshiki ron no tame ni (jō, chū, ge)." *Bungaku* 6, no. 4 (2005): 186–197; no. 5 (2005): 191–202; no. 6 (2005): 217–228.

Handler-Spitz, Rivi. *Symptoms of an Unruly Age: Li Zhi and Cultures of Early Modernity*. Seattle: University of Washington Press, 2017.

Hara Masako. "Mabuchi no 'masurao' kō." *Edo bungaku* 7 (1991): 113–126.

Hayot, Eric. *On Literary Worlds*. Oxford: Oxford University Press, 2016.

He, Yuming. *Home and the World: Editing the "Glorious Ming" in Woodblock-Printed Books of the Sixteenth and Seventeenth Centuries*. Cambridge, MA: Harvard University Asia Center, 2013.

Hedberg, William C. *The Japanese Discovery of Chinese Fiction: The Water Margin and the Making of a National Canon*. New York: Columbia University Press, 2020.

Heike monogatari. Ed. Ichiko Teiji. 2 vols. SNKBZ 46. Tokyo: Shōgakukan, 1994.

Henderson, Dan Fenno. "Introduction to the *Kujikata Osadamegaki* (1742)." In *Hō to keibatsu no rekishiteki kōsatsu*, ed. Hiramatsu Yoshirō hakushi tsuitō ronbunshū henshū iinkai, 490–544. Nagoya: Nagoya daigaku shuppankai, 1987.

Hino Tatsuo. "Engi suru shijintachi." In *Edo no jugaku*, vol. 1 of *Hino Tatsuo chosakushū*, 216–229. Tokyo: Perikansha, 2005.

Hiraide Kōjirō. *Katakiuchi*. Tokyo: Bunshōkaku, 1909; repr. Tokyo: Chūō kōronsha, 1990.

Hirano, Katsuya. *The Politics of Dialogic Imagination: Power and Popular Culture in Early Modern Japan*. Chicago: University of Chicago Press, 2014.

Hirosue Tamotsu. *Chikamatsu josetsu: kinsei higeki no kenkyū*. Tokyo: Miraisha, 1963.

———. *Saikaku no shōsetsu: jikū ishiki no tenkan o megutte*. Tokyo: Heibonsha, 1982.

Hōjō Hideo. *Shinshū Asai Ryōi*. Tokyo: Kasama shoin, 1974.

Howell, David L. *Geographies of Identity in Nineteenth-Century Japan*. Berkeley: University of California Press, 2005.

Hozumi Ikan. "Chikamatsu no gensetsu: *Naniwa miyage* hottanshō." In *Chikamatsu jōruri shū*, ed. Shuzui Kenji and Ōkubo Tadakuni, 2:355–359. NKBT 50. Tokyo: Iwanami shoten, 1959.

Hyde, Lewis. *Trickster Makes This World: Mischief, Myth, and Art*. New York: Farrar, Straus and Giroux, 2010.

Ibi Takashi. "'Shikubi no egao' no shudai." In *Kinsei bungaku no kyōkai: koga to hyōgen no hen'yō*, 185–200. Tokyo: Iwanami shoten, 2009.

Ihara Saikaku. *Budō denraiki*. 5 vols. Gofukuchō Shinsaibashi sujikado (Osaka): Okada Saburōemon, 1687. Waseda Daigaku Sōgō Kotenseki Dētabēsu (Kotenseki Sōgō Database: Japanese and Chinese Classics), https://www.wul.waseda.ac.jp/kotenseki.

———. *Budō denraiki*. Ed. Yokoyama Shigeru and Maeda Kingorō. Tokyo: Iwanami shoten, 1967.

———. *Budō denraiki*. In *Budō denraiki, Saikaku okimiyage, Yorozu no fumihōgu, Saikaku nagori no tomo*, ed. Taniwaki Masachika, Fuji Akio, and Inoue Toshiyuki, 3–255. SNKBT 77. Tokyo: Iwanami shoten, 1989.

———. *Kōshoku gonin onna*. In *Ihara Saikaku shū*, ed. Teruoka Yasutaka and Higashi Akimasa, 1:251–389. SNKBZ 66. Tokyo: Shōgakukan, 1996.

———. *Kōshoku ichidai otoko*. In *Ihara Saikaku shū*, ed. Teruoka Yasutaka and Higashi Akimasa, 1:15–250. SNKBZ 66. Tokyo: Shōgakukan, 1996.

Iikura Yōichi. "Akinari ni okeru 'ikidōri' no mondai: *Harusame monogatari* e no ichi shiten." In *Akinari kō*, 31–53. Tokyo: Kanrin shobō, 2005.

———. *Ueda Akinari: Kizuna toshite no bungei*. Suita-shi: Osaka daigaku shuppankai, 2012.

Ikegami, Eiko. *The Taming of the Samurai: Honorific Individualism and the Making of Modern Japan*. Cambridge, MA: Harvard University Press, 1995.

Inoue Keiji. *Kyōden kōshōgaku to yomihon no kenkyū*. Tokyo: Shintensha, 1997.

Ise monogatari. In *Taketori monogatari, Ise monogatari, Yamato monogatari, Heichū monogatari*, ed. Katagiri Yōichi et al., 107–226. SNKBZ 12. Tokyo: Shōgakukan, 1994.

Ishikawa Jun. "Akinari shiron." *Bungaku* 27, no. 8 (1959): 975–980.

Itasaka Yōko. *Edo no kikōbun: taihei no yo no tabibitotachi*. Tokyo: Chūō kōron shinsha, 2011.

Iwasaki, Haruko. "The Literature of Wit and Humor in Late-Eighteenth-Century Edo." In *The Floating World Revisited*, ed. Donald Jenkins, 47–61. Exhibition catalogue. Portland, OR: Portland Art Museum; Honolulu: University of Hawai'i Press, 1993.

Jackson, Michael. *The Politics of Storytelling: Variations on a Theme by Hannah Arendt*. 2nd ed. 2013. Reprint, Copenhagen: Museum Tusculanum Press, 2019.

Jinrin kinmō zui. Ed. Asakura Haruhiko. Tokyo: Heibonsha, 1990.

Kaibara Ekiken. *Yōjōkun*. Ed. Ishikawa Ken. Tokyo: Iwanami shoten, 1961.

Kamo no Mabuchi. "Ka'ikō." In *Kinsei shintō ron, zenki kokugaku*, ed. Taira Shigemichi and Abe Akio, 348–356. Nihon shisō taikei 39. Tokyo: Iwanami shoten, 1972.

———. Kamo no Mabuchi to Hōrai Garaku, Meiwa 6 [1769] 7.4. In *Takebe Ayatari zenshū*, ed. Takebe Ayatari Chosaku Kankōkai, 9:180–182. Tokyo: Kokusho kankōkai, 1990.

———. "Kokuikō." In *Kinsei shintōron, zenki kokugaku*, ed. Taira Shigemichi and Abe Akio, 374–393. Nihon shisō taikei 39. Tokyo: Iwanami shoten, 1972.

———. "Niimanabi." In *Kinsei shintōron, zenki kokugaku*, ed. Taira Shigemichi and Abe Akio, 357–373. Nihon shisō taikei 39. Tokyo: Iwanami shoten, 1972.

Kataoka Ryōichi. *Ihara Saikaku*. Tokyo: Shibundō, 1926.

Katsurajima Nobuhiro. "'Ka'i' shisō no kaitai to kokugakuteki 'jiko' zō no seisei." In *Kokka (jiko) zō no keisei*, ed. Edo no shisō henshū iinkai, 40–59. Edo no shisō 4. Tokyo: Perikansha, 1995.

Kawanishi Hidemichi. *Tōhoku: Japan's Constructed Outland*. Trans. Nanyan Guo and Raquel Hill. Leiden: Brill, 2016.

Kazama Seishi. "*Harusame monogatari* ron no tame ni: shiteki kenkyūshi to kasetsu, moshiku wa bōsō." In *Harusame monogatari to iu shisō*, 40–68. Tokyo: Shinwasha, 2011.

———. "*Harusame monogatari* to wa nanika." In *Harusame monogatari to iu shisō*, 14–21. Tokyo: Shinwasha, 2011.

———. "'Shikubi no egao' shiron." In *Harusame monogatari to iu shisō*, 69–93. Tokyo: Shinwasha, 2011.

Keene, Donald. *The Japanese Discovery of Europe: Honda Toshiaki and Other Discoverers, 1720–1798*. New York: Grove Press, 1954.

Kern, Adam L. *Manga from the Floating World: Comicbook Culture and the Kibyōshi of Edo Japan*. 2nd ed. Cambridge, MA: Harvard University Asia Center, 2019.

Kikuchi Isao. *Kikin kara yomu kinsei shakai*. Tokyo: Azekura shobō, 2003.

Kleinman, Arthur. "The Violences of Everyday Life: The Multiple Forms and Dynamics of Social Violence." In *Violence and Subjectivity*, ed. Veena Das, Arthur Kleinman, Mamphela Ramphele, and Pamela Reynolds, 226–241. Berkeley: University of California Press, 1997.

Kliger, Ilya. "Dynamic Archaeology or Distant Reading: Literary Study Between Two Formalisms." *Russian Literature* 122–123 (2021): 7–28.

Kobayashi Kin, Narasaki Muneshige, Kobayashi Ichitarō, and Takahashi Seiichirō. "Yoshitoshi tsuizen dan (3): Kobayashi Kinjo shi o kakonde." *Ukiyoekai* 5, no. 7 (1940): 20–24.

Koike Makiko and Ōuchi Mizue. "Yoshitoshi hitsu *Kaidai hyakusensō* no shosō." In *Kaidai hyakusensō*, by Tsukioka Yoshitoshi, 5–9. Ed. Machida Shiritsu Kokusai Hanga Bijutsukan, with commentary by Koike Makiko and Ōuchi Mizue. Nazotoki ukiyoe sōsho. Tokyo: Nigensha, 2012.

Kokin wakashū. Ed. Ozawa Masao and Matsuda Shigeho. SNKBZ 11. Tokyo: Shōgakukan, 1994.

Kominz, Laurence R. *Avatars of Vengeance: Japanese Drama and the Soga Literary Tradition*. Ann Arbor: Center for Japanese Studies, University of Michigan, 1995.

Konita Seiji. "Adauchi shōsetsu shiron." *Nihon bungaku* 38, no. 5 (1989): 75–83.

Konoe Noriko. "*Genji monogatari* e no manazashi: Akinari no monogatari to monogatari ron." In *Ueda Akinari shinkō: kusemono no bungaku*, 14–49. Tokyo: Perikansha, 2016.

Konta Yōzō. *Edo no hon'yasan: kinsei bunkashi no sokumen*. Tokyo: Heibonsha, 2009.

Kornbluh, Anna. *The Order of Forms: Realism, Formalism, and Social Space*. Chicago: University of Chicago Press, 2019.

Kornicki, Peter. *The Book in Japan: A Cultural History from the Beginnings to the Nineteenth Century*. Honolulu: University of Hawai'i Press, 2001.

———. "Narrative of a Catastrophe: *Musashi abumi* and the Meireki Fire." *Japan Forum* 21, no. 3 (2010): 347–361.

———. "*Nishiki no Ura*: An Instance of Censorship and the Structure of a *Sharebon*." *Monumenta Nipponica* 32, no. 2 (1977): 153–188.

Koyama Issei. "Utazaimon ni tsuite." In *Chikamatsu jōruri no kenkyū*, 125–146. Tokyo: Sōbunsha shuppan, 2000.

Kurachi Katsunao. *Tokugawa shakai no yuragi*. Zenshū Nihon no rekishi 11. Tokyo: Shōgakukan, 2008.

Kuroda Toshio. *Kenmitsu taisei ron*. Kuroda Toshio chosakushū 1. Kyoto: Hōzōkan, 1994.

Kuroki Takashi. *Meireki no taika*. Tokyo: Kōdansha, 1977.

Kyokutei Bakin. *Geppyō kien*. In *Kyokutei Bakin shū*, 1:1–107. Kindai Nihon bungaku taikei 15. Tokyo: Kokumin tosho kabushiki gaisha, 1927.

———. *Kinsei mononohon Edo sakusha burui*. Ed. Tokuda Takeshi. Tokyo: Iwanami shoten, 2014.

Le Guin, Ursula K. *The Carrier Bag Theory of Fiction*. [London]: Ignota, 2019.

Legge, James. trans. *Record of Rites*. In *The Sacred Books of China: The Texts of Confucianism*. Oxford: Clarendon Press, 1885; repr. Delhi: Motilal Banarsidass, 1968.

Levine, Caroline. *Forms: Whole, Rhythm, Hierarchy, Network*. Princeton, NJ: Princeton University Press, 2015.

Man'yōshū. Ed. Kojima Nobuyuki, Kinoshita Masatoshi, and Tōno Haruyuki. 4 vols. SNKBZ 9. Tokyo: Shōgakukan, 1996.

Marceau, Lawrence E. *Takebe Ayatari: A Bunjin Bohemian in Early Modern Japan*. Ann Arbor: Center for Japanese Studies, University of Michigan, 2004.

Matsuda Osamu. "Chūsei kara kinsei e: jikū ishiki to bungaku ishiki." In *Edo itan bungaku nōto*, 11–31. Tokyo: Seidosha, 1993.

———. *Nihon kinsei bungaku no seiritsu: itan no keifu*. In *Matsuda Osamu chosakushū*, 1:239–547. Tokyo: Yūbun shoin, 2002.

Matsumura Kōji. "Yōjōronteki na shintai e no manazashi." In *Shintai joseiron*, ed. Edo no shisō henshū iinkai, 28–47. Edo no shisō 6. Tokyo: Perikansha, 1997.

Matsuo Bashō. *Oku no hosomichi*. In *Bashō bunshū*, ed. Toyama Susumu, 106–157. SNKS 17. Tokyo: Shinchōsha, 1978.

Matsuzaki Hitoshi. "*Daikyōji mukashigoyomi* no saiginmi." In *Genroku engeki kenkyū*, 242–260. Tokyo: Tokyo daigaku shuppankai, 1979.

Mills, D. E. "Kataki-uchi: The Practice of Blood-Revenge in Pre-Modern Japan." *Modern Asian Studies* 10, no. 4 (1976): 525–542.

Minami Yōko. "Sakuhin no kenkyūshi: *Kōshoku gonin onna*." In *Saikaku to ukiyozōshi kenkyū*. Vol. 3, *Kinsen*, ed. Taniwaki Masachika, Sugimoto Yoshinobu, and Sugimoto Kazuhiro, 180–183. Tokyo: Kasama shoin, 2010.

Mishima Yukio. "Dekadansu bijutsu." In *Ketteiban Mishima Yukio zenshū*, 35:115–116. Tokyo: Shinchōsha, 2003.

——. "Jo ni kaete." In *Ketteiban Mishima Yukio zenshū*, 36:395. Tokyo: Shinchōsha, 2003.

Miyazawa Seiichi. *Akō rōshi: tsumugidasareru Chūshingura*. Tokyo: Sanseidō, 1999.

Mizue Renko. "Kanazōshi no kirokusei: *Musashi abumi* to Meireki no taika." *Nihon rekishi* 291 (1972): 87–100.

Moretti, Laura. "Adaptation as a Strategy for Participation: The Chikusai Storyworld in Early Modern Japanese Literature." *Japanese Language and Literature* 54, no. 1 (2020): 67–113.

——. "A Forest of Books: Seventeenth-Century Kamigata Commercial Prose." In *The Cambridge History of Japanese Literature*, ed. Haruo Shirane, Tomi Suzuki, and David Lurie, 396–402. Cambridge: Cambridge University Press, 2015.

——. "The Japanese Early-Modern Publishing Market Unveiled: A Survey of Edo-Period Booksellers' Catalogues." *East Asian Publishing and Society* 2 (2012): 199–308.

——. "Kanazōshi Revisited: The Beginnings of Japanese Popular Literature in Print." *Monumenta Nipponica* 65, no. 2 (2010): 297–356.

——. *Pleasure in Profit: Popular Prose in Seventeenth-Century Japan*. New York: Columbia University Press, 2020.

Morita Kirō. "*Harusame monogatari* no igi." In *Ueda Akinari bungei no kenkyū*, 379–524. Osaka: Izumi shoin, 2003.

Moriyama Shigeo. "'Masurao monogatari' no seiritsu." In *Gen'yō no bungaku: Ueda Akinari*, 198–210. Tokyo: San'ichi shobō, 1982.

Morris, David B. "About Suffering: Voice, Genre, and Moral Community." In *Social Suffering*, ed. Arthur Kleinman, Veena Das, and Margaret Lock, 25–45. Berkeley: University of California Press, 1997.

Morris-Suzuki, Tessa. "A Descent into the Past: The Frontier in the Construction of Japanese Identity." In *Multicultural Japan: Paleolithic to Postmodern*, ed. Donald Denoon, Mark Hudson, Gavan McCormack, and Tessa Morris-Suzuki, 81–94. Cambridge: Cambridge University Press, 1996.

——. *Re-inventing Japan: Time, Space, Nation*. Armonk, NY: Sharpe, 1998.

Mukunashi Issetsu. *Nihon bushi kagami*. In *Kanazōshi shūsei*, ed. Asakura Haruhiko, 29:83–165. Tokyo: Tōkyōdō shuppan, 2001.

Murakami Manabu. "Nichizō no jigoku meguri: *Dōken jōnin meidoki* to *Kitano Tenjin engi.*" *Kokubungaku kaishaku to kanshō* 55, no. 8 (1990): 79–83.

Murasaki Shikibu. *Genji monogatari.* Ed. Abe Akio et al. SNKBZ 20–25. Tokyo: Shōgakukan, 1994–1998.

Nagashima Hiroaki. "Akinari no chosho kaiki," *Bungaku* 8, no. 3 (2007): 26–38.

Naito, Akira. *Edo, the City That Became Tokyo: An Illustrated History.* Trans. H. Mack Horton. Tokyo: Kodansha International, 2003.

Nakamura Hiroyasu. "Akinari no bungaku ron." *Nihon bungaku* 13, no. 2 (1964): 1–22.

———. "*Harusame monogatari.*" In *Hanabusa sōshi, Nishiyama monogatari, Ugetsu monogatari, Harusame monogatari*, ed. Nakamura Yukihiko, Takada Mamoru, and Nakamura Hiroyasu, 609–619. SNKBZ 78. Tokyo: Shōgakukan, 1995.

———. "Kaidai." In *Hanabusa sōshi, Nishiyama monogatari, Ugetsu monogatari, Harusame monogatari*, ed. Nakamura Yukihiko, Takada Mamoru, and Nakamura Hiroyasu, 622. SNKBZ 78. Tokyo: Shōgakukan, 1995.

Nakamura Yukihiko. "Bungaku wa 'ninjō o iu' no setsu." In *Kinsei bungei shichōkō*, 56–94. Tokyo: Iwanami shoten, 1975.

———. *Gesaku ron. Nakamura Yukihiko chojutsushū*, vol. 8. Tokyo: Chūō kōronsha, 1982.

———. "Kaisetsu." In *Ueda Akinari shū*, ed. Nakamura Yukihiko, 3–27. NKBT 56. Tokyo: Iwanami shoten, 1959.

———. "Kata no bunshō." In *Nakamura Yukihiko chojutsushū*, 2:147–192. Tokyo: Chūō kōronsha, 1982.

———. "Saikaku bungaku ni okeru buke." *Kokubungaku kaishaku to kyōzai no kenkyū* 2, no. 6 (1957): 72–76.

———. "Ueda Akinari no monogatari kan." In *Nakamura Yukihiko chojutsushū*, 1:248–265. Tokyo: Chūō kōronsha, 1982.

Nakano Mitsutoshi. "Akinari no bungaku kan." In *Jūhasseiki no Edo bungei*, 270–283. Tokyo: Iwanami shoten, 1999.

———. "Gūgenron no tenkai: toku ni Akinari no ron to sono haikei." *Kokugo to kokubungaku* 45, no. 10 (1968): 108–120.

———. "Jūnana seiki no shōsetsushi: watakushi no gesakuron josetsu." In "Saikaku chōhatsu suru tekisuto," ed. Kigoshi Osamu. Special issue, *Kokubungaku kaishaku to kanshō* (March 2005): 19–27.

———. "The Role of Traditional Aesthetics." Trans. Maria Flutsch. In *18th Century Japan: Culture and Society*, ed. C. Andrew Gerstle, 124–131. Sydney: Allen & Unwin, 1989.

———. "Saikaku gesakusha setsu saikō: Edo no manako to gendai no manako no motsu imi." *Bungaku* 15, no. 1 (2014): 140–158.

Namura Jōhaku. *Onna chōhōki.* In *Onna chōhōki, Nan chōhōki: Genroku wakamono kokoroe shū*, ed. Nagatomo Chiyoji, 9–196. Tokyo: Shakai shisōsha, 1993.

Ngai, Sianne. "Interview with Sianne Ngai." By Kevin Brazil. *White Review*, October 2020. https://www.thewhitereview.org/feature/interview-with-sianne-ngai/.

Nishida Kōzō. *Shujinkō no tanjō: chūsei Zen kara kinsei shōsetsu e*. Tokyo: Perikansha, 2007.

Noda Hisao. "Tōkaidō meishoki ron." In *Kinsei shoki shōsetsu ron*, 129–164. Tokyo: Kasama shoin, 1978.

Noma Kōshin. "Iwayuru Genta sōdō o megutte: Ayatari to Akinari." In *Kinsei sakkaden kō*, 308–342. Tokyo: Chūō kōronsha, 1985.

———. "Ryōi tsuiseki." In *Kinsei sakkaden kō*, 105–147. Tokyo: Chūō kōronsha, 1985.

———. "Saikaku to Saikaku igo." In *Saikaku shin shinkō*, 33–75. Tokyo: Iwanami shoten, 1981.

Ogawa Takehiko. "Kanazōshi yonhen ni miru tenzai jihen no bungeisei to kirokusei." In *Kinsei bungei ronsō*, ed. Teruoka Yasutaka, 61–76. Tokyo: Chūō kōronsha, 1978.

Ōgimachi Machiko. *In the Shelter of the Pine: A Memoir of Yanagisawa Yoshiyasu and Tokugawa Japan*. Trans. G. G. Rowley. New York: Columbia University Press, 2021.

———. *Matsukage nikki*. Ed. Ueno Yōzō. Tokyo: Iwanami shoten, 2005.

Okada Morimasa. "Kantsū jōruri *Daikyōji mukashigoyomi* ni tsuite: igai na ketsumatsu ni miru Chikamatsu no sakui." *Aichi shukutoku daigaku kokugo kokubun* 31, no, 3 (2008): 69–84.

Oliver-Smith, Anthony. "Theorizing Disasters: Nature, Power, and Culture." In *Catastrophe and Culture: The Anthropology of Disaster*, ed. Susanna M. Hoffman and Anthony Oliver-Smith, 23–48. Santa Fe, NM: School of American Research Press, 2002.

Omuna kagami. In *Kanazōshi shūsei*, ed. Asakura Haruhiko and Fukazawa Akio, 10:3–77. Tokyo: Tōkyōdō shuppan, 1989.

Onzōshi shimawatari. In *Muromachi monogatari sōshi shū*, ed. Ōshima Tatehiko and Watari Kōichi, 91–118. SNKBZ 63. Tokyo: Shōgakukan, 2002.

Ooms, Herman. "Forms and Norms in Edo Arts and Society." In *Edo: Art in Japan, 1615–1868*, ed. Robert T. Singer, 23–47. Exhibition catalogue. Washington, DC: National Gallery of Art, 1998.

———. *Tokugawa Ideology: Early Constructs, 1570–1680*. Princeton, NJ: Princeton University Press, 1985.

———. *Tokugawa Village Practice: Class, Status, Power, Law*. Berkeley: University of California Press, 1996.

Ōtaka Yōji. "Edo: Kyōden, Bakin to 'haishimono' yomihon no keisei." In *Yomihon jiten: Edo no denki shōsetsu*, ed. Kokubungaku kenkyū shiryōkan and Hachinohe shiritsu toshokan, 51–52. Tokyo: Kasama shoin, 2008.

———. *Kyōden to Bakin: "haishimono" yomihon yōshiki no keisei*. Tokyo: Kanrin shobō, 2010.

Poch, Daniel. *Licentious Fictions: Ninjō and the Nineteenth-Century Japanese Novel*. New York: Columbia University Press, 2020.

Raiki. Ed. Takeuchi Teruo. *Shinshaku kanbun taikei* 27. Tokyo: Meiji shoin, 1971.

Rancière, Jacques. *The Politics of Aesthetics: The Distribution of the Sensible*. Edited and trans. Gabriel Rockhill. London: Continuum, 2006. Reprint, London: Bloomsbury Academic, 2013.

———. *The Politics of Literature*. Trans. Julie Rose. Cambridge: Polity, 2011.

Roberts, Luke S. "Governing the Samurai Family in the Late Edo Period." In *What Is a Family? Answers from Early Modern Japan*, ed. Mary Elizabeth Berry and Marcia Yonemoto, 149–173. Oakland: University of California Press, 2019.

———. *Performing the Great Peace: Political Space and Open Secrets in Tokugawa Japan*. Honolulu: University of Hawai'i Press, 2012.

Rooney, Ellen. "Form and Contentment." In *Reading for Form*, ed. Susan J. Wolfson and Marshall Brown, 25–48. Seattle: University of Washington Press, 2006.

Rowley, G. G. Introduction to *In the Shelter of the Pine: A Memoir of Yanagisawa Yoshiyasu and Tokugawa Japan*, by Ōgimachi Machiko, xi–xxxiii. Trans. G. G. Rowley. New York: Columbia University Press, 2021.

Ryōjin hishō. In *Kagurauta, Saibara, Ryōjin hishō, Kanginshū*, ed. Usuda Jingorō, 175–386. SNKBZ 42. Tokyo: Shōgakukan, 1994.

Sakamaki Kōta. "Kinsei shoki ni okeru sakusha shoshi dokusha no isō: sakusha Asai Ryōi shoshi Kawano Michikiyo o jiku ni." *Nihon bungaku* 43, no. 10 (1994): 1–9.

Sakamaki Kōta and Kuroki Takashi. "Asai Ryōi to *Musashi abumi*." In *Asai Ryōi, "Musashi abumi" kōchū to kenkyū*, ed. Sakamaki Kōta and Kuroki Takashi, 109–150. Tokyo: Ōfūsha, 1988.

Santō Kyōden. *Fukushū kidan Asaka no numa*. In *Santō Kyōden zenshū*, ed. Santō Kyōden zenshū henshū iinkai, 15:267–392. Tokyo: Perikansha, 1994.

———. *Katakiuchi ato no matsuri*. In *Santō Kyōden zenshū*, ed. Santō Kyōden zenshū henshū iinkai, 1:365–382. Tokyo: Perikansha, 1992.

———. *Katakiuchi Okazaki joroshu*. In *Santō Kyōden zenshū*, ed. Santō Kyōden zenshū henshū iinkai, 6:145–187. Tokyo: Perikansha, 1995.

Santō Kyōden zenshū henshū iinkai. "Kaidai." In *Santō Kyōden zenshū*, ed. Santō Kyōden zenshū henshū iinkai, 15:565–590. Tokyo: Perikansha, 1994.

Sasakawa Sachio, Shida Itaru, and Takahashi Kiichi, eds. *Manabon Soga monogatari 2*. Tōyō bunko 486. Tokyo: Heibonsha, 1988.

Sasaki Junnosuke. *Bakuhansei kokkaron*. 2 vols. Tokyo: Tokyo daigaku shuppankai, 1984.

Satō Miyuki. "Gisho to ihon." In *Ayatari to Akinari to: Jūhasseiki kokugaku e no hihan*, 127–148. Nagoya: Nagoya daigaku shuppankai, 1993.

———. "Harusame monogatari to iu sōchi." In *Ayatari to Akinari to: Jūhasseiki kokugaku e no hihan*, 171–196. Nagoya: Nagoya daigaku shuppankai, 1993.

———. "Junan suru kodomotachi: Kansei kaikaku go no Santō Kyōden." In *Dokusho to shakaishi*, ed. Edo no shisō henshū iinkai, 68–82. Edo no shisō 5. Tokyo: Perikansha, 1995.

Satō Satoru. "Jihon ron: Edo yomihon wa naze shomotsu na no ka." In *Yomihon kenkyū shinshū*, ed. Yomihon kenkyū no kai, 1:34–54. Tokyo: Kanrin shobō, 1998.

Satō Yukiko. *Edo no shuppan tōsei: dan'atsu ni honrō sareta gesakushatachi*. Tokyo: Yoshikawa kōbunkan, 2017.

Screech, Timon. *The Shogun's Painted Culture: Fear and Creativity in the Japanese States, 1760–1829*. London: Reaktion, 2000.

———. *Tokyo Before Tokyo: Power and Magic in the Shogun's City of Edo*. London: Reaktion Books, 2020.

Shimazaki, Satoko. *Edo Kabuki in Transition: From the Worlds of the Samurai to the Vengeful Female Ghost*. New York: Columbia University Press, 2016.

Shin kokin wakashū. Ed. Minemura Fumito. SNKBZ 43. Tokyo: Shōgakukan, 1995.

Shirane, Haruo. *Traces of Dreams: Landscape, Cultural Memory, and the Poetry of Bashō*. Stanford, CA: Stanford University Press, 1998.

Shively, Donald H. "Bakufu Versus Kabuki." *Harvard Journal of Asiatic Studies* 18, nos. 3–4 (1955): 326–356.

Shklovsky, Viktor. "Art as Device." In *On the Theory of Prose*, trans. Shushan Avagyan, 5–25. Dallas and Dublin: Dalkey Archive Press, 2021.

Smith, Henry D., II. "The Capacity of Chūshingura: Three Hundred Years of Chūshingura." *Monumenta Nipponica* 58, no. 1 (2003): 1–42.

Solares, Martin. "How to Draw a Novel." Trans. Tanya Huntington. *Literary Hub* (blog), April 8, 2015. https://lithub.com/how-to-draw-a-novel/.

Someya Tomoyuki. "'Fudan kokorogake no hayauma' kō: *Budō denraiki* to shi no yūtopia." In *Saikaku shōsetsu ron: taishōteki kōzō to "Higashi Ajia" e no shikai*, 368–391. Tokyo: Kanrin shobō, 2005.

Stanley, Amy. "Adultery, Punishment, and Reconciliation in Tokugawa Japan." *Journal of Japanese Studies* 33, no. 2 (2007): 309–335.

Sugawara Mayumi. *Tsukioka Yoshitoshi den: Bakumatsu Meiji no hazama ni*. Tokyo: Chūō kōron bijutsu shuppan, 2018.

Sugita Genpaku. *Nochimigusa*. In *Kikin akueki*, ed. Mori Kahei and Tanigawa Ken'ichi, 55–86. Nihon shomin seikatsu shiryō shūsei 7. Tokyo: San'ichi shobō, 1970.

Suwa Haruo. *Chikamatsu sewa jōruri no kenkyū*. Tokyo: Kasama shoin, 1974.

———. "Edo bungaku to wa nanika." In *Edo bungaku no hōhō*, 1–26. Tokyo: Benseisha, 1997.

———. "Utazaimon no kenkyū." *Kokugo kokubun* 31, no. 10 (1962): 40–57.

Suzuki Hideo. "Monozukushi no bungei." *Nihon no bigaku* 32 (2001): 55–68.

Tachibana Nankei. *Tōzai yūki*. Ed. Munemasa Isoo. 2 vols. Tōyō bunko 248, 249. Tokyo: Heibonsha, 2003.

Tagawa Kuniko. "'Saikaku no bukemono:' *Nanshoku ōkagami* to *Budō denraiki*." *Nihon bungaku* 19, no. 10 (1970): 1–13.

Taiheki. Ed. Gotō Tanji and Kamada Kisaburō. 5 vols. NKBT 34. Tokyo: Iwanami shoten, 1960.

Takada Mamoru. "Nishiyama monogatari." In *Hanabusa sōshi, Nishiyama monogatari, Ugetsu monogatari, Harusame monogatari*, ed. Nakamura Yukihiko, Takada Mamoru, and Nakamura Hiroyasu, 595–599. SNKBZ 78. Tokyo: Shōgakukan, 1995.

Takahashi Masaaki. "Yōwa no kikin, Genryaku no jishin to Kamo no Chōmei." *Bungaku* 13, no. 2 (2012): 48–60.

Takao Kazuhiko. *Kinsei no shomin bunka*. Tokyo: Iwanami shoten, 1968.

Takebe Ayatari. *Nishiyama monogatari*. In *Hanabusa sōshi, Nishiyama monogatari, Ugetsu monogatari, Harusame monogatari*, ed. Nakamura Yukihiko, Takada Mamoru, and Nakamura Hiroyasu, 191–267. SNKBZ 78. Tokyo: Shōgakukan, 1995.

Takase Baisei. *Ruisenshū*. 8 Vols. Teramachi Nijōagaru machi (Kyoto): Terada Yoheiji, 1677. Waseda Daigaku Sōgō Kotenseki Dētabēsu. https://www.wul.waseda.ac.jp/kotenseki.

Takeda Izumo II, Miyoshi Shōraku, and Namiki Senryū. *Kanadehon chūshingura*. In *Jōruri shū*, ed. Torigoe Bunzō, Nagatomo Chiyoji, Ōhashi Tadayoshi, Kuroishi Yōko, Hayashi Kumiko, and Inoue Katsushi, 11–161. SNKBZ 77. Tokyo: Shōgakukan, 2002.

Takemoto Chitosedayū. "Osan Mohei o tazunete." In *Saikaku to ukiyozōshi kenkyū*. Vol. 5, *Geinō*, ed. Hara Michio, Kawai Masumi, and Kurakazu Masae, 213–217. Tokyo: Kasama shoin, 2011.

Taniguchi Shinko. "Akō rōshi ni miru bushidō to 'ie' no meiyo." *Nihon rekishi* 650 (2002): 39–56.

———. *Bushidō kō: kenka, katakiuchi, bureiuchi*. Tokyo: Kadokawa gakugei shuppan, 2007.

Taniwaki Masachika. "*Budō denraiki* ni okeru fūshi no hōhō: sono ichi sokumen." *Edo bungaku* 1, no. 2 (1990): 34–52.

———. *Saikaku: kenkyū to hihyō*. Tokyo: Wakakusa shobō, 1995.

———. "Saikaku no jishu kisei to kamufurāju: ichiou no sōkatsu to kongo no kadai." In *Saikaku to ukiyozōshi kenkyū*, vol. 1, *Media*, ed. Nakajima Takashi and Shinohara Susumu, 117–131. Tokyo: Kasama shoin, 2006.

———. "Shuppan jānarizumu to Saikaku." In *Saikaku kenkyū ronkō*, 37–60. Tokyo: Shintensha, 1981.

———. "Ukiyo monogatari." In *Kanazōshi shū ukiyozōshi shū*, ed. Jinbō Kazuya, Aoyama Tadakazu, Kishi Tokuzō, Taniwaki Masachika, and Hasegawa Tsuyoshi, 28–33. NKBZ 37. Tokyo: Shōgakukan, 1971.

Thongchai Winichakul. *Siam Mapped: A History of the Geo-Body of a Nation*. Honolulu: University of Hawai'i Press, 1994.

Thornton, Sybil A. "*Meitokuki*: Earthquakes and Literary Fabrication in the *Gunki Monogatari*." *Japan Review* 28 (2015): 225–234.

Toby, Ronald P. "Contesting the Centre: International Sources of Japanese National Identity." *International History Review* 7, no. 3 (1985): 347–363.

———. *Engaging the Other: "Japan" and Its Alter Egos, 1550–1850*. Leiden: Brill, 2019.

Tsubouchi Shōyō. *Shōsetsu shinzui*. In *Tsubouchi Shōyō shū*, ed. Nakamura Ken and Umezawa Nobuo, 39–165. Nihon kindai bungaku taikei 3. Tokyo: Kadokawa shoten, 1974.

Tsukioka Yoshitoshi. *Kaidai hyakusensō*. Ed. Machida Shiritsu Kokusai Hanga Bijutsukan, with commentary by Koike Makiko and Ōuchi Mizue. Nazotoki ukiyoe sōsho. Tokyo: Nigensha, 2012.

Uchimura Katsushi. "'Masurao monogatari' ron: 'katari' to sono gaibu." In *Ueda Akinari ron: kokugakuteki sōzōryoku no ken'iki*, 158–195. Tokyo: Perikansha, 2007.

Ueda Akinari. *Akinari ibun*. Ed. Fujii Otoo. Tokyo: Shūbunkan, 1919.

———. *Harusame monogatari*. In *Hanabusa sōshi, Nishiyama monogatari, Ugetsu monogatari, Harusame monogatari*, ed. Nakamura Yukihiko, Takada Mamoru, and Nakamura Hiroyasu, 415–566. SNKBZ 78. Tokyo: Shōgakukan, 1995.

———. *Harusame monogatari: Bunka gonen bon*. In *Ueda Akinari zenshū*, ed. Ueda Akinari zenshū henshū iinkai, 5:147–240. Tokyo: Chūō kōronsha, 1992.

———. "Masurao monogatari." In *Hanabusa sōshi, Nishiyama monogatari, Ugetsu monogatari, Harusame monogatari*, ed. Nakamura Yukihiko, Takada Mamoru, and Nakamura Hiroyasu, 622–631. SNKBZ 78. Tokyo: Shōgakukan, 1995.

———. "Nubatama no maki." In *Ueda Akinari zenshū*, ed. Ueda Akinari zenshū henshū iinkai, 5:53–82. Tokyo: Chūō kōronsha, 1992.

———. *Shodō kikimimi sekenzaru*. In *Ueda Akinari shoki ukiyozōshi hyōshaku*, ed. Moriyama Shigeo, 24–177. Tokyo: Kokusho kankōkai, 1977.

———. *Tandai shōshin roku*. In *Ueda Akinari shū*, ed. Nakamura Yukihiko, 249–362. NKBT 56. Tokyo: Iwanami shoten, 1959.

———. *Ugetsu monogatari*. In *Hanabusa sōshi, Nishiyama monogatari, Ugetsu monogatari, Harusame monogatari*, ed. Nakamura Yukihiko, Takada Mamoru, and Nakamura Hiroyasu, 269–413. SNKBZ 78. Tokyo: Shōgakukan, 1995.

———. "Yoshiya ashiya." In *Ueda Akinari zenshū*, ed. Ueda Akinari zenshū henshū iinkai, 5:475–512. Tokyo: Chūō kōronsha, 1992."

"Ukiyo monogatari." In *Kanazōshi shū ukiyozōshi shū*, ed. Jinbō Kazuya, Aoyama Tadakazu, Kishi Tokuzō, Taniwaki Masachika, and Hasegawa Tsuyoshi, 147–281. NKBZ 37. Tokyo: Shōgakukan, 1971.

Utagawa Kuniyoshi. *Shōutsushi hyakumen sō*. In *Edo Meiji hyakumensō ehon hasshu*, ed. Mutō Sadao, 7–31. Kyoto: Taihei shoya, 1997.

Vaporis, Constantine Nomikos. *Breaking Barriers: Travel and the State in Early Modern Japan*. Cambridge, MA: Harvard University Press, 1994.

———. *Tour of Duty: Samurai, Military Service in Edo, and the Culture of Early Modern Japan*. Honolulu: University of Hawai'i Press, 2008.

Walker, Brett L. *The Conquest of Ainu Lands: Ecology and Culture in Japanese Expansion, 1590–1800*. Berkeley: University of California Press, 2001.

Walley, Glynne. *Good Dogs: Edification, Entertainment, and Kyokutei Bakin's "Nansō Satomi hakkenden."* Ithaca, NY: Cornell University East Asia Program, 2017.

Walthall, Anne. "The Life Cycle of Farm Women in Tokugawa Japan." In *Recreating Japanese Women, 1600–1945*, ed. Gail Lee Bernstein, 42–70. Berkeley: University of California Press, 1991.

Watanabe Hiroshi. "'Ōyake' to 'watakushi' no gogi: 'kō' 'shi,' 'public' 'private' to no hikaku ni oite." In *Kō to shi no shisōshi*, ed. Sasaki Takeshi and Kim T'aech'ang, 145–154. Tokyo: Tokyo daigaku shuppankai, 2001.

Williams, Raymond. *Marxism and Literature*. Oxford: Oxford University Press, 1977.

Woloch, Alex. *The One vs. the Many: Minor Characters and the Space of the Protagonist in the Novel*. Princeton, NJ: Princeton University Press, 2003.

Yamaga Sokō. "Shidō." In *Yamaga Sokō bunshū*, ed. Mukasa San, 45–206. Tokyo: Yūhōdō, 1914.

Yano Kimio. "*Budō denraiki*: katakiuchi o gyōshi suru." *Kokubungaku kaishaku to kanshō* 58, no. 8 (1993): 94–99.

———. "*Budō denraiki* no sekai: seido ni fūjikomerareta jōnen." In *Saikaku ron*, 285–313. Tokyo: Wakakusa shobō, 2003.

Yokota Fuyuhiko. "Imagining Working Women in Early Modern Japan." Trans. Mariko Asano Tamanoi. In *Women and Class in Japanese History*, ed. Hitomi Tonomura, Anne Walthall, and Wakita Haruko, 153–167. Ann Arbor: Center for Japanese Studies, University of Michigan, 1999.

Yonemoto, Marcia. *Mapping Early Modern Japan: Space, Place, and Culture in the Tokugawa Period, 1603–1868*. Berkeley: University of California Press, 2003.

Young, Blake Morgan. "A Tale of the Western Hills: Takebe Ayatari's *Nishiyama monogatari*." *Monumenta Nipponica* 37, no. 1 (1982): 77–88.

Zhuangzi. *Zhuangzi: The Complete Writings*. Trans. Brook Ziporyn. Indianapolis: Hackett, 2020.

Index

"Account of My Hermitage, An" (Hōjōki) (Kamo no Chōmei), 37–38, 46, 59
adultery, 82, 103–104, 110, 233n6, 240nn33,48. *See also* Osan-Mohei
Aeba Kōson, 213
Ainu people, 179, 182, 185, 195, 203
Akimichi, 237n60
Akō Vendetta, 23
allusive variation (*honkadori*), 18, 229n15
Appelbaum, Robert, 229n12
Aristotle, 21
Ariwara no Narihira, 161
"Art as Device" (Shklovsky), 9
"art for art's sake" (*geijutsu no tame no geijutsu*), 4, 222n7
Asai Ryōi: formal rearrangement and, 40; guidebooks by, 39, 40, 60, 229n21, 230n25; life of, 39–40; *The Pivot Stone*, 62; *Tales of the Floating World*, 60–61. *See also Stirrups of Musashi*
Asaji ga yado ("The House Overgrown with Grasses") (Ueda Akinari), 155

Asaka Marsh, The (Santō Kyōden). *See Revenge and Strange Tales: The Asaka Marsh*
associated words (*engo*), 78
audience, 122–124, 241nn65–66, 242n68, 243n86

Banquet of Blood: The Art of Taiso Yoshitoshi (*Chi no bansan: Taiso Yoshitoshi no geijutsu*), 217
Battle of Sekigahara (1600), 35, 215
Battle of Ueno (1868), 212, 213
Berry, Mary Elizabeth, 13, 38, 49, 51
blood revenge (*katakiuchi*): actual practice of, 66, 233n8, 234n17; Confucian origins, 70; idealization of, 67, 73–74; legalization of, 66, 233n7, 234nn12–13; liminality/ reintegration and, 72–73, 74–75; political authority and, 72; popular interest in, 66–67, 70; taxonomic social order and, 70–71, 72, 82, 235n22

[275]

"Bloodstained Robe, The" (Chikatabira) (Ueda Akinari), 172

bodies: cultural frontiers and, 194–195, 202–203; as signs of political authority, 99–101, 112–113, 124, 125. See also female body/sexuality

Boshin War (1868–1869), 212, 213, 214

Botsman, Daniel, 99, 100, 107, 124

Brown, Delmer M., 251n2

Buddhism: Asai Ryōi and, 39–40; death anniversaries and, 243n86; disaster literature and, 37; fiction and, 149; medieval literature and, 43; monozukushi and, 50–51; in Stirrups of Musashi, 45–46, 47, 54; Tokugawa politics and, 63

Budō denraiki (Ihara Saikaku). See Inheritance of the Martial Way

Buke giri monogatari (Tales of Samurai Obligation) (Ihara Saikaku), 232n3

bureiuchi, 233n6

Burns, Susan, 105–106, 141, 165

Calendar-Maker and the Old Calendar, The (Daikyōji mukashigoyomi) (Chikamatsu Monzaemon), 114–131; audience and, 122–124; calendrical system in, 129–130; cats in, 117–119, 241n52; empathy in, 103, 123–124, 125–127, 130; first performance of, 99; formal rearrangement in, 103, 127–128, 129; misrecognition in, 122, 124–125, 126–127; political authority in, 126–127, 242n80; restoration of subjectivity in, 116, 121–122, 124, 130; surprise ending in, 127–128, 243n85; The Tale of Genji and, 241n50; taxonomic social order in, 120–121, 131; truth vs. fiction in, 121, 123, 131, 132

"Calendar-Maker's Osan and Mohei, The" (Daikyōji Osan Mohei) (utazaimon), 99, 107–109, 114, 117, 128–129, 132, 239nn26,32

Catherine the Great (empress of Russia), 185, 253n29

cats, 116–119, 241n52

censorship, 187

Certeau, Michel de, 180

characterization: Genta murder and, 167–169, 250n112; normative social forms and, 10; Osan-Mohei and, 111–112, 240n38; typology and, 2, 10

Chi no bansan: Taiso Yoshitoshi no geijutsu (Banquet of Blood: The Art of Taiso Yoshitoshi), 217

Chikamatsu Hanji, 225n28

Chikamatsu Monzaemon: audience and, 122–124, 241nn65–66, 242n68, 243n86; The Chronicle of Great Peace Played Out on a Go Board, 227n62; Drum Waves of the Horikawa, 240n48; feeling and, 123, 124, 241nn65–66, 242n69; formal rearrangement and, 3, 10, 19–20, 225n28; Gonza the Lancer, 240n48; jidaimono and, 240n44; literature/life dialogue and, 227n62; The Love Suicides and the Two-Page Picture Book, 242n68; The Love Suicides at Amijima, 19–20; The Love Suicides at Sonezaki, 114; Lovers Pond in Settsu Province, 3, 10, 225n28; on megatakiuchi, 240n48; on realism, 131; Souvenirs of Naniwa, 241n65, 243n89. See also Calendar-Maker and the Old Calendar, The

Chikamatsu Tōnan, 225n28

Chikatabira ("The Bloodstained Robe") (Ueda Akinari), 172

Chikusai, 60, 229n21

China: calendrical system and, 128; cultural frontiers and, 189, 201; ka-i system and, 182; Kamo no Mabuchi on, 142, 143, 144; lost wholeness and, 141; *yomihon* and, 186–187. See also Confucianism; formal rearrangement

Chronicle of Great Peace, The (*Taiheiki*), 23, 32, 159–160, 212

Chronicle of Great Peace Played Out on a Go Board, The (*Goban Taiheiki*) (Chikamatsu Monzaemon), 227n62

Chronicles of Japan (*Nihon shoki*), 146–147

Chūdan ni miru koyomiya monogatari ("A Tale of the Calendar-Maker, Seen in the Middle Section") (Ihara Saikaku), 102–103, 110–114, 128, 132, 242n81

Chūshin suikoden (*The Water Margin of the Loyal Retainers*) (Santō Kyōden), 188, 190, 254n41

Classic of Poetry (*Shijing*), 141

classical poetics: cultural frontiers and, 184, 192–193, 195, 196–197; Edo school and, 245n26; *Inheritance of the Martial Way* and, 78, 81; *kokugaku* and, 141, 145; *monozukushi* and, 231n47; *utamakura*, 2, 83, 184, 196, 197, 202. See also formal rearrangement

Classified and Annotated Japanese Names (*Wamyō ruijū shō*), 147

Collection of Ancient and Modern Poems (*Kokin wakashū*), 141, 144, 184

Collection of Ten Thousand Leaves. See Man'yōshū

Collection of Treasures (*Hōbutsushū*), 247n64

commercial print culture: censorship and, 187; disaster literature and, 34, 35, 36; formal rearrangement and, 39, 41–42; genre and, 39, 187; information and, 35, 38–39, 49–50, 62, 228–229n12; *kanazōshi* and, 34, 38, 40, 228n8, 229n21; medieval-early modern transition and, 35, 63;

normative social forms and, 13–14, 105–106; political authority and, 49–50; taxonomic social order and, 177; women's roles and, 105–106

Companion Dolls (*Otogi bōko*) (Asai Ryōi), 39

Complete Biographies of the Drunken Bodhisattvas of Our Realm (*Honchō suibodai zenden*) (Santō Kyōden), 205

confession tale (*sangemono*), 43, 230n31

Confucianism: blood revenge and, 70; on feeling, 242n69; on fiction, 149, 150, 181; Kamo no Mabuchi on, 142, 143; lost wholeness and, 141, 142; *Record of Rites* and, 70, 234n15; travel narratives and, 185, 189, 200–201, 255n62

containment, 15, 71, 84. See also taxonomic social order

courtesan critiques (*yūjo hyōbanki*), 239n22

creativity. See innovation

cultural frontiers: closed borders and, 178–179, 185, 253n30; commodities and, 185, 194, 199–200, 202–203, 255n49; critical approach to, 182; early modern-Meiji transition and, 181–182; Ezo and, 182–183; foreign aggression and, 179, 184–185, 206, 253n28; formal rearrangement and, 186, 197–198, 206–207; *ka-i* system and, 182–183, 192, 194, 199; liminality and, 201, 255n63; normative social forms and, 179, 182–183; north and, 182–186, 252nn22–23; partitioning of space and, 180–181; political authority and, 179, 183, 199; ragged edges and, 178, 179, 181, 205, 206; revenge form and, 188–189; sameness and, 204–205; travel narratives and, 185, 189, 200–201; violence and, 179, 181, 195, 202–203, 207; visual art and, 251n10, 257n10

Daikokuya Kōdayū, 185, 253n29
Daikyōji mukashigoyomi (Chikamatsu Monzaemon). *See Calendar-Maker and the Old Calendar, The*
Daikyōji Osan Mohei ("The Calendar-Maker's Osan and Mohei") (*utazaimon*), 99, 107–109, 114, 117, 128–129, 132, 239nn26,32
Daoism, 150–151
disaster literature: Buddhism and, 37; comedy and, 35; commercial print culture and, 34, 35, 36; historical events and, 33, 228n4; as informational, 35, 228–229n12; medieval, 32, 33–34, 37–38, 56, 228n4; popularity of, 228n9. *See also Stirrups of Musashi*
Dokuyaku wa hakoiri no inochi ("Poison Put Her Life Into a Box") (Ihara Saikaku), 77
Drum Waves of the Horikawa (*Horikawa nami no tsuzumi*) (Chikamatsu Monzaemon), 240n48
Dutch studies (*Rangaku*), 204–205

early modern-Meiji transition: Boshin War, 212, 213, 214; cultural frontiers and, 181–182; late *yomihon* and, 181, 251n15; perceptions of time and, 214, 215; violence and, 215–216
Edo: construction of, 40–41; Great Meireki Fire, 34–35, 41; warfare in, 212
Edo meishoki (*A Guide to the Famous Places of Edo*) (Asai Ryōi), 40, 230n25
Edo-period Japan: adultery in, 82, 103–104, 238n11; Boshin War, 212, 213, 214; calendrical system, 128, 242n80; end of, 181, 212, 214, 215–216; foreign aggression and, 179, 184–185, 206, 253n28; foreign influences, 178, 204–205; geographical definitions and, 177–178, 251n2; isolationism, 177–178; military logic in, 9, 12; peace during, 1, 214, 215; perception of time and, 36–37, 214–215; Shimabara Rebellion, 74, 213, 214, 257n12; working women in, 91, 236n55. *See also* cultural frontiers; early modern-Meiji transition; medieval-early modern transition; Tokugawa shogunate
Edogawa Ranpo, 216
Eight Dog Chronicle (*Nansō Satomi hakkenden*) (Kyokutei Bakin), 187, 251n15, 253n34, 256n71
Eikhenbaum, Boris, 223n17
Eiko Ikegami, 104
Eiyū hyakushu (*Heroes: One Hundred Verses*) (Ryokutei Senryū), 212
Emishi people, 183, 252n23
Emmerich, Michael, 223n8
emotion. *See* empathy; feeling
empathy, 103, 109, 123–124, 125–127, 130
engo (associated words), 78
Essence of the Novel, The (*Shōsetsu shinzui*) (Tsubouchi Shōyō), 181, 206
etiquette. *See* normative social forms
European literature, 1–2, 8, 136, 181, 206, 217
Eyers, Tom, 176
Ezo (Hokkaido), 179, 182, 185, 189, 194, 252n22, 255n48. *See also* cultural frontiers
Ezochi. *See* Ainu people; Ezo

Fake Tales (*Nise monogatari*), 39
family politics, 11
feeling: Chikamatsu Monzaemon and, 123, 124, 241nn65–66, 242n69; fiction and, 152, 248n69; *kokugaku* and, 142,

148; *masurao* ideal and, 136, 144, 152; political authority and, 126–127. See also empathy

female body/sexuality: cats and, 116–117; household structure and, 104, 105–106, 107; male desire and, 106–107, 110, 117, 239n22

fiction: Buddhism and, 149; feeling and, 152, 248n69; healing power of, 208; Ueda Akinari's embrace of, 135, 136, 165–166, 171–172; Ueda Akinari's theorization of, 136, 149–150, 151–152, 154, 159, 248nn68–69; violence and, 136, 152, 153. See also truth vs. fiction

Five Amorous Women (*Kōshoku gonin onna*) (Ihara Saikaku), 99, 102–103, 109–114, 128, 132, 240n33, 242n81

Flueckiger, Peter, 143, 145

form: adaptability of, 113–114; afterlives of, 216–218; content and, 6–7, 21; defined, 6–8; flow and, 6, 223n17; instability/unreliability of, 69–70, 79, 84; *kata* and, 7, 224n18; literature/life dialogue and, 5, 15, 23–24, 227n62; models of the world and, 4–5, 223n9; obscurity of early modern use, 1–2; politics and, 22–23; as problematic, 24; relational nature of, 21; repetition and, 17; *seken* and, 110, 111, 113; truth and, 25–26; truth vs. fiction and, 131–132, 175–176; violence and, 8–9. See also formal rearrangement; normative social forms; taxonomic social order

formal rearrangement: aesthetic devices for, 20–21, 226n58; Asai Ryōi and, 40; Chikamatsu Monzaemon and, 3, 10, 19–20, 225n28; commercial print culture and, 39, 41–42; cultural frontiers and, 186, 197–198, 206–207;

Genta murder and, 147; imitation and, 19–20; in *Inheritance of the Martial Way*, 76; *kata* and, 7, 17–19, 191; Kyokutei Bakin and, 2–3, 6–7, 10, 225n28; late *yomihon* and, 188, 190–191, 254n44; normative social forms and, 6, 8; Osan-Mohei and, 100–101, 102–103, 107, 109–110, 127–128, 129, 132; repetition and, 17; setting and, 2, 225n28; time and, 214–215; typology and, 16–17; visual art and, 211–212, 213–214, 257n10

Fudan kokorogake no hayauma ("Never Let Your Guard Down on a Swift Horse") (Ihara Saikaku), 85–90

Fujii Otoo, 153

Fujimoto Kizan, 91

fukiyose, 20–21, 226n58

Fukushū kidan Asaka no numa (Santō Kyōden). See *Revenge and Strange Tales: The Asaka Marsh*

Furuike ya kawazu tobikomu mizu no oto ("Old pond: a frog jumps in—the sound of water") (Matsuo Bashō), 18–19, 20, 21

Furukawa Koshōken, 252n22

gender, family politics and, 11

Genji ipponkyō (*A Sutra for Genji*), 247n64

Genji monogatari (Murasaki Shikibu). See *Tale of Genji, The*

genre: commercial print culture and, 39, 187; late *yomihon* and, 186–187, 253n34

Genta murder: formal strangeness of, 135, 137, 146, 176; immediate responses to, 134–135; *kokugaku* and, 137, 147, 154–155; normative social forms and, 138–139; official version of, 137–140; original story of, 134; perceptions of *masurao* ideal and, 145–146; Ueda Akinari's meeting with Genta and,

Genta murder (*continued*)
134, 154. *See also* "Smile of the Severed Head, The"; "Tale of a *Masurao*, The"; *Tale of the Western Hills, A*; truth vs. fiction in Genta murder
Geppyō kien (*The Miraculous Destiny of Moon and Ice*) (Kyokutei Bakin), 2–3, 5, 6–7, 9–11, 221n2, 225n28
Gerstle, Andrew, 115, 243n86
gesaku, 187, 222n7
Girard, René, 117
Goban Taiheiki (*The Chronicle of Great Peace Played Out on a Go Board*) (Chikamatsu Monzaemon), 227n62
gōkan (bound books) genre, 187, 189, 223n8, 253n35
Gonza the Lancer (*Yari no Gonza kasane katabira*) (Chikamatsu Monzaemon), 240n48
"Good and the Bad, The" (*Yoshiya ashiya*) (Ueda Akinari), 151
Great Meireki Fire, 34–35, 41. *See also Stirrups of Musashi*
Great Mirror of Male Love, The (*Nanshoku ōkagami*) (Ihara Saikaku), 232–233n3
Great Mirror of the Way of Love (*Shikidō ōkagami*) (Fujimoto Kizan), 91, 106
Great Tenmei Famine, 185–186, 203
Great Train Robbery, The, 218
Griffiths, Devin, 21, 27
Guide to Famous Places Along the Eastern Highway (*Tōkaidō meishoki*) (Asai Ryōi), 39, 60, 229n21, 230n25
Guide to the Famous Places of Edo, A (*Edo meishoki*) (Asai Ryōi), 40, 230n25
Gundry, David J., 233–234n10
gunkimono genre, 228n4

Haidu, Peter, 8
haikai genre (linked verse), 78, 79, 80–81, 116, 147, 184
haishimono yomihon. *See* late *yomihon*
Hall, John W., 71
Hamada Keisuke, 190–191, 254n44
Handler-Spitz, Rivi, 96
"Hankai" (Ueda Akinari), 172–173
Hara Masako, 144
Harusame monogatari (Ueda Akinari). *See Tales of the Spring Rain*
Hayashi Shihei, 253n28
Hayot, Eric, 37, 38
"Heartstrings Plucked on Lake Biwa" (*Shintei o hiku biwa no umi*) (Ihara Saikaku), 235n31
Hedberg, William C., 188
Heike monogatari (*Tale of the Heike*), 33–34
hell tour (*jigoku meguri*), 46–47
Heroes: One Hundred Verses (*Eiyū hyakushu*) (Ryokutei Senryū), 212
hierarchy. *See* taxonomic social order
Hino Tatsuo, 14, 15, 17, 19
Hiraga Gennai, 254n41
Hirata Atsutane, 245n25
Hirosue Tamotsu, 76
Hishikawa Moronobu, 195
Hōbutsushū (*Collection of Treasures*), 247n64
Hōjōki ("An Account of My Hermitage") (Kamo no Chōmei), 37–38, 46, 59
Honchō suibodai zenden (*Complete Biographies of the Drunken Bodhisattvas of Our Realm*) (Santō Kyōden), 205
honkadori (allusive variation), 18, 229n15
Honshu, 183–184, 185–186, 189, 200, 252n23. *See also* cultural frontiers
Horikawa nami no tsuzumi (*Drum Waves of the Horikawa*) (Chikamatsu Monzaemon), 240n48
"House Overgrown with Grasses, The" (*Asaji ga yado*) (Ueda Akinari), 155
household structure: bodies-as-signs and, 100; cats and, 116–117; political

authority and, 100, 104, 107; vulnerability of, 103, 104, 132; women's roles in, 104, 105–106, 118–119, 238n15

Howell, David L., 183

Hozumi Ikan, 241n65

Hundred Articles (*Hyakkajō*), 138, 140. See also *Rules for Determining Legal Matters*

Hyakkajō (*Hundred Articles*), 138, 140

Hyde, Lewis, 75

identity. *See* personhood; taxonomic social order

Ihara Saikaku: on adultery, 240n33; *Five Amorous Women*, 99, 102–103, 109–114, 128, 132, 240n33, 242n81; *The Great Mirror of Male Love*, 232–233n3; innovation and, 65, 232n2; *The New Laughable Collection*, 232n3; on samurai, 232–233n3; style of, 78–79, 111; "Tale of the Calendar-Maker, Seen in the Middle Section, A," 102–103, 110–114, 128, 132, 242n81; *Tales of Samurai Obligation*, 232n3. See also *Inheritance of the Martial Way*

Iikura Yōichi, 248n69, 249–250n106

Illustrated Overview of Humanity (*Jinrin kinmō zui*), 13–14

Ima kagami (*The Mirror of the Present*), 247n64

Ima monogatari (*Tales of the Present*), 247n64

Imoseyama and the Women's Cultivation Manual (*Imoseyama onna teikin*) (Chikamatsu Hanji et al.), 225n28

In the Shelter of the Pine (*Matsukage nikki*) (Ōgimachi Machiko), 22–23

Inheritance of the Martial Way (*Budō denraiki*) (Ihara Saikaku): *Akimichi* and, 237n60; authenticity and, 96,

97; on boundaries, 75–76; collection as whole, 76, 79, 235n31; as commentary on samurai culture, 68, 87, 233–234n10; commercial logic in, 95; containment in, 84; criticisms of, 65, 67–68, 95–96, 233n4; distortion of revenge form in, 69, 75–78; formal rearrangement in, 76; on generative possibilities of normative social forms, 87–88; *haikai* and, 78, 79, 80–81; idealized revenge form in, 88–89; on instability/unreliability of form, 69–70, 79, 84; interruption of revenge form in, 93–94; invisibility in, 94–95; ironic inversions of revenge form in, 82–83; irony in, 82–83, 89, 90; on limits of revenge form, 95; new forms of relationship in, 89–90, 91–93, 237n63; normative social forms and, 84–87; plot in, 76–78, 80, 93, 236n33; strange realism in, 96–97; style in, 78–79; trickster play in, 75–76, 96. *See also* "Heartstrings Plucked on Lake Biwa"; "Never Let Your Guard Down on a Swift Horse"; "Poison Put Her Life Into a Box"; "Sudden New Year's of 'Knock Knock, Who's There?,' A"; "Vying Over Smoke at the Field Altar"; "Woman Can Write in a Man's Hand, A"

innovation: Asai Ryōi's life and, 40; idealized revenge form and, 74; Ihara Saikaku and, 65, 232n2; medieval-early modern transition and, 60; *mitate* and, 20; *monozukushi* and, 51; *shukō* and, 20; Ueda Akinari and, 135–136, 176. See also formal rearrangement

Inoue Keiji, 188

Instructions for Cultivating Life (*Yōjōkun*) (Kaibara Ekiken), 105
intersubjectivity, 102, 114, 131
intertextuality. *See* formal rearrangement
Inu kokon chomonjū (*The Mongrel Collection of Things Written and Heard in the Present and the Past*) (Mukunashi Issetsu), 233n4
Ise monogatari (*Tales of Ise*), 39, 141, 147, 161, 162
Ishihara Shintarō, 32, 229n13
Ishikawa Jun, 136
Itakura Shigemasa, 257n12
Itō Jinsai, 141, 242n69
Itō Tōgai, 242n69

Jackson, Michael, 101, 121
jealousy (*rinki*), 105
jidaimono, 115, 240n44
jigoku meguri (hell tour), 46–47
Jinrin kinmō zui (*Illustrated Overview of Humanity*), 13–14
jōruri theater, 19, 23, 99, 225n28
Journey to the East (*Tōyūki*) (Tachibana Nankei), 185, 189, 200–201, 255n62
Jōzan's Talks on History (*Jōzan kidan*), 212

ka-i system (*ka-i chitsujo*), 182–183, 192, 194, 199
kabuki theater, 15, 20, 134, 224n21
Kada no Azumamaro, 245n25
Kaibara Ekiken, 105
Kaidai hyakusensō (*One Hundred Selected Portraits of Those Who Dash Ahead*) (Tsukioka Yoshitoshi), 209, *210*, 211–217, 257n10
Ka'ikō ("Thoughts on the Meaning of Poetry") (Kamo no Mabuchi), 145
Kaitai shinsho (*New Book of Anatomy*), 204–205

kakekotoba (pivot words), 78
Kakinomoto no Hitomaro, 144
Kamigata *yomihon*. *See yomihon* (reading books) genre
Kamo no Chōmei, "An Account of My Hermitage," 37–38, 46, 59
Kamo no Mabuchi: on *kokugaku*, 142–143; on *masurao* ideal, 140, 143–144, 145, 154; "On the Meaning of Our Country," 142; origins of *kokugaku* and, 245n25; on poetry, 144–145, 246nn39,49; "Thoughts on the Meaning of Poetry," 145
Kanadehon chūshingura (*The Treasury of Loyal Retainers*), 23, 25, 188, 227n62
Kanameishi (*The Pivot Stone*) (Asai Ryōi), 62
kanazōshi (kana booklets), 34, 38, 40, 228n8, 229n21
Kanmei nikki, 231n57
Kanze Nobumitsu, 255n57
kata, 7, 17–19, 191, 224n18
"Kata and Literary Style" (Nakamura), 17–18
katakiuchi. *See* blood revenge
Katakiuchi ato no matsuri (*Revenge After the Fact*) (Santō Kyōden), 24–25
Katakiuchi Okazaki joroshu (*The Women of Okazaki: A Revenge*) (Santō Kyōden), 189
katarimono (oral performance), 43
katauta, 146–147
Katō Chikage, 245n26
Katō Umaki, 141, 145
Kawachi Yatasuke, 221n2
Kawanishi Hidemichi, 183
Kawano Michikiyo, 40
Kazama Seishi, 136, 164, 168, 250n112
Keichū, 245n25
Ki no Kaion, 19–20

"Kibitsu Cauldron, The" (Kibitsu no kama) (Ueda Akinari), 155
kibyōshi (illustrated fiction), 187, 189, 253n35
kikōbun, 153
Kinryū Keiyū, 147
Kinsei kiseki kō (Thoughts on the Wondrous Traces of Recent Ages) (Santō Kyōden), 189
Kiso Yoshinaka, 79
Kitashirakawa Yoshihisa, 213
Kiyomizu monogatari (The Tale of Kiyomizu), 63
Kleinman, Arthur, 114
Kliger, Ilya, 223n17
Koi no yama Gengobei monogatari ("The Tale of Gengobei, a Mountain of Love") (Ihara Saikaku), 240n33
Kojiki (Record of Ancient Matters), 146–147, 245n25
Kokin wakashū (Collection of Ancient and Modern Poems), 141, 144, 184
kokugaku: content of, 141–142, 245n26; Genta murder and, 137, 147, 154–155; Kamo no Mabuchi and, 142–143; masurao ideal and, 140–141, 143–144, 145, 154; origins of, 141, 245n25; poetry and, 143–145, 245nn25–26, 246n39; on truth vs. fiction, 150; Ueda Akinari and, 133, 136, 149
Kokuikō ("On the Meaning of Our Country") (Kamo no Mabuchi), 142
Komagine Hachibyōe, 209, 210, 211, 213–216, 257n12
Konoe Noriko, 155
Konta Yōzō, 232n2
Kornicki, Peter, 46, 128, 229n12
Kōshoku gonin onna (Five Amorous Women) (Ihara Saikaku), 99, 102–103, 109–114, 128, 240n33
Koyama Issei, 239n26
Kudō Heisuke, 253n28

Kujikata osadamegaki (Rules for Determining Legal Matters), 138, 238n11, 244n12. See also Hundred Articles (Hyakkajō)
"Kuka Heizaemon Avenges His Father" (Kuka Heizaemon chichi no kataki o utsu koto) (Mukunashi Issetsu), 74
Kurachi Katsunao, 71
Kyokutei Bakin: Eight Dog Chronicle, 187, 251n15, 253n34, 256n71; formal rearrangement and, 2–3, 6–7, 10, 225n28; late yomihon and, 179, 187, 253n34, 256n71; The Miraculous Destiny of Moon and Ice, 2–3, 5, 6–7, 9–11, 221n2, 225n28; normative social forms and, 5; Tales of the Spring Rain and, 249n104

language. See style
Laozi, 151
late yomihon, 179–180; The Asaka Marsh as foundation for, 189; early modern-Meiji transition and, 181, 251n15; formal rearrangement and, 188, 190–191, 254n44; genre and, 186–187, 253n34; genre frameworks for, 186–187, 253n34; interconnectedness in, 191; material form of, 187, 253n35; moral instruction and, 181, 206, 208; plot in, 190, 191; Santō Kyōden and, 179, 187, 190, 254n41; style in, 254n41; Tsubouchi Shōyō's critique of, 206, 251n15, 256n71
Laxman, Adam, 185, 253nn29–30
Le Guin, Ursula K., 96
Levine, Caroline, 7
linked verse (haikai genre), 78, 79, 80–81, 116, 147, 184
Love Suicides and the Two-Page Picture Book, The (Shinjū nimai ezōshi) (Chikamatsu Monzaemon), 242n68

Love Suicides at Amijima, The (Shinjū ten no Amijima) (Chikamatsu Monzaemon), 19–20
Love Suicides at Sonezaki, The (Sonezaki shinjū) (Chikamatsu Monzaemon), 114
Love Suicides at Umeda, The (Umeda shinjū) (Ki no Kaion), 19–20
Lovers Pond in Settsu Province (Tsu no kuni meoto ike) (Chikamatsu Monzaemon), 3, 10, 225n28
Luo Guanzhong, 149, 150, 247n63

macrocosmic social order. See political authority
Makura no sōshi (Pillow Book) (Sei Shōnagon), 50
Man'yōshū (Collection of Ten Thousand Leaves): The Asaka Marsh and, 197; cultural frontiers and, 184; Edo school and, 245n26; kata and, 224n18; kokugaku and, 145, 245n25, 246n39; masurao ideal and, 143–144; monozukushi in, 51; A Tale of the Western Hills and, 147; Ueda Akinari on, 248n68
masurao ideal: feeling and, 136, 144, 152; kokugaku and, 140–141, 143–144, 145, 154; linguistic origins of, 246n40; linguistic style and, 147; plot and, 171; self-possession and, 166; Takebe Ayatari's perception of Genta murder and, 145–146, 246n52; truth as intent and, 135, 152, 153, 154, 174; Ueda Akinari's perception of Genta murder and, 134, 135, 140, 145–146, 167; uncertainty and, 175
Masurao monogatari (Ueda Akinari). See "Tale of a Masurao, The"
Matsuda Baku, 225n28
Matsuda Osamu, 36–37, 38, 40, 63, 229n15

Matsukage nikki (In the Shelter of the Pine) (Ōgimachi Machiko), 22–23
Matsuo Bashō: The Narrow Road to the Interior, 184, 194, 198; "Old pond: a frog jumps in—the sound of water," 18–19, 20, 21
medieval-early modern transition: Battle of Sekigahara and, 35, 215; commercial print culture and, 35, 63; floating vs. sorrowful world and, 60–61, 232nn62–63; innovation and, 60; Stirrups of Musashi and, 60, 62; time and space and, 36–37, 72, 214–215
medieval literature: amplitude in, 37–38; on disaster, 32, 33–34, 37–38, 56, 228n4; honkadori in, 18, 229n15; jigoku meguri, 46; monozukushi, 51, 231n47; moral instruction and, 32–34, 56; on revenge, 73, 83; sangemono, 43, 230n31; Stirrups of Musashi's reworking of, 35, 43, 46, 47, 59; time and space in, 36–37. See also medieval-early modern transition
megatakiuchi (wife revenge), 104, 233n6, 240n48
Meiji Restoration. See early modern–Meiji transition
Miraculous Destiny of Moon and Ice, The (Geppyō kien) (Kyokutei Bakin), 2–3, 5, 6–7, 9–11, 221n2, 225n28
Mirror for Women, The: A Book of Secret Transmissions (Omuna kagami hidensho), 105
Mirror of Japanese Warriors, A (Nihon bushi kagami) (Mukunashi Issetsu), 65, 67, 68, 95–96
Mirror of the Present, The (Ima kagami), 247n64
Mishima Yukio, 217–218, 257nn17,19
mitate, 20, 21, 23, 188, 213

Miyoshi Shōraku, 225n28
Mizue Renko, 43
Mongrel Collection of Things Written and Heard in the Present and the Past, The (Inu kokon chomonjū) (Mukunashi Issetsu), 233n4
Monjushiri, 112, 240n41
Monomō dore to iu niwaka shōgatsu ("A Sudden New Year's of 'Knock Knock, Who's There?'") (Ihara Saikaku), 78–79
monozukushi (exhaustive list), 50–51, 231n47
moral instruction: in *Inheritance of the Martial Way*, 97; Kyokutei Bakin and, 11; late *yomihon* and, 181, 206, 208; medieval disaster literature and, 32–34, 56; as purpose of fiction, 149, 150, 159; revenge form and, 68, 89, 97
Moretti, Laura, 14, 222–223nn7–8, 228n12
Mori Osamu, 241n66
Morita Kirō, 135, 153
Moriyama Shigeo, 140
Moriyoshi, Prince, 213
Morris, David B., 123
Morris-Suzuki, Tessa, 178, 182
Motoori Norinaga, 164, 245n25
Mukashi goyomi sanjūsan nenki (The Old Calendar and the Thirty-third Death Anniversary) (Chikamatsu Monzaemon), 243n87
Mukashigatari inazuma byōshi (An Old Tale with a Thunderbolt Cover) (Santō Kyōden), 205
Mukunashi Issetsu: authenticity and, 96; criticism of *Inheritance of the Martial Way*, 65, 67–68, 95–96, 233n4; on idealized revenge form, 67–68, 73, 76; "Kuka Heizaemon Avenges His Father," 74; *A Mirror of Japanese Warriors*, 65, 67, 68, 95–96; The *Mongrel Collection of Things Written and Heard in the Present and the Past*, 233n4; normative social forms and, 86
Murasaki Shikibu, 149, 150, 247n64. See also *Tale of Genji, The*
Murata Harumi, 245n26
Musashi abumi (Asai Ryōi). See *Stirrups of Musashi*

Nagashima Hiroaki, 162, 249n98
naimaze, 20–21
Nakamura Hiroyasu, 171, 248n69
Nakamura Yukihiko, 17–19, 20, 222n7, 226n58, 241n66
Nakano Mitsutoshi, 3–4, 151, 222–223nn7–8
Naniwa miyage (Souvenirs of Naniwa) (Chikamatsu Monzaemon and Hozumi Ikan), 241n65, 243n89
Naniwa War Record, The (Naniwa senki), 212
Nanshoku ōkagami (The Great Mirror of Male Love) (Ihara Saikaku), 232–233n3
Nansō Satomi hakkenden (Eight Dog Chronicle) (Kyokutei Bakin), 187, 251n15, 253n34, 256n71
Narrow Road to the Interior, The (Oku no hosomichi) (Matsuo Bashō), 184, 194, 198
Nenashigusa (Rootless Grasses) (Hiraga Gennai), 254n41
Neo-Confucianism, 63, 141, 150, 159, 242n69
"Never Let Your Guard Down on a Swift Horse" (Fudan kokorogake no hayauma) (Ihara Saikaku), 85–90
New Book of Anatomy (Kaitai shinsho), 204–205
New Laughable Collection, The (Shin kashōki) (Ihara Saikaku), 232n3

Ngai, Sianne, 6
Nihon bushi kagami (*A Mirror of Japanese Warriors*) (Mukunashi Issetsu), 65, 67, 68, 95–96
Nihon shoki (*Chronicles of Japan*), 146–147
1930s Japan, 181–182, 216–217
Nise monogatari (*Fake Tales*), 39
Nishida Kōzō, 60
Nishiyama monogatari (Takebe Ayatari). See *Tale of the Western Hills, A*
Noda Hisao, 229n21, 230n25
normative social forms: alternative readings of, 122–123; commercial print culture and, 13–14, 105–106; cultural frontiers and, 179, 182–183; diversity within, 14, 178; formal rearrangement and, 6, 8; generative possibilities of, 87–88; Genta murder and, 138–139; interlocking nature of, 14; military logic and, 5, 9, 12; misrecognition and, 119–120, 122, 124–125, 126–127, 132; personhood and, 10, 14–15; political authority and, 179, 183; samurai culture and, 84–87; truth vs. fiction and, 15, 16; typology and, 19; women and, 105–106
Nozukue no keburi kurabe ("Vying Over Smoke at the Field Altar") (Ihara Saikaku), 90–95, 235n31
Nubatama no maki ("The Scroll of Darkness") (Ueda Akinari), 150, 151, 152

objectification: male desire and, 106; restoration of subjectivity and, 116, 121–122, 124, 130; taxonomic social order and, 121
Oda Nobunaga, 12
Ōgimachi Machiko, 22–23
Ogyū Sorai, 141

Oku no hosomichi (*The Narrow Road to the Interior*) (Matsuo Bashō), 184, 194, 198
Old Calendar and the Thirty-third Death Anniversary, The (*Mukashi goyomi sanjūsan nenki*) (Chikamatsu Monzaemon), 243n87
"Old pond: a frog jumps in—the sound of water" (*Furuike ya kawazu tobikomu mizu no oto*) (Matsuo Bashō), 19–20, 21
Old Tale with a Thunderbolt Cover, An (*Mukashigatari inazuma byōshi*) (Santō Kyōden), 205
Oliver-Smith, Anthony, 32
Omoiire onna shakuhachi ("A Woman's Shakuhachi, Played with Feeling") (Ihara Saikaku), 79–84, 90
Omuna kagami hidensho (*The Mirror for Women: A Book of Secret Transmissions*), 105
"On the Meaning of Our Country" (Kokuikō) (Kamo no Mabuchi), 142
One Hundred Selected Portraits of Those Who Dash Ahead (*Kaidai hyakusensō*) (Tsukioka Yoshitoshi), 209, 210, 211–217, 257n10
Onna no tsukureru otoko moji ("A Woman Can Write in a Man's Hand") (Ihara Saikaku), 235n31
Onzōshi shimawatari (*Yoshitsune Crosses the Isles*), 183, 194–195
Ooms, Herman, 13, 24, 63
oral performance (*katarimono*), 43
Osan-Mohei, 98–102, 107–132, 240n48; alternative readings of normative social forms in, 122–123; calendrical system and, 128–130, 242nn80–81; cats and, 116–119, 241n52; challenges to official version and, 112–113, 123–124; characterization and, 111–112, 240n38; empathy and, 103, 109, 123–124, 125–127, 130; execution

anniversary, 130, 243nn86–87; execution as performance, 98, 99–100; fallibility of political authority and, 115–116; female agency and, 111, 113, 114; formal rearrangement and, 100–101, 102–103, 107, 109–110, 127–128, 129, 132; intersubjectivity and, 102, 114, 131; irony and, 109, 239n32; male desire and, 110; misrecognition and, 119–120, 122, 124–125, 126–127, 132; official version of, 99–101, 112–113, 123–124, 125; plot variations, 103, 108–109, 110–111, 115, 127–128, 239n30, 243n85; political authority and, 100–101, 122, 126–127, 242n80; restoration of subjectivity and, 116, 121–122, 124, 130; *The Tale of Genji* and, 241n50; taxonomic social order and, 120–121, 131; truth vs. fiction and, 101–102, 121, 123, 131–132; *utazaimon* on, 99, 107–109, 114, 117, 128–129, 132, 239nn26,32

Ōtaka Yōji, 190, 254n41

Otogi bōko (*Companion Dolls*) (Asai Ryōi), 39

Ōzawa Shunsaku, 152

performance: political authority and, 16, 183; taxonomic social order and, 15–16, 183

Performing the Great Peace (Roberts), 15

personhood: normative social forms and, 10, 14–15; taxonomic social order and, 131

Pillow Book (*Makura no sōshi*) (Sei Shōnagon), 50

Pivot Stone, The (*Kanameishi*) (Asai Ryōi), 62

pivot words (*kakekotoba*), 78

Plato, 21

plot: Genta murder and, 147–148, 156–159; in *Inheritance of the Martial Way*, 76–78, 80, 93, 236n33; in late *yomihon*, 190, 191; Osan-Mohei and, 103, 108–109, 110–111, 115, 127–128, 239n30, 243n85

"Poison Put Her Life Into a Box" (*Dokuyaku wa hakoiri no inochi*) (Ihara Saikaku), 77

political authority: blood revenge and, 72; calendrical system and, 128, 129–130, 242n80; commercial print culture and, 49–50; cultural frontiers and, 179, 183, 199; differentiation and, 177; in disaster literature, 51, 52, 54–56, 59, 62, 63; fallibility of, 115–116; feeling and, 126–127; Genta murder official version and, 137–140; household structure and, 100, 104, 107; information and, 49–50, 51; misrecognition and, 115–116; normative social forms and, 179, 183; organization of Edo and, 41; Osan-Mohei and, 100–101, 122, 126–127, 242n80; Osan-Mohei execution anniversary and, 243n87; performance and, 16, 183; respect for, 3–4, 222n7; *Rules for Determining Legal Matters*, 138, 244n12; subversion of, 3, 22–23; taxonomic social order and, 71, 120–121; violation by, 124. *See also* taxonomic social order

Portraits of Loyal Retainers (*Seichū gishi shōzō*) (Utagawa Kuniyoshi), 213

print culture. *See* commercial print culture

puppet theater. *See jōruri* theater

rage (*ikidōri*), 136, 151, 152, 160, 248n69

Rancière, Jacques, 4, 63, 102, 223n9

Rangaku (Dutch studies), 204–205

Rashōmon, 160
Record of Ancient Matters (*Kojiki*), 146–147, 245n25
Record of Rites (*Liji*; *Raiki*), 70, 234n15
Revenge After the Fact (*Katakiuchi ato no matsuri*) (Santō Kyōden), 24–25
Revenge and Strange Tales: The Asaka Marsh (*Fukushū kidan Asaka no numa*) (Santō Kyōden), 180, 181, 182, 192–208; bodies as commodities in, 194–195, 202–203; cannibalism and, 203–204; classical landscape in, 196–199, 255n57; commodities in, 194, 199–200; criticisms of, 207, 256n72; formal rearrangement in, 197, 206–207; as foundation for late *yomihon* genre, 189, 254n41; interconnectedness in, 191, 206, 207; *ka-i* system and, 192, 194, 199; plot in, 190, 191; revenge form and, 188–189; sameness in, 204–205; sickness in, 207–208; style in, 196, 197; travel narratives and, 188–189, 200–201; *waka* poetry and, 192–193
revenge form: authenticity and, 96; boundaries and, 75–76; cultural frontiers and, 188–189; idealized shape of, 67–69, 70, 73–75, 88–89, 90; *Inheritance of the Martial Way*'s distortion of, 69, 75–78; *Inheritance of the Martial Way*'s interruption of, 93–94; *Inheritance of the Martial Way*'s ironic inversions of, 82–83; limits of, 95; moral instruction and, 68, 89, 97; taxonomic social order and, 93–94; travel narratives and, 189–190
Rezanov, Nikolai, 253n30
ritualized behavior. *See* normative social forms
Roberts, Luke, 15–16

Rōnin's Saké Cup, The (*Rōnin sakazuki*), 15, 225n40
Rooney, Ellen, 27–28
Rootless Grasses (*Nenashigusa*) (Hiraga Gennai), 254n41
Rowley, G. G., 22
Ruisenshū, 80–81
Rules for Determining Legal Matters (*Kujikata osadamegaki*), 138, 238n11, 244n12. *See also Hundred Articles* (*Hyakkajō*)
Russian Empire, 179, 184–185, 253nn28–29
Russian Formalists, 223n17
Ryōjin hishō (*Songs to Make the Dust on the Rafters Dance*), 50–51
Ryokutei Senryū, 212

Saigyō, 232n62
Sakai Zenpei, 225n28
Sakamaki Kōta, 40, 43, 229–230n24
samurai: authorized revenge for adultery and, 103, 121, 233n6, 240n48; Ihara Saikaku's works on, 232–233n3; *Inheritance of the Martial Way* as commentary on, 68, 87, 233–234n10; normative social forms and, 84–87; respect for, 4; taxonomic social order and, 121, 131; Tokugawa circumscription of, 66, 70, 82, 233n6. *See also* blood revenge
sangemono (confession tale), 43, 230n31
Santō Kyōden: *Complete Biographies of the Drunken Bodhisattvas of Our Realm*, 205; late *yomihon* and, 179, 187, 190, 254n41; *An Old Tale with a Thunderbolt Cover*, 205; *Revenge After the Fact*, 24–25; *The Tale of the Udumbara Flower*, 190; *Thoughts on the Wondrous Traces of Recent Ages*, 189; *The Water Margin of the Loyal Retainers*, 188, 190, 254n41; *The*

Women of Okazaki: A Revenge, 189.
  See also Revenge and Strange Tales: The
  Asaka Marsh
Satō Haruo, 244*n*8
Satō Miyuki, 164–165, 175, 249*n*106
Screech, Timon, 179, 251*n*10
"Scroll of Darkness, The" (Nubatama no
  maki) (Ueda Akinari), 150, 151, 152
Sei Shōnagon, 50
Seichū gishi shōzō (*Portraits of Loyal
  Retainers*) (Utagawa Kuniyoshi), 213
Seiichi, Miyazawa, 23
self-possession, 166, 172, 174–175, 250*n*122
senryū poetry, 212
seppuku, 217, 218
setting: formal rearrangement and, 2,
  225*n*28; psychological interiority
  and, 10, 225*n*27; revenge form and,
  73, 83; in *Stirrups of Musashi*, 43, 46
sewamono, 114–115, 240*n*44
"Shame!" (Tolstoy), 9
sharebon (wit and fashion books) genre,
  187
Shi Nai'an, 247*n*63
shibagaki, 58–59, 231*n*57
Shigeno (Sanada) Yozaemon, 213
Shijing (*Classic of Poetry*), 141
Shikidō ōkagami (*Great Mirror of the Way
  of Love*) (Fujimoto Kizan), 91, 106
Shikubi no egao (Ueda Akinari). See
  "Smile of the Severed Head, The"
Shimabara Rebellion (1637–1638), 74,
  213, 214, 257*n*12
Shin kashōki (*The New Laughable
  Collection*) (Ihara Saikaku), 232*n*3
Shinjū nimai ezōshi (*The Love Suicides and
  the Two-Page Picture Book*)
  (Chikamatsu Monzaemon), 242*n*68
Shinjū ten no Amijima (*The Love Suicides
  at Amijima*) (Chikamatsu
  Monzaemon), 19–20

Shintei o hiku biwa no umi
  ("Heartstrings Plucked on Lake
  Biwa") (Ihara Saikaku), 235*n*31
Shirakawa Barrier, 183–184, 198, 255*n*57
Shklovsky, Viktor, 9, 224*n*24
Shodō kikimimi sekenzaru (*Worldly
  Monkeys with Ears for All Ways*) (Ueda
  Akinari), 148–149
Shōsetsu shinzui (*The Essence of the Novel*)
  (Tsubouchi Shōyō), 181, 206
Shōutsushi hyakumen sō (*True to Life:
  A Compendium of One Hundred Faces*)
  (Utagawa Kuniyoshi), 213, 257*n*10
Shuihu zhuan (*The Water Margin*)
  (*Suikoden*), 149, 187, 188, 247*n*63
shukō, 20–21
"Smile of the Severed Head, The"
  (Shikubi no egao) (Ueda Akinari),
  153, 165–172; allegory in, 166–167,
  170–171, 173; characterization in,
  167–169, 250*n*112; embrace of fiction
  in, 135, 136, 165–166, 171–172;
  normative social forms in, 167;
  self-possession in, 166, 172, 174–175,
  250*n*122; style in, 135, 166, 169–170,
  171, 173–174; Ueda Akinari's turning
  point and, 249*n*98
Smith, Henry D., 23
social order. See household structure;
  political authority; taxonomic social
  order
Soga monogatari (*Tale of the Soga*), 73, 74
Someya Tomoyuki, 88
Sonezaki shinjū (*The Love Suicides at
  Sonezaki*) (Chikamatsu Monzaemon),
  114
Songs to Make the Dust on the Rafters
  Dance (*Ryōjin hishō*), 50–51
Souvenirs of Naniwa (*Naniwa miyage*)
  (Chikamatsu Monzaemon and
  Hozumi Ikan), 241*n*65, 243*n*89

Stanley, Amy, 104
Star Wars, 218
status (*mibun*), 12–13, 224*n*26
Stirrups of Musashi (*Musashi abumi*) (Asai Ryōi), 41–64; amplitude in, 38, 44, 46; confession narrative in, 43, 44–47; disaster as benevolent in, 51–52, 56, 57, 231*n*51; formal rearrangement in, 41–42; frame narrative of, 42–44; illustrations of, 35, 52–54, 53, 54–55, 55, 57; information in, 40, 47–50, 228–230*nn*12,24; medieval-early modern transition and, 60, 62; misreadings in, 44–45; *monozukushi* in, 50–51; narrative voice in, 43, 44; political authority in, 51, 52, 54–56, 59, 62, 63; popularity of, 34–35, 228*n*9; reworking of medieval modes and, 35, 43, 46, 47, 56, 59; setting of, 43, 46; *shibagaki* and, 58–59, 231*n*57; symbolic intentionality and, 35–36, 42
strange realism, 96–97
style: Ihara Saikaku and, 78–79, 111; in late *yomihon*, 254*n*41; truth vs. fiction in Genta murder and, 135, 166, 169–170, 171, 173–174
Su Wu, 201
subjectivity, restoration of, 116, 121–122, 124, 130
"Sudden New Year's of 'Knock Knock, Who's There?,' A" (Monomō dore to iu niwaka shōgatsu) (Ihara Saikaku), 78–79
Sugawara Mayumi, 215
Sugawara no Michizane, 33, 43
Sugita Genpaku, 228*n*9
"Suteishimaru" (Ueda Akinari), 172
Sutra for Genji, A (*Genji ipponkyō*), 247*n*64
Suwa Haruo, 19, 63

Suzuki Hideo, 51
symbolic intentionality, 35–36, 42, 229*n*13

Tachibana Nankei, *Journey to the East*, 185, 189, 200–201, 255*n*62
Tachibana no Moroe (Prince Kazuraki), 184
Taiheiki (*The Chronicle of Great Peace*), 23, 32, 159–160, 212
Takebe Ayatari, 141, 146–147. *See also* *Tale of the Western Hills, A*
Takechi no Kurohito, 144
Taketori monogatari (*Tale of the Bamboo Cutter*), 147
"Tale of a *Masurao*, The" (*Masurao monogatari*) (Ueda Akinari), 152–162; allegory in, 154–155, 156, 159–160, 166, 171; characterization in, 167; failure to express truth in, 136, 152, 160–161, 172; *kokugaku* and, 155; linguistic style in, 155–156; *masurao* ideal and, 152, 154, 174; plot of, 156–159; *The Tale of Genji* and, 155, 249*n*92; on *A Tale of the Western Hills*, 135, 148, 152, 153–154, 161, 165; titles of, 152–153; truth as intent of, 135, 152, 153, 154, 172, 174
"Tale of Gengobei, a Mountain of Love, The" (Koi no yama Gengobei monogatari) (Ihara Saikaku), 240*n*33
Tale of Genji, The (*Genji monogatari*) (Murasaki Shikibu): cats in, 116; formal rearrangement and, 20, 22–23; *Inheritance of the Martial Way* and, 81, 83; *kata* and, 224*n*18; negative power of fiction and, 149, 150, 247*n*64; Osan-Mohei and, 241*n*50; "The Tale of a *Masurao*" and, 155, 249*n*92
Tale of Kiyomizu, The (*Kiyomizu monogatari*), 63

Tale of the Bamboo Cutter (Taketori monogatari), 147
"Tale of the Calendar-Maker, Seen in the Middle Section, A" (Chūdan ni miru koyomiya monogatari) (Ihara Saikaku), 102–103, 110–114, 128, 132, 242n81
Tale of the Heike (Heike monogatari), 33–34
Tale of the Soga (Soga monogatari), 73, 74
Tale of the Udumbara Flower, The (Udonge monogatari) (Santō Kyōden), 190
Tale of the Western Hills, A (Nishiyama monogatari) (Takebe Ayatari): as example of yomihon, 134–135; formal strangeness of Genta murder and, 137; linguistic style of, 147; masurao ideal and, 145–146, 246n52; plot of, 147–148; Ueda Akinari on, 135, 148, 152, 153–154, 161, 165
Tales of Ise (Ise monogatari), 39, 141, 147, 161, 162
Tales of Moonlight and Rain (Ugetsu monogatari) (Ueda Akinari), 19, 133, 149, 154, 155, 254n41
Tales of Samurai Obligation (Buke giri monogatari) (Ihara Saikaku), 232n3
Tales of the Floating World (Ukiyo monogatari) (Asai Ryōi), 60–61
Tales of the Present (Ima monogatari), 247n64
Tales of the Spring Rain (Harusame monogatari) (Ueda Akinari): admiration for, 136, 244n8; innovation and, 135–136; material form of, 164–165, 249–250nn104,106; preface to, 163–164, 172, 173, 174; self-possession in, 172–173, 174–175; style in, 136; truth vs. fiction and, 163–164, 165, 173, 174; Ueda Akinari's turning point and, 162, 163; uncertainty in, 175. See also "Smile of the Severed Head, The"

Taniguchi Shinko, 23
Taniwaki Masachika, 61, 87, 88, 232n63
Tanizaki Jun'ichirō, 244n8
Tanuma Okitsugu, 253n28
taoyameburi, 144
taxonomic social order, 71–72, 87, 104, 224n26; adultery as threat to, 103–104; blood revenge and, 70–71, 72, 82, 235n22; commercial print culture and, 177; differentiation and, 177–178; establishment of, 12–13; geography and, 177; liminality/reintegration and, 72–73, 74–75; objectification and, 121; Osan-Mohei and, 120–121, 131; performance and, 15–16, 183; personhood and, 131; political authority and, 71, 120–121; relationships outside, 89–90; revenge form and, 93–94. See also political authority
"Thoughts on the Meaning of Poetry" (Ka'ikō) (Kamo no Mabuchi), 145
Thoughts on the Wondrous Traces of Recent Ages (Kinsei kiseki kō) (Santō Kyōden), 189
Toby, Ronald P., 178
Tōkaidō meishoki (Guide to Famous Places Along the Eastern Highway) (Asai Ryōi), 39, 60, 229n21, 230n25
Tokugawa Ieyasu, 12, 40–41, 133
Tokugawa shogunate: collapse of, 215–216; law enforcement issues in, 70; samurai circumscription and, 66, 70, 82, 233n6. See also Edo-period Japan; political authority
Tokugawa Tsunayoshi, 22
Tokugawa Yoshimune, 138
Tokugawa Yoshinobu, 213
Tolstoy, Leo, 9
Tominaga Heibei, 225n40
Toyotomi Hideyori, 34

Toyotomi Hideyoshi, 12, 34
Tōyūki (*Journey to the East*) (Tachibana Nankei), 185, 189, 200–201, 255n62
Treasury of Loyal Retainers, The (*Kanadehon chūshingura*), 23, 25, 188, 227n62
trickster, 75–76, 96
True to Life: A Compendium of One Hundred Faces (*Shōutsushi hyakumen sō*) (Utagawa Kuniyoshi), 213, 257n10
truth vs. fiction: form and, 131–132, 175–176; normative social forms and, 15, 16; Osan-Mohei and, 101–102, 121, 123, 131–132; performance and, 15; *Tales of the Spring Rain* and, 163–164; Ueda Akinari's theorization of, 148–149, 150–151; uncertainty and, 157, 161–162, 175. *See also* truth vs. fiction in Genta murder
truth vs. fiction in Genta murder: allegory and, 154–155, 156, 159–160, 170–171, 173; and, 154–155; characterization and, 167–169, 250n112; failure to express truth and, 136, 152, 160–161, 172; innovation and, 136; *kokugaku* and, 154–155; linguistic style and, 155–156; normative social forms and, 167; plot and, 156–159; rage and, 136, 160; reader's responsibility and, 166, 174; self-possession and, 166, 172, 174–175, 250n122; style and, 135, 166, 169–170, 171, 173–174; Takebe Ayatari on *masurao* ideal and, 246n52; titles and, 152–153; truth as intent and, 135, 152, 153, 154, 172, 174; Ueda Akinari on *A Tale of the Western Hills* and, 135, 148, 152, 153–154, 161, 165; uncertainty and, 157, 161–162
Tsu no kuni meoto ike (*Lovers Pond in Settsu Province*) (Chikamatsu Monzaemon), 3, 10, 225n28

Tsubouchi Shōyō, 181, 206, 251n15
Tsukioka Yoshitoshi, 217–218, 257n19; *One Hundred Selected Portraits of Those Who Dash Ahead*, 209, 210, 211–217, 257n10; *Twenty-Eight Famous Murders, with Verses*, 257n17
Twenty-Eight Famous Murders, with Verses (Tsukioka Yoshitoshi), 257n17
Tynianov, Iurii, 223n17
typology: characterization and, 2, 10; formal rearrangement and, 16–17

Uchimura Katsushi, 153, 162
Udonge monogatari (*The Tale of the Udumbara Flower*) (Santō Kyōden), 190
Ueda Akinari: formal rearrangement and, 19; innovation and, 135–136, 176; *kokugaku* and, 133, 136, 149; late *yomihon* and, 188, 254n41; *masurao* ideal and, 134, 135, 140, 145–146, 154; on rage, 136, 152, 160, 248n69; *Tales of Moonlight and Rain*, 19, 133, 149, 154, 155, 254n41; theorization of fiction, 136, 149–150, 151–152, 154, 159, 248nn68–69; theorization of truth vs. fiction, 148–149, 150–151; turning point of, 162–163, 249n98; works of, 133; *Worldly Monkeys with Ears for All Ways*, 148–149. *See also* "Smile of the Severed Head, The"; "Tale of a Masurao, The"; *Tales of the Spring Rain*
Ugetsu monogatari (*Tales of Moonlight and Rain*) (Ueda Akinari), 19, 133, 149, 154, 155, 254n41
Ukiyo monogatari (*Tales of the Floating World*) (Asai Ryōi), 60–61
ukiyozōshi (books of the floating world), 148, 232n2
Umeda shinjū (*The Love Suicides at Umeda*) (Ki no Kaion), 19–20
Utagawa Hiroshige, 20

[292] INDEX

Utagawa Kunisada, 20
Utagawa Kuniyoshi, *True to Life: A Compendium of One Hundred Faces*, 213, 257*n*10
utamakura, 2, 83, 184, 196, 197, 202
"*Utazaimon* of 'The Calendar-Maker's Osan,' The" (Utazaimon daikyōji Osan), 99, 107–109, 114, 117, 128–129, 132, 239*nn*26,32
utazaimon versions of Osan-Mohei, 99, 107–109, 114, 117, 128–129, 132, 239*nn*26,32

violence: afterlives of form and, 218; cultural frontiers and, 179, 181, 195, 202–203, 207; disaster and, 35; early modern-Meiji transition and, 215–216; Edo overdetermination of, 9; fiction and, 136, 152, 153; form as source of, 69–70; idealized revenge form and, 68–69; normative social forms and, 9; relationship to form, 8–9; samurai and, 66, 233*n*6; samurai circumscription and, 66, 70, 82, 233*n*6; sexuality and, 117; Shklovsky on, 9, 224*n*24; *Stirrups of Musashi* and, 35, 36, 43; as threat to authenticity, 96; visual art and, 216–217; warfare and, 212
visual art, 20, 211–212, 213–214, 216–217, 257*n*10
"Vying Over Smoke at the Field Altar" (Nozukue no keburi kurabe) (Ihara Saikaku), 90–95, 235*n*31

wabun, 22
Wajinchi. See Ezo
waka poetry: cultural frontiers and, 184, 192–193; Edo school and, 245*n*26; formal rearrangement and, 6, 18;

Inheritance of the Martial Way and, 81; *kokugaku* and, 141, 145; *monozukushi* and, 231*n*47; *utamakura* in, 202
Walley, Glynne, 253*n*34, 254*n*44
Walthall, Anne, 238*n*15
Wamyō ruijū shō (*Classified and Annotated Japanese Names*), 147
Wanderer's Willow, The (*Yugyō yanagi*) (Kanze Nobumitsu), 255*n*57
Watanabe Genta, 134. See also Genta murder
Watanabe no Tsuna, 159–160
Water Margin, The (*Shuihu zhuan*; *Suikoden*), 149, 187, 188, 247*n*63
Water Margin of the Loyal Retainers, The (*Chūshin suikoden*) (Santō Kyōden), 188, 190, 254*n*41
"What Is Edo Literature?" (Edo bungaku to wa nanika?) (Suwa), 19
Williams, Raymond, 6
Winichakul, Thongchai, 181
"Woman Can Write in a Man's Hand, A" (Onna no tsukureru otoko moji) (Ihara Saikaku), 235*n*31
"Woman's *Shakuhachi*, Played with Feeling, A" (Omoiire onna shakuhachi) (Ihara Saikaku), 79–84, 90
women: agency of, 111, 113, 114; household structure and, 104, 105–106, 118–119, 238*n*15; normative social forms and, 105–106; working, 91, 236*n*55. See also female body/sexuality
Women of Okazaki, The: A Revenge (*Katakiuchi Okazaki joroshu*) (Santō Kyōden), 189
woodblock prints, 1, 20, 35
Worldly Monkeys with Ears for All Ways (*Shodō kikimimi sekenzaru*) (Ueda Akinari), 148–149

Yamaga Sokō, 70
Yanagisawa Yoshiyasu, 22
Yano Kimio, 68
Yari no Gonza kasane katabira (*Gonza the Lancer*) (Chikamatsu Monzaemon), 240n48
Yōjōkun (*Instructions for Cultivating Life*) (Kaibara Ekiken), 105
Yokota Fuyuhiko, 91, 236n55
yomihon (reading books) genre, 135, 186, 188, 221n2. *See also* Kyokutei Bakin; late *yomihon*; Ueda Akinari
Yonemoto, Marcia, 178

Yoshitsune Crosses the Isles (*Onzōshi shimawatari*), 183, 194–195
Yoshiya ashiya ("The Good and the Bad") (Ueda Akinari), 151
Young, Blake Morgan, 139
Yugyō yanagi (*The Wanderer's Willow*) (Kanze Nobumitsu), 255n57
yūjo hyōbanki (courtesan critiques), 239n22

Zhu Xi, 150
Zhuangzi, 150–151
zuihitsu, 153

GPSR Authorized Representative: Easy Access System Europe, Mustamäe tee 50, 10621 Tallinn, Estonia, gpsr.requests@easproject.com

www.ingramcontent.com/pod-product-compliance
Lightning Source LLC
Chambersburg PA
CBHW022037290426
44109CB00014B/890